D1196620

THE COMPANY'S BIRTHPLACE

The State House, later called Independence Hall, as it looked in 1792 when the Insurance Company of North America was organized in the room in which the Declaration of Independence was signed. The now familiar spire in which the Liberty Bell hangs had been taken down because of structural defects. After 1800 it was rebuilt.

From an engraving by William Birch, 1799, owned by the Historical Society of Pennsylvania and reproduced by permission.

BIOGRAPHY OF A BUSINESS

1792—1942

INSURANCE COMPANY OF NORTH AMERICA

by

MARQUIS JAMES

THE BOBBS-MERRILL COMPANY

INDIANAPOLIS   *Publishers*   NEW YORK

COPYRIGHT, 1942, THE BOBBS-MERRILL COMPANY
PRINTED IN THE UNITED STATES

First Edition

CONTENTS

I   BORN IN INDEPENDENCE HALL 11

II   A CRISIS UNDER GEORGE WASHINGTON 25

III   PROSPERING IN THE FACE OF PERILS 40

IV   A FIGHT FOR LIFE 58

V   IN THE SECOND WAR FOR INDEPENDENCE 77

VI   FIRE INSURANCE COMING INTO ITS OWN 95

VII   CORPORATE FINANCES IN THE DAYS OF ANDREW JACKSON 110

VIII   THE ROAD TO LEADERSHIP 127

IX   THE CIVIL WAR 148

X   GROWING IN GOOD TIMES AND BAD 158

XI   THE MARINE BRANCH IN DIFFICULTY 174

XII   ENTER BENJAMIN RUSH 187

XIII   THE DRAMA OF SAN FRANCISCO 208

XIV   IMPROVING THE OTHER FELLOW'S BUSINESS 230

XV   THE FIRST WORLD WAR 242

XVI   NEW GROWTH 265

XVII   INLAND MARINE 283

XVIII   THE RISE OF CASUALTY 303

XIX   DEPRESSION AND RECOVERY 323

XX   HITLER FAILS TO SURPRISE THE UNDERWRITERS 341

XXI   UNFINISHED BUSINESS: SEQUEL TO PEARL HARBOR . . . 354

OFFICERS AND DIRECTORS 375

SOURCES AND ACKNOWLEDGMENTS 391

NOTES 395

INDEX 413

LIST OF ILLUSTRATIONS

The Company's Birthplace   *Frontispiece*

FACING PAGE

Samuel Blodget, Jr.   14
Ebenezer Hazard   16
The City Tavern   20
First Office of Insurance Company of North America   26
Minutes of the Company, 1792   32
Marine Insurance Policy, 1795   36

BETWEEN PAGES

Life Insurance Policy, 1813   44–45

FACING PAGE

Fire Insurance Policy, 1795   48
Colonel Charles Pettit   64
Joseph Ball   70
John Inskeep   80
The Company's Early "Fire Marks"   96
Hose Carriage, 1830   100
Fire Insurance "Survey," 1797   106
John Correy Smith   122
Arthur G. Coffin   134
Clipper "Black Warrior"   138
Early Fire Engine   144
Packet Ship "William Penn"   160
The Chicago Fire, 1871   164
Boston Fire   168

FACING PAGE

Sea-Going Tug "North America"   176

Charles Platt   182

The Company's New Home, 1880   188

"North America" to the Rescue   204

Greatest Fire "Shock Loss": San Francisco, 1906   224

Eugene L. Ellison   240

Benjamin Rush   256

The Company's Home, Completed 1925   280

Mississippi River Steamboat   284

Coming of the Railroad   288

Early "Engine-Side"   304

Seal of the Company, Adopted 1794   320

An Early Fireman and Fire-Insurance Man   332

John O. Platt   336

John A. Diemand   356

The Company's New York Property   368

BIOGRAPHY OF A BUSINESS
1792 — 1942

CHAPTER I

Born in Independence Hall

I

His restless imagination athrob with a new idea, Samuel Blodget, Jr., journeyed from his home in Boston early in 1791 to Georgetown, erstwhile in Maryland, but now in the lately established District of Columbia, where the new national capital, to be called Washington, was to rise on the marshy east bank of the Potomac. Blodget tramped over the extensive site of the city-to-be, watching Major L'Enfant and his surveying crew run lines.

There was criticism of L'Enfant's work on the ground that he was making the plan of the city too large. Indeed, a hundred thousand persons might be lost in it—which some thought preposterous, that being more than twice the population of Philadelphia, the country's largest city. Blodget did not join in this complaint. Like L'Enfant, he saw things large. In his mind he superimposed upon the vacant landscape by the majestic river a great and beautiful capital, a fitting seat of government of the young republic which he had seen born. The imaginative sightseer even went into the details of the public buildings which were to be, for Samuel Blodget's hobby was architecture, about which he knew as much as some practicing professionals.

So much for the vision of Blodget the artist, the pioneer and the dreamer. Blodget, the speculative man of business, also saw a few things. He saw fortunes to be made in Washington real estate. Riding back to Boston he combed his active mind to contrive a plan for getting his share.

But before anything could be accomplished along that line, Promoter Blodget's attention was drawn aside to something else. A group of local capitalists engaged him to manage a project called the Boston Tontine, which was a sort of lottery based on how long the individuals participating should live. Tontines were one of the ancestors of life insurance. They took the name from Lorenzo Tonti, a banker of Naples, who managed the first one on record in 1653. Each subscriber paid in a certain amount, the sum thus accumulated being invested for the benefit of all and an annuity paid to each participant. As subscribers died their annuities were distributed among the subscribers living. The last survivor took everything on the death of the next to the last.

Though tontines had been fairly successful in Europe, the English Government having operated one, Boston did not warm to the enterprise. A search for subscriptions elsewhere brought Samuel Blodget, Jr., in touch with an old acquaintance, Ebenezer Hazard, a prosperous merchant and broker of Philadelphia.

It seems likely that the friendship of these two unusual men dated from Revolutionary War days when Hazard was appointed surveyor of post offices and post roads throughout the United States and later postmaster general, an office he held until 1789. This employment carried Hazard from Georgia to New Hampshire. After two and a half years' service with the New Hampshire militia Blodget, at twenty-one, had resigned his captain's commission to go into business, at which he was not very successful until after the war when a Boston report had it that he had made himself rich in the China trade. However that may have been, Blodget was no longer in the China trade when he traveled to the site of Washington in 1791, and he was not rich. When the Tontine bogged down in Boston, Blodget was indeed thankful to receive an invitation from so well-connected a business-man as the former postmaster general to come to Philadelphia and discuss an extension of the life-insurance lottery to the Quaker City.[1]

With high expectations Blodget journeyed to Philadelphia in March 1792. He was hoping actually to kill two birds with one stone for he had not forgotten his Washington town-lots idea. Philadelphia was the temporary seat of government and the very place to see those in authority. Blodget lost no time approaching the highest authority in the land—President George Washington. They did not meet as strangers, youthful Captain Blodget having served on the staff of the Commander-in-Chief during the siege of Boston in 1775.

Blodget suggested the appointment of a superintendent to assist the Board of City Commissioners of the projected capital to direct the work of designing and constructing the needed public buildings. He laid before the President letters from Washington property owners recommending him for the post. The President was sufficiently impressed to write one of the commissioners, describing the applicant as "certainly a projecting genius."[2]

It was an apt description. Nevertheless the commissioners delayed action in the matter, thus giving Samuel Blodget more time to devote to the subject which Ebenezer Hazard had summoned him to Philadelphia to examine.

2

Ebenezer Hazard exhibited none of the externals ordinarily associated with the promoter type. He was forty-seven years old. A gentle manner and a mild, kindly face framed by a formal powdered wig hinted nothing of the youth of adventure on the high seas which had been his. Graduating from the College of New Jersey (now Princeton), of which his father, a wealthy merchant, had been one of the original trustees, Ebenezer had spent three years aboard British privateers and men-of-war. The later travels in the service of the post office had given Hazard a stirring vision of the future of the United States. A scholarly turn of mind and a passion for history set him to copying during these peregrinations all manner of local records, the first of two volumes of which were published in 1792 under the modest title of *Historical Collections, consisting of the State Papers and other Authentic Documents intended as materials for a History of the United States*. Generations of historians have reason to be grateful to Ebenezer Hazard for these and other works in the field of history, painstakingly carried on throughout a lifetime more than ordinarily filled with other concerns. At the time of Blodget's arrival Hazard was starting to build for his family a three-story brick domicile on Arch Street above Fourth, destined to stand for seventy years as one of Philadelphia's notable mansions.[3]

The lottery feature of a tontine may well have been one of the things which recommended the idea to Hazard. Lotteries were common money-raising devices of the time for projects public and private, including churches. They were especially popular among thrifty Pennsylvania Quakers who saw them as a means of keeping down taxes. The insurance feature was another recommendation. The richest commercial center of the country, Philadelphia was something of a headquarters for the writing of insurance against

losses at sea from all causes and to a lesser degree losses on land by
fire. Other types of insurance were almost unknown. But the country
was young, and, under the presidency of General Washington, serving his first term, it was growing strong and ready for fresh adventures. So why not a try at life insurance? Philadelphia would be the
seat of the national government until the dream city by the Potomac
was ready eight years hence. Nowhere could the pulse of the whole
country be felt better. Hazard thought Philadelphia the place and
the present the time to launch a pioneering life-insurance project.

Desk space was found in the quarters of Hazard's brokerage firm
at Third and Chestnut, and Blodget went to work. With a touch of
the grandiose, which suggests Blodget, the enterprise was rechris-
tened the Universal Tontine Association. A prospectus was printed
and advertisements soliciting subscriptions were placed in the Philadelphia papers. One hundred thousand shares were issued, 50,000
to be disposed of in Philadelphia and 50,000 in Boston. The latter
was a proposal of Blodget, undampened by his earlier failure in
Boston. The price of shares was graded according to age, in accordance with a crude table of life-expectancy. A share could be bought
in the name of a child of five for $22, whereas a person of forty
would have to pay only $15.50. A man of eighty-five could get one
for $3.20. Unlike earlier tontines, the Universal was not to be a last-
man club. At the end of twenty-one years, that is in 1813, the assets
were to be divided among the surviving shareholders and the Association disbanded. Advertisements stressed that "the Terms of
Admission are easy, being calculated particularly to favor the less
opulent Citizens."[4]

Yet opulent as well as less opulent citizens were drawn into the
promotion, forming, indeed, its directing inner circle. Among these
were John M. Nesbitt, merchant and all-round public-spirited citizen; Jasper Moylan, a leader of Philadelphia's famous Dancing
Assembly and attorney whose clients numbered some of Philadelphia's most socially eligible and financially solvent personages; General Walter Stewart, federal inspector of revenue and surveyor of the
port of Philadelphia; Alexander James Dallas, secretary of the Commonwealth of Pennsylvania; Matthew McConnell, merchant—all
friends or business associates of Hazard, who accepted the post of
secretary of the Tontine Association.

This left Blodget, who disliked office work, free to manage the

Samuel Blodget, Jr.

A leader among the original promoters of Insurance Company of North America and a director, 1792-1799. A pioneer developer of national capital, Washington, D. C. George Washington called him "certainly a projecting genius."

Likeness shows Blodget in uniform of captain New Hampshire militia during Revolutionary War. It is from a restoration by Henry B. McIntire of a photograph of a portrait attributed to John Trumbull. Photograph owned by and reproduced by permission of Yale University Art Gallery, which is unaware of whereabouts of original canvas. The portrait damaged by fire before photograph was made, rendering restoration necessary.

matter of rounding up subscriptions. He failed to make out very well, a circumstance which, however, did not prevent the buoyant promoter from effecting a quick conquest of the gay heart of Rebecca Smith, a daughter of the provost of the University of Pennsylvania. Fifty days after the adventurer's arrival in Philadelphia they were married. Luckily for his bride, she possessed an amiable disposition which found amusement more often than annoyance in her husband's perpetual hopefulness for his financial ventures. She thought his optimism gave his appearance a "comical look."[5] A month after his wedding Blodget went to Boston to try to revive the fortunes of the Universal Tontine by selling the 50,000 shares allotted to that city. Characteristically, on his departure Blodget neglected to sign some important papers Secretary Hazard had placed in his hands; and he went off without taking another document necessary to his work in New England.

The mission failed. The original supporters of the Boston Tontine used the funds subscribed to start a bank. Blodget sold only a few shares in the Universal and these on long-term installments.[6]

3

Over the summer matters did not improve. There was no disposition to blame Blodget. Some of Philadelphia's leading lights had succeeded no better than he at interesting the populace in the Tontine. By September only 187 Philadelphians had signed the articles of the Association for a total of 8,400 shares. To determine what to do, on November 3 a meeting of the subscribers was held at the State House in the room in which the Declaration of Independence had been signed. The historic chamber had been turned over to public use, any group of reputable citizens being permitted to gather there merely by reserving the time.

"Tontines in general appeared to be in disrepute," read the minutes of the disturbed Universal shareholders' meeting. "Many who had subscribed were dissatisfied & were desirous that either the Association be dissolved or the funds appropriated to some other use." What other use? "The Idea of a general Insurance Company had been suggested, & appeared to meet with public Approbation." Indeed, a motion was made and seconded to form an insurance company and invite Tontine shareholders to join. But more cautious counsel prevailed. This time the Philadelphians would look before they leaped. So the resolution was withdrawn and a committee, headed by John M. Nesbitt, was appointed to look into the project and report back to the body of Tontine subscribers at the same place on November 12, 1792.

At the adjourned gathering the Nesbitt committee submitted a formal endorsement of the insurance idea, and the meeting adopted a resolution "That the Universal Tontine Association be and is hereby changed from its original objects and converted into a Society to be called the Insurance Company of North America." Nesbitt probably had a good deal to do with this proposal, his mercantile firm of Conyngham, Nesbitt & Company, owner and charterer of ships, being in the marine underwriting business as a side line. For that matter practically all the leading Philadelphia merchants were underwriters. They banded together to insure one another's shipping ventures. The name proposed for the insurance company also may have come from Nesbitt, who had been an organizer of Philadelphia's Bank of North America. The committee submitted a detailed "Plan" calling for the subscription of 60,000 shares of stock at $10 each, which would make the new company an enormous concern of $600,000 capital when all shares should be taken and paid for.

No effort was made to thrust this Plan down the throat of the meeting. Caution was still the policy of Nesbitt. The Tontine subscribers were given a week to study the Plan, after which they were to come together again and speak their minds. So on November 19, 1792, they assembled a third time in the beautifully paneled Georgian room, with Nesbitt in the "rising sun" armchair in which John Hancock had sat while presiding over the momentous sessions of the Continental Congress in July 1776. On the desk before Hancock had been a draft of sandy-haired Thomas Jefferson's much-debated Declaration. On the same desk, before Nesbitt, was the Plan for the formation of the Insurance Company of North America. At the same hour, in another building of the Independence Square group, the Congress of the United States—lineal descendant of the Continental body of 1776—was in session. And rather curiously the Senate was considering a communication from Thomas Jefferson, now President Washington's Secretary of State, concerning "An act making provision for the Public Debt."

Probably every man Nesbitt saw before him could recall the ring-

EBENEZER HAZARD

Philadelphia merchant, scholar, historian. Surveyor General of Post Office during Revolution; Postmaster General United States 1782-1789. Associated with Blodget as original promoter of Insurance Company of North America; secretary of company, 1792-1800.

From a portrait, artist unknown, made in Huntsville, Alabama, 1816, when Hazard was seventy-two. Owned by Spencer Hazard of Philadelphia, a great-grandson and reproduced by permission.

ing of bells and the firing of guns which sixteen years before had announced the adoption of the Declaration of Independence. In the struggle of which it had been a part most of them had served, some of them conspicuously. The Irish-born Nesbitt, thirty-seven years old and well established as an importing merchant when the war began, fought in Washington's New Jersey campaigns as a cavalryman; but perhaps his most valuable service was in the domain of finance and provision supply for the hard-pressed Continental Army.

The meeting of November 19 seems to have been brief, suggesting ample beforehand preparation. The Plan "unanimously"—and it appears, enthusiastically—adopted, the career of the Insurance Company of North America was launched. A subscription book for stock was opened at the residence of Ebenezer Hazard.

People beat a path to his door, many of them shepherded by the ubiquitous Blodget, still in the role of stock salesman. This time he succeeded as brilliantly as he had failed dismally with the Tontine. In the clattering cobbled streets, the little cart-wide alleys, and along the teeming wharves of busy Philadelphia, the word spread to take the shares. In banks and counting houses, in lawyers' offices and in Government offices, in great stores and small shops, in sail lofts and at shoemakers' benches the word spread. In Hazard's book a ship carpenter's name went down under that of a shipowner; a stable keeper, a cobbler, a stationer, a War Department clerk and the secretary of the United States Senate signed along with bankers, merchants and barristers. Almost incredibly, in eleven days Hazard was able to report 40,000 shares taken, the minimum under which, according to the Plan, the company could proceed with the elections of officers and directors.

On December 10 the subscribers met—again in the Declaration of Independence room—to elect directors. When the votes were counted it was found that Samuel Blodget, Jr., had 4,136, or more than anyone else. This was, in part, a tribute to the esteem in which the promoter was held because of his energy and his fertility in ideas, and, in part, a result of the exceptional number of proxies Blodget had been able to bring to the meeting and vote for himself. Next on the list stood Joseph Ball, proprietor of an iron works which had made munitions for the American army, and currently a director of Alexander Hamilton's Bank of the United States which was doing so much for the prosperity of the new republic. He had 4,120 votes.

Nesbitt had 4,050; Matthew McConnell, 4,050; Jasper Moylan, 4,040; Charles Pettit, merchant and shipowner with a noteworthy military, civil and business record, 4,030; Thomas L. Moore, the mayor of Philadelphia, 4,016; General Walter Stewart, 3,920. Thirty-nine hundred and seventy votes elected John Ross, merchant and shipowner, at whose lavish town and country houses President Washington was sometimes a guest and whose manifold interests in sea-borne commerce included the writing of marine insurance. In all, fifteen directors were chosen and they made a strong Board.

The Board held its first meeting on the day following at the City Tavern, gathering place of the great and the near-great in local and in Government circles from Jefferson and Hamilton down. John Maxwell Nesbitt was elected president of the Insurance Company of North America and Ebenezer Hazard secretary. The directors split themselves into a number of committees to get the company under way at the earliest moment. On December 12 the committee charged with providing "suitable offices" leased a brick building at 119 (now 223) South Front Street, for £100 a year. That was the way it went down in the records, notwithstanding that the dollar and not the pound had been for more than a year our official unit of currency. A hundred Pennsylvania pounds were equal to $266.

4

"The Plan of a General Insurance Company" under which the North America set up in business empowered the company to write marine, fire and life insurance. Life insurance was a new and undeveloped thing, of which the public was skeptical, as proved by the fate of the Tontine. Probably on that account the directors laid the subject of life insurance aside when considering the opening activities of the North America. On the other hand fire insurance was a recognized business, with two Philadelphia companies prospering in the field. Perhaps this competition had something to do with the directors' decision to ignore fire insurance also, and, for the present at any rate, concentrate on marine risks. This, too, was an established line of business, representing, in fact, the oldest form of insurance known. As currently developed, the field was larger than that of fire insurance and the opportunities for profit were greater, especially in view of the present boom in American sea-borne commerce.

Demosthenes, the first historian of insurance, described the loans Greek capitalists made on ships or cargo to be repaid with large interest if the voyage prospered but not repaid at all if the ship were lost. In the twelfth century insurance on ships was a recognized feature of the maritime life of Lombardy. Latin domination of the business appears as late as the middle of the sixteenth century when the earliest policies on English ships were written in Italian. A hundred years later, however, the English wrote their own sea risks, and the great center was Edward Lloyd's coffeehouse on Tower Street, London. These policies were informally contrived affairs. Lloyd's was a social hangout for shipowners, merchants, brokers in goods and all manner of folk having to do with overseas trade. When a ship was preparing for the sea a paper would be left on a table at Lloyd's, giving particulars which included the nature and value of the cargo, and soliciting participants in the risk. *Under* this statement of facts was space for men to sign their names and to indicate how much of the total amount they, personally, would insure. For this they received an advance from the owners of ship or cargo, commissions running from 2 to 15 per cent, according to circumstances. If the voyage were safely made that ended the transaction. If disaster overtook the vessel, the signers, or "*under* writers," lost what they had pledged. At times it turned out that some of them did not have the money to lose.

The careful and scrupulous William Penn noted this circumstance. "I shall be glad if this dull sailor [*Cantico*] gets as safely [across] as the Hopewell," he wrote in 1702. "I am tender as to insurance and did nothing in it for the Hopewell." And in 1705 Penn noted: "J. Askew insured for £100, but the insurer broke and the twenty guineas [commission] lost. Ensurers fail much."

The majority of shippers had better luck than J. Askew, or the marine insurance business would have died a natural death. Instead it grew strongly. As early as 1721 John Copson of Philadelphia saw no use in local merchants and traders paying London underwriters for a service which might be performed as well at home, and the money kept on this side of the water. Setting forth this interesting fact in a newspaper advertisement, he announced the opening of "An Office of Publick Insurance on Vessels and Merchandizes . . . kept by John Copson *at his house in the High Street* [now Market Street]. . . . *Care shall be taken by the said* J. Copson *That all As-*

surers or Under Writers be Persons of undoubted Worth and Repu-
tation, and of considerable Interest in this City and Province."

Though no data are available as to how well Copson made out,
four years later in the print shop of Samuel Keimer, Benjamin
Franklin was setting the type for a book written by Francis Rawle,
founder of a distinguished Philadelphia family. It bore the attractive
title of *Ways and Means for the Inhabitants of Delaware to Become
Rich,* and contained a lengthy paragraph on the advantages marine
insurance opened before "the industrious Adventurer."

By 1760 a train of adventurers had followed the example of Copson
and the advice of Rawle. The insurance center of Philadelphia was
the London Coffee House, a hip-roofed building built in 1702, conveniently facing the smelly wharves at Front and High Streets. In
the Coffee House itself the Old Insurance Office, maintained by
Philadelphia underwriters, kept hours with two clerks in attendance
from twelve until one at midday and from six until eight in the evening. The "Old" office's rival was the New York Insurance Office
next door where Anthony Van Dam was clerk. Van Dam sent his
policies home to be underwritten.

The war saw the rise of the City Tavern as the gathering place
of soldiers and statesmen of the Revolution. There in 1781 Robert
Morris, ablest financier of the Revolutionary cause, brought together
the select little group which organized the Bank of North America
for which the Insurance Company of North America was probably
named. Incidentally, at Morris' bank meeting were seven men destined to become charter shareholders in the insurance company. In
the course of its elevation to prominence the Tavern virtually superseded the London Coffee House as the headquarters for marine underwriting. Imitating the more successful features of the Coffee
House, the Tavern posted arrivals and departures of vessels and all
manner of marine intelligence of interest to shippers or underwriters.

During the first decade after the war the Philadelphia underwriting community grew to a body of some fifty firms or individuals,
mostly shipping men themselves. They offered considerable competition to the agents of the London companies, which cut rates to
meet the challenge. The Americans' reply was that American money
should be kept at home to develop the country and not sent to London. Moreover, the American underwriters pointed out the months
which must elapse before English insurers could settle a claim, owing

THE CITY TAVERN

Famous in Philadelphia during the Revolutionary period and for thirty years after. Gathering place for private marine underwriters who preceded Insurance Company of North America. First meeting of company's Board of Directors held there, December 11, 1792. *From a drawing 1908 from contemporary sources by Joseph Preston*

to the slow ocean voyages. And as sometimes happened when liability was disputed, correspondence dragged out for years. The weakness of the native underwriters' position was a shortage of capital. They could not take on short notice the large risks that the London companies could underwrite with a stroke of a pen. Twenty-five thousand dollars was the outside limit the Americans could cover, and this would mean spreading the risk among most of the local underwriters; all of which took time.[7]

The Insurance Company of North America meant to change this aspect of things. Representing shareholders who had pledged $600,-000 on a permanent rather than a temporary basis, with it insurance was to be a full-time and not a part-time occupation. The largest marine risks of the day could be taken instantly. A wealth of experience at writing insurance as a side line supported the North America's organizers. President Nesbitt and his business partner and father-in-law David H. Conyngham had been for years perhaps the most active private underwriters in Philadelphia. Director John Ross, Director John Leamy, Archibald McCall and other leaders of the new company were conspicuous members of the City Tavern insurance crowd.

5

In this way it was that the Insurance Company of North America spread its sails with accustomed hands at the tiller. Yet the venture was begun most frugally. Nothing was done for show, but then show was unnecessary for a Nesbitt, a Pettit, a Hazard, a Ross or a score of others who had taken founders' shares; they were the cream of Philadelphia's commercial world.

The new offices which opened for business on December 15, 1792,[8] comprised two rooms on the ground floor of a small three-story brick building. Families lived above. The locality was an old residential district on which business had lately begun to encroach, Director Ross' fine town house, at Second and Pine, being only two and a half blocks away and Secretary of the Treasury Alexander Hamilton's, at Third and Walnut, about the same distance. The City Tavern on Second Street between Walnut and Chestnut, was under two blocks.

The little house at No. 119 being on the east side of the street, the insurance offices faced the town but from the back window one could overlook, a short block away, the pier-indented, ship-lined river on whose green bosom so much of the fortunes of the fledgling enterprise would lie. Perhaps it conveyed a feeling of assurance to Secretary Hazard to note that the largest and busiest wharf under his eye was owned by John Ross.

The absence of any recorded expenditure for office furniture or fixtures beyond a few miscellaneous items suggests that the new quarters may have been fitted out with loans or gifts from the ample establishments of the officers or directors. The first cash book mentions the purchase of "Paper & Quills, .75"; "Candles, .80"; "J. Gilpin for paper, $11.33"; "L. Alwine for Chairs, $37.50"; "Tho⁵. P. Cope for 7 yds. green Cloth, 8.40." The cloth was probably used to cover desks. Mr. Alwine, the cabinetmaker who turned out the chairs, was a neighbor, located at 99 South Front.

The Board empowered Hazard to employ a clerk "& it was agreed that the Preference should be given to Mʳ. William Coulthard, if, upon Conversation with him, he shall be found willing to engage on suitable terms." Mr. Coulthard's terms were $500 a year, which Hazard thought suitable. The remainder of the staff consisted of John Valentine Cline, the "porter," who was a gift from Director Charles Pettit. "John Valentine Cline . . . has been in my service the greater part of the last twenty years," Mr. Pettit wrote John M. Nesbitt. "He now comes to offer his services to the insurance company."⁹ He was never called John, always Valentine, and his pay was fixed by the Board "at Six p. [pounds per] Month [$10] & an hint of a Douceur at Christmass in Case of good Behavior." For the porter's immediate attention a cord of wood, a saw and an ax were bought for $5.95.

Before Valentine could have made much of an impression on that cord of wood, Secretary Hazard had interviewed the first applicants for insurance. In the first two days of business he wrote nine policies. As was fitting, Policy No. 1 insured "for Conyngham, Nesbitt & C°. at & from Philadelphia to Londonderry on the Ship America, James Ewing Mʳ. [master] valued at Twelve Thousand Dollars 5333.33 Doll⁵." This meant that the North America accepted a risk of $5,333.33 on a $12,000 ship. The premium was "2¼ p Cᵗ." or $120, with a charge of 50 cents for the policy. Policy No. 2 was on goods on board the *America*. The insurance was for $3,200 at a premium of

$72.50. Director John Leamy took out policy No. 3, on the brig *Margarita,* bound for New Orleans, "with Liberty to touch & trade at" Cape François on the Island of Hispaniola, now called Haiti. His premium was $45.50.

The largest premium for the first day's business was on policy No. 4 written "for Stuart & Barr, at & from Alexandria in Virginia to Falmouth in Great Britain, to trade between Europe (without the Streights) & America, for nine Months, commencing this Day, & to continue until the Ship's arrival at any safe Port in the United States . . . on the Ship Friendship, Samuel Hubbel, Master, 4000 Dollars & 7 p C^t. for the nine Months, & the assured to pay at that rate for a longer Time, until Arrival or Loss." Stuart & Barr's premium was $280.50. The rate was high because of the length of the voyage and the fact that the *Friendship* was to visit a number of ports. Underwriters did not necessarily view a port as a place of refuge. Carelessness and poorly equipped quays piled up unpredictable damages to vessels. Most frequent injuries were caused from bumping, either by another craft or against the wharves.

The plum of the first week's business was policy No. 13, issued on December 20 on the ship *Diana,* setting forth on a voyage of four months or more. Eight thousand dollars was taken on the vessel. Policy No. 14 insured the *Diana's* cargo for $2,666.67. The total premium, including the cost of two policies, amounted to $374.33.[10]

Premiums for December totaled $6,663.92, of which $4,120.06 was represented by notes payable in sixty, ninety or more days. In the face of these figures, it would appear that, after little more than two weeks in business, the Insurance Company of North America possessed a balance of $2,543.86 in cash from premiums. Actually Secretary Hazard had carried little more than $40 in currency to the Bank of North America for deposit to the account of the company.

In keeping its cash account the North America was following the custom of the times, which might confuse a modern bookkeeper. Cash accounts were often cleared off the books more slowly than accounts for which notes were given. As an instance policies No. 13 and No. 14—the largest written during the first week—were carried on the books as cash transactions, although the money was not paid over until May 8 of the following year, probably when the *Diana* completed her voyage. On the other hand Mr. Leamy gave a ninety-day note for his premium, redeeming it in March 1793. The advantage to the insurance company of the first transaction is not clear, but the explanation probably can be found in the way the purchasers of marine insurance were compelled to conduct their business. With few exceptions they were merchants who made collections slowly, usually having to wait out the round trip of a vessel before learning the disposition of their cargoes and the prices they brought.

In any event the North America must have been rather pleased with the way premiums were rolling in, whether in cash or in notes. Five weeks after opening the Front Street offices, the conservative Board busied itself with a scheme for building a new home for the company. From the Directors' Minutes, dated February 22, 1793:

"The President informed the Board that the Managers of the Dancing Assembly had found a Lot to build on, which they thought would accomodate both them and the Insurance Company; & proposed that the Company should unite with them for the purpose of building . . . each to advance £600. . . . Agreed that M^r. Nesbitt & Col. Pettit be a Committee to meet M^r. Moylan & endeavor to devise a Plan for building for the Accomodation of the Insurance Company, with a view at the same time, to the Accomodation of the dancing Assembly."[11]

It would not be hard for Messrs. Nesbitt and Pettit, representing the insurance company, to meet Mr. Moylan, representing the Dancing Assembly. They were looking at one another across the company's directory table at the time.

To those who know the Philadelphia of today as well as the Philadelphia of 1793, this item needs no elaboration. For the Dancing Assembly to propose to share quarters with the Insurance Company of North America was more than proof of the latter's solvency and material prospects. By rule-bound old-Philadelphia-family standards it was proof as well of the social impeccability of the North America's guiding lights.

CHAPTER II

A Crisis Under George Washington

I

The year 1793 opened with business thriving throughout the United States as well as in the little offices of the Insurance Company of North America, then a going concern for all of two weeks. People were joyful. On the night of the preceding fifteenth of December, when the North America had written its first policies, bells rang in Philadelphia, taprooms had a fine evening and revelers made the streets noisy late into the night. This was not a salute to the new firm at 119 South Front Street. Nor was it a celebration of the election returns which assured John Adams the vice-presidency of the United States over his rival George Clinton. (Washington's candidacy for a second term as President had not been contested.) The festivities were over news from France: the King locked up; a republic proclaimed; George Washington made an honorary French citizen. Street crowds coupled his name with the French revolutionary cry *"Ça ira!"*

All through the Christmas holidays Americans toasted French freedom. Names of the insurance company's officers and directors appeared on the rosters of several elite functions, while carpenters and shoemakers and shipwrights who held two or three shares apiece of North America stock joined the alehouse gatherings.

But as days stretched into weeks and weeks into two months no more news arrived from France for the valid reason that no ship arrived. Could this be due entirely to the westerly gales prevailing on the Atlantic? Rumor had it that the English had clamped an embargo on their own ships and were seizing French vessels. By the middle of March mariners up from the West Indies brought wisps of gossip which tended to confirm this. England and France, they had heard, were at war.

None got these reports sooner than the men of the Insurance Company of North America, and none acted quicker. During January of the new year, the company's first full month in business, premiums amounted to $2,491.79. Cash received, part for January and part for December business, was $255.73. But already the rumors from over the seas had had their effect.[1] As early as February 13 the following clause was being written into policies:

"It is mutually agreed that this Insurance is not made against any Risque or Loss occasioned by War; but only against such Risques & Losses as are usually insured against in Time of profound Peace."

At the same time a committee of the Board of Directors was at work on a comprehensive schedule of rates for "common" or peace risks. Further rumblings of war altered the occupation of this body when on March 25 it was ordered "that the President & sitting Committee take the rates of Premiums into consideration and form a table . . . having in view the chance of war."

Two days later the committee reported its inability, without more information, to frame a table of premiums for war conditions. Consequently the Board decided "to leave the determination of the Additional Premium to be required for *War* Risques to the discretion of the sitting Committee who will be governed by Circumstances." A table for "common Risques only" was adopted, however—to be used in event of peace but to be increased in case of war.

At the same meeting a proposed standard form of policy was submitted, debated and turned over to "M^r. Ingersol & M^r. Tilghman . . . two Gentlemen learned in the Law, for their Opinion whether it will secure the Property of the Individual Members (other than their Interest in the Company's Funds) from legal claims for losses."[2] Fees of $20 each were voted for these lawyers, who stood at the head of their profession in Pennsylvania.

It was the beginning of a long association with the insurance company for both of them. Jared Ingersoll, son of a Connecticut Tory, had been sent to England at the outbreak of the Revolution. He returned and joined the rebels. Settling in Philadelphia after the war, he married a daughter of Colonel Charles Pettit. In 1790 he became attorney general of Pennsylvania, an office he still held when engaged by the insurance company. Ingersoll's associate in the insurance work, Edward Tilghman, was a well-connected Marylander

FIRST OFFICE OF INSURANCE COMPANY OF NORTH AMERICA

119 South Front Street, Philadelphia. Used 1792-94. The company occupied two rooms on the ground floor.

From an etching, about 1880, from contemporary descriptions, by Joseph Pennell, then a member of the Philadelphia Etching Club.

who had fought in the Revolution. A short, spare man, he was distinguished for his plain speech and by the fact that he never wore black at the bar or powdered his hair on any occasion.

2

On April 3 a British packet, the first in three months, beat into New York harbor. After all, it had been the gales that had cut us off from European news. And such news! It was war and no mistake. The French Republic, in the hands of the radicals, had guillotined the King and the Queen, and had opened hostilities against England and Spain.

The startling intelligence was in Philadelphia by nightfall. As soon as desperately ridden horses could carry a courier there, it was in Mount Vernon where George Washington was enjoying a little vacation and getting his spring farm work started. Posting to Philadelphia, the President called a solemn meeting of the Cabinet to decide the question of war or peace for the United States. By the treaty of 1778 we were pledged to defend the New World possessions of France. Hamilton, who loathed the idea of the French revolution, was for immediate repudiation of the treaty. Jefferson, who loved the French and the democratic ideals their revolution expressed, did not wish war. But he was against a precipitous scrapping of the treaty which he said would be playing England's game. Washington pondered. He admired the French, and he shrank from war. The President could remember, probably better than anyone, the desperate plight of our country when France came to its aid with money, munitions and men, and exacted in return the mutual-aid treaty.

The French possessions were Caribbean islands. Without a navy, how could we defend them? Spain and restive Indians stood on our western frontier, England on our northern. To fight them all might bring terrible consequences. Deciding that in the circumstances we were not obliged to go to France's aid in a war of her own aggressive making, with a heavy heart Washington issued a proclamation of neutrality.

It was not well received. The common people of our country were pro-French and anti-British, and many of the wealthy class were pro-French. Only the profound respect felt among all classes for Washington kept the outbursts against the neutrality proclamation within bounds. Most of the insurance company's leading men—Alexander James Dallas being a notable exception—preferred the political and economic views of Hamilton to those of Jefferson. Yet not all found it pleasant to follow Hamilton in this matter of repudiating the treaty of alliance. But they would follow Washington, whom several of them knew well enough to break bread with. The President was striving to avoid plunging his country into a war which might prove disastrous. Such a war might easily visit similar consequences on business interests such as the Insurance Company of North America.

When Washington proclaimed our neutrality Edmond Gênet, the minister of the French Republic, was on his triumphal way overland from Charleston, South Carolina, cordially assuming that we would stick by the treaty. Crowds which huzzaed him en route assumed the same. News of the proclamation changed neither the attitude of Gênet nor that of most of the people. The French frigate *L'Ambuscade,* which had deposited Citizen Gênet on our shore, sailed up the coast, capturing seven British prizes and arriving at Philadelphia on May 2. The directors of the North America could have watched the tumultuous welcome from their back windows as the vessel dropped anchor off Ross' Wharf which was decked with flags for the occasion. On the official reception committee were two prominent insurance company stockholders, Dallas and William Barton.[3]

The scenes of welcome were repeated some days later when Gênet himself arrived. Coolly ignoring the neutrality edict, the minister distributed among American shipowners orders for a dozen French privateers and began to recruit armies among adventurous American spirits to attack the British and the Spanish. Hamilton put a stop to the land recruiting by refusing to honor Gênet's demand that installments on the debt owing France by the United States be paid to him.

The Government in Paris backed up its high-flying diplomat by according to neutral ships the rights of French ships. We jumped at this invitation to put to sea under the protection of France. Vessels which had prudently kept in port for weeks sailed forth, mostly bound for the West Indies with which we had built up a rich trade, exchanging fish, flour and hides for coffee, sugar and rum. The North America went in heavily for insurance on such vessels. The increased war rates and French naval activity on the western Atlantic made the business seem fairly safe. Men-of-war and privateers flying the tri-color, several of the latter manned by Americans, were banging up and down our coast seizing British merchantmen and bringing them into our ports. The captors were greeted with cheers. When a party of British seamen on shore got in a free-for-all with a gang of French sailors almost under the insurance company's windows, Americans pitched in and helped the French.

3

In these altered and uncertain circumstances the directors of the North America sat down to take stock of their first half-year in business. The figures Ebenezer Hazard spread before them were gratifying. To June 14, 1793, $62,114.33 had been received in premiums and $3,276.20 in interest. Against these stood two losses only, totaling $4,515.74. Both losses had been occasioned by the same storm and were reported in the May third issue of the Philadelphia *Advertiser*. The ship *Industry*, from Havre, France, was driven ashore at the mouth of the Delaware. Ten passengers and the crew of a lifeboat were drowned. This loss was $4,000. The other was on the cargo of the coastwise sloop *Betsey*, beaten to pieces on a shoal near Sandy Hook.

The directors declared a conservative dividend of 6 per cent of the paid-in capital. Subscribers were allowed to settle for their shares in installments and $60,000 of the $600,000 pledged had been turned in to date. The dividend, calculated on that amount, was $3,600. Forty thousand dollars, or more than two-thirds of the remaining funds of the company on hand, were invested in the stock of the newly chartered Bank of Pennsylvania, in which President Nesbitt and other leading characters of the North America were interested. And so was forged another link binding the insurance company to the principal financial institutions of Philadelphia.[4]

The wisdom of the directors' caution was soon apparent. England answered the French offer of safe-conduct to American ships with an order to the navy to bring in any ships laden with the produce of France or a French colony, or carrying goods to such destinations. The North America shortened sail, the directors refusing for the company at least one risk which some of them as individuals were willing to undertake. It is not surprising to find Samuel Blodget,

Jr., heading the group of directors, who, it appears, privately under-
wrote a policy on the brig *Nancy,* under charter of Thomas Patten &
Company of Philadelphia.[5] During these critical weeks his fellows
on the Board, meeting every few days, did not see much of Mr.
Blodget who had returned to his first love—the development of the
capital city of Washington. Although he had failed to obtain the
post of superintendent in charge of the erection of public buildings,
he raised some money and invested it in town lots. General Washington accepted the advice of Blodget in the selection of the lots
which the President himself purchased in the projected city that was
to bear his name.

The British navy and British privateers made broad use of their
new powers. Not only were American ships trading with France
and French possessions seized, but also many vessels plying peaceably
between our shores and British harbors. In the Caribbean the English had a holiday hauling American trading craft before sweating
prize courts sitting in tropical ports. Thomas Jefferson invited shippers to place statements of their claims in the hands of the Government.

4

When the Secretary of State took this encouraging action, business
and national problems were swiftly becoming secondary concerns in
Philadelphia. Late in July 1793 yellow fever appeared along the
congested waterfront north of High Street, four or five blocks above
the insurance offices. As it spread, inhabitants burned bonfires
and fired muskets to purify the air. They smoked tobacco, dipped
snuff, sprinkled vinegar about and had themselves bled white to resist
the contagion. In the stifling summer heat they closed their doors
and windows. The disease marched on until there were insufficient
hearses to carry the dead.

An exodus from the city increased to panic-stricken flight. Government officials swelled the stream of refugees. Yielding to the urgings
of his wife, Washington left on September 10. A week later Jefferson, last of the Cabinet to leave, was gone. Board meetings of the
Insurance Company of North America were suspended: no quorums.
President Nesbitt and family took up their abode at Clermont, the
country seat of Nesbitt's father-in-law, David Conyngham. But Sec-

retary Hazard stayed on with his family in his large house in Arch Street. With Coulthard, the clerk, and Valentine, the useful porter, he kept the office open. There was almost nothing to do there. Other American ports had laid an embargo on vessels from Philadelphia. Coaches, carriages and carts from the stricken town were halted on the roads.

On September 20 Hazard gave a picture of the scene in a letter to his friend Jedediah Morse, the celebrated geographer:

"The disease has spread all over the City, & if we may judge from the number of Funerals, its malignity has not abated much. Great numbers of the Citizens have shut up their houses, & fled into the Country;—so few are seen in our streets & so many houses are shut, that every Day has the appearance of Sunday. Business is almost entirely at a stand; almost every countenance is gloomy, & when two persons meet 'have you heard of any new Deaths today?' is among the first Questions that are asked; our Physicians differ in Sentiment both about the nature of the disorder & the mode of treating it, & have added to the general Distress by publishing their contradictory Opinions in the News Papers.

"Such are the Apprehensions of the Contagion, that a friend dares not visit a friend who is sick . . . & carry the disorder to his own family. No friends attend at Funerals, except perhaps two or three, who keep at a Distance from the Body . . . accompanied by three or four Negroes who bury it:—no Clergyman attends, no Ceremony is made use of, but the putrid corpse is committed to its kindred Earth, & covered up as expeditiously as possible. Our Situation has rendered such Sights as these both frequent & familiar to us;—yet they are distressing! how are the widows—how are the Orphans multiplied! This City truly mourns, & our inhuman neighbours, instead of sympathizing with us, tauntingly proclaim the healthfulness of their own Cities & refuse an Asylum even to healthful fugitives from ours. There are bitter Drops in the Cups of many . . . but we have among us some who can say of the Lord, he is our Refuge, & our Fortress, our God, in him will we trust. . . .

"Young, the Bookseller, his wife & a child are said to be very ill. Divine protection has hitherto preserved the Lives & health of my Family & I cannot say that we feel much alarmed on our own Accounts; but we cannot help being distressed for others. . . . You were misinformed about D^r. Rush; he is alive & very useful; he has lately been disordered, but has recovered so as to visit his Patients daily.

Mr. Bullock has lately lost another Child:—Mr. Markoes Family
are in usual health. . . . Remember me to my friend Belknap . . . and
remember me in your addresses to the Throne of Grace."[6]

Mr. Hazard referred to Doctor Benjamin Rush, signer of the Declaration of Independence and most renowned man of medicine in
Philadelphia if not in the United States. The "inhumanity" of neighboring cities formed an indictment to which Ebenezer's cousin,
Nathan Hazard, of New York, could not subscribe. In one sentence
Nathan defended New York for barring out Philadelphia refugees.
In another he demanded to know what could induce Ebenezer to
remain in the pestilence-ridden town and expressed the fervent hope
that he had sent his family away.[7]

But the quiet Hazard remained at his post, and his family stayed
with him. His letters minimized the distress. More than half of
Philadelphia's 43,000 people were now gone—thousands getting no
farther than the edge of town where they camped in thrown-up
shacks and hovels. On the streets men went about with vinegar- or
camphor-soaked cloths to their nostrils. Friends did not shake hands
on meeting and people tried to pass each other on the windward side.
The post office doused letters from Philadelphia with vinegar. Farm-
ers hesitated to venture into the city with food. Medicines, even the
indispensable vinegar, grew scarce. Hungry mobs plundered closed
houses and liquor shops. Deaths increased. Everyone in a house
might die and the bodies fester there for days. Cemeteries looked
like newly ploughed fields. Corpses of the poor were dumped in
ditches and covered over.

On September 23 Hazard wrote to Nesbitt:

"The Situation of our Neighbourhood I find has become truly
alarming . . . & it does not appear necessary to attend longer at the
office as so little Business offers. . . . M^r. Coulthard went a few miles
into the Country on Saturday afternoon, & intended returning this
morning; but as it is now one OClock, & I have not yet seen him,
I fear he is sick;—there are no Directors whom I can consult on
this Occasion:—thus situated, I have concluded to remove the Books
& Papers, for the present, to my own house . . . & from whence you
shall hear from me if any thing worthy of your Attention occurs;
in the meantime I remain Sir, Your mo: obed^t. Servt."[8]

The following Notification was pub:
:lished in Fenno's, Bache's, Dunlap's & Claypoole's Papers;
viz.:
       Agreeably to the Seventh Article of
their Constitution Notice is hereby given to the Members
of the Insurance Company of North America, that
Forty Thousand Shares are subscribed; and that a
general Meeting of the Subscribers is to be held
at the State House in this City, on Monday the
10th Inst. at 10 O'Clock, A. M. when the Directors are
to be chosen. —
                Eben. Hazard Secy

☞ The Holders of Certificates in
the late Tontine Association who
intend to become Members of the
Insurance Company, are desired
to call at No. 145 Arch Street where
their Subscriptions will be received.
Philª. Decr. 1st. 1792. —

                      Decr. 10th 1792.
The Insurance Company met, pursuant to the
above Notice.
    General Walter Stewart was appointed Chairman,
& the Meeting proceeded to the Choice of Directors. —
    Messrs. Hazard, Ingraham, & Fox, were appointed a
Committee to receive & count the Votes; which, upon Exami:
:nation stood as follows; viz:

For Samuel Blodget Junr.	4136.	John Ross	3970
Joseph Ball	4120.	Walter Stewart	3920
Magnus Miller	4090.	William Cramond	3916
Michael Prager	4090	John Leamy	3590
John M. Nesbit	4050	John Swanwick	2496
Matthew McConnell	4050	John Barclay	2420
Jasper Moylan	4040	Robert Ralston	2348
Charles Pettit	4038		
Thomas L. Moore	4016		

& some few Votes were given for other Candidates: —
upon the whole it appeared that the Fifteen Gentle:
:men first above mentioned were elected Directors, to
continue in Office until the second Tuesday of January
next.
                               A

MINUTES OF THE COMPANY, 1792

The first entry gives notice of a subscribers' meeting. The second the result of that meeting which chose the company's first Board of Directors. The handwriting is Ebenezer Hazard's.

When this arrived at Clermont, Nesbitt himself was on his way into town to have a look around. One look was enough. He galloped back to his father-in-law's, fumigated himself, read Hazard's letter (which Mrs. Conyngham had saturated with vinegar), and replied that the closing of the office was an act of "prudence." Coulthard, the clerk, was indeed ill. With Valentine, Hazard carried on, writing his chief on the twenty-seventh:

"The Disorder does not appear to me to abate much, if any. . . . Eleven graves have been, & are to be, dug in the Quaker burying Ground today. . . . Valentine says your wench & negro man are sick. . . ."[9]

Hazard began to look for a horse to carry Valentine to Clermont to keep Nesbitt in daily touch with things. Horses were scarce and dear and Hazard perceived the additional "risque" of a hired one's dying on his hands. So David Conyngham supplied a mount, with the stipulation that it be fed at company expense. It was also shod at company expense, Hazard noting the charge of eighty cents in his cash book. Thus equipped, Valentine began his tedious rides.

Coulthard's illness proved superficial, but no sooner had he reported for work at the Hazard residence than Hazard himself was taken down. He, too, escaped the plague and soon resumed his daily reports. A storm swept the coast. "We were D^s. 1100, for M^r. Vaughan, on the Betsey, which has arrived here." Other insured vessels were less fortunate, however. "We are D^s. 5000 on the Flora . . . it is probable that the Flora received some Damage. . . . M^r. Forde tells me that [the] McClenachan was on shore; we are D^s. 7000 on Vessel & Cargo" and also "D^s. 21500 on the Fanny." The letter concluded with a request for some buttermilk from the Clermont dairy for an ailing servant of the Hazard household.[10]

On October 24 the secretary sent hopeful news. "All accounts agree that the Sickness has very much abated. . . . Funerals in the Burying Grounds in Arch Street were, comparatively, a Rarity yesterday." And on the thirty-first: "People are beginning to return to the City; but I think they are too hasty." Nesbitt replied that he thought so, too. "M^r. Conyngham and myself dont mean to go in before next week or some rain to wash the Streets." "A charming Rain," wrote Hazard on November 1, "which I hope will enable our Citizens to return soon without Risque; a good frost after it will do the Business."[11]

People trooped back. Government offices, business offices, stores, shops and warehouses reopened. In the cemeteries were 4,044 new graves. A good authority placed the number buried elsewhere too hastily for careful record at nearly a thousand.[12] But Ebenezer Hazard had ridden out the plague without retreating, and without lowering the colors of the Insurance Company of North America. His last business letter from Arch Street:

"Phila. Nov. 9th 1793

"D[r] Sir,

     . . . . .

"Shall remove to the Office on Monday [November 11]; and send Notices to the Directors who are in Town. . . .
"Y[r]. very hum[l] Serv[t].
"EBEN HAZARD

"John M. Nesbitt, Esq[r]."[13]

5

The reassembled directors of the Insurance Company of North America found that in their absence business conditions had changed for the worse. Not only were the British taking our ships. The French, too, were taking them, in retaliation for our action on the treaty of 1778. The behavior of Gênet became so obnoxious that even Jefferson had enough of him. At our request, the French Government sent over another minister.

These happenings dimmed but by no means extinguished sympathy for France in the United States. Public meetings protesting seizures by the French were matched by meetings protesting seizures by the British and tranquilly overlooking what the French were doing. Over one such meeting, a mammoth affair, Stephen Girard presided. Philadelphia's richest citizen and largest shipowner, Girard was born in France, the son of a sea captain. His meeting noisily adopted a resounding set of resolutions enumerating the many and high crimes of the English and extolling "the arduous but glorious struggle of the French nation to establish a Free Republic." Two of the five members of the resolutions committee were Alexander James Dallas and John Swanwick, a director of the insurance company.[14]

Nevertheless, the North America continued to prosper, due to the increased premiums shippers were willing to pay, to Hazard's attention to business at the risk of his life during the epidemic, and to the all-round exercise of excellent and impartial business judgment in a difficult time. The company closed its second six months with premium receipts of $151,350 against $19,474 in losses paid. As other potential losses were outstanding, however, the second semi-annual dividend was a frugal 6 per cent on paid-up capital. It totaled $7,200, showing that stockholders had paid in $120,000 of the $600,000 capitalization.

A salary of $1,600 a year—the same as Hazard's—was voted to President Nesbitt and a second clerk hired for $500 a year. Valentine was rewarded for his services during the plague, his annual pay being increased from $100 to $250. The proposal to spend $32,000 to erect a building for the joint use of the company and of the Philadelphia Dancing Assembly had fallen through. With times as they were perhaps the directors did not wish to dip into the surplus. But as the business had outgrown the two rooms at 119 South Front Street, on March 1, 1794, the company moved half a block away to No. 107 South Front, at the corner of Walnut. The rent was $266 a year, the same as for the old premises, plus taxes. The location was better, however, being on a principal thoroughfare that merchants and seamen trod to and from the wharves.

A glance at some of the papers on Ebenezer Hazard's burdened desk would have indicated the reasons for the company's continued success in the midst of stress. Promptness was a rule of the office. Inquiries for insurance made before noon must be answered before three o'clock the same day, and inquiries left after three before ten the next morning. This did not mean that the insurance would be granted. First the vessel and its cargo must be inspected by the company's "surveyor," a retired sea captain named Smith. The particulars of the intended voyage would be scrutinized with care, and no insurance declared in effect until a well-secured note had been given for the premium or some other arrangement to pay had been approved by the Board.

Rates were high, and varied according to predictable chances of capture in addition to the other hazards of the sea. According to a schedule agreed upon March 7, 1794, the premium for a voyage to or from the French West Indies was 30 per cent, while that to or from the British, Spanish or Dutch Caribbean islands was only 12½. To Spain, or Portugal or Gibraltar 30 per cent; to the British Isles 12½; to Holland 15; to France 20; to Russia 17½; to the Madeira and Canary Islands 20; and, surprisingly, to or from New Orleans 12½. Higher premiums were usually collected for the privilege of calling at more than one port. At these rates casualties would have to be heavy to bring losses in excess of premiums.

The company continued to insure many of its stockholders and directors, showing them no favors. In February 1794 cargo in the brig *Mary C.,* in the service of John Leamy, was insured for $20,000, for a voyage from Cuba to Philadephia "& thence to one Port in Europe, say Rotterdam, Amsterdam, Hamburgh or Bremen." On reaching Philadelphia the brig was "making water" and the shipper required to transfer the cargo to another vessel. John Leamy was turning out to be one of the best customers of the company.[15]

6

The chaotic shipping situation was not the only problem with which the insurance company was obliged to wrestle. When news of the war crisis burst upon the United States in the spring of 1793 the North America already had a fight on its hands. Its application for a charter of incorporation from the State of Pennsylvania was meeting heavy opposition.

Incorporation of the company had been one of the items in the Plan under which the Insurance Company of North America was launched on November 19, 1792. On December 18, three days after the first policies were issued, a petition for incorporation was presented to the State Legislature, meeting in Philadelphia, then the capital of Pennsylvania as well as of the United States. This document was from the pen of Alexander James Dallas, a State official, who received a fee of $100 for his trouble. The petition recited what every patron of the City Tavern already knew: that the new firm, actively competing with European insurance companies, would tend to keep American money in America; its large capital would guarantee insureds against loss as "frequently [has] happened through the failure of individual underwriters"; a corporation would inspire greater public confidence than individual underwriters because "in case of disputed losses" insureds would enjoy "more convenient re-

By the President and Directors of the Insurance Company of North America.

No. 2639

WHEREAS *Jonathan Mifflin.*
as well in *his* own Name, as for and in the Name and Names of all and every other Person or Persons, to whom the same doth, may, or shall appertain, in part or in whole, doth make Insurance, and cause *himself* and them, and every of them to be insured, lost, or not lost, at and from.

Philadelphia to Barbadoes & Martinique, with liberty to proceed to any other Port or Ports in the West Indies (British or Neutral) & at & from thence back to Philadelphia

upon all kinds of lawful Goods and Merchandizes, laden or to be laden aboard the good *Brig called the Sally*

Ten per Cent to two Ports. and the Assured agrees to pay an additional premium of one per Cent for each Port the said Vessel shall proceed to or touch at more than two

And in Case of Loss, the Assured is to abate *Two per Cent.* and such Loss to be paid in Thirty days after Proof and Adjustment thereof; the Amount of the Note given for the Premium, if unpaid, being first deducted.

Kendall Hert

IN WITNESS whereof, The President and Directors of the Insurance Company of North America have, by the said President, subscribed the Sum insured, and caused this common Seal, and the Attestation of their Secretary to be annexed to these Presents, in Philadelphia, the *twenty first* Day of *November* One Thousand Seven Hundred and *Ninety five*

The Assured warrants the above Goods to be American property and the Vessel an American Bottom.

No. 2686. — *Two thousand six hundred & eighty six Dollars*

Ebe Pollit Pres. pro tem.

Dollars *2686.* — on Goods, *268.60*
Policy — *50*
269 10

MARINE INSURANCE POLICY, 1795

course to law." That was to say it would be simpler to sue a corporation than a collection of individuals.

The Legislature referred the memorial to a committee of five of its members one of whom, John Swanwick, was a company director, and another, Albert Gallatin, a budding master of public finance.

Opposition came at once from the private underwriters who inspired "a petition from a number of merchants and insurers of the port of Philadelphia . . . remonstrating against the prayer contained in the petition of the Directors of the Insurance Company of North America." The company countered with "Memorials from a number of merchants, Ship owners, Insurers and citizens . . . praying that the Company stiling themselves the Insurance Company of North America may be incorporated." Long communications to the newspapers further argued the matter, pro and con.

One correspondent signing himself A. Z. set forth that the two incorporated insurance companies in England had been parties to the wholesale corruption of British official life. With money they could get what they wanted. "I therefore sincerely hope the legislature of this state will not establish a precedent of so dangerous a nature, and which may eventually destroy the constitution of the country." A writer on the other side, using the initials A. B., alluded to the honorable characters of the North America's founders and asked if these men would be likely to act less honorably if joined into a corporation. He pointed out that the granting of a charter conveyed no privileges of monopoly. Individual underwriters could continue as before and if they should render better service to those wishing insurance they, and not the corporation, would get the business.[16]

When a month had passed without word from the legislators, the company's directors rather ostentatiously moved to ask for an act of incorporation in Delaware. This smoked out the legislative committe which returned a report favorable to incorporation, advancing, among other reasons:

"That insurance cannot be so well conducted by individuals as by an incorporated company, for want of that identity which would enable such a company to be sued in case of loss, where justice could be had more speedily than in suing every separate underwriter. . . .

"That solidity is also to be considered, which it is impossible to attain with certainty with private underwriters, whereas this Company's proposed capital of 600,000 dollars in the public funds will be a sufficient guarantee to those who employ them.

"That already the charges of insurance have been considerably abated since the establishment of this company, whereby a great saving to the mercantile body is effected. . . ."

It was recited that private underwriters had proved inadequate to care for the larger risks demanded by shippers, with a consequent drain of our money into the coffers of foreign companies.

A resolution giving leave to the petitioners to bring in a bill of incorporation was adopted by the committee and the measure was laid before the Legislature on April 1, 1793. The independent underwriters redoubled their efforts and with the war crisis in the air the Legislature adjourned on April 11 without taking action.

When with the passing of the yellow fever epidemic the lawmakers reconvened in December 1793, opposition to the incorporation of the North America came in stronger than ever, but on a new tack. The evils and dangers of corporations were forgotten. The alleged injustices to individual underwriters went by the board. In one fateful year the Insurance Company of North America had demonstrated a better way of protecting our imperiled overseas trade. It had opened a great and lucrative field which other Philadelphia capitalists, who had neglected to take stock in the North America, were now eager to till. The question no longer was "Shall we incorporate an insurance company?" but "Shall that company be the North America?" Thomas Willing, merchant, shipowner, private underwriter and president of the powerful Bank of the United States, gathered about him an influential group of moneyed and enterprising men. One of the number was George Latimer, Speaker of the Pennsylvania House of Representatives. Their plan was soon apparent.

On January 27, 1794, with the North America's petition again in the legislative mill, the committee considering it received "a petition from divers merchants of the City of Philadelphia . . . suggesting the impropriety of incorporating . . . the Insurance Company of North America and praying, that should the Legislature deem it proper to pass an Act for the incorporation of an Insurance Company, the same may be done in such a manner as those who are more immediately interested in commerce may have an opportunity of subscribing thereto."

Four days later the committee, in a lengthy resolution extolling the virtues of insurance companies, recommended the incorporation of the Insurance Company of North America and also "a new Insurance Company in the said city of *Philadelphia* to be carried on under the denomination of 'The Insurance Company of the State of *Pennsylvania.*'"

The projected new company represented the fruit of the labors of the Willing group. Then began a race to see which should get its charter first, and thus have the honor of being the first incorporated stock insurance organization in the United States. In the House the Pennsylvania Company got the inside track. Its bill passed on March 13, 1794, a day ahead of the North America's. Both bills passed the Senate on the same day and went back to the House for concurrence in amendments. Those in the North America's bill were ironed out three days ahead of those in the Pennsylvania's. That decided the race. On April 14, 1794, Governor Thomas Mifflin signed the act incorporating the Insurance Company of North America. The Pennsylvania Company achieved this goal on April 18.

Not until the following October, however, did the Pennsylvania elect officers and open offices at 137 South Front Street, a few doors from its competitor. Mordecai Lewis and Samuel W. Fisher, two good men, were chosen president and secretary, respectively. A number of North America stockholders, including nine members of the Board of Directors, took shares in the new concern. This was a minority of the Board, the number of directors having been increased from fifteen to twenty-five by the articles of incorporation. However, when John Swanwick and Archibald McCall accepted directorships in the Pennsylvania Company, their places on the North America's Board were declared vacant, in conformity with that company's charter which did not permit one of its directors to serve in a similar capacity for another insurance company.[17]

CHAPTER III

Prospering in the Face of Perils

I

With a strongly backed competitor in the field and difficulties assailing our ocean-borne trade increasing by the hour until they threatened to sweep that commerce from the seas, President Nesbitt and his colleagues of the Insurance Company of North America began to look into the possibility of developing their business in other directions. The first thing seriously considered was fire insurance. On April 28, 1794, ten days after the rival Insurance Company of Pennsylvania had received its charter, the North America's Board voted to investigate "a Plan for Insuring Goods, Wares, and Merchandises in Dwelling Houses, Warehouses or Stores and upon Buildings, against the Risque arising from Fire." Samuel Blodget, Jr., always attracted by the novel, was one of the committee of three named to look into the subject.

Though fire insurance was well over a hundred years old, with a Philadelphia company dating from 1752, the North America at one stroke proposed to carry the business into new channels. Existing Philadelphia companies wrote insurance on buildings only. The North America was looking into the matter of insuring goods as well, a great step forward.

Fire insurance does not go back to antiquity, as in the case of underwriting risks at sea. In the early part of the seventeenth century several efforts to set up fire insurance in London failed, which proved a sad thing for the property owners when in 1666 a blaze in the King's bake-house got out of hand and devastated the city. That catastrophe enabled Nicholas Barbon, a London dentist, to establish the Fire Office, the first fire-insurance company.

The first measures for protection against conflagrations in America were in the line of fire prevention. Disaster is a hard but a sure teacher, and after the first serious fire on this continent, in Boston in March

1630, Governor Winthrop ordered that no house in town should have a chimney of wood or a roof of thatch. In 1647 Pieter Stuyvesant directed householders of New York to clean their chimneys, and appointed four fire wardens to see that they did so. In 1653 after another fire Boston acquired a fire engine. In 1730 Philadelphia had a big fire and in 1736 Benjamin Franklin, thirty years old and a prosperous publisher, organized the Union Fire Company. In a way that has become a tradition among volunteer fire companies, its members mixed sociability with the business of fire fighting. Two years later at Franklin's suggestion the Fellowship Company was formed. Thereafter they multiplied: the Hand-in-Hand, the Heart-in-Hand, the Friendship, the Hibernia. Some were almost as socially exclusive as the Dancing Assembly. In later years the Hand-in-Hand had on its roster four signers of the Declaration of Independence, the chief justice of Pennsylvania, an Episcopal bishop and the head of the State university.

Seeing that physical protection was not enough, in 1752 Franklin lent a hand in the forming of the Philadelphia Contributionship for the Insurance of Houses from Loss by Fire. It was a mutual company wherein the profits were divided among the policyholders, there being no other stockholders. The popular name for the Contributionship was Hand-in-Hand—the same as that of one famous company of fire fighters. This derived from the four clasped hands on the Contributionship's metal badge given each policyholder to place on his house. The Hand-in-Hand got on cordial terms with the volunteer firemen by making contributions to their companies. The insurance company knew that fire-fighting organizations reduced the likelihood of losses. It shrewdly surmised that firemen might display a little extra zeal when fighting a blaze in the house of a financial supporter. In this way fire marks and contributions to fire companies became fixtures in the early history of fire insurance.

The Hand-in-Hand declined to insure houses surrounded by trees because of the increased hazard from lightning. This led to the formation of the Mutual Assurance Company for Insuring Houses from Loss by Fire in and near Philadelphia, whose policyholders, on payment of a slight additional premium, could have both insurance and shade. As the Mutual's fire mark, appropriately, was a tree in full leaf, the company became known as the Green Tree.[1]

2

On July 11, 1794, after about three months' deliberation, the committee of the Board reported favorably on the question of fire insurance. It was voted to insure houses and goods up to full valuation. A return of yellow fever—though not with epidemic violence—delayed action until fall. Then a form of policy was adopted, William Garrigues, a house carpenter, appointed surveyor of houses for which insurance applications might be made, and a fire mark adopted. This was a star with six wavy points executed in lead and mounted on a wooden shield. The Hand-in-Hand's and the Green Tree's fire marks had been skilfully designed and cast by John Stow of the metal-working firm of Pass & Stow, who had recast the Liberty Bell. True to its thrifty policy the North America went to no such expense. Its star badges were the work of Robert Haydock, a plumber at 38 South Second Street, who received $133.33 for a hundred of them.[2] His craftsmanship was crude by comparison with that of Pass & Stow.

The first fire insurance policy was issued on December 10 to William Beynroth "on German Dry Goods in House N°. 211 High Street for three years." The goods were valued at $8,000 and the rate was $3 per $1,000 per annum, making the premium $72 plus a charge of $2 for "Badge [the star] & Policy." By paying in advance for three years, however, Mr. Beynroth received a rebate of $8, enabling him to settle for $66.

Another policy was issued that day to "Lawrence Herbert on Sundries in House N° 161 on the North Side of High Street Viz—

"For one Year

"Dry Goods . . . . D^{rs}	5000
"Household Furniture including a looking Glass valued at Thirty Five Dollars and Linen . . .	500
"Wearing Apparel	400
"Silver plate	300
"China & Glass	100
	D^{rs} 6300
"at 30 Cents . . . . D^{rs}	18.90
"Badge & Policy	2.00
	20.90"

Mr. Herbert, insuring for one year only, received no rebate.

The sixth policy, on December 22, went to John Whitesides for $25,000 on the contents of "the Dwelling House and Store adjoining, both included in No. 136 on the South Side of High Street"—$23,000 being on linen, woolen and silk goods and $2,000 on furniture and wearing apparel. For some reason Surveyor Garrigues reported Mr. Whitesides' establishment a greater risk than Herbert's or Beynroth's, so the premium was double theirs, or $6 per $1,000. Nine days elapsed before the writing of another policy which was taken for $16,000 by the ironmongery, saddlery and hardware firm of Wells & Morris. The premium was $4.50 per $1,000.

These rates, ranging from one-tenth to one-fifth of 1 per cent of the face of the policies, were in keeping with the experience of the local mutual and the London fire insurance companies. Contrast these with the recent peacetime marine rates of from 1 to 7 per cent, not to speak of the current wartime rates which run as high as 30 per cent. A great deal of fire insurance would have to be written in order to make anything like the money the North America had been able to make on its marine business. At the end of the first month of the venture the aggregate in premiums received was $374.10.

While this beginning did not compare favorably with the earlier weeks of marine insurance, the North America had faith in fire insurance—especially on goods, which was a form of protection the mutual companies did not offer. But the public needed education in the matter. In January 1795 Secretary Hazard was directed to print and circulate 5,000 "proposals" advertising the virtues of North America's fire insurance. In March another step was taken. The North America offered to insure "Brick or Stone houses within ten miles of the City." Previously neither the mutuals nor the North America would take insurance beyond the reach of Philadelphia's fire brigades. A year later the company decided to accept fire insurance anywhere in the United States provided "premiums adequate to the risk . . . be paid." A tentative schedule fixed these to run as high as three-quarters of 1 per cent a year. In December 1796 a new fire mark, representing an eagle rising from a rock, was adopted and tastefully worked out by an artisan named Claudius F. Legrand.

These enterprising measures eventually began to take hold. Though business lagged throughout 1795, receipts being only $1,927.77, the following year premiums jumped more than five-fold to $10,600.28.

Another bright feature was that during this period of twenty-five months not a single insured property had been touched by fire.[3]

During the initial stages of the struggle to get fire insurance started the North America began experiments with life insurance. The ancients had placed money in speculations concerned with the duration of the lives of individuals. The tontine was a refinement of this idea, and in 1762 the Equitable Society of London had set up the first life insurance company in the modern sense of the term whose benefits were open to the general public. Preceding this by three years, however, was the Corporation for the Relief of Poor and Distressed Presbyterian Ministers, and for the Poor and Distressed Widows and Children of Presbyterian Ministers, organized by the Presbyterian Synod of Philadelphia. Later the name was conveniently shortened to the Presbyterian Ministers' Fund. The Fund did so well that in 1769 the Reverend William Smith, provost of the University of Pennsylvania and later the father-in-law of Samuel Blodget, Jr., formed the Episcopal Corporation for a similar purpose. The success of these limited organizations may have influenced the North America to retain, in its 1794 charter, power to write life insurance.

Indeed, when that charter was granted the company already was studying the feasibility of offering indemnity to the families of seafaring men in the case of death or capture at the hands of the Barbary pirates. On February 11 of that year a policy was issued insuring Captain John Collet "against Algerines and other Barbary Corsairs in a Voyage from Philadelphia to London, in the Ship George Barclay, himself Master, valuing himself at $5,000." For this Captain Collet paid a premium of 2 per cent, or $100, for the one voyage only. No harm came to him. In March Captain Samuel Hubbell of the ship *Eagle,* Baltimore to Oporto or Lisbon, insured himself in a like manner for $4,000 at 5 per cent, and returned to tell the tale. In May Thomas Baker, master of the brig *Hector,* Bordeaux to Philadelphia, was insured for $4,000 at 5 per cent.

In 1795 Director Blodget got behind an attempt to expand this phase of the business. John Holker applied for a policy of $24,000 on his life for the period of June 6 to September 19. He was willing to pay a premium of 1½ per cent. How John Holker meant to spend his time does not appear, but the Board turned down the application. It accepted, however, a $5,000 policy at 10 per cent "on the natural

LIFE INSURANCE POLICY, 1813

In its early years the North America wrote a small amount of life insurance, usually on sea captains or travelers. The three-year policy above on the life of Thomas Greeves, was taken out by the firm of Comley & Wright which wished to be indemnified in event of the loss of

Greeves' services. Greeves was not a traveler. Indeed, by the terms of the policy, he could not go south of Maryland during the summer or sickly season. Space limitations oblige the omission (page 2 of the reproduction) of part of the policy including a statement of the company's liability—$800—should Greeves die during the third and last year of the policy's life.

life of Bon Albert Briois de Beaumez who attained the age of Forty-
one years in the month of December now last past and is about to
sail for India for and during the term and space of Eighteen Calendar months." For that period he was insured against death from
any cause excepting suicide and "the hand of justice."

One Colonel Tousard was willing to pay $640 or 8 per cent for an
$8,000 policy covering a year's stay in the West Indies, but the insur-
ance does not appear to have been granted. A General de Noailles
was more fortunate. He obtained insurance for six months, at 5 per
cent, with the proviso that he steer clear of "military expeditions."

But the game was hardly worth the candle from a business point
of view. It developed no volume and the sporadic applications from
world-roving adventurers yielded returns incommensurate with the
trouble of making the requisite investigations of their characters,
plans and purposes. Efforts to promote this branch of the business
ceased. Within a few years companies writing life insurance as we
now understand it gained slippery footholds in the United States,
unchallenged by the North America which had its hands full of other
matters. Occasionally, however, a term policy on a life would be
made as a favor to a stockholder or customer of the company. Elias
Boudinot was both. The kindly old Revolutionary statesman from
New Jersey, spending his declining years in near-by Burlington looking after his considerable estate and reading the Bible, asked for
small five-year policies on two servants. The second of these, granted
in 1817, appears to be the last life policy written by the Insurance
Company of North America until 1941.[4]

3

With life insurance dying on its feet and fire insurance coming
along slowly, early in the portentous year of 1794 the North America
realized that its hope of survival lay in the domain of marine risks,
beset though this was by mounting hazards.

Upon the ocean also rested our hope of survival as an independent nation, for the seas held the answer to the question whether
we or England or France or Spain should be the dominant power
of this continent. The issue was twenty years being decided—in
our favor. During those years the fate of the United States teetered
in the balance, tipped first this way and then that by concussions

from the fierce conflict between England and France. The freedom of the seas was necessary to our life and prosperity and there were dark days and years when it seemed as if that freedom were impossible for us to win or to keep. Its own future at stake on the sea, the interests of the Insurance Company of North America and those of the United States were one. In the long fight the fortunes of the firm on Front Street were tied to those of the United States as a tail to a kite. Every American flag the company helped to keep afloat was a blow for our side in the battle for national existence.

The country was divided as to how we should wage this battle. The majority of the people—including a few, though a minority, of the leading men of the North America—still were for taking the part of France in armed conflict. Despite the unsavory memory of Gênet, and the harassment by the French of our sea-borne commerce, Washington's proclamation of neutrality, now a year old, remained unpopular with the masses, though not so much so as it had been at first. Against the pleadings of old soldiers with whom he had fought the Revolution, the President continued unflinchingly a policy of peace, in the belief that war would prove our ruin. Yet he began to fortify our principal seaports and to build a navy. This cheered the populace. An embargo on foreign shipments was proclaimed for sixty days. This, too, cheered the populace but not the merchants. When the two months were up in May 1794, a meeting of sea captains and mates at Barnabas McShane's Harp and Crown Tavern in Philadelphia defied their merchant employers by voting to refuse to go to sea for ten days. "Why feed the English?"

The English, however, eased restrictions on our commerce, the French following suit. Our ships took to the seas again with a somewhat greater degree of safety. One large convoy of American vessels slipped through the British blockade into Brest in time to avert hunger in France. Under these brightening skies Washington sought to improve our situation by sending James Monroe to Paris and John Jay to London to negotiate an alleviation of our difficulties.

Heart-filling reports came of Monroe's reception. Robespierre and the Terror being things of the past, a more moderate spirit ruled the republic. An American flag was hung in the hall of the French Convention and the Yankee sea captain who brought it thither was made an honorary French admiral on the spot. Yet other American flags and other Yankee skippers fared not so well at the hands of the

French, whose behavior at sea did not comport with their fair assurances to Monroe. French cruisers and privateers still overhauled our vessels engaged in English trade. Other American ships were herded into French ports and made to accept depreciated assignats in exchange for cargoes destined elsewhere. Nevertheless, aside from the suffering ship owners and merchants, most Americans remained pro-French and anti-British.

Not much was heard at first from Mr. Jay in London, and then it was reported that he had kissed the Queen's hand at a reception. This was enough to justify popular suspicion that Jay, despite his Huguenot ancestry, was toadying to the English. In March 1795 when his treaty arrived in Philadelphia the country was on the *qui vive*. Washington read the document in private and straightway summoned the Senate, which had adjourned and its members gone home, to reconvene in secret session. "Why secret session?" demanded the people. "Is the treaty *that* bad?" Washington offered no reply; nor could any amount of importunity bring from him a syllable on the contents of the Jay agreement.

In tense sessions behind closed doors the President won the Senate's approval of the treaty, with a single reservation. Though secrecy was still enjoined, Senator Mason of Virginia could not restrain himself. Having voted for rejection he made the document public on June 29. Reprints swept the country. From Boston to Savannah flared wild demonstrations of disapproval: Jay burned in effigy; Hamilton stoned in person; Washington lampooned.

The treaty was, indeed, a resounding British victory. Even in the hostile atmosphere of London a diplomat less inept than Mr. Jay could have done better. Our gains were the British promise to evacuate the military posts she held in our northwestern territory; adjudication of certain boundary disputes; a mixed commission to pass on American claims for indemnity arising from ship seizures; right to trade with the British West Indies in vessels of under seventy tons. The last item was valueless as most West Indian ports were open to ships of any size by local proclamations, so dependent were the islands on American goods. For the real concessions we paid a humiliating price. The old British doctrine of contraband and neutral rights at sea were upheld. This meant the same rough treatment of our commerce as before. Nothing was said of the impressment of American seamen into the British naval service. We submitted to a one-sided arrangement to settle private debts owing Englishmen prior to the Revolution. A further stipulation prohibited the export, from the United States, in American ships, of cotton, sugar, cocoa and coffee. At this outrageous article the Senate rebelled, striking it out.

With the denunciations of the greater part of the nation ringing in his ears, George Washington affixed his signature to an order declaring the treaty in force. In the light of history this stands as one of the wisest and bravest acts of a life filled with such acts.

France struck back at once. Courtesies to Mr. Monroe ceased. He was told that his country had sold out to England and that its commerce must take the consequences.

Though this cured more Americans of their devotion to France, the country remained vigorously divided. On February 22, 1796, the President was sixty-four, and for the first time in his life beginning to show his years. The House of Representatives evinced its displeasure of the Executive's stand by declining to adjourn on his birthday as a mark of respect. In the beginning the division over the treaty had invaded the councils of the Insurance Company of America, though at all times a majority supported the President. Now this support became more positive, as when the Board of Directors named a committee of three to call on the Secretary of State—Edmund Randolph who had succeeded his distant cousin, Jefferson. The ostensible mission of the committee was to inquire concerning the truth of "a Report . . . that the French Cruizers have orders to Capture all Vessels bound to British ports."[5] Actually the visit seems to have been more than one of mere inquiry. It well may have been a quiet way of conveying assurance that a powerful body of Philadelphia citizens had its fill of the French and would stand behind the hard-pressed Executive in the taking of forthright measures to protect our ships.

Moreover the company's Board, giving the Jay treaty close scrutiny, perceived, as had Washington, possibilities of good in the reviled contract. There was a clear agreement by Britain to negotiate concerning seizures and confiscations beginning in 1793. By proper handling of the American case much might be made of this. The House of Representatives, however, stubbornly held up an appropriation to pay our members of the British-American commission which was to hear the claims for indemnity. Officers and directors of the insurance company took increasingly active parts in a campaign to

[H O U S E.]

By the President and Directors of the Insurance Company of North America.

Nº 5.

WHEREAS *Anthony Butler of the District of the Northern Liberties* hath paid to the President and Directors of the Insurance Company of North America *Six Dollars for Insurance of Two Thousand Dollars on his Three Story Brick Dwelling House situate in the District of the North. Liberties on the West Side of Front Street, & between Front Street and Quality Court*

Attest
Eben Hazard Sec.

from Loss or Damage by Fire, for *One Year* from this *Thirteenth Day of August One Thousand seven hundred & Ninety five* NOW KNOW ALL MEN BY THESE PRESENTS that in consideration thereof the Capital Stock, Estate and Securities of the said Corporation shall be liable to pay unto the said *Anthony Butler his* Executors, Administrators or Assigns any Loss or Damage which shall or may happen by or by means of Fire, to the said *Dwelling House* In as good a State of Repair as it was before it was so injured by Fire; or shall make good the said Loss or Damage by paying thereof according to the Estimate thereof to be made by *Two disinterested persons chosen by the Parties* or provided the *Dwelling House* shall be wholly destroyed by or by means of fire within the term aforesaid then the said Capital Stock, Estate and Securities of the Corporation shall be subject to pay to the said *Anthony Butler his* Heirs, Executors, Administrators or Assigns the entire sum of *Two Thousand Dollars* and so shall continue, remain and be subject as aforesaid from time to time to be computed from the *Thirteenth Day of August* in every year so long time at the said *Anthony Butler* shall well and truly pay, or cause to be paid the sum of *Six Dollars* on or before the said *Thirteenth Day of August* which shall be in each succeeding Year, and the said Corporation shall agree thereto by accepting the same, which said Loss or Damage shall be paid or indemnified in manner aforesaid within thirty days after proof thereof; and if any dispute shall arise respecting the same between the Corporation and the ASSURED, such difference shall be submitted to the judgment and determination of Arbitrators indifferently chosen, whose award in writing shall be conclusive and binding to all parties. PROVIDED always nevertheless, and it is hereby declared to be the true intent and meaning of this Policy, that the said Stock, Estate and Securities of the said Corporation shall not be subject or liable to pay, or make good to the Assured, any loss or Damage by Fire, which shall happen by Invasion, Foreign Enemy, Civil Commotion, or any Military or usurped power whatever; And provided also, that this Policy shall not take effect, or be binding to the said Corporation, in case the said Assured shall have already made, or shall hereafter make any other Assurance upon the *Dwelling House* aforesaid, unless the same shall be allowed of, and specified on the back of this Policy: Or if the *Dwelling House* abovementioned shall, at the time when any such fire shall happen, be in whole or in part occupied by any person who shall use or exercise therein the Trade of a Carpenter; Joiner; Cooper; Tavern-keeper, or innholder; Stable Keeper; Bread or Biscuit Baker's; Sugar Baker; Ship Chandler; Rosin Builder; Malt Dryer; Brewer; Tallow Chandler; Apothecary; Chemist; Oil and Colourman; China, Glass or Earthen Ware Seller; or shall be made use of for the Storing or keeping of Hemp, Flax, Tallow, Pitch, Tar, Turpentine, Rosin, Salt-Petre, Sulphur, Gun-Powder, Spirits of Turpentine, Shingles, Hay, Straw, Fodder of any kind, Corn unthreshed, Oil, Wax, Distilled Spirits,

but that in all, or any of the said cases, this Policy, and every clause, article and Thing herein contained shall be void and of none effect; otherwise it shall remain in full force and virtue. IN WITNESS whereof the said Corporation have caused their Common Seal to be hereunto affixed on the *Thirteenth* Day of *August* in the Year of our Lord one thousand seven hundred and *Ninety three*. N. B. This Policy to be of no force if assigned, unless such assignment be allowed by an entry thereof in the Books of the Company.

2000 Two thousand Dollars

J. M. Nesbitt, pres.

Dwelling House D. 2000

FIRE INSURANCE POLICY, 1795

spur the House to action. At a meeting of shippers four of ten members of a committee named to petition the House were directors of the North America. "Property of the Merchants of the United States," declared this body, "amounting upon a moderate computation to more than five millions of dollars have been taken from them by the subjects of Great Britain, the restitution of which, they verily believe, depends, in great measure, upon the completion of the treaty on our part."[6]

Stephen Girard, who owned more money, more merchandise and more ships than anyone else in Philadelphia, led the opposition. Although a purchaser of marine insurance from the North America, he got up a meeting which called the treaty "unequal and unfair" and upheld the stand of the recalcitrant representatives. Mr. Girard lost out. After an oratorical marathon the House voted the appropriation in May 1796.

Ebenezer Hazard was as near a state of excitement as he ever got about anything. "You have doubtless heard the Issue of the Debate about the Treaty & are pleased by it," he wrote a friend. "[Congressmen] Ames & Tracy behaved well upon the occasion—their Speeches have gained them immortal honor."[7]

4

Five million dollars lost in three years as a result of British depredations alone give an idea of the extent to which our trade had suffered. The Insurance Company of North America's interest in these losses seems impossible to state exactly, for when "war risques" were not written into a policy the company bore no liability for captures or condemnations. War-risk, as distinguished from "common-risque," policies carried this all-embracing clause:

"Touching the adventures and perils, which the assurers are contented to bear, and take upon them in this voyage, they are of the Seas, Men of War, Fires, Enemies, Pirates, Rovers, Thieves, Jettisons, Letters of Mart, and Counter Mart, Surprisals, Takings at Sea, Arrests, Restraints and Detainments of all Kings, Princes or People, of what Nation, Condition or Quality soever, Barratry of the Masters and Mariners, and all other perils, losses and misfortunes, which have or shall come to the hurt, detriment or damage of the said vessel or part thereof."

As the country's largest single insurer of ships and cargoes it is certain, however, that the North America's stake in the $5,000,000 in question was considerable.[8] Surviving in the company's archives is an obviously fragmentary list, representing special cases only, of bottoms covered by North America policies which had been taken by the British in a space of twenty-two months ending April 1795. The vessels number nineteen, with war-risk insurance aggregating $149,000.[9]

The action of the Congress opened the way to possible relief. What this would amount to in actuality depended on a number of things. Should the American members of the Anglo-British commission prove no better bargainers than Mr. Jay our chances of recovering anything substantial would be slim.

But before the Insurance Company of North America had much time to speculate on these probabilities another crisis was on its head—and on the country's.

In May 1796 when the House implemented the mixed-commission part of the Jay treaty, a French privateer, the *Flying Fish,* was enjoying the hospitality of the port of Philadelphia. Though French privateers no longer made our harbors bases for operations as during the heyday of Gênet, the sight of one watering and provisioning under approving American eyes was not altogether rare. The *Flying Fish* in particular felt at home in the Delaware as she was supposed to be owned by French-sympathizing Philadelphians who received their share of the booty.

The Delaware was crowded with ships at the time, several of them taking cargo for the British Isles. Late in May the *Flying Fish* hauled anchor and dropped down to sea. On June 8 the ship *Mount Vernon,* 424 tons burden and heavily laden with valuable cargo for London, followed. Two days later Captain George Dominick of the *Mount Vernon* was back in Philadelphia with a story that stood the town on end. In sight of the Delaware capes the *Flying Fish* had taken the *Mount Vernon* and sent her under a prize crew to St. Domingo. Obligingly Captain Dominick had been permitted to return in the pilot boat which had escorted his vessel through the treacherous Delaware Bay shoals. This act of consideration seems to have cost the *Flying Fish* several other prizes, for Dominick had heard aboard the privateer that she possessed a list of ships at Philadelphia marked for capture. The *Philadelphia,* London bound, was already under way. She put about in the river, and other vessels can-

celed preparations to depart. After waiting in vain for its expected
quarry the *Flying Fish* at length sailed away and Philadelphia's
trade with Britain was resumed.

The *Mount Vernon* was insured for $50,000, of which the North
America had taken only $15,000. The Insurance Company of Penn-
sylvania had a like amount and a private underwriting firm the balance. This division of a risk represented a recent departure from the
original policy of the North America, dictated by the perils of the
times. Although a loud cry was made over this daring capture, a
look at the facts in the case revealed particulars about which not so
much was publicly said. Insured and cleared as an American ship,
the *Mount Vernon* had sailed under charter of the mercantile firm
of Willing & Francis, the senior partner of which was one of the
founders of the Insurance Company of Pennsylvania. Nevertheless
the ship was British, and therefore legitimate French game. Lately
it had been purchased by an Englishman residing in Philadelphia.
To contend that the insurers were unaware of this imposes a strain
on credulity. The American clearance was merely one of the common subterfuges of the period.[10]

These technical flaws in our claim to outraged virtue notwithstanding, the *Mount Vernon* case became a cause célèbre which widened
the breach between the United States and France, diminishing the
number and vocality of that republic's American supporters. Because Washington did not think him displaying a sufficient amount
of backbone, Monroe was recalled from Paris and C. C. Pinckney
sent in his stead. France refused to receive Pinckney and withdrew
its own minister from Philadelphia. The Insurance Company of
North America continued to push for aggressive action. Another
committee of the Board was dispatched to the State Department to
give Secretary Randolph the benefit of disturbing private advices the
company had received from England bearing on further contemplated French depredations against us. At the same time the Board
voted a temporary suspension of "sea risques," British ports only
excepted.[11] The last words were significant.

Nor were these the only indications that events were driving us
away from our long-cherished but fading French sympathies into the
arms of England. The temper of the country was visibly changing
when on March 4, 1797, George Washington gave the burdens of
the presidency into the keeping of John Adams.

For four days more the retired Executive lingered in the big house on High Street, between Fifth and Sixth, which had been his official residence. The animosities of recent years fell away as men of all shades of political opinion streamed in to say farewell. Among these, certainly, were the North America's leaders who knew Washington best—Nesbitt, Hazard, Blodget, Pettit, John Ross, Jared Ingersoll, who was the company's attorney, and Walter Stewart. On the field of Monmouth the General had seen Stewart fall wounded leading a Pennsylvania regiment in the counterattack which redeemed the day. On March 9 throngs braved a raw wind to cheer the coach on its way as the Father of His Country, with a grateful sigh, turned his face toward Virginia.

5

The boom which blessed the country when the Insurance Company of North America began business in the closing days of 1792 had been snuffed out. Times were growing hard. Men of proved sagacity who had extended themselves in the view of earlier glowing prospects retrenched desperately, their fortunes in peril. Yet so high were the premiums shippers were willing to pay for insurance, so carefully did the North America select its risks and so shrewdly did it dispose its surplus funds that the company continued to prosper, and prosper enormously.

In 1794 premium receipts were $290,656 and losses $167,494, but dividends were held down to a modest $21,600 or 12 per cent of the paid capital. On January 1, 1795, all shares bought on time had been paid for and the full capital of $600,000 was in the hands of the company and presumably invested at interest. That year premium receipts continued to outrun losses by $303,128 to $139,192 and at the Board meeting to determine the semi-annual dividend payable in January there was sentiment for a more liberal treatment of the stockholders. A motion was made and seconded for a 12-per-cent dividend, which would have been $1.20 a share. It did not prevail and fifty cents a share, or 5 per cent, was voted.[12] But at the July meeting a real melon was cut, in the form of a 17½-per-cent dividend, making a total of 22½ per cent for the year or a total distribution of $135,000—a handsome return on an investment at any time, and more remarkable still when money is tight. It is no wonder that North America shares which had cost the original purchasers

$10 were changing hands for $13 and probably more.[13] But better things yet were in store for the stockholders. Dividends for 1796 totalled 28¾ per cent on receipts of $467,122 against $261,803 in losses. And the year 1797 was ushered in with the declaration of a January half-year dividend of 20 per cent.

Regarding the figures foregoing it should be understood, however, that the difference between losses paid and premiums taken in did not always represent certain profit to the company for the period named. There were cases of ships seized and carried away before prize courts on which the company did not pay the losses for a term of years, pending determination of its liability. For example the figure given for 1796 includes the premium received for the *Mount Vernon's* insurance, whereas the North America did not pay that loss until April 4, 1798, nearly two years after it was seized by the *Flying Fish*.[14] Money had to be set aside to meet such contingencies.

The employment of surplus funds presented a problem, enhanced by business uncertainty. An application for a loan by the Philadelphia & Lancaster Turnpike Company, the toll road over which so many emigrants passed toward the frontier West, was turned down though sponsored by William Sansom, a new director of great financial acumen. The company did, however, purchase eighty shares of Turnpike stock. It voted also to purchase, in the conservative amount of $15,000, its own shares provided they could be obtained for $13 or less. That shares in a company returning such dividends could be had for this price is evidence of the prevailing money stringency.

Lotteries continued to be a favorite method for promoting certain public improvements. While the directors turned down numerous opportunities to participate in them, they eagerly subscribed in June 1794 to two hundred tickets in the "Lottery for building Piers at New Castle." Here was a project which would benefit marine insurers. The North America thought so well of the scheme that fifty additional tickets were bought in the fall.[15]

An important use for idle funds was found in bottomry and respondentia loans—terms used to designate a maritime practice of the day which became more active in times of stress when shippers and shipowners were likely to be hard up. Such loans were made on ships or cargoes or both. In the case of a respondentia loan the lender advanced the shipper a sum at high interest—sometimes as much as 25 per cent. If the cargo reached its destination the shipper repaid the loan out of the proceeds. If the cargo were lost the lender was out his principal amount and the shipper out both the value of his cargo in excess of the loan, if uninsured, and the interest he had paid in advance. A bottomry loan, on a hull, operated the same way. The North America loaned only up to 50 per cent of the value of ship or of the cargo and only on vessels or cargoes carrying the company's insurance. By this means the North America doubled its hazard on many craft, doubling also its profits in case of a successful voyage.[16]

Already the company owned one hundred shares in the Bank of Pennsylvania. In 1794 it engaged to buy fifty more at $460 a share. The seller was Robert Morris, the country's foremost capitalist. In recognition of the prodigies of finance Morris worked during the Revolution President Washington had offered him the post of Secretary of the Treasury, but Morris suggested Hamilton instead and took a seat in the Senate. Before his term was to expire in 1795 he made great investments in unoccupied western lands, certain the day would come when they would be filled with settlers. He bought real estate in the townsite of Washington on the Potomac and in several lesser enterprises all of whose prosperity depended on the country's growth. He began the construction on Chestnut Street, between Seventh and Eighth, of a marble palace on a scale not before attempted by the builder of a residence in America.

Then had come the European wars and the closing in of hard times. When Morris engaged to sell his bank shares he was in urgent need of money, though this was a fact few suspected. The North America did not suspect it and advanced Mr. Morris $23,000 on his word to deliver the stock. Nearly anyone would have done the same for the credit of Robert Morris was probably as good as that of any man in the United States. Yet, amazingly, when nearly four months passed and the stock had not been produced, Secretary Hazard wrote asking, at least, for security. After some backing and filling, security was obtained in the form of a mortgage on Morrisville, a landed property the financier had purchased on the Delaware opposite Trenton, with a view to its industrial development.

By early 1795 Robert Morris was known to be in trouble, and creditors descended upon him in a cloud. The depression in trade and the rascality of a partner made his western lands unsalable.

Everything he had was mortgaged. Construction on the Chestnut Street palace stopped. Morris defaulted the interest on his mortgage to the North America. Probably a third of the twenty-five directors of the company were Morris' warm personal friends. Some, like Nesbitt, had worked with him in the struggle to finance the Revolution. Robert Morris' predicament was due to the dishonesty of a man he had trusted and to overconfidence in the immediate future of the nation he had helped to establish. The directors of the North America were disposed to be lenient, but, as Hazard wrote in one of his letters, the question was not a personal one. The directors were trustees of funds belonging to others. They were lenient, nevertheless. At meeting after meeting of the Board the matter was discussed and action postponed, though Hazard confessed he "could not obtain anything more than *promises*" from Mr. Morris.

Morris' promises, once as good as gold, were depreciating rapidly. Yet, realizing they were dealing with one of the great personal tragedies of the time, the Board of the North America hesitated to press its claim. Other creditors had no such compunctions. With the beginning of 1797 the financial empire of Robert Morris was in a state of collapse. On January 9 the Board adopted a resolution which must have cost its sponsors a tug at the heart. "If the Interest shall not be paid within fifteen Days from this Date the necessary Steps shall be taken, without further Delay, for foreclosing the Mortgage given for the Security of the Debt from M^r. Morris." Nevertheless, when the fifteen days passed there was no foreclosure.[17]

6

The company was less generous with some of its own people. The increase in business had brought about an expansion of personnel—both in the office and outside. Boatmen under fee were kept at Cape May, New Jersey, and at Lewes, Delaware, to pilot vessels through the dangerous shoals of Delaware Bay. By resolution of the Board the office hours were lengthened—from 9 A.M. to 2 P.M. and from 4 to 8 P.M. The secretary was supposed to be on hand from 10 to 2 and 4 to 8, the president from 11 to 2 and 5 to 8, the Committee of the Week, composed of Board members, from 12 to 2 and 6 to 8 daily. Hazard's hours were frequently longer than the requirements indicated, and sometimes he complained of the confinement. "It is now near Ten O'clock at night," he wrote a friend, "and I have not left the office yet."[18]

On May 9, 1794, "the Draft of a Device for Seal presented by Mr. Blodget was approved." Blodget, the amateur architect who loved to draw, probably made the draft with his own hand. Thus came into being the seal of the Insurance Company of North America, which remains unchanged today. It represents Justice with her scales seated beside a box of salvaged cargo, on which rests a horn of plenty. The goddess is giving money to a seaman whose ship has been wrecked on the rocky coast in the background.

Salary raises within the company were notable for their smallness, Hazard's pay being increased from $1,600 to $2,000 a year and President Nesbitt's from $1,600 to $2,500. Valentine, the porter and general factotum, was a personage of sufficient importance to claim the attention of the Board of Directors. In 1796 his application for a salary increase—from $250 a year—was refused "but the Board unanimously agreed to give him one hundred Dollars extra for the present year." One Kenney, who hung about the City Tavern and the wharves gathering marine tidings, was voted $20 "for his assiduity," with a promise of $50 "if he will in future regularly leave at this office the earliest Intelligence as it arrives." Another marine investment was the purchase from Clement Biddle, "notary public, scrivener and broker," of two volumes of sea charts for which the North America paid "Twenty six & two thirds dollars."

An indication of the steps the company was taking to reduce the likelihood of disasters in Delaware Bay may be gathered from a note signed "William Eldredge, Pilot, Cape May, Dec.[r] 22, 1797." He claimed that the men manning the boats "attending and Roweing from the Shore to Vessels at the Capes in Winter season find our Selves so illy paid that the Cervice ondoubtedly will be neglected." He went on to indicate what might happen in that event. "Frequently in the Coldest of the Winter we Send of[f] A bote maned with 5 or 6 ores to giv Infermation to Vessels beating of[f] the Capes—without such infermation ... Sum times wold Accasion the Loss of both Ship and Cargo or ablige them to leave the Capes with the loss of their Ankers and Cables." Pilot Eldredge thought the boatmen should have more money, and added a constructive suggestion. "I believe it wold be advantages to this Navigation to have Sum Supplies at the Capes for the Relief of Vessels in Distress. . . . I leave to the Consideration of whom it may Concearn the Purport of what hath been Said."[19]

The action on Eldredge's request and recommendation does not appear, though steps must have been taken to keep the boatmen on their jobs and satisfied. Their work was too important for it to have been otherwise, the company being deeply interested in measures for making safer the passage in and out of the Capes, which had such a bad name among seamen.

The first important change in the governing personnel of the North America came in January 1796, when John Maxwell Nesbitt resigned the office of president on account of ill health and was succeeded by Colonel Charles Pettit.

The second head of the company, like the first, belonged distinctly to the Revolutionary generation. As a colonial official, rising to secretary of his native province of New Jersey, Pettit had been close to the events which as early as 1760 were drawing America apart from the mother country. Ineffectually he strove to avert this, but, when the break came, threw his lot with the Revolutionary cause. A boyhood friend of General Nathanael Greene, Pettit became Greene's first assistant as quartermaster general of the army. Entering business in Philadelphia after the war, he maintained his interest in public affairs, serving in the State Legislature and in Congress. He was the author of Pennsylvania's funding system and an authority on questions of public finance. Fifty-nine years old when he accepted the presidency of the North America, Colonel Pettit was in appearance an old-school gentleman of the Revolutionary era: powdered wig, knee breeches, silk stockings and silver-buckled shoes. Gilbert Stuart and Charles Willson Peale, to whose brushes we owe likenesses of so many of Pettit's contemporaries of renown, painted portraits of him.

CHAPTER IV

A FIGHT FOR LIFE

I

FLUSHED by the feats of arms of her latest prodigy, Napoleon Bonaparte, France met the hardening temper of the United States with increasing hostility. Ever more severe grew the restrictions imposed on sea-borne commerce in an effort to isolate her island adversary, England. French ports were closed to vessels which had so much as dropped anchor in a British harbor. Countering move for move, England blockaded Holland as well as France, even interdicting trade between the Dutch and Spanish colonies and the mother countries.

These officially proclaimed impediments to our commerce did not tell the whole story, though. Vessels of the French and the British navies frequently exceeded their authorized powers. Privateers of both nations, swarming the seas, customarily did so. The practice of paying privateersmen in booty was an incentive to a broad interpretation of authority. Scores of American vessels were taken without a shadow of justification. Moreover, the neutrality of Spain was a farce. French privateers were fitted out in Spanish ports, their prizes condemned by French consuls on Spanish soil. Not to be left out of the free-for-all looting, under a pretext of blockading Gibraltar Spain herself began seizing American ships passing through that strait.

The provisions of the Jay treaty and a shrewd evaluation of the recent drift of American sentiment away from France did something to mitigate the offenses committed by the British, however. They often paid for confiscated cargoes; London attempted to restrain the greed of British West Indian prize courts; treaty machinery looking toward indemnification in the case of wrongful seizures slowly took form. On the strength of this the Insurance Company of North America named agents in London and in some of the British colonies to establish friendly contacts with officialdom.

Nevertheless, immediate losses mounted alarmingly, the North America's going to $804,458 in 1797, against $261,000 for the year before. Premiums reached figures which would have been prohibitory in many cases except for the respondentia loan policy which enabled shippers to borrow (at high rates, it is true) on their cargoes in advance of sailings. Some examples of premiums charged by the North America in 1797:

"Jany 28—John Wilcocks at & from Montseratt to touch and trade at all Ports and places for Six Callendar Months . . . on the Brig Three Brothers John Briggs master . . . and the assured agrees to pay a further Premium in proportion for the time the Risque shall continue . . . after the said Six Months D^{rs}. 6000 @ 25 p C^t—1500. . . .

"Feby 20 David Easton at & from Rappahanock River to Martinique . . . on the Schooner Charming Betsey . . . freight . . . D^{rs} 1600 @ 20 p C^t—320. . . . The assured warrants [the cargo] . . . to be American Property and that the Vessel is an American Bottom. . . .

"Augt. 15 Samuel A. Otis at & from St Iago De Cuba to Jamaica and at and from thence to Philadelphia . . . on the Brig^e. Neutrality William H. Nicholls master Vessel D^{rs}. 3000 @ 30 p C^t—900. . . . The above vessel is declared to be an American Prize purchased at St Iago de Cuba."[1]

But we were doing something about this. More money for fortifications was voted; the frigates *Constitution, Constellation* and *United States* were hastened to completion and manned; the militia strengthened. At the same time President Adams took a line looking toward a peaceable solution by dispatching a three-man commission to France to try for an agreement which would include payment for seizures.

The commissioners departed in the fall of 1797, and in March 1798 Adams gravely announced to Congress that the mission had failed. The country must prepare for the worst, he added. In general the country was ready for the worst and heartily approved of further defensive measures. The pro-French minority put in a noisy dissent, however, the situation being aggravated by partisan politics. Whereupon Adams, who had briefly reported the ill success of our envoys, published their full report, substituting the initials X, Y and Z for the three French dignitaries who had approached the Americans with demands the fulfillment of which should precede any negotiations. These were a disavowal of certain strong words President Adams had used toward France, a loan to France and a gratuity of $250,000 to Talleyrand, the French foreign minister.

The X Y Z Papers, as they were called, brought a storm against France as great as some of the demonstrations in her favor a few years earlier. "Millions for defense but not a cent for tribute!" The street in front of the offices of the Insurance Company of North America filled with young men converging upon the City Tavern where 1,200 of them formed up and marched past the house of the President in a demonstration of loyalty. Subscriptions to build and arm ships were started in every coastal city, three of the seven committeemen in charge of the Philadelphia fund being directors of the insurance company. The North America suspended war risks on vessels bound for France.

Congress issued privateer commissions and authorized the arming of merchant ships. It began to raise an army and recalled Washington to active duty with the rank of lieutenant general. The undeclared war with France opened in August when the naval sloop *Delaware,* Captain Stephen Decatur, the elder, captured the French privateer *Le Croyable.* Hostilities lasted two years, with a series of brilliant exploits for our arms on the sea. Without these victories it appears that the Stars and Stripes would have been swept from the oceans. Even with them the perils continued real enough. In 1798 the business of the Insurance Company of North America was the biggest in its history thus far, net receipts from premiums totaling $1,304,218—a stupendous sum for the time. But losses also were the highest in the company's experience—$1,195,724—reducing the favorable balance to $108,494. The year before on a smaller volume this balance had been $423,000.

This was only the beginning of adverse tidings. The Insurance Company of North America closed the year 1799 with an actual deficit of $120,549 on marine insurance operations—net premiums aggregating $830,976 and losses $951,525. In 1800 this deficit continued—on receipts of $912,510 against losses of $954,767. Worse was to come. In 1801 the volume of business dropped more than 50 per cent, with outgo exceeding income by the alarming figure of $224,-000. The majority of the sea losses responsible for these figures was the work of the French.

Assuming the statistics foregoing to be fairly reflective of American shipping conditions as a whole, it would appear that the effects of our naval operations against France have been exaggerated by some historians. Yet without them our overseas trade must have been virtually extinguished.

Adams sent another commission abroad and this time Napoleon listened to reason. The result was a peace treaty signed in September 1800 and ratified in December 1801. France promised to abandon some of her more pernicious interferences with our commerce. But whereas the Jay treaty with England had provided for reciprocal adjudication of private claims, the French compact bartered these away. To give satisfaction for our defaults under the treaty of 1778 the United States Government relieved France of responsibility in the matter of the claims of American citizens arising from the recent confiscations at sea. Thus the United States took private property for public use. The Insurance Company of North America computed its stake in this property to be $1,952,000—representing marine losses the company asserted it had sustained at French hands. It believed our Government honor bound to make restitution.

In the interim between the signing and the ratification of the treaty President Pettit took the lead in a move to bring the matter before Congress. Common cause was made with the Insurance Company of the State of Pennsylvania. During the recent crisis these companies had been working closer together, dividing risks and consulting on rates. Seeking the strength of a further united front, Pettit corresponded with the heads of insurance companies in New York, Baltimore and Charleston. On the initiative of Pettit, a fortnight after the treaty had been declared effective a meeting of individual losers was called at the City Tavern and a committee of seven named to represent their interests. Four of the members, including the chairman, Joseph Ball, were directors of the North America. Another member was Stephen Girard whose persistent French sympathies had hitherto placed him in opposition to the general policy pursued by the North America.[2]

The result was a memorial to Congress requesting reparation. A committee of the House acted promptly, calling the claims just and recommending their payment from the Treasury.

2

The naval warfare against France engendered friendlier feelings toward England. British naval vessels and privateers were welcomed to our ports as once French vessels had been. No better example of this altered sentiment could be cited than a communication from the president of the Insurance Company of North America to Captain Joseph Larcom of the British man-of-war *Hind*. Seeking shelter in the Potomac River from heavy weather, the *Hind* had found the American merchantman *Sally* aground and pulled her free. As the *Sally* had been insured by the North America this act resulted in a considerable saving to the company. Hence this letter:

"The President and Directors of the Insurance Company of North America, having been informed of the extraordinary exertions made by the crew of the ship under your command to effect the preservation of the ship Sally, Capt. Gelston, and her crew, when in iminent danger of being lost, have requested me to present their sincere acknowledgments and thanks. . . .

"From the well-known character of the seamen of your nation, for benevolence, generosity and bravery in their general conduct, they may consider their exertions on this occasion only as a duty that a brother Seaman owes to another; yet we cannot forego the pleasure of expressing the sense we entertain of their merits on this occasion.

"You will permit me, Sir, to request the favour of your acceptance of one thousand dollars, to be distributed in such manner as you shall think proper, among the crew of your Ship."[3]

The Anglo-British commission was at work on our Jay treaty claims for losses antedating 1795. The High Court of Admiralty, sitting in London, passed on claims of later dates, including appeals from the findings of the colonial prize courts in various quarters of the globe. The claims in which we were chiefly concerned were dealt with by the courts that sat in the West Indies and at Halifax, Nova Scotia. To represent the North America's interests before these bodies a number of "settling agents" were appointed. Busiest of these was the London agent, John Fry, Jr., a Philadelphian and a former director of the North America, who had entered business in England. Other agents were named in Jamaica, Halifax, Nassau and Bermuda. On the latter island the agents were James and William Perot, recommended by their brothers Elliston and John Perot, North Water Street merchants who insured their shipments of "callico, cottons, Irish linen, flannels" with the North America.[4]

Agents in France and in Spain also were appointed to see what could be done about our claims against those nations. Though it appears that the North America took the initiative in appointing them, these agents worked on the claims of other insurers as well. Frequently several companies or private underwriting groups would be interested in the same case, as the practice of dividing risks became more common all the time.

Correspondence between the home office and its overseas agents affords interesting glimpses into the maritime history of the period. From a single memorandum to John Fry, Jr., epitomizing the circumstances of twenty-one captures, the following examples are cited as representative:

"Brig John Jay, Wm. Broad M^r., a New England Ship chartered by Mr Dupuy, a Citizen of New York, bound from Aux Cayes to New York in 1798; Captured by the King's Ship Adventure, Capt. Chelcott, condemned at Jamaica; appeal ent^d & admitted in 1799. Insured in this Office for M^r. Dupuy $8000, on Goods, & $2000 on freight. Loss paid on proof of being American property.

"Brig Hopewell, Henry Dandelot M^r., owned by R^d Gernon of Philad. Captured by the French on her way to Barracoa, in April 1799; recaptured the same day by a british Cruizer; Salvage only Supposed to be due, having clear Documents of American Bottom & Property; but Vessel & Cargo were totally condemned as prize at Jamaica. Appeal ent. & papers forwarded to England. We have paid a total loss of $10,795 on Goods, & suppose it to be a clear case for recovery, subject to Salvage.

"Brig Eagle, from Philad^a. for Havanna; Vessel & Cargo owned by Richd Gernon of Philad^a Captured & taken to New Providence about June 1799; full & clear Documents of Am^n. Bottom & Property. But the Wisdom of the Judge decided a few Casks of Sugar box Nails to be contraband, & thereupon condemned them as prize. The Vessel & the rest of the Cargo indicated no other cause for condemnation. An Appeal entered, & papers forwarded to England—total loss paid by this Office on $16,800 Goods, of $2000 Super Cargo's Commissions. The Penn^a Insur^e C^o. are also interested in this cause.

"Brig Currier, McKeever, from Philad^a for Havanna, about June 1799 taken to N. Providence [Nassau]; final judgment delayed, & Commission issued to obtain farther proofs; no decision yet made known here. In the meantime, Mr. Tarasion, the owner of the Vessel had been paid by us a total loss of $3500. on Vessel, & $2000 on Freight, on abandonment [to the insurance company by the owner of all interest in claims for recovery.] Several Insurances were also made in this Office on Goods to the amount of $12000, or $15000, payment of which is demanded and some actually made.

"Ship Gadsden, Capt. Gardner, from Rh. Island to Port Passage in Spain, insured 12 Octr. 1799 for Fred^k Kohne, Owner of the Ship & Cargo, $15,400 Goods American property—taken & carried to Halifax. Part of the Cargo taken in at Charleston, S. Carolina, released; but part appearing to be taken in at Laguira condemned, together with the Ship. Appealed for Pretty large Sums insured in several offices. An abandonment has been offered, and, it is said, accepted by the Penns^a. Office. This office have not thought proper to accept it nor to acknowledge the loss, tho' a suit is threatened, & we may ultimately become interested.

"Ship America, Ja^s. D. Burger M^r., insured in July 1799 for J. & B Bohlen from Amsterdam to New York—said to be captured & carried into England; $1400, on Goods & Profits.

"Schooner Aquedita—Spanish Property from New Providence to a Spanish Port, under Licence from the Governor pursuant to the King's instructions—Captured, carried to Jamaica, acquitted—appealed for by the Captors. Insured in this Office $25,000 on Goods and $3500 on Vessel. A Loss is demanded & part of the money has been advanced."[5]

Thus it appears that, friendly feelings notwithstanding, our commerce still suffered materially at the hands of the English. True, means of possible redress were available. But like the mills of the gods, this machinery ground slowly. To settle a single case it was often necessary to assemble testimony and a host of papers from distant parts of the world at a time when ocean travel was slow and precarious. "We are lately informed," Hazard wrote to Fry, "of the Capture [by the French] of the Ship William Penn on her passage home from London. She carried with her a large Bundle of Papers in the Case of the Brig Friendship, Capt Gallagher, and additional Documents in the case of the Hector, Capt. Connell. This loss will prove a Serious Inconvenience." It would be necessary to send to Jamaica for duplicates of the *Friendship* papers. As an additional safeguard an appeal was made to the French to deliver them from the captured vessel which had been taken to Bordeaux.[6] These inconveniences, delaying consideration of the case of the *Friendship*

COLONEL CHARLES PETTIT

Assistant Quartermaster-General Continental Army, member Congress from Pennsylvania, merchant and private marine underwriter in days before incorporated companies. President Insurance Company of North America, 1796-1798 and 1799-1806. Saw company through its greatest financial crisis arising from naval war with France, 1798-1800.

From a portrait by Charles Willson Peale, owned by Worcester (Massachusetts) Art Museum and reproduced by permission.

for months, were in addition to the payment of insurance on the
William Penn.

In the fulness of time this state of affairs reflected itself in that consideration vital to stockholders: dividends. In 1797 the bonanza character of the company's dividends had been maintained despite the
narrowing margin between income and outgo. One hundred and
eighty thousand dollars or 30 per cent of par was paid. In January
1798 the rate was maintained with a 15-per-cent semi-annual dividend but in July of that year the Board voted to pass a dividend for
the first time. In January 1799, however, a 20-per-cent dividend was
announced and the stockholders felt easier. Their feelings went
down six months later, though, when the July dividend was again
passed. And in 1800 the January dividend was passed. Despite an
enormous amount of business done, losses had exceeded receipts for
the year of 1799 by $120,549.

The year 1800 opened more brightly. In March came word from
Fry in London that the first claims had been paid by the British
Government. The amount was small but it cheered President Pettit,
who wrote: "That you have actually received *Some* money & may
expect more Somewhat revives the Spirits of the Stockholders."[7]
The year proved a better one than 1799, with the excess of losses
over premiums cut to $42,000. But no dividend was voted, and the
spirits of the stockholders sank again. Some of them sold their
shares.

Eighteen hundred and one was a year of ups and downs. It started
badly, with losses far outrunning receipts. No dividend was paid in
January or in July. Shares sank to 5. In October the picture was
more comforting. Writing that he had invested $40,000 of the com-
pany's funds in United States three-per-cents, Colonel Pettit said it
was better off by $100,000 than in the January preceding. The blow
of the French treaty began to wear off as hope grew that surely the
United States would meet the claims of its citizens which had been
bartered away. Pettit heard of a man selling for 7¼ two thousand
shares he had lately bought for 5½.[8] Despite these promising signs
a heavy burden of losses during the last quarter made 1801 the
worst year yet for marine operations, the deficit being $224,000. A
January 1802 dividend was out of the question, making the sixth consecutive semiannual omission.

3

After the treaty of 1801 it was no longer possible to lay the bulk of our sea troubles at the door of the French. Our ardor for the English began to cool. The tortuous course of events which drew us into the War of 1812 were in train. Instead of the agreeable expressions in the company's letter of 1799 to Captain Larcom, eighteen months later President Pettit was writing in this vein on the subject of an American ship, insured for $25,000, overhauled near Charleston, South Carolina, its destination:

"The late Captures made by the British Ships are truly alarming, and none more So than those made by the Halifax Squadron, as we cannot discern the principles or pretences on which Some of them are made, & of course know not by what precautions to guard against them. They Seem to imply Some new rule of conduct of which we are uninformed."[9]

Colonial courts were notoriously severe and frequently corrupt. Something better was expected of the High Court of Admiralty in London, but even there Colonel Pettit found the expense of prosecuting claims high and the red tape hard to get through. To Fry:

"One would suppose that a Government whose servants have been permitted so wantonly and carelessly to injure innocent neutrals and load them with losses and difficulty, would, when they are pretending to restore the plundered property, remove the difficulties and impediments which legal forms and customs seem to plant in the way. . . . A mere award, clogged with insuperable impediments [to collection of the money] is but a mockery of justice."[10]

Colonel Pettit had cause for dismay. In 1802 marine premium receipts dropped to $103,902, which was less than the figure for 1793, the company's first full year in business. Losses stood at $331,-944, giving a deficit of $228,042, the largest in the company's history and the fourth annual deficit in a row. But it seemed that the bottom had been reached. While receipts for 1803 were only $134,901, losses dropped to $145,029, reducing the adverse balance to $10,128. The next year the corner was turned. Premiums went to $197,255 and losses were $159,759, yielding the first profit on marine insurance since 1798.

During these lean years the company had kept its head above water only by heroic measures. Fortunately it had begun the period with its finances in good condition—though that condition would have been better had not a dividend of $120,000 or 20 per cent been distributed in January 1799, the year the North America first ran behind. To meet the early deficits, however, were the earnings of surplus and capital, including sizable receipts from respondentia loans and bottomry bonds. There was also a comparatively small but very welcome income from a slowly expanding fire-insurance business. Moreover, the company pressed its debtors, proceeding, at length, against Robert Morris—though not until another creditor had thrown that unfortunate man into a debtors' prison, rendering his financial affairs hopeless of redemption.

The time soon came when money from all these sources was insufficient. The company had to take from the principal sum of its surplus. Next the capital account was encroached upon. An example:

"For loss of the Brig Molly, Capt.ⁿ Harding . . . to be paid on twenty days notice: The President Stated that in order to meet this contingency it may become necessary to dispose of a part of the Capital Stock of the Company. It was left to the discretion of the President to dispose of as much Stock as may be necessary for this purpose. . . ."[11]

This went on until, in January 1804, a deeply concerned committee of share owners, examining the records of the company, reported to the main body of stockholders that "actual Capital which may be fairly relied upon and which is in the possession of the Company is not equal to half its original Stock after payment of the claims against it."[12] This means $300,000 of the original $600,000 capital gone or immobilized. A less courageous man than Charles Pettit might have thrown in the sponge, and a less resourceful one failed in any event.

Other revenue which had gone into the maw of deficit consisted of reparations paid by the British for, notwithstanding Colonel Pettit's complaints about expense and delay, $411,605 had been received by the end of 1803. This was duly reported by the stockholders' committee, quoted above, which added "the flattering prospect" that perhaps $494,066 more would come in from that source.[13]

There were also claims against the French in the amount of the magnificent sum of $1,952,000, traded away by the treaty of 1801, which the company looked to the United States to refund. Receipt of any considerable part of this money would restore the finances of the North America at one stroke. Yet no action by Congress had been taken on the report of the committee of the House which had declared the money due. That the Government would eventually honor the obligation, however, remained a confident expectation which helped to carry the company through dismal days.

4

An unfortunate outcome of the North America's crippled financial condition was its inability to take proper advantage of a sudden boom in American shipping. England was now supreme on the water, with the sea power of France and Holland at her mercy. We were also at her mercy, but the opportunities in the carrying trade were so plentiful and the world so wide that we profited despite the risks. Our shipyards were busier than ever before and our flag waved over every ocean. The British could not intercept them all, and much trade went through legitimately by the practice of technically "neutralizing" cargoes in the United States. From Africa, from China, from the rich Dutch East Indies and from the Philippine Islands, from South America and from the familiar ports of the Caribbean, cargoes were carried to the United States and duty paid on them. Then, sometimes without unloading, they were re-exported as American goods. Spain even transported specie and bullion from her treasure house of Mexico in American hulls.

The shipping boom brought an insurance boom. Seven new companies, dating from 1797 to 1804, were in business in New York and four in Philadelphia. In addition a novel practice sprang up in New York with the appearance of the "out-of-door underwriter," a sort of free-lance salesman whose office was the curb. He was a trial to the established insurance companies, always shading their rates a fraction, and winding up by giving them his business at his price, for he peddled his policies among them and invited their competitive bids. On top of this the out-of-door underwriter collected a commission. Curiously the out-of-door underwriters had built up good reputations, and Philadelphia merchants had already got onto the pecuniary advantages to be gained by shopping for their marine insurance in New York.[14]

This competition as well as that offered by the new insurance companies made the North America's road to recovery a rocky one. The first of the new local companies was the Union which in 1803 began business under imposing auspices. On the Board of Directors was Stephen Girard, whose business prestige was as high as that of any other man in the United States. Three directors of the North America resigned to try their fortunes with the Union: Joseph Ball, who became president; Richard Dale, an ex-naval officer under John Paul Jones; and Lewis Clapier.

On February 6, 1804, the Phoenix Insurance Company obtained its charter. While this organization drew off no directors from the North America, its presence was felt in another way. The charter of the Phoenix provided for capitalization of $600,000 with the following proviso: "one-half of the capital stock to be in shares of the Insurance Company of North America."[15] That would be half of the North America's capital stock, also. Whether the ambition of the incorporators of the Phoenix was fully realized in this particular seems unascertainable, though it is known that they got hold of a good deal of North America stock. In 1806 the directors of the North America admitted the Phoenix' ownership of "a considerable proportion of the Capital Stock" of the older company.[16]

On March 10 the Delaware Insurance Company was formed. Thomas Fitzsimons, who had quit the North America in 1794 to join the Insurance Company of the State of Pennsylvania, was elected president. Two directors of the North America, Samuel Keith and Andrew Bayard, became members of the Board of the new organization. Bayard was a son-in-law of President Pettit of the North America.

Ten days later the Philadelphia Insurance Company made its debut with an impressive list of backers, including five who were or recently had been directors of the North America. Three new companies in six weeks probably still constitute a record for swift expansion in the marine-insurance field.

Before the smoke of these exertions had cleared away, President Pettit gave his settling agent in Jamaica, William Savage, a candid account of the North America's position. Losses at the hands of the English and French, tardiness in adjudicating foreign claims and the great expense of the process "had so far diminished the Capital Stock of the Company, tho' large, as to oblige them to refrain from making dividends for a number of years past. This incapacity Still continues as we are restrained by our Charter from making dividends till the capital shall be restored to the amount of $600,000.

"We are gradually approaching this degree of restoration," continued Colonel Pettit, "and hope to accomplish this, partly by retributions [for British and French losses] and part by growing profits of current business." Then Pettit touched the latest complication of his hydra-headed problem. "But a great increase in rival institutions will considerably retard the progress of the latter resourse [profits from current business] because no less than four new Companies, free from incumbrances of former losses, have been organized within a few Months past. These circumstances have induced our Company to be more circumspect in taking Risques of uncommon hazard, and also in the expenses of the office till the time shall arrive at which they may recommense the making of dividends, which we have a flattering hope may happen in the course of a year or two."

With these statements the Colonel came down to the business immediately at hand. The Union Company had started off with a flourish which was to put 1,198 policies on its books in twelve months' time. Though the amount of the premiums flowing from this enterprise is unavailable, it seems very likely that the sum exceeded the North America's receipts for the same period. Joseph Ball was proving an energetic captain of the Union's affairs, one of his first moves being to try to hire away the North America's Jamaica agent, William Savage. Pettit met the challenge with dignity. After sketching the North America's situation and prospects he said that Savage's work in Jamaica had been satisfactory. The directors held him in esteem, and it had been as a director of the North America that Mr. Ball of the Union had learned to value the services of the Jamaica agent. In closing Colonel Pettit said that the North America "wishes to preserve your friendship and a continuance of your aid," but there was no appeal to decline the offer of Mr. Ball.[17]

Savage remained with the North America.

Thus the old soldier who remembered the dark-before-dawn of the Revolutionary War fought to retain intact his business organization, spread now over half of the world, and to keep his embattled company afloat during the most difficult years of its experience.

JOSEPH BALL

Proprietor of an iron works which made munitions for Continental Army. Member original Board of the Directors Insurance Company of North America, he served as president between January, 1798, and July, 1799, while Colonel Charles Pettit was incapacitated by injuries in a carriage accident.

From a portrait by Gilbert Stuart, owned by the North America.

As it happened he had been a little oversanguine about the early prospect of restoring the capital, permitting the resumption of dividends. Stockholders were restive and the directors appealed to Jared Ingersoll for an opinion as to the "propriety" of asking the Legislature for permission to declare dividends on the capital in the company's hands. The lawyer said such an application would be proper. The subject seems to have been debated at some length, the conservatives carrying the day. There was no application and consequently there were no dividends.[18]

It was perhaps as well, for the North America had to reinforce itself against still further competition when, in 1806, the Marine and Fire Insurance Company of Philadelphia was formed. John Leamy, an original stockholder, an incorporator and a member of the Board of Directors of the North America since the founding in Independence Hall, resigned his office to take the presidency of this latest rival. The loss of so experienced and useful a man was bound to be felt.

5

Other familiar faces were missing from the directors' table. In 1799 Samuel Blodget, Jr., in debt to the company and heavily involved in Washington real estate and promotion ventures, resigned to try to straighten out his affairs on the Potomac. He failed and in three years was imprisoned for debt, though the North America had no part in this action. It remained the task of a later generation to recognize the soundness of his vision of the future of the capital city and to couple his name with that of Robert Morris as one who had been in advance of his time.

In January 1800 Ebenezer Hazard relinquished his post as secretary, giving ill health as the reason. It seems also that Hazard, who had long complained of the confining nature of his insurance duties, wished leisure to continue his historical and other scholarly pursuits which included collaboration on a translation of the Bible from the Greek. Unlike so many of his acquaintances, Hazard had brought his large personal fortune through the upsetting times without impairment. Retiring to the tranquillity of his library in the big house in Arch Street, the genial Hazard retained a heavy stock interest in the North America and was frequently consulted by his friends on the Board. Moreover, he wound up the company's interest in the sad affairs of Robert Morris, and after three or four years' patient effort seems to have collected about all that was due. Robert S. Stephens, first clerk, took over Hazard's duties but was not given the title of secretary until 1806.

To the places vacated by those who left its service from one motive or another, the North America fortunately was able to attract some excellent men. They were younger than their predecessors. The day of the Revolutionary veteran was passing. Washington died in 1799. True, John Inskeep, who became a director in 1802, and immediately made his presence felt, had served in the Continental Army as a youth of nineteen. But his reputation and his fortune had been made as a merchant after the close of the war. He was mayor of Philadelphia when he joined the North America's Board.

Alexander Elmslie, another influential new director, had landed in Philadelphia from Scotland in 1780 as a lad of twelve. Going to work in James Oldden's dry-goods importing house in South Second Street, he became a partner shortly after his twenty-first birthday. In 1801 he succeeded Oldden on the Board of the North America. A stranger would not have guessed Director Elmslie, living frugally and dressing plainly, to be the rich man that he was. Another addition to the Board was William Waln, valuable both on his own account and because of the Waln family's connection with the China trade. The Waln account was a profitable one and William was the first of three Walns to sit on the North America's Board.

The tedious work in connection with the settlement of foreign claims obliged the company to engage another attorney to help Jared Ingersoll. He was lively and energetic Joseph Hopkinson, six years old in 1776 when his father, Francis Hopkinson, had signed the Declaration of Independence. During the stirring days of 1798 Joseph had composed the words of the song "Hail Columbia." The following year his legal talents were employed in trying to save from ruin his father-in-law, Governor Mifflin, who had signed the North America's charter of incorporation. Mifflin had been caught up in speculations akin to those of Morris and Blodget. Creditors drove him out of Philadelphia and in 1800 the old statesman, who had been a quartermaster general of Washington's army, died heartbroken and penniless. The State of Pennsylvania paid the expenses of his funeral.

In such times the Insurance Company of North America stood in

need of all the sagacity and the levelheaded leadership which Charles
Pettit could muster. The Colonel responded to the call. His children
grown and gone, the welfare of the company became his very life.
Badly injured in a carriage accident, Pettit had himself carried to the
offices of the company which, in December 1797, had been transferred to a building of its own at the southwest corner of South Front
and Walnut. But his injuries were too serious to permit of direction
of the affairs of the company from his bed as he had hoped. Consequently Director Joseph Ball was chosen president, though the
Board attested to the value of having Colonel Pettit close at hand by
permitting him to fit up two rooms on the third floor of the building
as living quarters. Ball held office from January 1798 until July 1799,
when the Colonel had recovered sufficiently to come downstairs and
resume the helm. Mr. Ball returned to the Board, serving until he
quit to head the Union in 1803.

Having grown accustomed to them during nearly two years of
invalidism, President Pettit continued to make his home in the rooms
above his office, the only other resident of the building being Valentine; the porter. When yellow fever returned in 1799 president and
porter moved with the company's offices to temporary quarters in
Germantown. In 1804 the North America left Front Street for
good and took quarters in a rented building at 98 (now 204) South
Second Street, just off Walnut and half a block from the City Tavern
which had been Pettit's favorite haunt for more than thirty years.
The Front Street property was advertised for sale: "A three story
Brick House, well adapted to business of various kinds . . . [and]
nearly equal to new, having been built Since the Revolution." The
purchaser, too, would acquire the fireproof vault which the insurance
company had commissioned Antoine Ratshillar, a blacksmith in
Apple Tree Alley, to install.[19]

6

The new location formed a part of what was already being called
"Insurance Row." Next door, at 96 South Second, was the Phoenix
Company; at the corner of Walnut and Second, the Philadelphia; at
42 Walnut, the Delaware; at 45, the Union; at 47, the Marine, and
at 49, a newcomer, the United States Insurance Company. The
presidents of three of these companies had learned much of what

they knew about marine underwriting in the service of the North America. Officers and directors of the rival institutions saw each other every day at the City Tavern. Since his accident had left him lame, the thump of Pettit's heavy cane on the brick sidewalk was familiar to every man, woman and child in the neighborhood. It announced the Row's most venerated personage—from the buckles on his shoes to his three-cornered hat, a specimen of the fading Revolutionary epoch.

All the companies were doing good business and all except the North America gladdening the hearts of their stockholders with dividends because the new firms had no disaster-year losses to work off. The working off of those losses became the old Colonel's passion. To see them diminish did his ailing frame more good than all the doctors. The effort required no end of disagreeable decisions. The firm of Conyngham, Nesbitt & Company had gone under with the fall of Robert Morris, owing the North America money. John M. Nesbitt, the first president of the insurance company, did not long survive this crash. It became the unpleasant duty of Pettit to dun Conyngham for payment.[20]

The North America made progress on the road to recovery not only because of the president's strict attention to detail but because his Board of Directors knew its business. Is it likely that a man who had not been to sea could have written this:

"Having examined the Protest & Surveys relative to the loss of the Ship Anna Maria, whereof Jonathan Coffin Rathbone was master, it appears: That the Said Ship sailed from Cadiz on the 25th. day of December 1802 with a Cargo of Merchandize for Antwerp; that they continued their course till the 28th when it came to blow very hard at SW, accompanied with a very heavy Sea; that they continued with a boisterous Sea and Strong Gale of Wind, the Sea occasionally making a free passage over the Vessels Decks, and Striking with such violence as to make every part of her Shake, until the 2d January when the weather became more moderate, but a prodigious heavy swell continued which occasioned the Vessel to pitch and make much water. On Sounding the pumps found twenty two Inches of Water in the hold, on the 3d light and variable winds, on the 4th blowing very hard and a heavy swell at 6 P.M. the Carpenter aft on Quarter deck complained to the master the Ship had Suffered so much and

Strained from the Gales they had been in that it was his opinion they should bear away for the first port they could fetch, for the Water ways had Strained so much fore and aft and the Ship had worked so much round the Bows that the Oakum had Started out and Several of the Planks began to Start off.

"Whereupon they held a consultation and were unanimously of opinion they should make for the first port for preservation of Ship, Cargo and lives, that in effecting this they arrived at Gibraltar on the 6th Jany 1803 at 2 PM. . . .

"It appears from the Report of the Surveyors upon the Said Ship under date of 26th January 1803 that they found in the Run abaft, the floor and Futtock Timbers, as far as the Mizen Mast, *decayed and Rotten,* and having caused the Starboard and Larboard Sides to be opened in Several places, we found many of the Timbers Started *and decayed and Rotten,* so as to render them perfectly *unserviceable and irrepairable,* and the Apron forward is also in the Same State, and having then examined between Decks, and caused several places to be opened, we found some of the Timbers on both Sides *rotten,* and many of the Knees twisted and the *whole frame of the Ship* Strained and *decayed.* . . .

"From the above Statement the Committee are of opinion that the Ship Anna Maria, was not Sea worthy at the time of her Sailing and consequently that the Underwriters are not liable for the loss, the contract being void from the origin."[21]

The year 1805 closed with a favorable balance of $50,000 in the marine account—the best showing since 1798. But there was no dividend, the Colonel steadfastly persisting in his policy of building up a surplus and recapturing the company's capital. Early in 1806 the Phoenix Company, in a brief note, requested of Colonel Pettit "a general Statement of the Stock and situation of the affairs" of the North America, "and such further information as the interests of this Company may require." Pettit turned the letter over to a committee of his Board which pointedly suggested that the Phoenix be treated as any other stockholder.

"Considering, however," added the committee, "that it may probably afford pleasing gratification to the Directors of the Phoenix Insurance Company, for whom the Committee cherish great respect, to perceive that the affairs of the Insurance Company of North America affords a prospect, which would not be depreciated by a comparison with that of other institutions of the like nature, your Committee recommend that the President be authorized to furnish the Phoenix Company with a Copy of the general account current Stated at the last half yearly period, together with a Statement of the funds of the Company appropriated as capital Stock."[22]

A little later the Colonel was able to announce that the long fight for the restoration of the capital had been won. The tidings were suitably celebrated in July by the distribution of a 4-per-cent dividend—the first dividend in seven and a half years.

Into the battle Charles Petit had thrown the last reserves of his strength. On September 1, 1806, infirmities compelled him to ask the Board to appoint one of its number "to Supply the place of the President during his indispotion [sic] and Act as Pres^t. pro: Tempore."[23]

The Board named the Colonel's son, Andrew Pettit, who had become a director only a few months before.

On September 4 the need was for a permanent rather than a temporary president. Colonel Charles Pettit was dead, aged sixty-nine.

CHAPTER V

IN THE SECOND WAR FOR INDEPENDENCE

I

ON October 1, 1806, John Inskeep was elected the fourth president of the Insurance Company of North America. An extremely modest man who never shed all the traces of his country rearing, he had attained a place among Philadelphia's first citizens by almost imperceptible steps. Born on a farm in Burlington County, New Jersey, in 1757, Inskeep was forty-nine when he succeeded the late Colonel Pettit.

During the Revolution he had risen to a captaincy of New Jersey militia. Though married and with a young family coming on, like many another ex-soldier after the war, he had come to the city to try to enlarge his fortunes. In 1785 he was able to buy the George Tavern, at Second and Mulberry Streets, distinguished as the starting point of the stage which "sets off precisely at half-past eight o'clock in the morning, and on Saturday at 6 o'clock, and arrives at New-York the succeeding day at 1 o'clock." Certain it is that Nesbitt, Hazard, Stewart, Moylan, Ross, Ball, Leamy and other prospective founders of the North America from time to time made their ways to that house of entertainment to take the coach to New York. Such casual calls probably constituted the extent of their acquaintance with the proprietor. The travelers represented the best in Philadelphia's upper crust of business, politics and fashion. John Inskeep did not belong to their milieu.

But he was on the way up, and in 1794 left tavern-keeping to engage in the china and glassware business at 31 South Front Street, not far from the North America's lately established office. As he prospered his acquaintance expanded. In 1799 he succeeded John Barclay, an original director of the North America, as a city alderman. The following year he was elected mayor, succeeding John Wharton, another member of the North America Board. He made an energetic and progressive municipal executive, building the first bridge across the Schuylkill and giving the city increased protection against the hazard of fire. In 1801 he made his first insurance connection as director of the Mutual Assurance Society, which handled fire risks only. In 1802 he joined the board of the North America, retaining his Mutual post as the two companies were in different lines of the business.

Then followed a term as associate judge of the Court of Common Pleas. Without legal education or training, sound common sense and an innate instinct for fairness guided the one-time tavern-keeper in formulating his decisions, the most revolutionary of which was upheld by a higher court. This was the liberation on a writ of habeas corpus of Ben, a slave, brought to the city by United States Senator Pierce Butler, of South Carolina, who maintained a residence in Philadelphia. John Inskeep was again chosen to head the city government and closed his public career with the conclusion of a second memorable term as mayor twenty-one days after assuming the presidency of the Insurance Company of North America.[1]

A favorable prospect confronted the new president. Thanks to his predecessor, the company was again in possession of its whole capital of $600,000, a dividend had been paid, and plenty of business for a marine underwriter was at hand, despite competition. The total of our foreign commerce had grown from $148,290,477 in 1802 to $230,946,963. Ninety-one per cent of this was carried in American bottoms as against 86.5 per cent in 1802. More American ships than ever before flew the Stars and Stripes, the tonnage registered for foreign trade having risen in four years from 557,760 to 798,507. The United States was profiting where it had once suffered from the convulsions in Europe.

More than half of the goods sent from our shores represented re-exports—cargoes brought from other parts of the world and sent out again as American. This subterfuge to beat the British blockade represented a war business purely, and would disappear when Europe quieted down. Another form of wartime trade was a rise in the flow of American-grown foods to unhappy Europe. The immediate profits were great. Already the American merchant marine was second to England's, and not all the goods brought to these shores were sent away again. Domestic use of Chinese silks increased and the coffee trade from Brazil, begun largely as a re-export venture, gave us a taste for that pleasant stimulant which has made us the greatest coffee-drinking country in the world. Though no disciple of Thomas Jefferson, now President of the United States, Colonel Pettit had felt a surge of optimism over the Louisiana Purchase, doubling our national area. As potential new markets beckoned from the vast interior, the commercial seaboard caught once again the spacious feeling of empire and of illimitable destiny which the frontier West had never lost.

Though the Insurance Company of North America finished the year 1806 with $312,115 in net receipts from premiums against $286,278 in losses, Inskeep preferred to invest the profit instead of declaring a January (1807) dividend. He put the case before a meeting of the stockholders which approved the action in a resolution thanking "the President & Directors for their good management and attention to the concerns of the Company."[2]

The confidence of the stockholders and of the investing public generally in the North America was reflected in the prices posted for Philadelphia insurance stocks in the third week of March 1807:

	Current price	Capital paid in per share
Insurance Company of North America . .	$ 12	$ 10
Insurance Company of State of Pennsylvania	185	400
Union	71½	60
Phoenix	114	100
Philadelphia	172.50	100
Delaware	70	80
Marine	35	60
United States	21½	50[3]

Considering that the North America had paid only one dividend in seven and a half years these figures are rather eloquent. And another fact should be borne in mind. No longer the political capital of the United States, Philadelphia also saw her commercial supremacy threatened. Though the Pennsylvania port's business increased, that of the metropolis on the Hudson increased faster. Ten marine insurance companies were doing business there. Yet New York shippers still placed a large share of their risks with the Philadelphia underwriters. To the Row's reputation for solvency, soundness and superior management, the North America had made a conspicuous contribution.

2

The fair prospects upon which John Inskeep gazed at the commencement of his term as president ended before a year was out. The growing intensity of the conflict between England and Napoleon was biting into our re-export trade as Britain, asserting the doctrine of "continuous voyage," outlawed traffic between the French West Indies and France via the United States. Inskeep had been in office less than two months when Bonaparte proclaimed the British Isles in a state of blockade and revived the rule that no ship which had touched an English port could enter a port of France.

French and British privateers were on the oceans again, with our commerce their principal quarry. Seizures, confiscations and underwriters' losses were everyday news. Insurance rates, which competition and a period of comparative calm had driven down to peace-time levels, went up, the Philadelphia companies uniting on a set of emergency regulations.

On June 23, 1807, came the most momentous tidings yet. This time no mere merchantman flying the American flag had been attacked, but a United States ship of war. The *Chesapeake,* her mainmast gone, her rigging a tangle and her flag missing, limped into Norfolk with eighteen wounded below decks. Three dead had been buried at sea. Bound for the Mediterranean and wholly unprepared for action, the American frigate had refused a demand by the British man-of-war *Leopard* for the surrender of alleged English deserters. Twenty minutes after the *Leopard* opened fire the *Chesapeake* struck her colors and surrendered four seamen, three of them Americans.

The effect on popular emotions in the United States was like that of a match on powder. Joseph Hopkinson acted as secretary of a mass meeting which filled Independence Square and expressed the preponderant sentiment of the country in a resolution declaring that submission to such an insult would debase us as a nation. Jefferson resisted this pressure for war and when England consented to discuss possible reparations for the outrage American tempers began to cool a trifle. John Inskeep was very glad to see this. Like most of the

JOHN INSKEEP

Captain New Jersey militia during Revolution. Successively tavern keeper, merchant, judge and mayor of Philadelphia. Fourth president Insurance Company of North America, 1806-1831. Thomas Jefferson's embargo and the War of 1812 created major marine problems. Inskeep promoted fire insurance, founding forerunner of modern agency system.

From a portrait by Rembrandt Peale owned by Mrs. Bodine Wallace, Chestnut Hill, Pennsylvania, and reproduced by permission.

seaboard mercantile interests, he had not joined his company's attorney in the popular outcry for war.

"The fears of a Rupture between England and this Country have very much subsided," he wrote. "It is confidently expected that some arrangement will be made to avoid war, that horrid alternative being so repugnant to the interest of both Countries."[4]

And again:

"The British Government on the receipt of [word of] the unfortunate affair of the Chesapeak has evinced a very pacific disposition, which circumstance affords strong hopes that all Matters at variance between the two Governments will be amicably adjusted."[5]

These protestations, doing England full justice to say the least, fairly represented the mercantile point of view of the eastern part of the United States.

Small were the thanks received. In November the British gave the screws another turn with Orders in Council putting all French and French colonial ports under blockade. No neutral vessel could trade with them unless it first entered a British port and paid re-export duties. Napoleon, who did nothing by halves, replied with the most sweeping decree of all. Any ship bound to or from a British port anywhere on earth was declared a lawful prize. The same applied to any ship submitting to English dictates concerning trade or navigation. Between the two of them, England and Bonaparte had ordered our ships off the ocean.

But before news of these latest blows could cross the Atlantic, Congress beat our European tormentors to it by invoking an absolute embargo on foreign commerce, effective December 22, 1807. Only coasting vessels were allowed to put to sea.

3

Thomas Jefferson long had yearned to try this economic weapon against a hostile Europe. He believed the embargo would prove the glory of his second administration as the Louisiana Purchase had of his first. It did not work out that way. Although the stoppage of

American supplies inconvenienced England and France, we were the real sufferers. Grass sprouted between the cobblestones of Philadelphia's Water Street. Ships were tied up, their rat- and worm-infested hulls rotting. The inverted tar barrels atop the masts to protect them from the weather were derisively called "Mr. Jefferson's nightcaps." Hungry seamen, sailmakers and rope-walk workers prowled the town. The Insurance Company of North America contributed $500 to a fund raised by the Chamber of Commerce to organize a program of relief work.

Nor were mariners the only victims. Shipping firms were ruined and debtors' prisons filled to overflowing. Farm prices fell as the exportable surplus became a drug on the market.

That, and more, on the debit side. On the profit side was a stimulus to domestic manufacturers, fabricating the things we had hitherto obtained overseas in exchange for our exports. But the embargo lost popularity steadily. It split Mr. Jefferson's own Republican party, becoming, in everyday parlance, the "dambargo." To circumvent a statute so oppressive was reckoned no crime by ordinarily law-abiding men. The simplest artifice was for a ship to clear for a coastwise voyage and wind up in a foreign port. Philadelphia was quite a center for this kind of trade before the Government slapped on every coasting vessel a bond of twice the value of ship and cargo. Still, surreptitious voyages were made, often with the connivance of local officials. Canadian and Floridian borders teemed with smugglers.

Whether vessels violating the embargo were able to get insurance does not appear, though it seems certain they obtained none from the North America, opposed though that company was to the law. The decrees of foreign governments were something else. As in times past the North America contributed to the efforts to get around them.

As opposition to the embargo continued to gain, John Inskeep wrote his agent in Jamaica, William Savage:

"A more interesting crisis than the present has scarcely ever been witnessed in this Country—at least not since the Revolutionary War. The long suspension of Commerce which has borne extremely hard on some and been more or less felt by all. The hopes and fears of every person depending on or in any respect concerned in Commerce are compleatly awakened. This dreadful state of anxiety however cannot continue much longer, as Congress have the subject now before them; various resolutions relative to the Embargo having already been proposed but the result is altogether uncertain; the prevailing opinion however is that the Embargo will be provisionally raised."[6]

Much as John Inskeep abominated the embargo, he seemed to have a keener appreciation than before of the gravity of the condition it endeavored to correct. This is not to say that he had joined the swelling ranks of those who proclaimed the respect of England could be won only at cannon's mouth. Inskeep thought the differences would be removed by negotiation. But his choler was rising. Unlike a considerable proportion of the eastern commercial and maritime community, he was no advocate of peace at any price. If peace were to be preserved, England would have to come down from her high horse. He favored a proposal to arm merchant ships for defense, bluntly writing James Mackenzie and A. Glennie, who had succeeded Fry as London representatives of the insurance company:

"Should your Government evince a conciliatory disposition towards this & permit our Commerce to float without much interruption War may yet be averted, but should they adopt a different course that event is inevitable."[7]

Congress repealed the embargo in March 1809, that futile statute and Thomas Jefferson terminating their official careers together. Yet our ships were not permitted to brave the dangers of the deep and of British and French sea power as they would have pleased. Nor were they permitted to arm. A non-intercourse act took the place of the embargo, interdicting trade with Britain and France. There was rejoicing, for a crust of bread is something to a starving man. But, as John Inskeep wrote his London agents, commerce revived sluggishly. The Board of Directors of the North America took a cautious view:

"On the subject of the recommencement of Marine Insurances to Foreign Ports it was agreed to write such risques as may be offered (out only) and which shall be safely within the Laws of our Country, and not endangered by any decrees of Orders of Foreign Powers."[8]

The following month, however, brought great news. A proclamation of President Madison, dated April 19—the anniversary of Lexington and Concord—declared British ports the world over open to American shipping, beginning June 10. This was the result of negotiations at Washington with the British minister, Erskine, who pledged his government to withdraw the Orders in Council of 1807. The American concession was to reopen our ports to British men of war. Inskeep took up his pen to write his London agents of the "immediate Spring to Commercial enterprise" in Philadelphia.[9] Off came Mr. Jefferson's nightcaps from the tall masts as the water-front rang with the work of fitting ships for the sea. Great fleets sailed from all the Atlantic ports, the merchants of Philadelphia toasting England at a lavish banquet.

It all ended in abrupt disillusionment. July brought word of the British government's refusal to ratify the compact its minister had made in Washington. The Orders in Council stood. Erskine was recalled and Francis James Jackson sent over in his stead. Mackenzie and Glennie wrote assuringly from London that Jackson had directions to enter into new engagements which would preserve "the harmony, just restored" between the two countries. John Inskeep was not mollified. "This Country is in an uproar," he replied. "I must confess that if M^r. Jackson comes with the same instructions alleged to have been M^r. Erskine's I have no hopes that 'the harmony, just restored' will remain uninterrupted."[10]

John Inskeep had called the turn exactly. Jackson's instructions were such that we could not deal with him and within a few months he had his passports. The non-intercourse act gave way to a law allowing trade with the European belligerents. Thus matters drifted back approximately to where they had been before the embargo. Our merchantmen were at sea—taking their chances.

4

During the fourteen months the embargo was on, the Insurance Company of North America suspended the writing of marine risks. In the year 1807—the only full calendar year of the embargo—net receipts from marine premiums were $5,842 while losses paid on insurance written earlier aggregated $108,568. A glance at the activities of the company during those deadly fourteen months, and during the unsettled periods immediately preceding and following them, is revealing. The reason the North America came through this crisis in such excellent condition could be stated very briefly: competent management.

With the shipping world prostrate John Inskeep devoted his time to fortifying the internal financial position of his company. A standing Committee on Finance, consisting of himself and Directors William Poyntell and James Boggs, was appointed. Funds were judiciously husbanded and the portfolio of investments watched with care. The assets of the company during this period ran in the neighborhood of $750,000. Of this amount about half was kept in United States Government bonds. Cash in the Bank of Pennsylvania, now the company's depository, would run close to $100,000 and notes deposited for collection close to $200,000. Other investments were in the stocks of local toll roads, bridges, canals, banks and in mortgages. Eighty-three shares of stock in the Phoenix Insurance Company were bought at par and 180 shares in the Delaware at 40. Moreover, the Finance Committee displayed confidence in itself by purchasing, for the company's account, 6,230 shares of the North America's own stock which the stress of events had driven to $9.17. Presently most of this was sold at a profit.[11]

Administrative improvements were introduced. The bylaws were amended and codified, the system of records and accounts reorganized, fuller and clearer semiannual statements were made available to stockholders. More attention was paid to fire insurance with the result that this business was nourished to a point where its profits took care of the overhead of the home office.

Looking forward to happier times, the North America examined proposals for decreasing the hazards to navigation in Delaware Bay. It studied a project to install a telegraph line from Philadelphia to the bay, by which intelligence of the arrival of ships might be brought to the city more quickly. This telegraph line, the enterprise of a New England schoolmaster named Jonathan Grout, was one of the excitements of the day. Grout belonged to the circle of pioneer experimenters with electrical current of which Benjamin Franklin had been a founder. He proved that intelligible signals could be sent over a wire. A line was run from Philadelphia to Reedy Island at the head of Delaware Bay. The North America contributed $250, but declined further investment because the temperamental inventor proved so hard to get along with. This first successful electrical telegraph operated for several years and was a boon to Philadelphia underwriters. The British bottling up the mouth of the Delaware stopped it in 1813. Owing to the inventor's quarrelsome disposition it never got going again.[12]

Statements of the company's assets were on a solid basis. They did not include such expectations as indemnity for spoliations sustained at the hands of the British, French, Spaniards and Danes, though such expectations were justifiable and they ran into large sums. Only actual receipts from such sources were accounted assets. To date these had come solely from the British who despite their highhandedness at sea still paid over reparations, though on a diminishing scale. The company's claim of $1,950,000 against the United States for French losses growing out of the treaty of 1801 remained much alive, however. In 1807 another committee of the House of Representatives had recommended payment, but, with so many other demands on the nation's revenue, nothing had been done. The company's claims against Spain, largely for vessels captured by the French and taken to Spanish ports, were $768,959. Moreover, it had a share in claims against Denmark for $1,500,000. And there were additional claims against the French for depredations after 1801. All these claims were in the hands of the United States Government, and some eventual return on some of them surely seemed probable.

This probability was not valued at one cent, however, in the statement of assets drawn up by the Finance Committee on July 11, 1808, when the embargo had been in operation nearly seven months. The "whole property of the Company" was placed at $766,185. Deducting $600,000 to keep the capital entire and $112,198 more as a reserve for known or possible losses, a surplus of $53,987 remained. "Inasmuch as they conceive it will highly tend to add to the Character of the Company," the Committee recommended the distribution of $30,000 as a 5-per-cent dividend.[13]

Six months later, without a single new marine-insurance premium having been received, the surplus was again in excess of $30,000 and another 5-per-cent dividend was declared.[14]

A company able to make money and to pay dividends in such times was a company that would bear watching. The Finance Committee was correct in its assumption that the feat tended to "add to the character" of the North America. The company felt sufficiently secure to add to its real-estate holdings by buying its fifth home at 40 (now 136) Walnut Street, in the center of Insurance Row. In January 1810 these quarters were occupied. Two neighboring houses were part of the property purchased. The one adjoining on the west was promptly rented to the Delaware Insurance Company. The other, around the corner on Dock Street, already had a tenant, Nicholas Biddle, a young attorney-at-law. Mr. Biddle signed a lease with the North America, agreeing to pay "$250 p annum until any further arrangement can be made." In October Mr. Biddle achieved a new "arrangement" which reduced his rent $50 a year.[15]

With the lifting of the embargo, and the resumption of ocean trade at great risk, the company pursued a cautious policy. Though volume of business remained small three profitable years ensued. Net marine premiums for the period totaled only $141,000 against losses of $91,500, indicating that the greater part of the company's earnings were from investments, including respondentia loans. Dividends distributed were 9½ per cent in 1809, 10 per cent in 1810 and 15 per cent in 1811.

Caution was not so much in evidence, however, when a 5-per-cent dividend was voted at the semiannual meeting in January 1812. Tension between the United States and England was increasing. During the month of May preceding, the American frigate *President*, patrolling the coast to protect our commerce, had fallen in with the British man-of-war *Little Belt*. The British said we fired first and we said the British did. In any event the *Little Belt* was soundly beaten and the country applauded. Philadelphia seemed especially proud that the first gun aboard the *President* had been touched off (without orders, as it was later admitted) by Third Lieutenant Alexander James Dallas, Jr. The war party swept the ensuing elections in the West and, despite considerable eastern opposition, Congress began to prepare for a conflict.

This was the situation when the January 1812 dividend was declared. A committee of stockholders, after examining the company's books, explained why it was no larger than 5 per cent. Bright hopes were held out for the immediate future. "Before the next periodical Report they Antisipate an handsome acquisition to their Funds (should no War arise between this Country & Great Britain) from the termination of Loans on Respondentia to Canton & back, in the sum of $90,000 at premium & Interest of 25 p Cent."[16]

The next periodical report would be due in July. On June 18 we went to war.

5

A pioneer in Philadelphia insurance, Benjamin Franklin, whom some of the founders of the North America had known well enough to visit in his home, once remarked that while Americans had won their personal freedom national independence remained to be gained. Our second war to that end started with a series of victories at sea which amazed the world. The tradition of invincibility which Nelson had given the British navy sustained considerable impairment when in six months' time in five separate engagements three of our ships put six English ships out of action. Later on we had a few reverses but taking the war as a whole British naval forces have never been so badly outclassed. Our privateers were also successful. Operating at a disadvantage in distant oceans, they destroyed or captured 1,300 British merchantmen while the British who dominated our Atlantic seaboard were doing away with 1,400 of ours, including fishing vessels.

Yet these figures give a most misleading picture of the war, up to nearly the very end of it. During the first six months we did as poorly on land as we did well at sea. An American invasion of Canada, which should have taken Montreal, failed ingloriously. Detroit surrendered without a shot. Fort Dearborn (Chicago) was lost. New England, whose Congressmen had voted 20 to 12 against the war resolution, gazed on these humiliations with apathetic eyes. Under the shrewd encouragement of Britain, which until 1814 exempted New England from the blockade, this lukewarmness toward the war changed to a clamor for peace on nearly any terms.

Though ship for ship we demonstrated our superiority over the English, the United States Navy was too small to attempt fleet action to protect our commerce. Our privateers, quickly driven from local waters, took most of their prizes off the coasts of Europe and in the South Pacific. In February 1813 a British fleet appeared off the Atlantic seaboard. Delaware Bay was cleared of shipping and the town of Lewes, traditional home of Delaware River pilots, bombarded. Stephen Girard's China packet *Montesquieu,* captured off the Delaware capes, was ransomed by him for $180,000 specie. Our foreign commerce dropped from $115,557,000 in 1812 to $49,861,000 in 1813. Most of this went through New England ports as part of the British scheme to foment American disunity.

The scene on the Philadelphia waterfront grew reminiscent of the embargo. "The few vessels that remain to us," one newspaper said, "are hauled up in the docks, prey to the weather and worms, and the wretched portion that is permitted to enter and depart bears the colors of other nations." The enthusiasm with which Philadelphia had greeted the declaration of war began to wane. With tacit approval the *American Daily Advertiser,* leading journal of the commercial interests, reprinted from the Portland (Maine) *Gazette,* this typically New England commentary:

"When the present war was declared its advocates declared that American privateers within one year would be so numerous and efficient as in a great measure to annihilate the British: 'two for one' was the lowest calculation. . . . The result is that the Commerce of the United States has been swept from the ocean, except a little which has been permitted by special license of the British, while the commerce of England has greatly increased. When insurance on British vessels can be made for 3 or 4 per cent., it could not be made on United States vessel short of 50 per cent. In consequence of this England enjoys the commerce of the world, with the exception of the little that is carried on by the Swedes, Portuguese and Spaniards who are at peace with her."[17]

6

The war had come at an awkward moment for the Insurance Company of North America. The previous six months had brought unduly heavy losses, paring down to $18,174 the "surplus"—the term employed in the current financial statements—available for dividends. On top of this had come a decision of the Supreme Court of Pennsylvania in a suit against another insurance company which the North America feared might have an unfortunate bearing on the so-called Antwerp cases. The Antwerp cases comprised certain French seizures on which the North America, by advice of counsel, had declined to pay losses and had made no financial provision for their payment. The recent court ruling supported the contention of the company's liability in this matter. The amount involved was $64,500. Consequently there was no July 1812 dividend.[18]

In a letter to his London agents John Inskeep spoke his mind on the subject of the war:

"Last Winter we suffered severely by the Capture of several American Vessels insured by us, bound from France to the United States. As these Captures were made under the orders in Council, then in full force, we are apprehensive that unless indemnification should be provided for by a subsequent Treaty, we shall be without redress.

"Long ere this reaches you, you will no doubt have received (& with no small degree of surprise) the declaration of War by our Government against England. A War commenced at a period inauspicious to success even were it ever so just or necessary—a moment that put it in the power of an Enemy (most unfortunately selected) to avail itself of some Millions of the Property of our Citizens by Capture, which might and no doubt would have been saved by a delay of two or three months. The certain loss, too, of our Seamen, about whom so much ridiculous sensibility has hitherto been manifested, is a consideration of no trifling import especially if the War shall continue any length of time, which however does not now appear at all probable inasmuch as the repeal of the Orders in Council the account of which reached us a few days since, will afford an opportunity to our Government to put an end to the direful calamity which they so hastily & unnecessarily entered into.

"The attentions paid to my son by your M^r. Glennie & Family, are highly gratifying to me & which is hightened in no small degree by your remark that he appears to be deserving of them."[19]

John Inskeep had been a member of neither the war party nor the peace party. At times he had written as if he would not shrink from war to preserve our right to sail the seas. Insofar as his complaint was directed at official negligence in the matter of warlike preparations, it rested on firm ground. With years in which to get ready, Mr. Madison had done next to nothing. But after one experience with an embargo, whether the country would have permitted the President to do anything very effective in the way of clearing the seas of our richly laden merchantmen in advance of a declaration of war seems unlikely. The weight of the shipping and insuring interests would have been against him.

In the second half of the year 1812 the Insurance Company of North America was required to pay the Antwerp claims. It also paid $35,000 on the loss of a single ship, the *Pekin*. These adversities were the major factors in bringing the assets of the company down to

$522,027, or $77,973 less than the $600,000 owing the stockholders who had paid in the company's capital.

Economies introduced included sharp salary cuts for all the personnel. Later these were extended to take in the officers. With shipping at a low ebb little marine insurance was written the first half of 1813. Even this proved a losing venture. The combined operations of the company represented a loss of $8,404 for the period. Thereafter the marine field was abandoned entirely and during the last half of the year the company made (from fire insurance and investment income) $20,361. This cut to $66,016 the deficiency of assets to capital.

No marine insurance was written during the entire year of 1814. The mid-year statement showed a further reduction of the deficit to $50,649. During this interim the company had been able to make its first fresh investment of any consequence since the beginning of the war—$40,000 in United States 6-per-cent obligations which were purchased directly from the Treasury at 85.[20]

7

When July came the feeling was this would prove an excellent purchase, for rumors of peace filled the air. Not even the late unexpected violence of the British toward New England stilled this talk. In a sweeping set of forays Admiral Cochrane had captured Eastport and Nantucket, laid the Cape Cod towns under tribute and made a foray into Long Island Sound. The peace talk stemmed from a mission headed by Albert Gallatin which had been sent to St. Petersburg at the invitation of the czar. Nothing accomplished in Russia, on receipt of an unofficial intimation that Britain would treat directly, the envoys had set out for England. John Quincy Adams, Henry Clay and Jonathan Russell were sent to join them there. Then came the surrender of Paris and Napoleon's exile to Elba. Peace in Europe after twenty-one years! Surely peace in America would follow quickly.

Echoes of our jubilation over Napoleon's fate had scarcely died away when the news took on a different color. Fourteen thousand of Wellington's veterans had landed at Quebec for an invasion via the Hudson valley. Cochrane was in the Chesapeake.

John Inskeep showed no alarm, however, writing on August 19 to his London representatives:

"The time I hope and trust is fast approaching when our correspondence will be more active & with less reserve."[21]

Probably many another complacent Philadelphian felt the same until seven days later when a hard-riding courier dashed in from the south with tidings that brought the war to the city's door. The British had struck in the Chesapeake. Washington was taken and the Government in flight. The enemy was moving on Baltimore. Philadelphia would be next.

The town frantically fortified. At noon on September 14 the Board of Directors of the Insurance Company of North America gathered for a hurried meeting. The minutes are brief:

"The President proposed taking into consideration the propriety, under present Circumstances, of making preparation for the removal of the Books, Papers and Effects of this Company for safe keeping from injury which may be done thereto, Should the Enemy enter this City. Whereupon He was authorized to adopt such means, and at such time as he may think fit. . . ."[22]

Baltimore halted the invaders, however, who re-embarked and sailed for the south. Philadelphia had time to take two or three long breaths before the next dose of bad news, which was of an American defeat at Plattsburgh by the invaders from Quebec. It was false! An astonishing land and water victory on the shore of Lake Champlain had sent Wellington's veterans reeling back into Canada.

Yet our troubles were not over. In the Gulf of Mexico the British were concentrating the mightiest military expedition of all for the subjugation of the Mississippi Valley. To oppose them was a man of whom the learned East knew nothing: a lantern-jawed Indian fighter from Tennessee named, as it appeared, Andrew Jackson. No repetition of the Plattsburgh miracle was expected of this Jackson. The Government sitting beside the ashes of the White House and the Capitol could help him little. The Treasury empty, the Secretary of that Department threw up his hands and the North America's old attorney, Alexander James Dallas, took over the thankless post.

Dallas scraped up $100,000 for Jackson. With the defeatist Hartford Convention demanding that our Government make peace, gloomily we awaited word of disaster in Louisiana.

In this state of affairs the Board of Directors of the Insurance Company of North America made its semiannual report to the stockholders under date of January 9, 1815. This indicated a gain in assets to $590,938, reducing the capital deficiency to $9,062. The report told how these figures had been determined:

"The Directors ... do not present it as containing properties which at the actual Value of the present Market rates would produce within a considerable Sum of what is the apparent amount of them, but that they have been guided by a View of what would be consider'd a correct Statement under a return of the relations of Peace, and other favouring Circumstances; leaving it to the Stockholders to make their own Deductions therefrom. . . .

"The Directors will State, that Should an estimate be made at the present Market prices . . . the Said deficit would rise to $113,000 nearly."[23]

Events justified the optimism of the Directors so speedily that all one can say is that they, in common with the rest of the country, were mighty lucky in having a man of Jackson's stamp in Louisiana. On February 5 came the almost incredible news that the Tennessean had obliterated the British at New Orleans. On February 13 Philadelphia learned that the war had ended the December preceding with a treaty signed at Ghent, Belgium. This compact itself ended little but the war. The maritime questions which had brought on the war were left to future negotiation. But the lessons of the battle of New Orleans (fought though it was after peace had been signed), of Plattsburgh and of our prodigious little navy were to leave their mark. They gained respect for the United States at the Court of St. James's. The second War of American Independence had been won.

Our commerce again on the oceans, with insurance rates at peacetime levels, prices rebounded. "In the last Semi-annual Statement," declared the Board of the North America, "a valuation was put on the United States Stocks predicated on a contemplated State of Peace, which, having happily taken place, they are consider'd as confirm'd in said Valuation."[24] Prudent preparations for expansion were made:

"The Board authorized Insurances to be made on Risques beyond the Cape of Good Hope to an Amount of Doll[s]. 35,000 or thereabouts."[25]

Another item denoting expansion:

"Cap[n]. Arthur Stotesbury to be appointed Surveyor of Vessels in this port ... for this Company at a Salary of $200 p annum."[26]

Captain Stotesbury was sixty years old and the father of seventeen children. Born in Ireland, he had fought under John Paul Jones in the action between the *Bonhomme Richard* and the *Serapis*. He served the Insurance Company of North America for nineteen years. His work was important, if not highly paid. Some of Captain Stotesbury's descendants were destined to leave their impress on Philadelphia.[27]

CHAPTER VI

Fire Insurance Coming into Its Own

I

The restoration of peace and the resumption of marine underwriting brought some relaxation of wartime economies. It was necessary to spend more money in order to make more money. During the six months ending in July 1815 the overhead of the Insurance Company of North America was $3,453.37, of which $2,113.30 were paid in salaries. Transmitting these figures to the stockholders, who had been without a dividend since January 1812, the directors noted that the operating costs had been taken care of without touching a dollar of the company's revenues from the reviving marine business or from investments. The "Fire Insurance Business still continues to far exceed ... the amount of *all* Expences ... in and out of the Office." Clear profits from fire business for the six months past had aggregated $3,879.64—enough to take care of running expenses and contribute $426.27 to the patient work of extinguishing the war-made deficit.[1]

This showing was the result of no natural phenomenon. It was the result of twenty years of pioneering labor, the more remarkable because of the distracting circumstances in which it was carried on. From its inception marine risks constituted the venture on which the Insurance Company of North America was prepared to stand or fall. Since the spring of 1793 these risks had been involved with the violent challenge to the principle of the freedom of the seas which for twenty-two years thereafter threatened the life of the United States as an independent nation. More than once during the storm and stress of the long conflict the existence of the North America, likewise, was threatened.

During that travail another phase of our evolution as a nation was going on far from salt water: the settlement of the West—land pioneers pushing into the heart of the continent with their axes and their long rifles. Historians have devoted a great deal more space to this than to the basic conflict which was waged on the sea. The land pioneers contended against the forces of Nature, against the Indians, against British and Spanish intrigue. The Louisiana Purchase gave a leaping impetus to this spirit of conquest. The end of the Napoleonic wars, of which our War of 1812 was a part, confirmed the land pioneers in the possession of their gains, and opened before them enticing new vistas. Yet had the fight for maritime freedom been lost our land freedom would have gone along with it, suffocated for the want of a breath of sea air.

Long before the struggle on the water was decided the Insurance Company of North America had found time for a look at the land phase—at the green Allegheny passes through which a leather-shirted race of frontiersmen was pouring westward. It believed the shares of toll bridges and of toll roads, pointing westward, and bonds of the new Territory of Louisiana to be good investments in the future of America. It bought such securities. Moreover, it was the first insurance company to follow the pioneers into the settlements they were carving from the wilderness of Ohio and Kentucky and Tennessee with a specific offer of participation in the westward march of empire. The offer took the form of insurance against fire.

2

By the close of 1796, two years after writing its first fire policy, the North America had made a number of contributions to fire insurance which were destined to have permanent effects on the business. It insured goods as well as the structures which housed them. It reached far afield for business. The metal "fire mark" of the North America, depicting an eagle taking flight from a rock, appeared on houses in localities as widely separated as New Hampshire and Georgia. Some of the twenty-odd other American fire insurance companies then in existence wrote more risks than the North America, but it seems doubtful if the business of any was scattered over so large an area. The two oldest Philadelphia companies, Hand-in-Hand and Green Tree, confined their risks to the city's limits. The greatest of the North America's early contributions to the science of fire insurance flowed from this extensively distributed activity. It was the germ of the local agency system.

THE COMPANY'S EARLY "FIRE MARKS"

Insurance companies once marked with distinctive insignia houses they insured against fire. The North America's first "fire mark," designed in 1794, was a six-pointed star. Its second, adopted 1796, showed an eagle arising from a rock.

On January 28, 1797, Colonel Charles Pettit wrote the following letter to John Hollins, a well-known merchant of Baltimore:

"Divers applications have been made to this office for Insurances against fire, on buildings in the Town and Neighbourhood of Baltimore, and on Furniture & Merchandize contained in Buildings. The descriptions of the Buildings proposed to be Insured, as to materials, Stile, finishing, local situation, neighbourhood, and various other particulars requesite to be made known, are often deficient. The kind of Goods to be Insured, in what part of the Building kept, whether in entire packages, or open and dispersed on Shelves &c are apt to be also too imperfectly described.

"To remedy these inconveniences it is proposed that a Suitable person be appointed in Baltimore to whom persons desirous of making Insurance on property there, should apply to See that their applications are put into proper form, accompanied by a drawing or Sketch of the ground plan of the Premises to be Insured, and of the neighbouring adjacent buildings, annexed & referred to in the description, to be extended as far as the next Cross Street on both sides of the Front and a particular description of the Back Buildings as well as of the House to be Insured as of those in or near a line with the Front, for One hundred feet each way, naming the Streets and their Directions, and marking the distances by common estimation. The materials of which the neighbouring Back buildings are formed, & a general description of the manner & purposes for which these are occupied is necessary, especially if there be any extra Hazardous business carried on, or extra Hazardous Goods Stored in them.

"In Philadelphia an Officer appointed by the Company who Surveys and Reports in writing upon every House Insured: for which he receives a Fee from the Applicants of Two Dollars each whether the Application be for Insurance on the Building or on Goods contained in it.

"If a person of Suitable talents and integrity could be engaged in Baltimore who would undertake this Agency for such Fees as the Applicant would pay him, the Insurance Company would appoint him, and Stipulate not to Act upon any application but Such as should be Signed by him and they would expect on his part that every application he should Sign would be accompanied by a drawing & description answering all the essential particulars of their Directors or requisitions. Neither perfect accuracy nor elegance will be required in those Drawings. Substantial information necessary to give an adequate Idea of the Risque is the object desired. A Master Carpenter would be most likely to do the Business with ease to himself."[2]

Colonel Pettit concluded by asking Mr. Hollins to help him in selecting "a person of Suitable talents" to be the Baltimore agent.

This communication throws interesting light on the conduct of fire insurance in the closing days of the presidency of George Washington. It defined a local agent's duties according to Charles Pettit's conception, including the feature of exclusive agency and mode and amount of the agent's remuneration.

When the survey of the applicant's premises was forwarded to Philadelphia, the company itself established the premium rate in conformity with the degree of risk involved. Clients of the company were notified of the approaching expiration of their policies, most of which were written for three years, by advertisements periodically published in the Philadelphia papers. Surely this uncertain means of communicating with a policyholder even no farther away than Baltimore, was something an alert local agent would be quick to improve.

While displaying considerable originality in the development of its fire business, the Insurance Company of North America made good use of what had been learned by its predecessors. It emphasized fire prevention and adopted the habit of standing contributions to the various volunteer fire companies of Philadelphia. It kept up with the latest in fire-fighting apparatus and helped the companies to acquire it. "Agreed to give 40 Dollars . . . towards the purchase of a Fire Engine called the Hope." "Forty Dollars to the Columbia Fire Company to assist them in procuring an Engine."[3] Such items studded the records of the North America, as they did of all other fire-insurance companies. As a consequence the volunteer fire fighters were usually well, and sometimes handsomely, financed.

The social aspect of these organizations was preserved. Membership in many was an honor difficult of attainment, and a mark of a man's standing in his community. Money was spent for fancy uniforms and for decorative trimmings for the engines and hose carts. Rival companies vied particularly over the elegance of their "engine-sides" as they called the decorations that lent distinction to the different engines. In New York the Aetna Engine Company hired Thomas Sully to paint its engine-sides. No Philadelphia Company could boast of a "side" decorated by so eminent a master of the brush, though John A. Woodside, a better-than-average portrait painter, made for the Washington Company a passable copy of Trumbull's "Washington at the Battle of Trenton." Woodside seems to have been the popular fireman's painter of the day. His work appeared on several engines in Philadelphia and elsewhere. An unknown artist placed an entirely recognizable likeness of Benjamin Franklin, in full fire fighter's regalia including hat, on the engine of the Union Company which Franklin once served as chief. The visage of Robert Morris decorated the cart of a hose company named in honor of that unfortunate financier.

Hose companies sprang into being in Philadelphia in a peculiar way. The social aspirations of a few young fellows who had failed on account of their youth to gain admission to one of the engine companies was responsible for the first one, called the Philadelphia, organized in 1803. The initial equipment was a small box-bed wagon and a few lengths of leather hose. When the fire bells rang the boys grabbed the handlines and, dragging their wagon, raced after one of the engine companies. Connecting their hose—so called because of the resemblance to a stocking—to a hydrant near the fire, the boys filled the engine's cistern in a minute and a half. By the old bucket-line method this would have taken fifteen minutes.

So it was that the Philadelphia Hose Company won its spurs and gained admission to the Philadelphia Fire Association, which governed the recognition of new fire companies. Two other hose companies—the Good Intent and the Neptune—followed quickly. The Philadelphia blossomed out in uniforms and acquired a brilliantly adorned wagon to which was added a bell to distinguish it from the wagons of the Johnny-come-latelys. The Neptune, too, ordered a bell, whereupon the Philadelphia appealed to the Fire Association which was a sort of supreme court made up of a representative from each of the fire companies. The Association found in favor of the Philadelphia. The Neptune did not get to use its bell.

Within four years the number of hose companies had increased to nine and the North America's Board of Directors formally considered the subject of their support:

"Some have 800 feet of Hose and none less than 450. They are all set on foot by a number of Young Citisens, the expence of which has been very considerable. Each Hose and Carriage costs with all the apparatus from Eight hundred to One Thousand Dollars each, and from the perishable nature of the Leather which constitutes the Hose, the annual expence of keeping one of them in repair is about $200. Your Committee knowing the great utility of these Machines in extinguishing fires, and fearing the weight of expence attending them, might damp the ardour of our meritorious young men, We think it would be money well laid out by the office, to Subscribe Two hundred and fifty Dollars per annum, to be paid for the use of the Nine Hose Companies."[4]

Four years later, in 1811, the Philadelphia fire companies received their first contribution from the public funds when the City Council appropriated $1,000.

3

At first the Board was divided on the question of local agencies. In the summer of 1797 an experimental contact was made with the firm of Davis & Reid in Charleston, South Carolina, who seem to have been hustlers. In behalf of the North America, Davis & Reid inserted advertisements in the local newspapers. They convinced people of the advantages possessed by the Philadelphia company over European competitors, notably the Phoenix of London. They transmitted several applications, with surveys, to Philadelphia, along with the following inquiries:

"Will the Company Insure Merchandize and Household furniture against fire & what are the Conditions—
"Will the Company Insure Buildings in the Country—Rice Machines, Barns, & produce against fire & at what Rates—
"Will the Company Insure Buildings in Georgia, North Carolina, and St Augustine East florida & on what Conditions—
"Will the Company Insure Distilleries and Manufactories & Saw & Grist Mills."

Then Davis & Reid asked that their relations with the company be placed "upon a more sure footing, that we may not disappoint people." The directors decided, however, "that it is not expedient to have an Agent at Charleston authorised to take Risques against Fire."[5]

J. Riegel, Jr.

EARLY HOSE CARRIAGE

Contemporary model of carriage made in 1830 for the Fame Hose Company of Philadelphia. Original in the North America's collection.

The argument against the appointment of representatives in such a distant place probably was the same argument that was advanced when the question was revived a few years later. This held that the agents would favor the interest of the policyholders, who were neighbors, over the interests of the insurance company. Preoccupations with marine concerns in 1798 also may have had something to do with the Charleston decision. Further, fire losses were running heavy for the first time. In 1797 they had been $8,821 against $12,090 in premium receipts. There was also the case of supposed incendiarism in New York, the Board authorizing "a Reward of from D^{rs}. 100 to D^{rs}. 1000 for discovering and prosecuting to conviction the person or Persons who set M^r. Sperry's store on Fire, as there is some reason to suspect that the Fire was not accidental."[6]

Nevertheless, the agency question would not down. With the plan working satisfactorily in near-by Baltimore and Wilmington, in 1804 Colonel Pettit proposed to extend it to Washington. His inquiries brought from Andrew Ross a proposal which was interesting in several particulars. Sprawling, unfinished, inconvenient and ugly, the hamlet euphemistically called our capital city was having hard sledding. L'Enfant's grandiose plan had placed the public buildings miles apart. Travel from one to another was a time-wasting task in any season, and during wet weather it was an adventure. Hogs rooted in the muddy "streets" and cows grazed on lots speculators had sold for fortunes. Such frontier towns as Lexington, Kentucky, and Nashville, Tennessee, were centers of civilized comforts by comparison. Not all the speculators were happy, however, Robert Morris and Samuel Blodget having gone to jail. Members of Congress and other officials hesitated to bring their families to such a place, and already there was talk of the Government's abandoning the site. Andrew Ross, a retired businessman who seems to have been in easy circumstances, wished to avert this. Possibly he had investments in Washington. At any rate he conceived that fire insurance as a factor might be helpful to the struggling city's development. He offered his services, without pay, to the North America, writing:

"You are correct Sir in understanding that it is my wish to become the Company's Agent in this place. . . . I know you have a number of Insurances against fire in this City and Geo. Town—indeed it was seeing the Badge [fire mark] of the Comp^y. on some of these houses, which from circumstances, in my opinion, render them verry extra hazardous, that first induced me thus to Volunteer my service. My desire is if possible to put you on your guard against imposition. There are a number of well built houses both in this City and Geo. Town, but there are others that seem to have been built that they might be burned.

"I find in your printed proposals that the description of the property proposed to be insured must be made by a master Carpenter, and attested to, both by the applicant & said Carpenter. In the first place I am no Carpenter, altho' I have no doubt of being able to describe & value a House or other property to your satisfaction. In the second place I am not going to require from Magistrates or others Certificates of my credibility (particularly in this place) nor shall I subject my self to make oath to every application. If it be neccessary that I should be under oath let one suffice during my Agency which I will do agreeably to the form you may prescribe and transmit it to your Office. Again that the agency may not be merely nominal, let it be required that all applications shall come through me. Lastly as I expect no pay let the mode of making remittances be so arranged that I shall run no risque. . . . If some such arrangement as here proposed meets your approbation; only enclose me a Short advertisement to be published in this City of my appointment & I will cheerfully undertake the task."[7]

Chary as so experienced a man of business as Charles Pettit must have been of gratuitous offers, Andrew Ross' terms were accepted. Taking his obligations to the community seriously, he proved an energetic agent. The eagle badges of the North America multiplied along the Potomac. One appeared on the brick barn at Mount Vernon, which Bushrod Washington insured for $4,000 for a premium of 1 per cent.[8] Whether Judge Washington applied for insurance on the mansion house and the numerous other buildings which made up the plantation community is not known. Under a rule of the company then in force, which declined risks on frame structures outside of Philadelphia, they were uninsurable.

The eagle emblem on the big brick barn was an excellent advertisement, for already Mount Vernon had become a place of pilgrimage. The current tenant, Bushrod Washington, was an Associate Justice of the United States Supreme Court under John Marshall. Old Revolutionary soldiers, who had known his distinguished uncle, were apt, on first sight, to be a little disappointed in the appearance of Bushrod, a small, sharp-faced man, careless of how he dressed. The late commander of the armies had been six feet three inches tall, with the unmistakable stamp of chieftainship upon him.

4

At the end of 1802, when the Insurance Company of North America completed its first ten years in business, receipts for that period from fire insurance stood at $81,253. Losses aggregated $31,116. The percentage of profit far exceeded that of the much larger marine business which exhibited the following totals: receipts $6,037,456; losses $5,500,887. And lately marine losses had exceeded receipts.

The fire business continued to move along at about the same gait, while mounting of marine losses encompassed the company with serious difficulties, taking half of its capital. No sooner had the capital been recovered than the maritime situation once more became acute, with the embargo in prospect. This was the state of affairs when on October 6, 1807, Alexander Henry in a vigorous address to his fellow members of the Board called for a march to the frontier, beginning with the establishment of an agency in Lexington, Kentucky.

It seems rather curious that Henry, who apparently had never been west of Philadelphia in his life, should have been so far ahead of some of his colleagues in perceiving the opportunities open to the company in the Ohio valley. Born in Northern Ireland he had emigrated to the New World in 1783 at the age of twenty. Nine years later he invested a part of his savings in the original issue of North America stock. In 1799, an exporter and importer on his own, he was elected to the Board of Directors. From the first the fire branch of the company's business had interested him.

Henry's spirited advocacy of an invasion of the West resulted in the appointment of a committee, with himself as chairman, to "consider the benefit and propriety of extending insurance against Fire generally to other Cities and Towns in other States beyond what it is now Customary to take." The committee's favorable report aroused opposition on the ground that the company would never know the true character of its liabilities in such distant places owing to the partiality of agents in favor of the local policy holders. Nevertheless, the Henry committee's report prevailed and on December 1, 1807, President Inskeep was directed to appoint "trusty persons . . . at such places as he shall think advisable to act as Surveyors and Agents of this Company whose duty it shall be to Survey and Certify the situation of all Buildings and property on which insurance is required, at the expense of the persons applying therefor. But no insurance to be made without the return of such survey and Certificate to the office, and the sanction of the President, Provided, however, that where there is no Agent acting for the Company, the Survey and statement of the parties or others may be accepted as heretofore."

From this it will be seen that nothing new was added to the functions of the local agent. He solicited business and surveyed property. Whether this business was accepted and at what rate was determined in the home office—usually by the president himself. Not until the Civil War was business accepted on the ground.

In 1807 the Board also ordered that "a suitable address by way of advertisement be prepared by the President and transmitted to such places as he may deem advisable." This seems to have been the first approach to a national advertising campaign inaugurated by an insurance company.

John Inskeep acted with characteristic promptitude, and within sixty days the West was opened up. On January 26, 1808, Thomas Wallace was appointed agent at Lexington, Kentucky, John Bustard at Louisville, Jephthah Dudley at Frankfort, Peter Lee at Washington, Pennsylvania, near the Ohio line, and Jesse Hunt at Cincinnati. A fortnight later James M. Caldwell was designated to represent the company at Wheeling, Virginia, John McCoy at Chillicothe, Ohio, Doctor John McDowell at Steubenville, Ohio, and William Tate at Nashville, Tennessee. At the same time representatives were named in a number of places nearer to hand in eastern Pennsylvania and in New Jersey, Virginia and Maryland. The local-agency system had been born.[9]

This line of outposts proved a very substantial factor in helping the company weather the fourteen months' embargo as well as it did. The western expansion was made in the nick of time for the North America was pressed by competition from the newer Philadelphia companies and others.

The work added to the burdens of John Inskeep whose quill was seldom idle. He carried on all correspondence with the agents and personally passed on each survey that came in. He also fixed the premium. The result was an intimate acquaintance with persons and their affairs the country over. To Agent Wallace in Lexington:

"Your Survey of Mess.rs. Geo. Trotter & John Tilford's buildings in the Town of Lexington was presented at this Office a few days ago. . . . [We have] . . . effected insurance for their account on Said buildings (the Stable excepted) to Amo.t of $8,000. at ½ per Cent for one year. The Stable was not included, because it could not be taken at the same premium, Such risks always being considered more hazardous than dwellings or Store houses built of the Same materials. . . .

"Considering this Survey as your first essay it is certainly very well, and indeed you have succeeded better than many others; I could not, however, comprehend some parts of it. After a very minute and proper discription of the front house you go on to say that 'adjoining and about 14 feet back of the front house is a two Story Kitchen.' Again you Say that 'adjoining and about 14 feet further back is a Smoke house built of brick.' Now as I understand the word adjoining to be the same as connected, or contiguous, I could not reconcile the idea of these buildings being adjoining and yet 14 feet back of each other & I find by enquiry [of a Philadelphia man acquainted with the property] that they are not connected or adjoining to each other. Again, you do not mention in the discription of the Surrounding buildings Whether the wooden buildings, east and West, are adjoining or at some distance. These are circumstances of the first importance, as the risque may be materially affected by them. In the present instance, however, no inconvenience arose from this omission as I found no difficulty in obtaining correct information on the Subject.

"When buildings stand distinct from each other it is always desirable to have a valuation put upon each, especially when they are built of different materials, or . . . [are used] for different purposes, as in such cases the premium will necessarily vary and in some instances will require a different policy. You will observe by our proposals that not more than $10,000 can be taken on one Risque; the rules of the office therefore will not permit us to take more than $2,000 on Mess.rs. Trotter & Tilfords goods, $8,000 being already insured on the Building in which they are contained, it being considered the same Risque. This circumstance you will please bear in mind on other occasions. The foregoing Risque would have been taken at a lower rate had it not been surrounded by combustable buildings and in which hazardous occupations are carried on.

"I observe by Messrs. Trotter & Tilford's Letter that they seem to entertain an idea that, in the event of a fire where part of the property is destroyed and part saved that the Comp^y. would only pay a partial loss; this being an erroneous understanding of the subject, you will please explain to them as well as to others wishing to make insurance, that the Comp^y. consider themselves bound and would pay the whole loss, provided it did not exceed the sum insured; notwithstanding part of the property might be saved.

"The foregoing remarks are merely for your Government, and

"I am

"With Much Respect &c

"J^no. INSKEEP Pres^t"[10]

From Mr. Inskeep's concluding lines it will be observed that the theory of co-insurance was as yet unknown.

"Your Survey of M^r. Cramer's property and the buildings in which it is contained is very minute and satisfactory," he wrote another agent, "but the risk is of a nature which we consider as being among the most hazardous, inasmuch as that printers and Book Binders are generally in the habit of working by Candle Light, surrounded by combustable matter and the business too often intrusted to boys and other inconsiderate persons. Books and Stationery are also considered very hazardous not on account of their combustable quality but the difficulty of removal in case of fire and being so very Susceptable of injury by Water. The property being contained in wooden buildings, also serves to encrease the risk; which I am of opinion cannot be taken under 1¾ per Cent for one year on a sum not exceeding ⅔ of the whole value of the property."[11]

To James Ewing, at Trenton, concerning a house of entertainment famous during the Revolutionary era:

"The premium on the City Tavern will be 70 cents, the tremendous wooden Stables situated so near the house makes this an extra hazardous Risk."[12]

Again to the same agent:

"When Insurance is wanted on personal property it is necessary to describe the Building in which the property is contained, with the

Hagley on the Waters of Brandywine State of Delaware

Belonging to R. & A. Dawes.

Fire-Insurance "Survey," 1797

The company's early fire agents submitted "surveys" of properties offered for insurance. Part of each survey was a "drawing & description" in which, according to company instructions, "neither perfect accuracy nor elegance" was required; merely a "Substantial . . Idea of the Risque." Above is a drawing, dated January 5, 1797, of property near Wilmington, Delaware, belonging to Rumford and Abijah Dawes. Guided by this and other data the company accepted $1,200 on the dwelling (No. 1); $1,500 on the flour mill (No. 2); $500 on the slitting mill (No. 3) and $500 on the stone stable (No. 4). In accepting the stable a standing prohibition against structures containing "Hay, Straw & Fodder" was set aside. A few years later this property became a part of the Du Pont powder works, which were uninsurable.

adjacent Buildings &c precisely the same as though the Building itself was to be insured. . . . It is desirable in all cases of Insurance on *Personal property in particular* to know something of the Moral character of the assured. . . . You will therefore confer a favour by giving me a confidential *hint* where circumstances may in your opinion require it."[13]

Thus an early perception of the vital factor known as "moral hazard."

5

The second decade of the North America's history, closing with the year 1812, brought $98,649 in fire insurance premiums, against an outgo of $23,873 for losses. The second war with England was on, marine business at a standstill. Again the fire business, meeting the operating expenses of the company, was proving its worth in a time of trial. The agency system, which Director Alexander Henry watched grow as a father would watch the progress of a favorite child, was proving its worth. None of the dire prophecies concerning the unreliability of agents was realized. Additional cities and towns were added to the North America's agency chain, until the greater part of the country was covered. Though the volume of fire business did not grow, profits grew because of Inskeep's insistence on conservative risks and measures of fire prevention. A large amount of business was refused as too hazardous, or because the applicant declined to meet conditions looking toward fire prevention. Every year these conditions grew more stringent.

With Washington made a little more habitable and the danger of the removal of the capital past, Andrew Ross had retired from his agency. In 1816, however, he resumed the post, this time accepting the surveying fees which constituted an agent's remuneration. The old gentleman's object seems to have been to build a business to hand to his son-in-law. Almost at once Ross ran into some of the company's new regulations.

"Yours of 13th Instant with a Survey of the Washington Hotel &c, just receiv'd," wrote the tireless Inskeep. "By a rule of long standing in this office (which perhaps was never made known to you) We are not permitted to insure more than three adjacent buildings together; nor to an Amount exceeding Doll'. 10,000 on the main building, and those used & connected with it on the West Side of the 15 feet wide alley, at 55 Cents, if the ashes are provided for agreeable to the Clause in the policies. The other Buildings on the East Side of the Alley and likewise the Furniture, we would rather decline taking at present."[14]

Inskeep was immovable on his rule calling for fireproof traps for ashes. Over and over he reminded agents of this, and would accept no insurance in which the presence of such traps did not appear in the survey. Though extremely useful, Andrew Ross was a strong-minded old man more accustomed to giving orders than taking them. He sometimes exceeded his powers, and to a certain point John Inskeep was indulgent but never on the ashes-trap issue.

"As you are of opinion that the house should be insured at 40 cents, we have no objections, in case the ashes are provided for, which you do not mention. We have to regret that the people of your place cannot See the necessity of, or have such an aversion to, making provision for the safe keeping of their ashes. We cannot however dispense with the rule. Indeed it is a measure forced upon us by imperious necessity, the destruction of Some public and many private buildings having been traced to the carelessness of servants and others in placing the ashes in wooden Vessels."[15]

Although John Inskeep was in advance of his time in the matter of using newspaper space to acquaint the public with the virtues of fire insurance, he was not so far in advance as Andrew Ross. After resuming the Washington agency Ross ran an announcement for a solid year in the *National Intelligencer,* and then called on Philadelphia for payment.

"With respect to the Printer's bill for advertising your agency &c," wrote John Inskeep in reply, "we have to regret that it has been permitted to accumulate to such an amount. A few insertions would have made the Subject sufficiently notorious and we hoped that our instructions would have been So understood. The Bill, however, must be paid, altho' it amounts to about $\frac{1}{4}^{th}$ of the whole annual premiums we receive in the District."[16]

Nevertheless, Andrew Ross was doing a good job. In the same letter Inskeep found occasion to congratulate the agent for obtaining "one of the best risks" in the city. This was a $10,000 policy on the handsome new residence Stephen Decatur had just built with his wartime prize-money, on Lafayette Square, which faces the White House. Indeed, the eagle badge on that house, as on the barn at Mount Vernon, constituted a prestige item which the North America could not have purchased for money. When the naval hero was killed in a duel the following year, his widow found the mansion a source of livelihood. The Baron de Neuville, minister of France, was the first renter. The names of the distinguished tenants who have followed him would fill half of this page.

The vigor with which the company acted when a fire was reported and its indisposition to split hairs in the matter of settlements is set forth in a letter to another excellent agent, Frederick Fritz of Reading, Pennsylvania:

"The account of the Fire at Reading having reach'd us on Saturday, We prevail'd upon M^r. Mifflin, One of our Directors, to Start immediately for that place to ascertain how the Company might be affected. . . . This morning Your favour of the 6th. was receiv'd, and We are much gratified to find that our Loss is not likely to be So fatal as we at first apprehended; and indeed it is questionable whether We are in Strictness liable for any damage Mess^s. O'Brien's Goods may have sustain'd in the removal of them. . . . As it may have been a prudential Measure however we are not at all inclined to make any difficulty in the Settlement."[17]

When Andrew Ross died in 1822 he was succeeded by his son-in-law, Samuel I. Potts, making the Washington agency the first of many North America agencies to become family legacies. Although Potts was no stranger to the business, the detailed instructions Mr. Inskeep, in his own hand, sent to Potts is evidence of the scrupulous care taken to keep agents informed. Fire-resisting doors and window shutters were among the new things the company was recommending to its patrons. The value of fire walls, extending above the roofs, and of trapdoors in the roofs with stairs leading thereto, had been proved and their presence or absence was noted on surveys.

The company's third decade, ending with 1822, was to be the most remarkable in its century and a half of history for low fire losses. During the ten years these were only $1,569, against receipts of $69,224. In such a discrepancy luck, of course, played a part; but that was not the whole story. The Insurance Company of North America had achieved mastery of the fire business.

CHAPTER VII

Corporate Finances in the Days of Andrew Jackson

I

Before 1820 the trend had begun which eventually was to make fire insurance a bigger enterprise than marine insurance in the United States, though another thirty years were to elapse before that trend was to become apparent. Therefore it was fortunate that the Insurance Company of North America had been forehanded enough to establish its fire business on a sound footing. As we have seen, the profits of that business paid the company's overhead and a little more. So far so good. Yet, if an adequate return were to be earned on the company's large capital, it must come in the main from marine underwriting, which had entered a new era.

November 12, 1815, the North America celebrated its twenty-third birthday, though "celebrated" may not be the right word. If any formal observance of the anniversary were made, record does not appear in the surviving archives of the company. The probability is that John Inskeep, not much of a hand to look backward for sentimental reasons, was too busy wrestling with the circumstances of a profoundly altered world. Twenty-two of the North America's twenty-three years of life had been passed under wartime conditions at sea. It had become used to them: to great risks and great losses but also great rewards; to violent ups and downs; in other words, to the mercurial fortunes of war. Now, with Napoleon out of the way, the world was tranquil and the seas unvexed. Insurance men were confronted by the fact that peace has its problems no less than war. These problems had not taken John Inskeep unaware. He had foreseen them and prepared.

The dawn of peace had set trade moving the world over. Europe was in sore need of finished goods. Much of the rest of the world also was short of them, and the raw-material-producing countries were glutted with produce they had been unable to move. Now everything was in motion to and fro across the oceans. The foreign trade of the United States leaped from $19,000,000 in 1814 to $165,-000,000 in 1815 and $229,000,000 in 1816. Our ships were busy again, and new ones were coming off the ways—not alone for foreign trade, but also for the coastwise and inland waters, for whaling and fishing.

Internally the country throbbed with commercial activity as the first of our great national booms got under way. "A great speck'l [speculation] on the allabama. I have been making some conditional contracts for land on the [Gulf] coast, and am . . . [contemplating] the purchase of a sugar estate."[1] Though these lines were penned by General Andrew Jackson of Nashville, Tennessee—his name a household word—they might have come from a Boston merchant on the hunt for quick profits. The focal point of the boom was the rich domain comprising most of the present states of Alabama and Mississippi which the same Jackson had wrested from the Creek Indians, British allies in the War of 1812. The whole western frontier, however, was included in the land craze. Moreover, American eyes were definitely on Spanish Florida. Eastern real estate responded to the spell, particularly in New York City, which had unmistakably succeeded its old rival, Philadelphia, as the first port of the United States.

It is not without significance, therefore, that the Board of Directors of the North America "Order'd That The President may purchase for the Company Kimber & Co's Map of the United States lately published."[2] In addition to the mariner's charts, with which he was well supplied, John Inskeep needed a map of the United States where so many concerns of interest to his company were going on. He needed a new one; a map two years old would have been out of date.

2

Speaking broadly, the problems which peace brought to the Insurance Company of North America fell under three heads:

First was the decline of Philadelphia as a port. In 1816, 599 foreign and 1,218 coastwise vessels docked along the Delaware waterfront. The figures for New York were 1,172 foreign and 1,832 coasters. Twenty years before, Philadelphia had led New York by about the same margin. The change diminished the amount of business to be picked up at home. The scramble for that business sharpened rivalry among the Philadelphia companies. Nor was it so easy as it had been in the past for Philadelphia companies to get business elsewhere. With the revival of ocean trade a crop of new marine companies was springing up in New York, Boston and Baltimore.

This brought to its evening the day of the private underwriter, and of the informal coffeehouse groups from which the North America and, indeed, all the incorporated companies, had stemmed. Yet the tavern tradition was too pleasant and too convenient to be abandoned. Every seaport had its gathering place for insurance men, with a marine diary chalked on a blackboard, register of vessels for sale and ships' letter bags. Philadelphia's was the Merchants' Coffee House, new name for the City Tavern which carried on at the old location in Second Street above Walnut, a veritable part of Insurance Row.

The second part of the postwar insurance problem concerned rates. What would be a fair premium for a voyage free of war hazards to the West Indies, to China, to the Mediterranean? It had been long since underwriters were required to consider the matter. And now the North America had to take into account factors which did not exist when it had begun business, in peacetime, in 1792. It had to consider competition at home in Philadelphia, in New York, Boston, etc.; and from the English companies which were quick to send agents here. There was a constant shaving of rates. Some of the newer companies shaved them below the safety point.

Though the North America avoided this error, it collected only $33,000 in premiums on $900,000 worth of insurance written during the last six months of 1815. The average rate was about 3.5 per cent. In 1811, $100,000 in premiums would have been collected on a similar amount of business. Though the chances of loss would have been greater, they would have been discounted by the higher premiums. Some of the company's most prosperous years had been when the dangers were greatest. Now much more insurance must be written to bring in a respectable return. Owing to the number of new companies, the volume of business the North America had once enjoyed was no longer obtainable. Inskeep must make money out of a smaller volume at lower rates.

And he must make enough to keep his stockholders satisfied during a speculative period of abnormal returns on capital. This introduced his third group of problems. American businessmen have faced similar problems during every boom in our history. With the records of several national and innumerable regional booms available, they still make mistakes. When one considers that Inskeep was facing the first national get-rich-quick era in our annals, the comparative dimensions of this phase of his difficulty increase. With definite limits to premium income, investment income was important. With the country flooded with quick- and large-profit enterprises, all tied in one way or another to fictitious western land prices, the path of the true investor was not an easy one.

Caution was the note upon which Inskeep had resumed normal activities following the restoration of peace with England early in 1815, and caution the note upon which he continued despite the flurry of speculation about him. By the end of the year the damage which the war had done to the capital structure of the company was repaired, and a "surplus" existed for the first time since the beginning of 1812.

In January 1816 a committee of the Board recommended the payment of a 4-per-cent dividend—the first dividend in three and a half years. As 58,976 shares were outstanding the dividend suggested would have aggregated $23,590, leaving a surplus balance of $9,984.

The Board revised the committee's recommendation, however, and distributed a dividend of 3 per cent, leaving a balance in the "surplus" account of $15,882. Six months later the Board "again deemed it prudent to exercise caution," though the dividend was increased to 4 per cent, making a total of 7 per cent for the year. Care was taken not to stimulate unduly the optimism of the shareholders. There was talk along the Row about the rosy prospects of indemnity for the Napoleonic spoliations. Indeed a committee of the Board was of the opinion that "the Claims on the Spanish & French Governments for Captures & Seizures seem to wear a more favourable aspect." In passing this information on to the stockholders the language was toned down as follows: "A small hope now exists that Something may at some future day (tho perhaps remote) be recover'd." The whole effort seems to have been to dissociate the Insurance Company of North America from the prevailing boom psychology, with its gilded expectations of great profits.[3]

The following year, 1817, dividends were raised to 10 per cent, and would have been more except for $30,000 lost on a single ship, the *Marcellus* which sailed from Calcutta for Philadelphia and was never heard of again. In 1818 the 10-per-cent rate was maintained.

These disbursements could not have been made from the proceeds of marine underwriting, on which the income and outgo for the three years mentioned had been as follows:

	Net Premiums	Losses
1816	$38,701.76	$31,965.84
1817	32,697.61	51,450.93
1818	27,627.28	8,679.80
	$99,026.65	$92,096.57

These slender sums represented not so much a decline in the volume of business since before the war as a decline in rates. The largest single source of income for the period was respondentia loans, to which the Finance Committee gave particular attention. During 1818, $58,000 was realized from this quarter. Fire insurance was adding from $1,000 to $2,000 a year after absorbing the company's operating expenses. The rest came from investments of capital, reserves and surplus.

Thus the old company moved gingerly through the temptations and pitfalls of easy money in most other lines of business. Wages and salaries were increased somewhat, John Inskeep's being raised from $2,500 to $3,000 a year. The company began the practice of footing the bills for "refreshments" at directors' meetings. Beyond these items, however, there was little to indicate that the North America contributed to the free-spending character of America's first all-out boom.

3

If stockholders felt like grumbling—as some of them must—over 7- to 10-per-cent returns on their money during a period of lush prosperity, they were glad to have their funds in a safe place when the boom burst in 1819. With the collapse of fantastic real-estate prices went the whole artificial price structure. Bank failures virtually denuded the West of banking facilities. In Philadelphia the Bank of the United States, of which the Federal Government owned one-fifth of the stock, was saved from ruin only by the appointment of a new president, Nicholas Biddle of Philadelphia, the lawyer who had once rented an office of the Insurance Company of North America. Foreign trade was cut in half and the merchant marine tonnage in use fell to the lowest figure in more than twenty years, barring the embargo and the War of 1812. The country was in its first general depression. It lasted four years.

During those years the North America paid dividends as follows: 1819, 10 per cent; 1820, 9 per cent; 1821, 8 per cent; 1822, 10 per cent. When the clouds lifted its stock was selling at $14.50 a share or 45 per cent above par. The investments portfolio was in good shape, after writing off as much as 50 per cent of the former book value of some of the securities. In 1820 when the Government had floated a $2,000,000 loan at 6 per cent, the North America had taken 5 per cent of the total issue, or $100,000, paying a premium of 1½ per cent.[4]

Only the closest attention to business had made this showing possible. The instance has been cited of dispatching a director forthwith to the scene on report of a fire in Reading. When news came that the ship *Emma Mathilda* was aground on the Jersey coast, the same director, Samuel Mifflin, was sent with a pilot and a crew of able hands to lighten the distressed vessel and haul her free.[5]

Another factor which helped to sustain the price of North America shares could be classified under the head of great expectations. These arose from claims resulting from the abuse of our maritime commerce during the Napoleonic epoch. The North America asserted its own stake in the French claims prior to 1801 to be $1,952,000; in the French claims after 1801 to be about $500,000; in the Spanish claims to be $768,959. The British claims had been settled and paid over a period of nearly twenty years, that procedure ending, so far as the North America was concerned, in 1817, when its current London agents, Alexander Glennie Son & Company, failed owing the company £524. Just what altogether had been received from the English seems impossible to ascertain, but the aggregate may have been around $600,000, or perhaps a third or a fourth of what the company had contended for. Should it do no worse with its French and Spanish claims the result would be a bonanza.

The sensibilities of stockholders were not excited with bonanza-like predictions, however. The soft pedal was deliberately applied and the attractive figures foregoing kept as much in the dark as possible. But behind the scenes, John Inskeep was unremittingly busy.

The French claims prior to 1801 were not only the largest but, it would appear, the easiest to realize on. One dealt not with foreign governments, rarely distinguished for their candid dealing with United States citizens, but with our own Government, which had signed away the claims of its citizens. The Constitution says private property may not be taken for public use without compensation. Two committees of the House of Representatives had found for reimbursement in this instance. Yet the matter got no farther. The Government seemed always short of money. War had added to the national debt. In good times as well as bad people complained of the taxes. All the North America and all the other interested underwriters could do seemed to amount to exactly nothing. They took what consolation they could from the fact that our Government was making diplomatic representations to France in the matter of the claims *after* 1801.

That left the claims against Spain, in which the North America professed an interest of $768,959. Over the years the company's own efforts in its behalf had spun out a tangled narrative, garnished with typically Spanish touches of delay, intrigue and futility. First the company had dealt through "The Widow of Maurice Roberts, Merch^t., Cadiz," as Colonel Pettit addressed her. It appears that John Leamy, then a member of the Board, had known her husband.

Mrs. Roberts has the honor of being the first woman connected with the Insurance Company of North America. It would be pleasant to record her success. However, she proved a trial to Colonel Pettit by her irregular correspondence and the tardiness with which she forwarded reports and statements. The Chesterfieldian old Colonel was very patient, and so it remained for John Inskeep to write Mrs. Roberts summarily that "Our Board having been so long disappointed" it would be necessary to make other arrangements to handle the company's Spanish affairs. The new agent likewise proved a disappointment. He was an enigmatic personality named Stephen Kingston who had dropped "mysterious hints" of "influence" in "certain directions." The man of mystery having accomplished nothing in four years, Inskeep sought to get rid of him, too. But Kingston refused to accept dismissal or to return the company's papers which had been entrusted to him.[6]

Matters were at this stand in 1817 when the claims became a pawn in the diplomatic chess game Secretary of State John Quincy Adams was playing to wrest Florida from Spain. Andrew Jackson simplified matters by marching an army through the province—after which Spain let go. A part of the eventual settlement was the renunciation of American indemnity demands, the United States agreeing to satisfy claims of its citizens to an aggregate of $5,000,000.

The year this agreement was ratified, 1821, the North America recovered its papers from Stephen Kingston and turned them over to Daniel Webster.[7] Other underwriters in Philadelphia and elsewhere likewise engaged Webster. It is doubtful if they could have found a better man to represent them. Though at this juncture temporarily without a seat in Congress, the Boston lawyer knew the ropes in Washington and he was aggressive. Within a few months he had good news for his clients, which included $100,000 in claims of the North America marked for reimbursement. The sum steadily mounted until the final settlement was made in June 1824. The North America received a check on the Bank of the United States for $332,933.49, which increased the wealth of the company about 50 per cent.

4

There was joy at 40 Walnut. In high good humor the Board paid Daniel Webster his "commission," which appears to have been about $20,000. Samuel Jaudon, a Philadelphia merchant and former private underwriter, who had assisted the attorney, was voted $6,600. Robert S. Stephens, secretary of the company, received a bonus of a year's pay, $2,000, and old Valentine $150 "for extra employment under the directions of Mr Jaudon & Mr Stephens."[8] For some time past Valentine had occupied the more or less honorary position of doorkeeper, from which the need for a messenger to carry confidential papers between Philadelphia and Washington temporarily rescued him. The last surviving employee who had seen the Insurance Company of America spread its sails in 1792, Valentine retired on a pension in 1828 at the age of eighty-two. When he died five years later the company helped to bury him.

After expenses had been subtracted the claims money amounted to $303,190. Coming at the end of a half-year during which only $6,200 had been paid in marine- and fire-losses combined, this boosted to $350,000 what the company called its "surplus." The term "surplus" as used in the insurance business then is not to be confused with the present-day definition. By "surplus" was meant anything in addition to the $600,000 capital plus a "reserve" consisting of the premiums on "undetermined" risks, on which policies were still in force. If losses among such undetermined risks proved to be only normal the "reserve" would cover them. If they proved abnormal the "surplus" would be eaten into. If they proved abnormal to a great degree the "surplus" would be insufficient and it would be necessary to tap the capital. This had happened during our naval war with France at the turn of the century and the company was several years getting back its full capital. It had happened again at the outset of the War of 1812, after which the capital had been restored more promptly.

When the "surplus" was not needed to meet immediate losses the practice was to pay out nearly all of it in dividends twice a year. This was not regarded as an extravagant dividend policy. The conception of a reserve or a surplus as modern business knows them had not dawned. In the old days of personal underwriters an insurer's private fortune and his credit stood back of his share in a risk. Incorporated companies considered their capital in the same light. It was "working capital" in the literal sense of the words. The necessity for a heavier wall of protection between the capital account and the demands of unexpectedly heavy losses had not been made clear by experience. That the North America's capital should have been broken into only twice in thirty-two years was the mark of an expertly and safely conducted organization. Comparatively few businesses of the day appear to have been more conservatively managed. This was revealed by the failures following the collapse of the postwar boom in 1819 when the Bank of the United States nearly went under.

Consequently the possibility of using a part of the Spanish claims manna to establish a reserve and a surplus such as are known today was not given a thought, so far as any record discloses. Stockholders had been following with avid interest the progress of the claims drama. Appetites for a whopping dividend were on fine edge. The directors, who also were stockholders, were none the less ready to comply. One director voted against delaying the distribution for a month, or until the date of the regular July dividend meeting. When that time arrived the Board was unanimous in declaring an extra dividend of 60 per cent, or $6 a share. This took $296,600 of the claims money. Then the pre-existing "surplus" was tapped for $24,550, representing a regular dividend of 5 per cent. After these record-breaking disbursements, a "surplus" of $31,071 remained— an amount so much larger than usual that the Board felt the necessity of explaining it. With the hurricane season in the West Indies near at hand an addition to the "reserv'd Excess" would "the better assure a Dividend in January next."[9]

The hurricanes were worse than usual that autumn and the ship *Columbian* was lost on the passage from China. Surplus, undetermined premium reserve, and current receipts were unequal by $17,-225.47 to the damage done. For the third time in the company's history the capital account was tapped, and there was no January 1825 dividend. By the following July the capital had been restored, with a "surplus" of $14,849—all but $2,587 of which was taken to pay a 2½-per-cent dividend.

After declining to act on a resolution to allow him an extra year's salary, the thrifty stockholders recognized John Inskeep's services in relation to the French indemnity with a set of silver plate "of the value of $500." It became one of the prized possessions of the president who altered his will to provide for its division among his children.

Regardless of what a present-day corporation executive would think of such a dividend policy, the North America's shares were still quoted above par, as were those of its Walnut Street neighbors with two exceptions. Indeed, the Philadelphia marine group, now numbering nine companies, was by no small odds the strongest and best-run insurance community in the country. Much had been learned in a quarter of a century of underwriting. Measures calculated to avoid a repetition of circumstances which had resulted in losses were steadily introduced. Through the directors' minutes of the Insurance Company of North America are scattered recommendations and subscriptions for innumerable accessories and devices which one by one have reduced the hazards of water-borne traffic: "Agreed to join . . . in the expense of dispatching a Pilot Boat with provisions &c to cruise off the Capes." "Order'd that $20 be contributed . . . towards the use of the signal establishment at the Light House at Cape Henlopen." "The meeting of citizens yesterday afternoon . . . upon the subject of the Breakwater at the mouth of the Delaware was numerously

attended. . . . A committee was . . . appointed to draft a memorial
to Congress . . . praying for appropriations for the Breakwater."[10]

This last project had occupied the attention of the directors for
many years. The severe winter of 1825 which was particularly hard
on vessels entering Delaware Bay brought matters to a head. Late
in December Philadelphia merchants and underwriters held a meeting and adopted resolutions asking Congress to build an artificial
harbor in the bay. Horace Binney, attorney for the North America,
presided over the gathering. His predecessor, Joseph Hopkinson,
presented "a very lucid explanation of the Nature of the meeting."
Three years later Congress made its first appropriation for the Delaware Breakwater. By 1833 close to 2,000 feet of stone barrier
stretched into the Bay. During a disastrous northeast gale twenty
vessels, many of which might otherwise have been doomed, found
safe anchorage.[11]

All this helped the Philadelphia insurance companies. Elsewhere
insufficient managing experience and rate-cutting had begun to tell.
The stock of only four of New York's twelve marine companies was
above par. For the shares of two no offerings were quoted. Of thirty-
one fire companies in New York the stock of five was above par,
twelve below and fourteen without any offered price. Boston's
twenty companies, with average annual incomes of no more than
$18,000 apiece, were in even worse case. An exception to the prevail-
ing condition was the Connecticut group of well-conducted fire companies. As yet, however, it was too small to make much of an impression on the general situation.

The July 1825 dividend was the last the North America's stockholders received for two years. Then business mended. Six and a
half per cent was paid in 1829, 3 per cent in 1830 and 6 per cent in
1831. The future seemed more promising than in several years past,
but the realization of this promise meant the mastery of a host of
new insurance problems. John Inskeep was seventy-four years old.
Having piloted the company for a quarter of a century he resolved
to leave the solution of the new problems to someone else. He had
decided who the someone should be. At the annual meeting in January 1831 John Correy Smith was added to the Board of Directors,
and Inskeep informed his colleagues that he would retire before the
year was out. On May 21 he offered his resignation.

"In thus taking leave of you Gentlemen, most sincerely do I feel the obligations imposed upon me by the repeated and flattering proofs of your kindness & confidence, for more than a quarter of a century, as well as for your uniform urbanity. . . . Wishing you present & eternal happiness,

I am very sincerely your friend. . . ."[12]

John Correy Smith was chosen president. Robert S. Stephens, who had been Ebenezer Hazard's chief clerk, retired from the secretary-ship which he had held for twenty-six years. His successor was a young New Englander named Arthur G. Coffin.

5

The fifth president of the Insurance Company of North America was a native Philadelphian, forty-six years of age. His father, William Smith, had been a well-known apothecary during the Revolutionary period. But the bottles and vials in the elder Smith's shop held small attraction for young John who began work as a shipper's clerk on the waterfront. The eventual result was a fortune acquired in the China trade.

Smith and Coffin tackled their jobs with vigor. A healthy increase in the volume of fire business, hitherto unfailingly a money maker, was the first visible sign of their efforts.

Several new factors whose ultimate bearing on fire risks remained to be determined were appearing on the scene. Coal was supplanting wood for fuel in Pennsylvania. Friction matches were becoming common. Gaslights appeared in Philadelphia and other cities. A few years of experience were to show gaslights safer than candles and coal safer than wood. Matches, however, increased the fire hazard.

Monopolistic legislation, sponsored by the insurance companies, threatened the local agency system, which the North America had originated. This started in 1827 when Massachusetts imposed a 10-per-cent tax on the premiums of out-of-state companies. Moreover, it barred outside companies of less than $200,000 capital and prohibited the writing of single risks exceeding 10 per cent of the capitalization. The last two provisions protected the policyholder and were a first step in the direction of regulation to insure solvency.

Pennsylvania came back immediately with a similar law, and two years later raised the tax on out-of-state companies to 20 per cent.

Seven other states levied taxes ranging from 4 to 10 per cent. One result was a fresh crop of home-grown fire-insurance companies, often inadequately financed and amateurishly managed. This made hard sledding for the sound companies. The thriving and competent Aetna of Hartford, Connecticut, found itself excluded entirely from Pennsylvania and Massachusetts because it did not possess $200,000 in capital. The 4-per-cent tax in Ohio induced it to close all its agencies there excepting the one at Cincinnati. While the North America discontinued a few smaller agencies, generally speaking it was able to meet the situation in the taxing states with an increase of rates.

This was in agreement with the company's conception of the importance of the local agent to the insurance structure. From the first the North America had endeavored to attract good men into its agency service by making their jobs worth while. In 1823 the survey-fee mode of payment was abolished in favor of a 5-per-cent commission on premiums. By 1830 this had been increased to 10 per cent, and presently was extended to include renewals as well as new business.

New York City was the first conspicuous sufferer from the uneconomic tax policy. In 1835 fire swept the city, burning for three days because water drawn from the river froze in the hoses. Six hundred and forty-eight houses were destroyed, entailing a loss of $18,000,000. Nearly the whole insurance burden fell upon the tariff-protected local companies. They were unequal to the strain, twenty-three out of twenty-six joint-stock corporations going to the wall. Thereafter New York reduced its tax on outside companies to 2 per cent.

The shrewdest of insurance men make mistakes, especially when, like Smith, they push their business forward during a period of transition. Though the amount of single risks had been increased from $10,000 to $50,000, and other regulations of the Inskeep regime liberalized, the $10,000 limit on isolated country houses remained. The North America declined to accept a $15,000 policy on the mansion of Arlington, across the river from Washington and owned by George Washington Parke Custis, adopted son of the first President.[13] That house is standing today. Yet other and greater risks

JOHN CORREY SMITH

An importing merchant of Philadelphia, like his predecessors as president of the Insurance Company of North America, Coffin's first contact with underwriting was as a buyer of insurance. Head of company, 1831-1845. Salient contribution was creation of large surplus, a safety factor little known to corporations of day. Enabled company to weather panic of 1837 which wrecked many other underwriters.

were accepted. For the ten years ending in 1832 fire receipts had totaled $61,639 and losses $17,973. Under Smith's pressure receipts for the decade following nearly doubled—to $114,326—while losses more than quadrupled—to $78,949. The rapid increase in losses constituted a real problem of the company's fire business as the North America entered the sixth decade of its career in 1843.

6

Though Smith's expansion of the fire business was being pressed at the expense of a narrowing profit ratio in that field, at the same time he had taken measures to protect the company's capital from this as well as from other untoward events. The safety device was a progressive increase of the "surplus" or "excess in hand," as it also sometimes was called, remaining after the distribution of a dividend.

John Correy Smith had not been in office three months when the July 1831 dividend period was at hand. After deducting undetermined premiums the company's assets stood at $619,765 or $19,765 above the capital fund. A dividend of 3 per cent, or $13,962, was declared, leaving an "excess" of $5,803—a mere cobweb against the uncertainties of the coming hurricane season in the Caribbean. It was, however, in keeping with former dividend practice.

But the following January 1832 the "excess" was increased to $10,532, concerning which the following explanation was offered to the stockholders:

"The directors have, when taking into view the amount of undecided premiums being inadequate to any heavy demand, deemed it most advisable to retain a larger surplus than usual—particularly as this has not lessened the dividend to which the stockholders have been for several terms accustomed."[14]

In July, though the dividend was increased to 4 per cent, the "excess" was nearly doubled—to $19,144. The semiannual report in which this figure appeared also contained the following interesting note: "Some changes have been made in the investments of funds by the sale of 570 shares of the U. S. Bank Stock . . . and the increase of the Amount loaned on Mortgages."[15] Since its early days the company had been a considerable investor in Bank of the United

States stock. The sale of 570 shares represented all the shares in the company's possession at the time. They brought $70,854, which was $2,762 above cost.

It would be interesting to know what prompted the company to get rid of its United States Bank holdings at this particular time. The bank was a Philadelphia institution and its president a Philadelphia man, Nicholas Biddle. Together with most of the conservative financial interests the North America's directors were on the bank's side in its battle with President Andrew Jackson to obtain a renewal of its Federal charter. Nicholas Biddle had boldly taken the offensive. It was a presidential year and he was backing Henry Clay to defeat Jackson for re-election. Thus the bank was in politics, always a bad place for a bank.

Jackson beat Clay hands down, and then he turned furiously on Nicholas Biddle. The result was the most desperate fight over a domestic issue the country had witnessed to that time. The sole depository of Government funds, on which it paid no interest, the great bank, through its twenty-seven branches, controlled the economic life of the nation. Jackson believed no institution not responsible to the people should have such authority.

In 1833 he electrified the country and dumfounded conservative financiers with the announcement that Government deposits would be removed to a series of state-chartered institutions which immediately, and appropriately, became known as "pet" banks. This obliged Biddle to contract his credit. He contracted it far beyond necessary requirements, bringing on the country a financial panic and a standstill in commerce. His expectation was that blame for the panic would fall on Jackson and ruin him. Instead, it fell on Biddle. Unable to obtain a renewal of its charter, the Bank of the United States went out of business.[16]

7

The artificially created depression ended and good times returned as soon as the bank question was settled. Though the North America's leading men regretted the outcome of that issue, they had cause to congratulate themselves on their timely disposal of bank stock. Moreover, they had cause for satisfaction with the excellent state of the company's business all through the bank turmoil. From

1832 to 1835 our foreign trade increased from $176,000,000 to $251,-000,000, our merchant marine engaged in that trade from 614,000 tons to 788,000. Nor do the tonnage figures tell the whole story. We were building safer and faster ships. The *Ann McKim,* launched at Baltimore in 1832, was the first of the clippers destined to rule the waves until the ascendancy of steam. All this was good news for a marine underwriter.

Other good news came from the White House. Much as the Insurance Company of North America might deprecate General Jackson's bank policies, it could applaud his vigorous conduct of our foreign affairs. For twenty-five years France had been dilly-dallying about paying the Napoleonic claims originating *after* 1801. Jackson declined to be put off. He threatened to go after France as he had gone after Nicholas Biddle. France paid up—25,000,000 francs. Though this amount was not enough to cover all verified claims, it was more than many of the claimants had expected to get. Commissioners whittled the North America's $500,000 claims to $111,000, on which $59,362 was paid in 1836.

An indication of the pleasing trend of events was the removal of the company into its sixth home in 1834. Philadelphia's business center was moving westward, and the North America needed larger quarters. It found them a block and a half away in a building just erected at the corner of Walnut and Dock Streets by Thomas P. Cope, a director of the company.

The French award was made occasion for two extra dividends of 5 per cent each, giving the company the following dividend record over the period just reviewed: 1832, 7 per cent; 1833, 9 per cent; 1834 (bank panic year), 7 per cent; 1835, 8 per cent; 1836, 15 per cent; 1837, 15 per cent. In the face of these disbursements the "surplus" had grown from $19,144 in 1832 to $47,311 in January 1837. In their semiannual statements the directors no longer apologized for the size of this item. In addition to "surplus" and undetermined premiums the capital account was further guarded by an item called "claims, reservations &c" which in January 1837 amounted to $19,920, thus affording the capital a degree of protection not known before in the company's history.

As matters fell out these prudential measures could not have been taken at a better time. In the spring of 1835 the healthy business recovery crossed the line into speculation. The second national boom in our history was on. The impetus came in part from a speculative wave in Europe, in part from the momentum of an over-rapid recovery from the Biddle panic, in part from a Treasury surplus which was creating an excess of loanable deposits in the "pet" banks. Signs of inflation began to appear.

Everyone was spending. State legislatures voted millions to finance turnpikes, canals and railroads. City folk gambled in the stocks of these corporations, and in commodities, houses and rentals. Everyone gambled in the most abundant of all American resources—land. Public land sales jumped from $4,000,000 to $14,000,000 in a year. Paper towns and paper railroads began to dot the vacant spaces, all to be paid for with paper money.

The whirligig lasted about eighteen months before a tightening of the situation abroad began to draw European funds home. Jackson took steps to curb the capers of wildcat banks. Thirty million dollars in Treasury deposits were withdrawn and presented to the states. The banks had that much less to loan for speculative purposes.

Land prices tumbled, carrying other prices with them. Western banks, clogged with mortgages made on fictitious valuations, began to topple. On May 10, 1837, the banks of New York City suspended specie payment. Next day the Philadelphia banks followed suit. The reckoning was at hand.

CHAPTER VIII

THE ROAD TO LEADERSHIP

I

WHEN the panic of 1837 struck, Pennsylvania was the richest state in the Union, its securities honored abroad as gilt-edge. Insurance Row was the soundest and best-managed underwriting group in the country. Philadelphia was regarded as the financial capital of the United States. When the city's banks resumed specie payments in the summer of 1838, the worst of the crisis seemed to be over—at any rate as far as Philadelphia was concerned.

Far from being over, Philadelphia's money troubles had only begun. The period of distress was to last six more years, and to play havoc with the Row.

When Andrew Jackson brought an end, in 1836, to the Bank of the United States he did not interrupt Nicholas Biddle's career as a banker. The Philadelphian continued to operate by means of a state-chartered institution called the United States Bank of Pennsylvania. The preponderant majority of Philadelphia's financial community, having opposed Jackson, wished Mr. Biddle well. Confidence was expressed in the new bank. Its suspension of specie payments in 1837 was taken as a part of the ills of the times rather than as a special mark of weakness of the Biddle bank. All other Philadelphia banks had suspended as well. But in October 1838—two months after resumption—when the Biddle bank suspended again the fact was not so easily explained. This suspension started a general bank run obliging the other Philadelphia depositories to suspend or limit hard-money payments to small change.

The second wave of local suspensions, plus the depressed state of the country at large, had a distressing effect on Insurance Row. The "surplus" after dividends with which the Insurance Company of North America had entered the troubled period shrank from $47,000 in 1837 to $7,954 in January 1839. In July this was gone and

127

there was a deficit of $1,694 in the capital account—consequently no dividend. The next two years brought a profit on operations which would have restored the capital account but for the decline in security values. In January 1841 only four of Insurance Row's eleven marine companies paid dividends. Though the North America was not among the payers, its shares, for which $9.50 was bid, stood higher in relation to par than those of three of the four companies which distributed dividends. The company continued to make money on its operations and to lose it through the downward plunge of the securities in which its capital was invested.

By decree of the Legislature all Philadelphia banks resumed specie payments on January 15, 1841. By this time, however, unpleasant rumors concerning the United States Bank of Pennsylvania were afloat and a run on it promptly began. Biddle made a brave show of strength. In twenty days he paid out $6,683,000 in gold and silver. Some of the other Philadelphia banks paid out as much as $1,000,000. On February 4 the Biddle bank suspended for the third time. The remaining banks were forced to limit specie disbursement to $5. A little later some were able to resume the payment of coin with legislative aid, some without it. But there was no aid for Mr. Biddle's bank. An investigating committee of its directors reported sensational findings: the bank involved in wild speculations; evidence of misapplication of funds and participation in political corruption. The bank closed, insolvent.

By January 1842 the deficit of the Insurance Company of North America was close to $300,000. President Smith reduced his salary from $2,500 to $2,000 a year. Stockholders were asked to consider "whether their interests would not be promoted by a reduction of the capital of the Co. to an amount which would correspond with the present actual value of the assets."[1]

Stockholders consenting, the Board on January 26 petitioned the Legislature for permission to reduce the par of shares from $10 to $5 which was declared to be "what it is really worth." The same day the financial crisis took a turn for the worse when the Girard Bank again discontinued specie payments. Stephen Girard was dead, and his fortune was not behind the bank which used his name. The action of the Girard Bank forced the other Philadelphia depositories to suspend—for the fourth time. Unable to procure funds to meet the interest on its public debt, the Commonwealth of Pennsylvania defaulted. The shock went around the world. The credit of Pennsylvania tumbled. The Legislature promptly complied with the North America's request, cutting the capital in half to $300,000. Having thus written off its depression losses in securities the company, still making a profit on operations, was able to resume dividends on a 6-per-cent annual basis in July 1842. It had survived the crisis.

2

Other companies were not faring so well. The latest comer to Insurance Row was the first to go. In 1838, when Philadelphia's money troubles seemed almost over, the Washington Insurance Company had been organized. In April 1842 it went out of business. The Atlantic, established in 1825, wound up its affairs in October. In 1843 the Washington Insurance Company came back into the field as a mutual company. "Mutualism was in the air," observed one chronicler of the scene.[2] The mutual companies, which divided their profits among the policyholders, usually operated with less capital than joint-stock corporations. In New York mutualization seemed to offer hard-pressed and sometimes indifferently managed companies a hope of continued existence, though an exception to this general statement was the prosperous and well-run Atlantic of New York which became a mutual in 1842. While the North America was getting on a secure basis in 1843 the other Philadelphia companies, with two possible exceptions, barely weathered the year.

In 1844 the weaker ones dropped like autumn leaves. On January 1, the United States Insurance Company, founded in 1807, gave up the ghost. In February the Philadelphia, dating from 1804, and the Marine, dating from 1806, folded their tents. In March the Union, 1804, the Phoenix, 1803, and the American, 1831, mutualized. The Delaware, 1804, held out until March 1845 when it became the Philadelphia Mutual. The Union may be cited as an example of the shrinkage in assets thse operations involved. The capital of the old Union was $500,000, that of the Union Mutual, $100,000.

Thus in 1844 Pennsylvania pulled itself out of the depression, about a year behind the rest of the country. An incidental echo of the passing distress was the Lehigh Coal & Navigation Company's offer to pay interest on a loan in coal, which the North America accepted.

It will be noted that of all the tenants of Insurance Row only the

North America and its oldest competitor, the Insurance Company of
the State of Pennsylvania, survived the holocaust in original joint-
stock form. And, like the North America, the State of Pennsylvania
had sacrificed half its capital. Not only did the North America survive. It came out head and shoulders the largest and strongest organization in the depleted Row. Comparative statements of assets follow:

Insurance Company of North America (July 1, 1845) . . $393,160
Insurance Company of the State of Pennsylvania
   (January 1, 1846) 240,683
Union Mutual (January 1, 1846) 163,371
Phoenix Mutual (January 1, 1846) 159,660
Philadelphia Mutual (January 1, 1846) 133,730
Delaware Mutual Safety (a new company, October 31, 1845) 114,974

One result of the recent hard times was a forward step by the
Massachusetts Legislature for the protection of fire-insurance policyholders. A law was passed obliging companies to maintain a fund to
guarantee the fulfillment of their contracts. Thus was inaugurated
the unearned premium reserve and the beginning of state supervision
of fire insurance. Another outcropping of the depression was the rise
of the insurance broker, despite the opposition of the old established
companies. As times improved the broker demonstrated his ability
to get business. It was apparent that he had become a permanent
fixture.[3]

3

After dividends and proper reservations the North America's surplus in 1844 was $70,115, the largest in the company's history.[4] The
reasons for the old company's fine showing were not far to seek: an
enlightened and conservative surplus policy, begun in the prosperous thirties; superb management, which included a realistic attitude toward security losses; skillful and energetic attention to fire
insurance. The Insurance Company of the State of Pennsylvania, for
instance, did not enter this profitable field until 1844.

Under the head of good management was a definitely established
policy of reinsurance. This was another mark of conservatism, a
buffer against the shock of sudden enormous loss, which has become

one of the guiding principles of modern insurance. In a way it represented a return to the practice of coffeehouse days when all risks were spread among a number of individual underwriters. Hitherto the North America had been accustomed to divide risks among the other Philadelphia companies. The recent changes along the Row induced it to seek other connections. The eyes of John Correy Smith fell upon the Atlantic Mutual, the strongest of the New York companies. He wrote to Walter R. Jones, its president:

"This Company has been in the practice of effecting re-insurances to a considerable extent. . . . Under these circumstances, it has occurred to us that we might establish a correspondence with your Co. which would prove mutually advantageous.

"As it is desirable, in the outset, to have a clear understanding with each other, we would state that we shall offer those risks only which we consider *good,* and are willing to assume for ourselves in such sums as we think prudent, & we would expect in all cases to give you the same premium that we receive. This in some instances, would exceed your rates & sometimes might fall below them:—the average however would probably exceed the rate charged in your city. . . .

"We presume that you are sufficiently acquainted with the standing of this Company, to have implicit confidence in all our representations. We claim precedence of all similar institutions here in respect of age & solidity of capital: and in other particulars we hope that we do not fall behind. Of this, however, you can satisfy yourself. . . .

"Should you be disposed to re-insure for us, the risks we should offer would be principally by Inland transportation, to & from New Orleans, and to & from Brazil."[5]

This interesting letter was mailed on April 8, 1844. The Atlantic lost no time accepting the proposal, and on April 11 two applications for reinsurance went from the Philadelphia to the New York office. Such was the beginning of a business association which, as this is written, has lasted for ninety-eight years.

A few months after the reinsurance agreement with the Atlantic Mutual had been made the Walnut Street companies bound themselves closer together in the Philadelphia Board of Marine Underwriters. This organization undertook to prepare and keep current a tariff of premium rates; to prepare a standard form of policy; to gather helpful statistics "relative to insurance, marine affairs, commercial regulations, maritime law, &c." It was empowered to appoint agents abroad to represent all the companies, and to set up a board of five experienced "surveyors and reporters," whose duty would be to examine each vessel arriving at Philadelphia and make detailed reports on its fitness for sea service.

Heretofore these labors had been performed separately by the various companies, with obvious duplication of expense. Another matter the Board of Underwriters dealt with successfully was that of fraudulent wrecks, particularly along the Atlantic and Gulf coasts. During the past fifteen years these had constituted a growing problem.

On June 22, 1845, John Correy Smith died suddenly, and the presidency of the Insurance Company of North America was assumed by Arthur Gilman Coffin. This was a natural choice. Coffin had entered the corporation's service in 1832 as secretary, restoring to that office much of the authority Ebenezer Hazard had brought to it. As his successor to the secretaryship, Coffin chose a young man of promise and capacity, Henry D. Sherrerd, who had held the same position with the late Atlantic Insurance Company of Philadelphia.

Arthur G. Coffin was forty-five years old when he took office. After he had left Harvard College on the death of his father, a Gloucester, Massachusetts, physician, Coffin's job was on the Philadelphia waterfront. After eleven years with the shipping firm of Havens & Smith he joined the North America. Celebrated for tact and diplomacy, he was to accomplish a number of administrative improvements so quietly that many seemed almost unaware of them. In the same noiseless way A. G. Coffin became in time one of Philadelphia's notable humanitarians. He served as a trustee of Girard College, established by the will of Stephen Girard for the education of poor orphan boys. For more than a quarter of a century, he virtually managed the activities of the Union Benevolent Association, the House of Refuge, the Magdalen Society, the Pennsylvania Bible Society and the Seaman's Friend Society.

4

Mention of "inland transportation" as one variety of risk on which the North America desired reinsurance is significant. Steam as the

motive power of water carriers had come to stay. It had revolutionized inland travel and was making itself felt on the oceans. Men of
the North America had seen the steamboat born and had seen it
grow. In 1786 the Connecticut mechanic, John Fitch, had built in
Philadelphia a steamboat that would run. Then came Fulton on
the Hudson in 1807 with the first commercially successful craft. In
1811 a boat built in Pittsburgh journeyed to New Orleans, and the
transformation was on. In 1834 there were 230 steamers on western
rivers, and more than double that number in 1835. In 1836, $432,-
621,000 worth of goods were transported by steam on western streams
alone. This was more than double the value of our foreign commerce.

In 1818 an ocean steamship plied between New York and New
Orleans. The following year the American-built *Savannah* crossed
the Atlantic. Coastwise and transatlantic service developed slowly,
however. Financial and engineering difficulties were great.

Prior to the advent of steam river traffic had been by sail, flatboat
and raft. In the West losses were so heavy that practically no insurance could be obtained by these carriers from any source. Yet in 1805
the North America departed from what appears to have been almost
a fixed rule against such risks and covered for $13,000 "the body,
tackle and apparell" of the brig *Kentucky,* bound from the Ohio river
to New Orleans. Perhaps the characters of the owners had something to do with it. Samuel Mifflin, Henry Nixon and John Lassley
were well-known Philadelphia merchants, Mifflin being a North
America director and Nixon a stockholder. The venture was an
unfortunate one for the company, which paid a claim of $12,000.[6]

While steamboats moved passengers and freight much more expeditiously and more safely than sail on flatboats, the paddle-wheelers
also were very questionable underwriting risks. The North America
adopted an attitude of watchful waiting, letting other insurers blaze
the trail in this chancy field. Particularly on our western rivers were
accidents frequent and captains and pilots a reckless lot. Even in
1844 when river boats were far and away our heaviest carriers, the
North America preferred to share its risks with the Atlantic Mutual.
Only after careful consideration was the first agency created expressly
to go after river and other inland transportation risks. This was in
St. Louis in 1849. The agent, Edward Brooks, was experienced in
river and western overland traffic. Nevertheless he operated under

very particular instructions from the home office. Boats were to be insured on no account—only cargoes.

"You may insure goods on board of first class steamboats not over two years old, to the extent of $15,000, when the waters are high and no ice is to be encountered. But when the waters are low, you must not exceed $10,000. When the navigation is obstructed by ice, we should prefer, if you can do it, that you would avoid taking risks altogether. By Steamboats of inferior grade, you will reduce the amount at risk in proportion to their age and character, avoiding, if possible, the lower class entirely. Be careful in all cases to exercise prudence and caution. Especially would we have you make yourself thoroughly acquainted with the standing of your Masters and Pilots. No premium is adequate to the risk of insuring property under the care of an intemperate or unprincipled man. . . .

"You may adopt the same rates of premium which the Companies of your city are charging, not submitting to any reduction for the purpose of securing business. The latter is bad policy. With regard to the settlement of premiums you can follow the course usually pursued in your city. All premiums under fifty dollars ought to be paid in cash. However, do in this matter as your neighbours do."[7]

Brooks asked for instructions concerning an application from Pierre Chouteau & Company, the greatest fur traders in the West. By every means of primitive land and water transportation pelts were brought from as far as the summits of the Rockies. In St. Louis they were graded, sold and forwarded via New Orleans or Pittsburgh to the ultimate markets. The account of this firm, then in the third generation of the Chouteau family, would have been a feather in the cap of any insurance agent. "The Board decided to decline whatever applications that might be made for insurances of this character," was the crisp word that came from Philadelphia.[8] It must have been a blow to Agent Brooks. There was no question of the financial responsibility, the integrity or competence of the Chouteaus. The North America simply acknowledged itself insufficiently versed in the multiple hazards of fur transportation over a thousand miles of Indian country. It preferred to leave the honor of insurance pioneering in that particular to others. All in all, the restrictions imposed on Mr. Brooks were such that he does not seem to have been able to write a great deal of insurance.

ARTHUR G. COFFIN

Sixth president Insurance Company of North America and first professional insurance man to assume that office. Had been company's secretary for thirteen years. President from 1845 to 1878, he saw age of modern marine and fire insurance born. In its development he played a notable part.

From a portrait by S. B. Waugh, owned by the Insurance Company of North America.

The investment portfolio of the company likewise reflected a policy of reserve toward steam projects. When other underwriters were taking the shares of early railroads and river boats, the North America held off and usually saved money. Its only losses in ventures of this kind appear to have aggregated $400, spent for shares in two steam towboat corporations. One motive of these small but ill-fated investments was to help the port of Philadelphia.

A similar motive prompted the company's first railway investment in 1847 when it took fifty shares at $50 each in the projected Pennsylvania Railroad. The persuasions of Thomas P. Cope also had something to do with it. Thomas P. Cope had come a long way since 1792 when he sold the Insurance Company of North America seven yards of green cloth for $8.40 to cover desks in the office. In 1807 Mr. Cope built his first ship, christened *Lancaster* after the Pennsylvania town in which the owner was born. The *Lancaster* proved a "lucky ship" in the manner in which she escaped the perils of the deep, including hostile commerce raiders. Of course, maritime men knew such persistent luck to be a matter of skillful handling by her master. By all accounts, Mr. Cope was not a lavish purchaser of insurance, depending largely on the competence of his captains to save his vessels from loss or injury. For a generation the story was related of the *Lancaster's* passage from China at the beginning of the War of 1812. Full war rates had just gone into effect. Cope thought them too high. His partner did not. The partner insured his half of the ship and cargo. Cope took a chance on his half. In the fullness of time the *Lancaster* appeared, full sail, in the Delaware.[9]

In 1821 Thomas P. Cope established the first line of sailing packets to make voyages on schedule between Philadelphia and Liverpool. It was eminently successful. In 1829 he joined the Board of the Insurance Company of North America, where his knowledge of the personal qualifications of sea captains and of other precautions for preserving ships from injury was of the greatest value. Over the years the North America's consistently good knowledge of such details had been an important factor in its success. Note the injunction to Agent Brooks of St. Louis concerning captains.

The Erie Canal, connecting the Hudson and the Great Lakes, had opened the port of New York to the great western grain trade. The Baltimore & Ohio railroad promised to tap the Ohio valley for Baltimore. Cope argued that Philadelphia had to establish its own

line with the West. And it must act quickly because the Baltimore
& Ohio, already running trains to Cumberland, Maryland, had a
franchise for right-of-way through Pennsylvania to Pittsburgh.

At the age of seventy-five, when most men look forward to a
tranquil evening of life, Thomas P. Cope launched his fight to build
a railroad from Philadelphia to the West. Whipping up an apathetic
and skeptical public, drumming in the dangers to the city's commercial prosperity, he set out to obtain pledges in the prodigious sum of
$2,500,000. In the teeth of staggering obstacles the old man drove on,
and after two years, in 1847, remarkable success had crowned his
efforts. The Baltimore & Ohio had permitted its right to a route
across Pennsylvania to lapse. From the State Legislature Cope had
obtained the abandoned franchise. Track was started between Philadelphia and Harrisburg. By 1849 the capital subscriptions pledged
amounted to $5,500,000, the Insurance Company of North America's
cautious contribution being fifty additional shares.

5

The fire business into which John Correy Smith had infused new
life in the 1830's continued to grow. The ascending curve of losses
in relation to premiums, which had been the disquieting feature
of that period of expansion, was checked.

The woes following the panic of 1837 had decimated the ranks
of insurance companies in New York as well as in Philadelphia.
In July 1845 New York suffered another great fire, putting a further
strain on the underwriters. The Aetna Company of Hartford, hit
for losses of $120,000, saved itself only by means of a personal assess-
ment on its directors. The North America, which had never made
an especial bid for New York business because of the rate-cutting so
long practiced there, lost only $8,000. Shortly after this fire Joseph
Hoxie, vice-president of the Mercantile Mutual Insurance Company
of New York, called on Mr. Coffin in Philadelphia. He said the
Mercantile wished to retire from the fire business in favor of marine
exclusively. He proposed the sale of its line of fire risks to the North
America, and argued that by establishing an agency in New York the
Philadelphia company could reap a rich harvest.

Mr. Coffin laid the matter before his Board which declined to
make the purchase and declined to open an agency in New York.

Thirteen months later the latter action was rescinded, however, and an agency established. The agent, James Wright, proved to be a hustler. His jurisdiction was enlarged to include Brooklyn, Williamsburg and Jersey City with the proviso that "risks would be of the first character and no concentration." The no-concentration policy had saved the North America from embarrassing losses in several extensive fires. When Wright submitted an application for $30,000 on a bonded warehouse, Coffin himself made a trip to New York to survey the property. He took the risk. In a year Wright wrote $2,900,000 worth of insurance for premiums aggregating $13,500. He was given wider powers and the salary of his clerk, which the company paid, was raised $100 a year.[10]

During this year occurred another event worthy of mention in connection with the North America's fire business. On August 13, 1847, Director Alexander T. Henry died at the age of eighty-two, after forty-eight years on the Board. As much as any one man, Mr. Henry was the creator of the local agency system when, in 1807, his spirited advocacy of a policy of expansion led to the posting of North America representatives on the western frontier.

In May 1849 half of the business district of St. Louis and twenty-seven steamboats lying at the wharves were burned. The disaster wrecked several western insurance companies which had neglected to lay up sufficient reserves and had ignored the no-concentration rule. Some eastern companies were hard hit, Aetna losing $130,000. It was able to pay without resorting to extraordinary measures because, having profited by the New York experience, it had created an ample reserve. The North America, which maintained no fire agent in St. Louis, had exactly four policies aggregating $26,500 in that city. Had it been willing to cut rates and to discard other safety devices to meet competition it could have had many times that amount. The fire cost it two losses, for $11,000. One was on merchandise owned by Edward Brooks, the company's agent for inland transportation risks. These were promptly met from current funds, without touching the company's surplus of $200,000.

As always happens after a great fire, there was a scramble for insurance. Nevertheless, the North America continued to scrutinize applications as carefully as before. A number of eastern companies sent representatives to a meeting in New York to consider the lessons of St. Louis. "Uniform, sound rates were adopted," note the his-

torians of Aetna, adding wryly: "For a time serious attempts were
made to sustain them." Aetna was not one of the backsliders,
however.[11]

6

Despite the increased attention to fire risks, the Insurance Company of North America regarded itself primarily as a marine organization. Marine underwriters remained the aristocrats of the insurance
world. Nor did the North America lose sight of the fact that of all
the marine underwriters in the United States it was the oldest. The
smell of tar had been all over that first little office in South Front
Street, with its view of Director John Ross' wharf. Sea captains,
straight from the decks of ships they had brought from every quarter
of the globe, dropped in and out, most of them with a worth-while
tale to tell. They were made to feel at home. More than one of the
company's leading men had, like Ebenezer Hazard, sailed before
the mast. And all earned their livelihoods from the sea as shippers
or shipowners. Looking back in 1842 over its first half century, the
North America was proud of the part it had borne in the do-or-die
fight to keep open the sea lanes during the desperate early years
when the true frontier of this republic was on the blue.

Consequently the sense of satisfaction flowed from the recent
encouraging revival of our merchant marine. Between 1840 and
1861 American tonnage in the foreign carrying trade rose from
762,838 to 2,496,894, a figure not exceeded until the first World War.
The remarkable performances of our clipper ships led the way to
this golden era. Long and slender and spreading a cloud of lofty
canvas, clippers set records which to this day are unsurpassed by
sailing craft. The *Lightning's* run of 436 miles in a day rivals that of
many modern steamers. Twice the *Flying Cloud* made the passage
from Boston to San Francisco in eighty-nine days. Some clippers
could make three round trips to Europe while broad-beamed Brit-
ishers were making two. Distances everywhere were shortened.
Clippers were more economical to operate than old-time sailers and
less likely to injury from stress of weather. The character and capacity of American captains, who often owned a share in the ships they
sailed, contributed to the preference of shippers the world over for
American vessels.

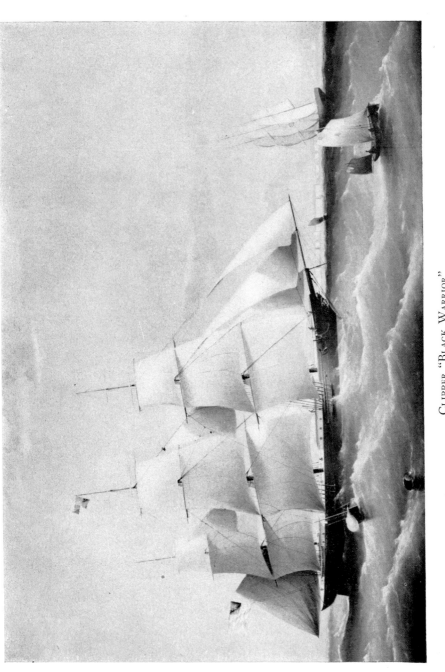

Clipper "Black Warrior"

No sailing vessels in history have equalled the records of American clippers, 1840-1870. Their performance created a boom in American shipping which helped establish Insurance Company of North America in front rank in marine field. The *Black Warrior*, built in Maine in 1853, was owned in Baltimore.

From a painting owned by the North America.

The Insurance Company of North America's marine business kept pace with this development. In 1843 its marine premium receipts were $94,191; in 1858, $306,572, roughly a three-fold increase. During the same interval fire insurance had increased about five-fold, though from smaller beginnings. In the decade ending in 1852 marine receipts were $2,885,189 and losses $2,153,679. Fire income for the same periods was $554,267, against $382,407 losses. Though gains from respondentia loans materially raised marine profits above the figures foregoing, fire insurance was the better payer of the two considered on a percentage basis. The narrow margin of profit in marine operations demonstrated the need for increasing the surplus which John Correy Smith had begun to build to respectable size ten years before.

Dividends were scaled accordingly. Twenty per cent was paid in 1844, 15 per cent in 1845 and 10 in 1846; and it should be borne in mind that these payments were based on shares which had been devalued from $10 to $5. There seems to have been some talk among the stockholders as to whether mutualization might not have been the better way out of the difficulties which had followed the 1837 panic. At any rate in their semiannual statement of January 1846 the directors discussed the mutual question. It was too early, they said, to decide whether the relief sought by the Philadelphia companies which had mutualized would be permanent. At present the directors were satisfied to "adhere to the old system. . . . Time only can determine whether at any subsequent period a necessity for a change may arise." The directors went on to add their word of excuse for continuing to enlarge the surplus at the expense of dividends. One of the reasons given was the "aspect of our foreign relations."[12]

The ensuing May the United States declared war against Mexico. Wartime rates went into effect immediately, except where insurers specifically relieved the company from responsibility in case of loss by hostile action. These precautions proved almost needless. Mexico's weak naval forces were securely bottled up, and no European powers which could have menaced us on the sea were drawn into the fray. It appears that the North America's only war loss was $7,500 on a vessel which ran aground off Tampico and was burned to keep the Mexicans from getting her. The war ended in February 1848 with the relinquishment by Mexico of vast western territories, including California.

7

A week before California became part of the United States gold was discovered near San Francisco. The news reached Washington the middle of September and by November the Gold Rush was on. On December 18 a newspaper reporter counted sixty vessels loading at New York for California. Between December 14 and January 18, 1849, sixty-one vessels cleared from New York, Philadelphia, Baltimore and Boston. In February the departures were 130. Nearly anything that could float was fitted with bunks and advertised as a crack sailer. From factory benches, countinghouse desks, farms and colleges men swarmed to fill these craft. "An oyster house will be sold low, proprietor is going to California." Advertisements like this could be found in almost any eastern paper. The melting of the winter snows found another army moving toward the jumping-off places on the Missouri River to attempt the overland journey to the promised land.

From the world over the gold-hungry headed for California. In Hong Kong, China, was a lad of twenty, named Charles Platt. He had sailed to the Orient in a ship owned by his father, a China trader of Philadelphia, to learn about the overseas end of the family enterprise. The California craze put young Platt in business for himself. Buying space in available vessels he began sending goods to sell to the fortune hunters in San Francisco.

"Here am I," he wrote a friend at home, "living on board the Heber in this beautiful harbor, attending to her being loaded for the 'Land of Gold.' Excitement continues and numbers are going. I myself would like to go for I think fortunes are to be made there. But as I can't leave very well now, I have contented myself with shipping to the extent of my ability, all sorts of things,—hats, chow chow ware, etc. Last night, a young fellow, by name Bruce, and myself chartered the between decks of a brig bound there and are filling them up with furniture of all sorts, chairs, tables, etc. It will pay I think...."[13]

It did pay. The fortune hunters were willing to pay fabulous prices for anything. And to pay in gold, of which $3,000,000 worth was taken from the earth in 1848, $25,000,000 in 1849, $40,000,000 in 1850 and $60,000,000 in 1851. These sums were greater than the revenues of the United States Government. Though young Platt did not get to San Francisco at this time, he will reappear in the course of this narrative.

For every clipper queen which could make the passage around the Horn in a hundred days, some dull sailer of questionable seaworthiness might take 150 or 200 days to reach the land of sudden riches. Yet on the whole it was easier to take a vessel through the Golden Gate than to bring one out again. Seamen deserted and took to the diggings the instant ships dropped anchor. By the end of 1849 five hundred crewless vessels rode helplessly in the Bay of San Francisco. Until the fever abated somewhat, hands to sail them home could not be hired for any wage. Some of the abandoned craft were destined never to get to sea again. A number became waterlogged and sank. Others were towed on the mud flats near the shore and converted into hotels, warehouses, stores and offices.

The problems the Gold Rush posed for underwriters were many. The North America met them with its customary policy of conservatism in the selection of risks and an extensive use of reinsurance. Much of the latter appears to have been made with the Atlantic Mutual of New York. Premium receipts rose from $355,000 in 1847 to $416,000 in 1848, $474,000 in 1849, and $494,000 in 1850. Losses rose in rather higher proportion though respondentia loans seem to have redressed the balance.

Company records afford fragmentary glimpses of the trials of the gold adventurers:

"The brig Encarnacion put into Rio in distress having lost every compass on the way."

"Ship Robert Fulton, Chase [Master], from New York, 5th May [1849] for San Francisco, was totally lost on the E. Falkland Islands. . . . The Captain, passengers and all hands were saved."

"Brig Saldana, formerly of Baltimore, totally lost Sept. 21 [1849], at Cerro Azul. She parted both chains and went ashore."

"On the 20th [January, 1850], the Hanoverian ship 'Kronprincessin' in going out of the Harbor [of San Francisco] ran upon the 'Blossom Rocks.' She will probably have to be abandoned."

"Ship Venice, of Philadelphia, Young, Master, put into Rio de Janeiro on the 16th of March [1850], having taken fire between her decks."

"Schr. Boreas, hence for Chagres [Panama], ran ashore on the reef at the entrance of the harbour and was a total loss."[14]

It was one thing to conduct a sane insurance business on the eastern seaboard, and another to obtain similar representation three thousand miles away where, in the early days of the Rush, even captains abandoned their ships. Repairs cost a fortune and loss-adjustment and salvage difficulties were innumerable. The North America, therefore, could thank its lucky star for Joshua P. Haven. This robust character, who had tried his hand at underwriting in Philadelphia, arrived in California ahead of the gold strike. When the strike came there was need for a man who could handle the rough-and-tumble underwriting situation that developed. Haven set out to be that man and succeeded brilliantly. As early as April 1849 he advertised in San Francisco's newspaper, *Alta California,* as "agent for the under-writers of Philadelphia and Baltimore,"[15] which meant principally the North America. The pioneer insurance agent became a figure in the life of San Francisco—city alderman and brigadier-general of militia. His remittances of premiums reached Walnut Street in the form of gold dust, which Secretary Sherrerd exchanged for currency at the United States mint.

8

Nothing more was heard from the stockholders about mutualiza-tion. The abundant prosperity of the company seems to have been accepted as confirmation of the wisdom of the directors in retaining the joint-stock system. Dividends in 1847 were 15 per cent and in 1848 they were 18. During the first six months of 1849 the North America's business exceeded that of all the other Philadelphia marine companies combined.

At four o'clock in the morning on July 9, 1850, a warehouse at 141 North Water Street, Philadelphia, on which the North America had a policy, was discovered on fire. Two explosions of stored salt-peter brought down walls killing several persons, blew others into the river where they drowned, and spread the fire. Firemen and apparatus were summoned by telegraph from New York, Newark and Baltimore. At three o'clock the following morning a shift in the wind assisted in getting the blaze under control. Thirty persons were dead or missing, one hundred injured; eighteen acres on which 367 houses had stood were in ruins representing a destruction of property worth more than a million dollars, less than half of which was covered by insurance.

The largest losses to insurance companies were: American Fire, $103,000; Franklin, $94,000; Fire Association of Philadelphia, $93,000; Hand-in-Hand (Philadephia Contributionship), $77,000; Green Tree (Mutual Assurance Company), $65,000; North America, $19,083. The Fire Association was a company formed by volunteer firemen. It escaped bankruptcy by action of the trustees who signed a joint note to secure payment of the losses.[16] Thanks to the no-concentration rule, the North America had survived another great fire with small loss.

Assets at the close of the year stood at $1,001,255 and in 1851 ten thousand shares of capital stock, owned by the company, were canceled. The other shares were restored to their former par of $10. Two hundred thousand dollars of the surplus was capitalized, raising the capital to a half-million dollars. With finances in such good shape the company in December moved into its seventh home, the first of its own building. The property at 60 (now 232) Walnut Street was bought for $16,000. It was 17 feet 3 inches wide and 138 feet deep, running through to Pear Street. Existing buildings were demolished and a three-story structure erected at a cost of $5,350. It had a depth of 85 feet, leaving a pleasant garden on the Pear Street rear.

Also lending a bright tinge to the company's financial outlook was the hope that eventually the French spoliation claims would be collected. Like the trail of a lost legacy, references to the expected payments continued to thread the records of the directors' meetings. Daniel Webster, Edward Everett, Edward Livingston, Caleb Cushing, Rufus Choate, John M. Clayton and John J. Crittenden were among the statesmen who had one time or another advocated reimbursement by the United States. In 1846 a bill appropriating $5,000,000 had been passed by both houses of Congress. Faced with the Mexican War expenses President Polk vetoed it on grounds of expediency. Counsel for the insurance companies and for private claimants immediately revived the issue. Congress passed a new bill which President Franklin Pierce vetoed in 1855. The claimants began their labors anew.

In the spring of 1852 the North America was tapped for its largest single loss sustained to that time—$65,000—when two neighboring Philadelphia warehouses were destroyed by a fire. This led to an immediate reconsideration of the concentration aspect of the company's fire risks. The finding was that, despite "this extraordinary occurrence," the risks were "generally well distributed." Yet, "in a few localities too large an amount was found to be concentrated, which had been reduced by re-insurance when practicable. The cases that remain will receive attention." Mindful that this policy would have a "tendency to abridge the amount of our fire risks in this City, the President suggested that it might be expedient" to look more briskly for business elsewhere. Accordingly the Cincinnati agency, abandoned in the face of local taxation, was reopened. The Pittsburgh agency which the Board had ordered closed was continued after Mr. Coffin made a trip to look over the ground.[17]

This renewed attention to the West came in good time for other strong eastern companies were doing the same thing. All over the country new companies were setting up at such a rate that presently they outnumbered the old. Our flourishing merchant marine and the free spending and speculation which accompanied the discovery of gold in California invited an expansion of the insurance business. Another spur was the national railroad boom. In 1852 the Pennsylvania Railroad was completed to Pittsburgh. Its success was more than its founder had prophesied. Within a generation the Pennsylvania was the richest and most powerful corporation in the United States. Two years after the first train ran into Pittsburgh Thomas P. Cope, at eighty-four, laid down his burdens. The country lost the first of a legendary line—the great railroad builders—and the North America one of the giants among its directors.

Some few of the new insurance companies that sprang up were properly financed and properly run. At the other end of the line some few were out-and-out frauds. The bulk came in between: typically hopeful and well-meaning products of flush times whose main dependence for success lay in a continuation of those times. Experience-tested organizations like the North America were obliged to contend against the vicious practices of the frauds and the rate-cutting of the optimistic amateurs.

And so, in 1852, when the best ideals of insurance stood in need of a fighting champion, American insurance journalism was born in Philadelphia with the appearance of *Tuckett's Monthly Insurance*

J Riegel, Jr.

EARLY FIRE ENGINE

Contemporary model of a hand pumper made in 1825 for the Fairmount Fire Company of Philadelphia. Original in the North America's collection.

Journal. The publication was the creation of Captain Harvey G. P. Tuckett, an English adventurer who had been obliged to flee British soil after a duel with a member of the House of Lords. A brilliant and imaginative mathematician, the refugee found employment with American life-insurance companies. By 1848 he had carried actuarial calculations into realms hitherto unknown. As a free-lance actuary and statistician, he saved enough from his earnings to launch the *Journal.* The early Philadelphia insurance historian, John A. Fowler, pays Tuckett this tribute:

"He could not become a mere gazetteer of unwarranted pretense, official audacity and ignorance, trade quackery and scheming knavery. He understood the underwriter to be an instrument for insurance—he did not understand insurance to be an instrument for the underwriter. He had no faith in insurance as a trade; he believed in it only as a systematic, scientific economy."[18]

The *Insurance Journal* immediately began a campaign against the irresponsible companies. The financial rewards were meager, but Harvey Tuckett was setting down a code of ethics for the insurance business. Tuckett died in 1854, mourned as "a knightly spirit," says Fowler, by those who appreciated his worth. His *Journal* courageously carried on in the path blazed by the founder. When the Philadephia companies writing marine and fire risks had increased to twenty-six, the periodical boldly grouped them into four categories. Nine of the twenty-six corporations were listed as "reliable"; ten as having "insufficient assets"; one as "unsafe for business"; and six as "fraudulent."[19]

The *Journal's* tabulation caused a stir in Philadelphia. Criticized companies were loud in their protests. The Philadelphia Board of Trade warned insurers to look to the soundness of the firms with which they placed their business. The Legislature, which had granted insurance charters with such airy freedom, began to ponder the situation. The panic of 1857, however, applied the immediate corrective.

A break in the riot of speculation caused by the railroad-construction and California gold booms was overdue. It came when the over-extended Ohio Life Insurance Company of Cincinnati failed. In the convulsion that followed fifteen of the twenty-six Philadelphia insurance companies went under.

Unlike the 1837 panic which inaugurated a depression lasting for years, reaction from that of 1857 was sharp. By the end of 1858 sound securities had recovered most of their values. The North America scarcely felt the storm. Its 1857 dividends were 11 per cent against 9 for 1856 which had been a disastrous year for marine risks. In 1858 dividends were 12 per cent and in 1859 they went to 18.

The company had prepared for the crisis. In 1856 when the country was flooded with inflated securities, stockholders were reminded "that there exists not One Dollar of Doubtful Assets in the list which we have the pleasure of presenting for your consideration." In January 1858 shareholders were assured that, despite "disasters happening to Companies pursuing business of like character," the North America had nothing to fear. Eighteen fifty-nine was begun with a net surplus of $212,599, and in January of 1860 the directors reported:

"At no previous period in the history of the Company has its affairs been in a more prosperous state."[20]

When these words were written no such happy conclusion could have been drawn from a truthful account of the state of affairs in the nation at large. Signs pointing to the "irrepressible conflict" between North and South had multiplied over the years. Noting the shrill crescendo of fighting talk that poured forth in the congressional debates over the Kansas-Nebraska Bill, as early as 1855 the North America had taken an ominous precaution. The Board had directed that the "clause in our Fire policies designed to protect the Company from loss in event of fire resulting from foreign invasion and civil commotion" be drafted in more explicit language.[21]

Threats of disunion and of civil war continued to drown out the voices of moderate men. There was no stemming the tide. On November 13, 1860, ten months after issuing its satisfying report to the stockholders, the Board of Directors sat down to a regular meeting. One week before, to the day, the country had cast its ballots in the most fateful national election in our history. It was known that a country lawyer from Illinois whose name, Abraham Lincoln, few Easterners had ever heard until lately, had carried all the free states and lost all the slave states. The free states were enough to elect him President. A large part of the South was in tumult. With steps toward secession under way, armed men were drilling in the streets of southern towns. But Walnut Street was calm; Philadelphia was calm; the North was calm. The North was even apathetic. It did not believe the southern extremists would execute their threats. And the hotheads of the South were sure the North would never fight to preserve the Union.

A consciousness of this state of affairs must have weighed on every man present at the Board meeting. For more than a year, while the signs of trouble grew more and more distinct, the company had been devoting close attention to westward expansion. The principal item of business at the November 13 meeting was a report by President Coffin on a trip he had made "to the interior of Pennsylvania." After a short debate authorization was voted to establish as many more western agencies as Mr. Coffin "may deem advisable."[22] Thus the North America made preparation to compensate for a possible loss of southern business.

CHAPTER IX

The Civil War

I

THE North got ready for war very slowly, and for a long time refused to believe there was really going to be any war. In the South the same belief was widespread, for different reasons. Popular conviction had the Yankees too interested in money-making to take time off to fight. Yet the South made ready—enlisting volunteers, assembling military stores. The Federal Government did nothing. In the White House old Mr. Buchanan seemed thankful only that each winter sunset brought his administration that much nearer its inglorious end. Out in Illinois President-elect Lincoln had made no pronouncement of policy, no reply to the South's bellicose preparations. The Yankees were, indeed, making money and liking it. The last thing they wished was a war to interrupt that pleasant occupation. Most Northerners seemed to think that the crisis would peter out somehow.

On January 2, 1861, the day after Alabama, the fourth state, had seceded, the governing body of the Board of Philadephia Marine Underwriters held a meeting. Henry D. Sherrerd, who had left the secretaryship of the Insurance Company of North America to accept the presidency of the Insurance Company of the State of Pennsylvania, offered a resolution "that the following clause be introduced into all Policies of Insurance to any U. S. Port or Ports South of the Chesapeake: 'Warranted free from claim for loss or damage arising from riot or civil commotion or from seizure, Capture or detention, or the consequences of any other hostile act of the Government or people of any State of this Union.'"[1]

Two days later the directors of the North America held their January dividend meeting. The minutes make no allusion to the national situation unless something can be read into the remark that no alteration had been made "in the value of the investments as they stand on the books of the Company" though "they are worth at the Market price Fifteen thousand Dollars more than represented."

Attention was drawn to "the exhibit which . . . shows that the business of the Company has been well sustained, and its results cannot but prove satisfactory to all concerned." Assets stood at $1,254,720. Profits from marine insurance in 1860 had been $30,755, from fire insurance $60,768. Capital was formidably protected, the reserve fund standing at $355,921, the surplus at $321,758. "Resolved that a dividend of Six per cent be declared . . . and also an extra dividend of Six percent." The 12-per-cent distribution amounted to $60,000.[2]

On January 18 the Board of Underwriters took more particular notice of the gathering clouds. Channel buoys had been removed from the harbor at Charleston, South Carolina, "increasing thereby the risk of navigation." It was decided "that the Question of rate of premiums to & from Ports in States that have or shall secede be referred to the Committee of Risks & Premiums who are requested to correspond with the New York Board of underwriters upon the subject."[3]

The New York Board replied that it had done nothing, though some of the individual companies had increased their premiums.

On April 12 Fort Sumter was fired on. President Lincoln called for 75,000 ninety-day volunteers. On April 17 Virginia seceded, bringing the scene of impending conflict to Pennsylvania's border. On April 19 a regiment of Massachusetts militia, marching through Baltimore to the defense of Washington, was fired on by a mob and several soldiers killed. The secession of Maryland seemed imminent. This would isolate the national capital and lay Philadelphia open to invasion.

2

The North began to wake up. A blockade of Confederate ports was proclaimed and in retaliation lighthouses were extinguished on southern coasts. The day of the Baltimore "massacre," the North America put a war clause in all its new marine policies (the action of January 12 had applied only to southern United States ports), holding the company harmless from losses caused by the civil conflict unless an additional premium were paid. The additional premium amounted to about 1 per cent, doubling the prevailing rate. At the same time the Board resolved to take no new fire risks in

Washington nor to renew risks in the New Orleans office. Moreover, the attention of policyholders was directed to the civil-commotion clause which the company had put in its fire policies in 1855. One of the company's employees, J. Chester White, had responded to Lincoln's call for troops. The Board voted to continue his salary "during his absence and that he should have the privilege of resuming his place in the Office on his return." The company as well as Mr. Lincoln, who had asked for three-month men, seems to have expected Chester White to be back shortly.[4]

By the end of May, however, things had taken a turn for the worse. Confederate privateers were loose in the Atlantic and in the Gulf. The *Jeff Davis* captured the bark *Rowena,* on which the North America had a share of the insurance.[5] New York boosted its war rate to 5 per cent, Philadelphia following suit. The presidents of the six companies comprising the Board of Philadelphia Underwriters petitioned the Secretary of the Navy for a cutter and a gunboat to protect the entrance to Delaware Bay. The Navy had other uses for its vessels, however. The blockade began to assume an aspect of reality, and it was the turn of southern shipping to suffer. The first in many prizes was brought into Philadelphia in September. The summer scare died down and in response to a hearty protest from shippers the war rate dropped to 2½ per cent, only to go to 5 again when the Confederate steam privateer *Nashville* was reported at Southampton, England, ready to ambush the transatlantic trade routes.[6]

By now a firmer purpose had taken hold of the North. With the debacle of Bull Run behind him, Lincoln set out to build an army of three-year men, and, on land and on sea, to fight the war to a finish. The Board of the North America appointed a committee to pass on applications for contributions toward the equipment of volunteers and the relief of soldiers' families. This body would have a long work to do.

As has been seen, in the late fifties forehanded steps had been taken to extend the company's fire business in the rich western territory north of the Ohio River. Before it could be foretold to what extent the conflict might develop into a naval war—with the possibility of England, destitute of cotton, intervening on the side of the South—this was pushed with determination. In May policies in Washington (threatened with capture), Baltimore and St. Louis

were canceled. Elsewhere in the South they might run to expiration—bearing in mind the civil-war clause. No southern agency
except the one in Lexington, Kentucky, (established in 1808) might
accept new business or renewals. In October "the extension of the
Fire business being the special order of the day," William Buehler,
of Harrisburg, was appointed "general superintendent" of agents
in central Pennsylvania. He left immediately on a trip to "nominate
agents in the various [new] localities which he shall consider desirable." The company granted $300 a year to its Cincinnati agent to
enable him to move his office to "a more prominent position in that
city." An agency was opened in Boston.[7]

The expansion was undertaken too late in the year to have any
effect on the figures for 1861. The loss of southern business reduced
the fire profits to $32,206. Marine business had shrunk also and losses
had been heavy, though it does not appear that the war had contributed particularly in this regard. The marine department finished the year in red figures to the amount of $7,269. Nevertheless,
after charging $25,000 to depreciation on investments, reserving
$282,120 for unadjusted losses and increasing the surplus to $333,928,
the company was able to begin 1862 with another 12-per-cent
dividend.

3

On October 10, 1862, J. R. Wucherer, president of the Phoenix
Mutual Insurance Company and president also of the Board of
Philadelphia Marine Underwriters, wrote a letter in great haste to
Secretary of Navy Gideon Welles:

"By the arrival of the Steamer Persia, intelligence has been rec[d].
from Flores [Azores] that the rebel Steame[r] Alabama has been com-
mitting great depredations on our whalers and other Shipping near
the Western Islands.

"On behalf of this Board I beg leave respectfully to enquire if we
have any naval force at present in that quarter to check these out-
rages; or if not to solicit that immediate Steps may be taken to send
a sufficient armament for that purpose."

The following day Mr. Wucherer wrote again:

"I now beg leave to give you an extract from a letter just received from an intelligent Master & owner of a Vessel at Glasgow—

" 'The Rebels are having some fine plated War Vessels built over here. . . . I am afraid that our Commerce will suffer before long.' "[8]

Such was the manner in which Insurance Row received the news that the Confederate cruiser *Alabama* had begun its career with British connivance. Secretary Welles did what could be done without weakening the blockade as the Confederate authorities had hoped. After destroying the whaling fleet off the Azores, the *Alabama* headed across the Atlantic and took nine prizes on the way. At a point two hundred miles off New York the raider swung southward, and, burning two vessels as she went, appeared at Martinique for coal which had been sent from England. Next she was reported across the track of the California and China traders.

The flurry of these events sent war rates to 5 and 6 per cent and kept underwriters tied to their desks night and day lest they miss first word of the *Alabama's* latest reported whereabouts. Charts were scanned and naval strategists consulted in an effort to divine the future intentions of the cruiser's bold and resourceful commander, Raphael Semmes. In the North America office the ticklish task of matching wits with Semmes fell upon an attractive young man by the name of Charles Platt. As a strapping, good-looking boy fresh from the University of Pennsylvania Charles Platt had already demonstrated a capacity for thinking and acting on his own when the Gold Rush caught him serving an apprenticeship in the China office of an American trading firm at Hong Kong. Engaging on his personal account space in San Francisco-bound vessels he shipped across the Pacific supplies which the forty-niners were glad to buy at handsome profits. In the midst of this success he wrote a boyhood friend in Philadelphia:

"If you want to know what my ideas of life are I'll tell you, premising that they are not the romantic castles which 'boys' are apt to build, but good, solid, sober structures which will stand for time to come. What are they? An income of about $3000 per year *clear,* a nice little place with a few acres around it, near a city but not so near as to be in its way for 'improvements'; pleasant society in the neighbourhood, not too much, but *enough!* A house, tasty and neat, with arrangements of its 'internals' to suit *my* taste, and now to come to the all important part, a good library of books, not bought in a heap but chosen by myself. Chairs fit to sit in, to read the said books. A billiard table for recreation; with one or two horses, and finally, last of all, but far from least, a wife to my taste and of my own choice to grace the whole."[9]

Home from China young Platt endeavored to realize his goal in the shipping firm founded by his father. He did not succeed and after liquidating the firm became secretary of the Insurance Company of North America in 1860. He was thirty-one years of age, married and drawing a salary of $2,000. Long hours waiting for news of the Confederate raider did not trouble Charles Platt, a giant in size and in mental and physical vigor. He thrived on work which would have worn out many another. A magnetic personality and an easy camaraderie had quickly established him as a figure on the Row where his friends ranged from bootblacks to bankers.

The transatlantic cable which in 1858 promised to revolutionize the transmission of marine intelligence had ceased to work after a month. Consequently tidings of the *Alabama* were anywhere from a week to two months old when received. Inasmuch as Federal men-of-war were scouring the seas for the raider, Semmes could not stay long in one place no matter how good the pickings. Platt counted on this. When Semmes was reported in the North Atlantic Platt did not hesitate to insure vessels for that crossing, in the belief that Semmes would be elsewhere when the insured vessels appeared. When Semmes was reported on the California track Platt confidently accepted insurance for San Francisco. Simple as the device was, it worked. By the end of 1863 Semmes, on the loose for sixteen months, had sailed and steamed the *Alabama* around the world. Of the forty vessels which had fallen prey to him not one was insured by the North America.[10]

Platt's stratagem was helpful only to outward-bound vessels. That no incoming ships came within reach of the *Alabama* could be attributed only to luck. When the second British-built Confederate cruiser appeared early in 1863 Platt's luck did not hold so well. After taking fourteen prizes in the North Atlantic and spreading consternation along the New England coast the *Florida* headed toward Brazil. On May 28, 1863, Captain Jesse F. Potter, late of the ship *Oneida,* Shanghai to New York with tea, arrived in New York

as a passenger on another ship from Pernambuco, Brazil. Potter
reported that the *Oneida* had been overhauled on April 24 and
burned by the *Florida*. The North America held $7,500 in insurance
on the *Oneida*. It was the company's first loss to one of the British-
built Confederate commerce destroyers. A month later the second
loss of $3,069 was chalked up on an outward-bound vessel when it
was learned that the *Florida* had caught, off Brazil, the San Francisco-
bound *Crown Point*.

By comparison with other companies these losses were astonishing-
ly small. The Atlantic Mutual of New York, with which the North
America did much reinsuring, lost $818,296 to the Confederate raid-
ers in 1863. The North America's losses from all causes for the year
were only $205,687. Premium receipts were $364,117, leaving a
profit, after deducting expenses, of $154,101. Fire profits were
$72,401. The company distributed $90,000 in dividends, which was
at the rate of 18 per cent. Its stock sold for $29 a share.

4

The year was also eventful on land. In Virginia the Confederates
had been able to sustain the precedent of Bull Run, repeatedly beating Union armies superior in numbers and equipment. Crowning
these feats of arms, in June 1863 General Lee crossed the Pennsylvania line and invaded the North. The mayor of Philadelphia called
upon business houses to close so that employees might enlist for the
defense of the city. At a meeting which filled Independence Square
the enrollment of "minute men" began. The North America limited
office hours from 10 A.M. to noon and contributed $2,000 to the war
chest. Thousands fled northward. The Pennsylvania Railroad rushed
rolling stock in from the West as Lee's cavalry threatened the line
at Harrisburg. Spades in unaccustomed hands made dirt fly in the
improvisation of breastworks.

On July 1 Lee found the Union army under Meade athwart his
path at the village of Gettysburg and attacked. Two agonizing days
for Philadelphia followed. On July 4 a rumor that Lee was in retreat
found mainly disbelievers. But on the fifth confirmation came—
along with the first of many trainloads of wounded. On the Fourth
of July Vicksburg had fallen in the West and the military fortunes of
the Union were in the ascendancy.

No less cheering were the prospects which confronted the Insurance Company of North America. Its decisive stroke for fire business had been eminently successful. Receipts rose from $116,000 in 1862 to $207,000 in 1864, when the net profits reached $104,503. This was largely due to the conquest of the West.

The first steps toward administrative decentralization of this widely spread business were taken. In 1861 William Buehler of Harrisburg had been given the title of "general superintendent" over local agents in middle Pennsylvania. This led to the creation of the Pennsylvania State Central Agency under Buehler with headquarters at Harrisburg. In October 1864 the Western Department, with headquarters at Erie, Pennsylvania, was organized under Jerome F. Downing. Downing was a lawyer, thirty-six years old, who had been writing insurance as a sideline. Having been elected district attorney of Erie County in 1863, he hesitated to devote any more time to insurance. But the offer of the Department, embracing an empire of thirteen states bounded on the west by Kansas, Nebraska, Iowa and Minnesota, was too much to resist.

Within this broad jurisdiction Downing exercised important powers hitherto reserved to the home office. He could accept risks on the surveys of local agents and adjust losses. This authority was not misplaced. J. F. Downing was to become one of the great agency men of his time. Looking over his vast territory, he went immediately to Cleveland, Ohio, to set up his first agency in the office of Runnells & Manchester which carries on today under the name of the James-Manchester Company. Agencies two, three and four were established in the Ohio towns of Newark, Mansfield and Akron. Shortly Downing journeyed into Michigan, reporting the opening of an agency at Paw Paw, for which he received his first adverse criticism from Philadelphia. The home office thought no office could hope for success in a town with such a name. Downing reassured Philadelphia and thereafter referred to his critics in the home office as the "old folks." "What do the old folks think?" he would write after proposing a new agency. Downing traveled into Colorado and located an office of the North America in the little town of Denver. The "old folks" cautioned the head of the Western Department against getting too far from civilization.[11]

With his domain stretching to the Rockies, it was natural that Downing shortly would have to devise a scheme for keeping track of the work of his agencies. To meet the situation in 1864 he inaugurated the daily report, presently to become a standard practice of the insurance world, the means by which the companies keep in continuous touch with the state of business in every quarter they serve.[12]

Eighteen sixty-four saw the end of the *Alabama* and of the *Florida.* The former was sunk off Cherbourg, France, by the U. S. S. *Kearsarge,* and the latter captured in a Brazilian harbor. This left only one Confederate raider at sea, the British-built *Shenandoah,* which remained in the Pacific until after the surrender of Lee in 1865. After all, it had not been a naval war with destruction of shipping on a scale such as the country had suffered in the Napoleonic struggles. Losses inflicted by the British-built Confederate cruisers were later found by an international tribunal sitting at Geneva, Switzerland, to total $15,500,000. Damage by home-built vessels in the service of the South was much less than that.[13]

Losses of the North America were a pittance of the $15,500,000 total for which the British Government eventually reimbursed the United States. All the North America claimed of that sum was $11,169 on two victims of the *Florida* and one of the *Alabama.* By contrast the Insurance Company of the State of Pennsylvania, doing a much smaller business, lost $36,971, the Union Mutual, $16,397 and the Delaware Mutual, $48,934. The Atlantic Mutual of New York lost $1,653,889.[14] The directors thought enough of Charles Platt's work to raise his salary to $5,000 and give him a bonus of $1,600 for "services in the year 1864."

The return of peace found the North America in a much stronger position than at the start of the war. Assets were $1,669,245, with its capital safeguarded by a reserve of $600,831 and a surplus of $456,567. Marine business had increased by about 25 per cent. Fire business had more than trebled. After a backward glance at the war years the Board of Directors addressed the stockholders in a tone of solid self-assurance:

"The future of the Company as far as can be foreseen promises well.

"The large business now transacted is well distributed, and the management under the executive officers, in competent hands.

"The age and standing of the Company, give great advantages in the present competition for business, and it is not unreasonable to look for a still further healthy growth."[15]

5

Considering the uniform modesty of the Board's utterances over a period of nearly three-quarters of a century the prophecy foregoing was noteworthy. On the fire side, however, there seemed nothing to prevent its realization. A company that could make such remarkable strides in the face of the preoccupations, the economic dislocations and drains and the high taxes of wartime should do even better with a million men home from the armies to turn their hands to productive employments.

But on the marine side the picture was confused and cloudy. The war had taken hundreds of our ships and thousands of our seamen from the trade lanes to serve in the Navy. The needs of naval construction pre-empted our shipyards so that few merchantmen were turned out. The tax on hulls and on marine engines, the duties on cordage, copper and iron increased the operating cost of those in the merchant service. An even greater handicap to merchantmen flying the American flag were the war-insurance rates. Foreign ships, in no danger from Confederate cruisers, obtained insurance on hull and cargo for 1 or 2 per cent. On top of this England began building steamers which could compete with the American clippers.

To escape the disadvantages of American registry one-third of our merchant ships was sold to foreigners, mostly English. Our tonnage dropped from 2,496,000 in 1861 to 1,387,000 in 1866. Foreign commerce in 1866 surpassed that of the prosperous year of 1860, but only 25.1 per cent of it was carried in American ships against 63 per cent in 1860. After the war Congress refused to readmit to American registry vessels which had been sold abroad.

These were the factors, rather than losses from hostile action at sea, which had caused the Civil War to bear heavily upon the marine-insurance companies. Weaklings having been shaken out by the panic of 1857, all the Philadelphia companies came through the war in a way that contributed to the prestige of Insurance Row. On the other hand four companies failed in New York, including the Columbian which left unpaid losses of $3,470,000. In 1865 only one of the eleven companies doing business in New York State made money.

Yet in the face of all this the North America looked to the future with mettlesome confidence.

CHAPTER X

Growing in Good Times and Bad

I

"They talk of millions as confidently as formerly of thousands," Senator John Sherman of Ohio wrote his brother, the general, a few months after Appomattox.[1]

It was as if a dam had been thrown across a mighty river in 1861— the river of American enterprise. For four years a large part of the energies of the nation had gone into the wasteful business of war. But not all. John D. Rockefeller was creating the foundations for Standard Oil. The Pennsylvania Railroad was laying the first steel rails in the United States. In New York Cornelius Vanderbilt, turning from water to land transportation, began to piece together the line that was to become the Pennsylvania's classic rival. Gold strikes in Nevada and in Colorado preserved something of the illusion of easy wealth.

In 1865 the dam was cut. Prosperity burst upon the country in a torrent. The postwar boom which had begun in 1815 was re-enacted on a vastly magnified scale, and with an important change in fundamentals: the industrialization of the United States and the beginning of monopolies were at hand. With all the essentials so readily accessible, this time it seemed as if prosperity should last forever. We had the resources: gold, silver, coal, iron, copper, lead, petroleum, grains, cotton, tobacco. We had the labor to take them from the ground. We had the capital and the inventive skill to transform the raw material. We had the population lustily growing by natural increase and by immigration to provide a home market. And there were, of course, the markets beyond the seas.

In ten years the number of manufacturing plants increased from 123,000 to 252,000. The Bessemer steel process, imported from England, revolutionized that industry. An Armour and a Morris were packing meat in Chicago. The invention of the refrigerator car enabled them to send it fresh to Boston. Nearly half of the country still public domain, boundless ranges were open to the budding cattle barons. A Pillsbury and a Washburn were milling flour by water power in the frontier town of Minneapolis. Homesteaders flowed upon the plains, built sod houses and planted wheat. McCormick was making reapers. The Pennsylvania Railroad pushed through to Chicago, tapping the Mississippi Valley granary for Philadelphia. Vanderbilt's New York Central followed and a rate war began.

In this hurly-burly it was railroads that really captivated popular imagination. The Baltimore & Ohio and the Erie were building to Chicago. The junction of the Union Pacific and the Central Pacific in Utah completed the first transcontinental track. Three others were building or projected. Lesser lines were going down everywhere.

An impetus to these promotions was cheap money. To help finance the war currency had been inflated: greenbacks with no metal back of them. There were also the issues of some 1,500 national banks. With the restoration of peace the Government began to retire the greenbacks, but the promoters raised such a howl that this was stopped. With easy money went easy morals. Carpetbaggers frankly looted what of value they found in the South. Elsewhere railroad (and other) promoters bought up state legislators at so much a head. They also bought a good many congressmen, and others even more highly placed. In return they received a variety of official favors, including land grants of astronomical dimensions.

Double the size of any other railroad grant—44,000,000 acres—was that obtained by the Northern Pacific, financed by Jay Cooke & Company of Philadelphia. This banking house was a product of the war. Founded in 1861, it first attracted attention as a handler of Government bonds. By 1865 Jay Cooke & Company, as fiscal agent of the United States Treasury, was regarded as the leading American banking firm. Cooke had expected to keep his large organization employed after the war in the work of refunding the greenbacks. When speculators blocked the refunding Cooke, too, turned to railroad speculation.

2

With business marching forward in every other line it seemed not unreasonable to suppose that our merchant marine should regain the ground lost during the war. The year 1867 gave promise of this when the tonnage rose from 1,300,000 to 1,500,000. In its annual report to the stockholders the Insurance Company of North America predicted a good year. This expectation was not realized. Though a little more marine insurance was written than in 1866, losses were proportionately greater and the company finished with a marine profit of only $51,978, or $2,100 less than the year preceding.[2] In 1868 American tonnage declined again and there was less insurance to write. Year by year this slump continued, shrinking the volume of business available. All the while our foreign commerce was growing. In 1872 it was more than double that of 1865. But 70 per cent of the whole crossed the oceans in foreign ships, mostly British.

The prospering British marine underwriters were in considerable part the authors of their prosperity. By a series of distinctions in classification they favored vessels of their own flag with lower rates which made British bottoms more attractive to shippers. Iron steamships, in the construction of which the British led the world, received preference over wooden sailing vessels. And British sail were invariably rated above our sail, regardless of seaworthiness or of performance. Lloyd's scale gave the best white oak we could put into a ship two-thirds the years of usefulness that it gave British oak.[3] These measures were effective. By 1872 American tonnage was less than it had been in 1850.

Several of our marine companies closed their doors. Others barely held on. Not so the North America, which in 1850 had collected $84,633 in marine premiums and rated it a good year. With less business to be had, in 1872 the company's marine premiums aggregated $1,232,437, of which $231,609 was net profit. This remarkable growth placed the North America in a position where the most powerful London companies could no longer omit it from their calculations. It was a growth that bore no relation to the haphazard boom which had passed the safety point—a growth achieved against international competition in the one major field where American enterprise was steadily losing.

For his share in this accomplishment Charles Platt was advanced to the office of vice-president, created for him in January 1869. A little later when President Coffin went abroad for six months for his health, Mr. Platt assumed temporary direction of the company's affairs.

PACKET SHIP "WILLIAM PENN"

Full-rigged ship built in Philadelphia, 1791, for Waln & Company. Three members of the Waln family were early directors of the North America.

From a painting owned by the North America.

3

In the meantime fire business moved apace though without increasing its contribution to the company's net gain in revenue:

Year	Premiums, less return premiums & reinsurance	Losses, less reinsurance recovered & salvage	Expenses	Gain
1865 ......$	385,813.73	$160,245.51	$ 71,720.93	$153,847.29
1866	644,692.98	506,751.39	164,564.15	26,622.56*
1867	849,417.77	438,308.17	138,428.88	272,680.72
1868	938,004.68	525,642.95	301,841.14	110,520.59
1869	1,038,413.64	616,968.79	282,623.09	138,821.76
1870	956,024.48	616,531.29	304,814.22	34,678.97

*Loss

Thus volume grew two and one-half times, profits not at all. The situation was a repetition of the spurt in the thirties. Causes were numerous. Business was more expensive to get because of the increase in local companies and consequent rate-cutting. In 1866 the North America raised the commissions of agents from 10 to 15 per cent. In 1868 it organized the Eastern Department, with headquarters in the insurance center of Hartford, under C. C. Kimball. His jurisdiction included all New England except Boston, whose agent reported directly to the home office. The New York State Department was erected under Charles R. Knowles of Albany, of which the metropolitan New York City area was independent.

The increase in losses was not peculiar to the North America's clientele. It was general. "The past year," stated the directors in their annual review of 1866, "will long be remembered among Insurance Companies as a year of disaster. The losses by fire alone in the United States having been one hundred millions of Dollars against Sixty millions in 1865 and Forty millions in 1864. . . . Many companies have wound up their affairs and retired from business. Many more will follow. Competition is diminished, premiums are materially enhanced and will be raised still more."[4] This prophecy was not borne out by events. For every company that failed two new ones seemed to spring up, and rate rivalry went on.

The year 1866 had seen only one big fire—in Portland, Maine. This cost the North America $65,000. The real drain was from thousands of small fires. New methods of heating and lighting and the neglect of elementary fire precautions in the hasty construction of boom times contributed to this. The *North America Almanac* which the company put out to bring its name and qualifications before the public, had a good deal to say on the subject:

"CHIMNEYS—See to it that they are well constructed, plastered inside and out, and built on a firm foundation to prevent settling. A large portion of the chimneys built these days are first class incendiaries.

"STOVEPIPES—Allow no stovepipes to pass through floors or partitions not properly protected by tin thimbles or by earthen crocks. No wood should come nearer to the pipe than six inches. . . .

"HOT AIR FURNACES . . . [are] seldom altogether safe even when the most scientific care and mechanical skill are bestowed on their construction. . . .

"LAMPS—Use only those protected by a glass chimney and have them trimmed and filled by daylight only. . . . Never take an open light into a Barn. . . .

"COAL OIL—*Sell by Daylight* only Kerosine, or Coal Oil, Alcohol, etc., never go near them with a light for you may do so at your cost both in life and property."[5]

Fire-fighting equipment had improved, but in the hands of volunteers it was inadequate to the new hazards. Yet the volunteer companies were socially and politically so strong that their displacement could not be achieved overnight. Cincinnati, without the traditions of older places, led the way in 1853 with the first paid professional fire department. New York followed in 1865. In 1868 the North America espoused the unpopular cause of superseding Philadelphia's volunteers, and this was accomplished in 1871.

The record showed that the company was writing poor fire risks. It maintained its preparation to meet losses by keeping investments sound and liquid—the former a more difficult feat than the latter during flush times. At the end of 1870 the fire reserve alone was $325,000; the surplus, $619,000. Steps were taken to check losses at their source. Early in 1868 President Coffin announced to the Board that the agency in Chicago had been discontinued.[6]

4

The boisterous, money-mad municipality on Lake Michigan was little more than an overgrown frontier camp. Shooting up in ten years from 136,000 people to 308,000, Chicago had taken little time to construct anything to last. Gaudy marble fronts on State Street, where ground sold for $1,000 a foot, were façades for jerry-built wooden barns: "miles of fire-traps, pleasing to the eye, looking substantial, but all sham and shingles," acknowledged the Chicago *Tribune.* Forty thousand of the city's 60,000 edifices were frame. No fire law was observed. A few banknotes in the palm of an alderman took care of anything. For quick business regardless of risk this was an insurance man's paradise, as Chicago's money kings were punctual to perceive. A dozen home companies, backed by locally impressive names, paid big dividends. Reserve? Surplus? Chicago economists brushed such inconsequentialities aside and went on to launch more insurance companies, as flimsy as the false fronts on State Street.[7]

In this dispensation of affairs Mr. Coffin decided his company was carrying enough Chicago insurance. A prompt remonstrance came from J. F. Downing, manager of the Western Department. In March 1868 the Board modified the president's order, given in February, and permitted the writing of additional risks on dwelling houses. In May, the restriction was further relaxed to include "risks of the first class," apparently in any category.[8]

On Sunday evening, October 8, 1871, someone neglected the admonition of the *North America Almanac* and carried a lamp into the little cow stable of Jeremiah O'Leary who lived in a frame house on the West Side of town. Mrs. O'Leary, who had done the milking, later said she had not used a lamp though the remains of one was found in the ashes of the stable. Lamp or no, whatever happened in the O'Leary stable that evening cost the Insurance Company of North America $650,056.33.[9]

At 9:25 P.M. a drayman saw the stable on fire and gave the alarm. It was too late. A strong southwest wind whipped the flames among the pine shanties of the West Side. They blazed like grass on a prairie. In an hour the conflagration was its own master. At midnight it leaped the Chicago River and attacked the business district. Monday night the fire burned itself out on the North Side. Two hundred and fifty persons were dead, 2,124 acres in ruin entailing a loss of

$190,526,500. This was insured for $100,225,780 by 202 companies.

Four days later, on Friday, October 13, a little group of eastern insurance men stood amid the scene of desolation on the bank of the Chicago River. A haggard crowd pressed about them. The dominant question among Chicago's 100,000 homeless was "What will the insurance companies do?" Already it was apparent that many of them could do nothing. General Agent E. J. Bassett of the Aetna mounted a barrel. As nearly as he could tell at the time his company's obligations would run about $3,500,000. No American company had ever met such a liability. Mr. Bassett had a message from Hartford for the people of Chicago and he delivered it.

"The Aetna will pay every dollar of loss," he said, "and I will pay now the first claim to be presented."

A policy for $7,350 was thrust in his hands. Using the barrel head as a desk Mr. Bassett wrote a check for the amount.

Former Governor Marshall Jewell of Connecticut, a large stockholder in the Phoenix of Hartford, spoke next, and on the spot paid a claim for $10,000.[10]

Whether representatives of the North America participated in a scene of comparable dramatic value is not known, though they were on the job settling claims as fast as they could be verified. More fortunate than some of his insurance colleagues, North America's Chicago agent, C. H. Case, had saved his papers when his office, at 170 Washington Street, fell to the flames. Having reestablished himself at 65 South Canal Street, Case was joined by Charles H. Reeves from the home office. In Philadelphia Vice-President Platt seemed to think his emissaries on the scene of destruction needed cheering. He wrote them nearly every day, stressing the financial solidarity of the company and the influx of new business the fire had brought. Daily Case or Reeves scratched hurried reports to Downing at Erie. A few excerpts:

From Case, October 23, 1871: "Mr. Platt writes me that we are doing a rushing business as you have doubtless heard. Let the 'good work go on.'"

From Case, October 24: "We are nearly out of drafts—having but six left and have just wired you to send supply at once."

THE CHICAGO FIRE, 1871

Largest fire-insurance loss in history to that time, $100,225,780, underwritten by 202 companies. Sixty-eight went bankrupt, eighty-three settled in part, fifty-one in full. The North America's loss, $650,056, was paid on the spot and in full.

Illustration from Frank Leslie's Illustrated Weekly.

From Reeves, October 25: "Reports from all parts of this State are very encouraging—increase in business at advanced rates. Popularity of the old North America unbounded!"

From Reeves, October 30: "Mr. Platt writes me that our business is tremendous!"

From Reeves, November 1: "We are entirely out of receipts (total loss) and wired you yesterday for supply. Proofs [of loss—an insurance form] received today—also your telegram that more will be sent. We shall not have too many."

From Reeves, November 3: "Mr. Platt writes me the Enterprise have closed their doors. So we go!!"[11]

The Enterprise, of Philadelphia, was one of sixty-eight companies bankrupt by the fire. Eighty-three others settled in part. Fifty-one of the 202 involved paid in full. Chicagoans received about 40 per cent of what they had coming. Among the bankrupts were seventeen home concerns.

"The feeling is very strong here that the local insurance companies have outrageously swindled their policyholders," telegraphed a correspondent of the New York *Tribune* on October 22. "The names of old and wealthy citizens are mentioned for their prominent connection with the stupendous frauds. Under cover of these names an enormous business has been done, and very large profits divided on a very small paid-in capital, with a result now of losses exceeding tenfold their entire assets."[12]

5

The Insurance Company of North America was able to pay its losses of $650,000, representing 180 claims, without resorting to the heroic measures adopted by some of the companies which settled in full. There were no assessments, no encroachments on capital, no borrowing. The surplus more than covered everything. The regular semiannual dividend of 10 per cent was distributed in January 1872. This left assets totaling $3,212,000, including a surplus conservatively stated at $182,985.

"To this [surplus]," noted the Annual Report, "must be added the difference [in our favor] between market value of the securities and book value which is $103,107.50/100. . . . [Moreover], it should be stated that the surplus of the Company is ascertained by deducting from Gross Assets all unpaid losses and all premiums not terminated. The rule adopted by all American and English Companies, tested by experience and sanctioned by law, only requires that 50% of Fire Premiums not terminated should be deducted as a liability. If this rule were applied to your Company there would be added to the above surplus the large sum of $708,000.00.

"Your directors while fully aware that the 50% basis could be used with entire propriety prefer to continue the plan heretofore used by the Company, conscious that the large reserve which could be availed of, should necessity require, renders the Company amply able to meet any probable disaster."

There is nothing like catastrophe to recommend insurance to the average property owner, and no advertisement like settling in full at such time. The flood of applications which Charles Platt had mentioned continued to pour in. "We have obtained [in ninety days] a business which under ordinary circumstances would have required ten years to secure."[13] Take the case of L. J. Bonar, local agent at Mansfield, Ohio, for five companies, all wiped out by the Chicago fire. "The day was among the darkest of my life," Mr. Bonar later said. Submitting a list of his policyholders to the agent of the North America he requested that they be protected. This stroke of initiative led to Mr. Bonar's employment as a field agent by the North America in whose service he continued for more than fifty years.[14]

In several states the disaster furthered legislation looking toward the enforced solvency of insurance companies and the public supervision of their finances. Cities tightened fire-prevention ordinances and bettered their fire departments. The arm of the National Board of Fire Underwriters was strengthened. This body, formed in 1866 by the leading companies to deal with such questions as rates, compensation for agents, arson and incendiarism, introduced a national program of increased rates. Though the sounder companies adhered to it, the increased demand for insurance was too much of a temptation for some of the others.

English companies, which had paid $6,000,000 or 93 per cent of their total obligations in Chicago, began weeding out American risks. A large amount of insurance was canceled in Chicago and in San Francisco. The New York and Boston situations were under review when, a year after the Chicago fire, Julius L. Clarke, Insurance Commissioner of the State of Massachusetts, made a trip to England. A London underwriter remarked that the report on Boston, just received, would result in heavy cancellations there.

"Mr. Clarke, we look upon your Boston as the next most likely place for a Chicago fire."

The astonished American's attention was directed to a map showing the narrow, crowded streets of the wholesale district. Though well constructed, too many buildings were surmounted with what the Londoner called "tinder boxes on their tops," meaning mansard roofs.[15]

Mr. Clarke sailed for home on November 7, 1872.

November 9, being Saturday, the wholesale district in Boston closed early. The Old South clock had just struck seven when a pedestrian, hurrying along deserted Sumner Street, glanced at the top of a four-story granite building. Flames were licking from the windows of the mansard roof. The ground floor was occupied by a dry-goods house, the second and third floors by vendors of hosiery, gloves and laces, the top story by a manufacturer of ladies' hoop skirts. Every floor was chock-full of winter stock. The Boston fire department, a professional organization, was rated the equal of any in the country. An electric signal box stood a few feet from the burning building. The discoverer of the fire turned in an alarm. But the engines were slow in responding. An epidemic among the horses obliged firemen to drag their apparatus. The delay was fatal.

"Blocks of granite weighing tons were split as if by powder and hurled across wide streets, and planks sent flying through the air as if they were feathers," wrote the correspondent of the Philadelphia *North American* in a dispatch filed at 1 A.M., Sunday. "The firemen erected barricades and worked behind them but they were burned as soon as erected. An hour had hardly elapsed before it was evident that Beebe's block, the finest business structure in the city, built of granite, five stories high, with the cursed mansard roof over all, must go.... Pieces of dry goods went whistling across the square, lodging on the sills of the magnificent stores on Devonshire street. Beebe's block stood a solid wall of granite several minutes after the inside fell, but the heat warped it and two million dollars, its cost, soon lay a heap of stone."[16]

All day Sunday the conflagration roared, breaking the Sabbath calm of Insurance Row in Philadelphia. A reporter for the Philadelphia *Press* noted the "anxious knots of various officers, from presidents down through the various grades of vice presidents, actuaries, directors and even clerks." But the newspaperman could venture "no approximation of the insurance held by the different companies, but only the startling intelligence that the Philadelphia underwriters were more heavily stricken than they had been by the Chicago fire."[17] Hardest hit of all was the North America. As telegraphic bulletins came from the company's Boston agents, Foster & Cole, Messrs. Coffin and Platt saw the total of their obligations mount by the hour.

Monday's New York morning papers published a tabulation of Boston liabilities given out by the *Spectator,* an insurance journal. In the case of the North America these were truly startling. Boston risks were stated at $35,589,326 and the company's total assets as $3,212,000. A reporter for the Philadelphia *Inquirer* showed the figures to Mathias Maris, secretary of the North America. Mr. Maris explained their misleading character. The company's fire risks in Boston were only $3,000,000—the rest being marine insurance. Maris estimated the loss at $900,000, which he said would be speedily paid. The officers, he added, did not feel "the least apprehension."[18]

Another insurance periodical, the *Chronicle,* did not let its careless contemporary off so easily. The data broadcast by the *Spectator* were "worse than falsehood," it said. "The *effect,* if not *intent,* of these publications is to destroy the credit of these companies and create a panic in the public mind."[19] This in turn was an exaggeration which showed the tension existing in insurance circles.

The fire cost Boston $75,000,000, of which $50,000,000 was covered by insurance. Thirty millions were carried by thirty-three Massachusetts companies, twenty-two of which were obliged to suspend, demonstrating once more the weakness of the local organizations which did not properly distribute their risks. Of sixty-eight New York companies involved, three suspended. All other companies paid. The North America's contribution was $988,530.

This reduced the surplus to $8,707, and in January 1873, the first dividend since 1855 was passed.

BOSTON FIRE, 1872

Insured losses, $50,000,000. Of more than one hundred companies involved all seem to have paid in full except twenty-five which suspended, paying part or nothing. The North America promptly paid in full, $988,530.

From a Currier & Ives engraving.

6

The Chicago fire had caused a wave of selling on the New York Stock Exchange and nervous talk of the bursting of the boom. The Boston disaster brought a repetition of this on a larger scale, the *Chronicle* being not the only periodical to throw out the fear-inspiring word "panic." Again the markets rallied, but the old-time buoyance was gone. The timorous and the wise resumed selling. In the spring of 1873 associates warned Jay Cooke not to commit himself more deeply in the Northern Pacific venture. The banker went on, as he had to do or see the Northern Pacific crash. Money was tighter in the summer. The failure of a bank and of Daniel Drew's brokerage house unhinged the New York stock market on September 17. President Grant hastened to Philadelphia to spend the night at the country place of Jay Cooke, whose bank was considered unshakable.

But at eleven next morning Jay Cooke & Company closed its doors and the panic broke.

"FINANCIAL CALAMITY"

announced the headline in the *Inquirer*. Two other banks failed and with frightened crowds filling Chestnut Street, a run was started on the Fidelity Insurance Trust and Safe Deposit Company. This was a great bank, not an insurance company, and its collapse would have pulled down twenty other Philadelphia depositories. In five hours on the nineteenth the Fidelity paid $800,000 across its counters.

Next day the run continued. At the time of the Chicago fire the Fidelity had volunteered to advance the Insurance Company of North America any amount it might need. The offer was repeated after the Boston fire. On neither occasion did the insurance company have to borrow. During the second day of the run the directors of the North America, at a special meeting, offered the besieged bank $300,000 "as a reciprocal act of friendship as well as a general duty."[20] It was accepted.

The run lasted through September 21, and on the morning following the *Inquirer* reported:

"CONFIDENCE RESTORED
THE FIDELITY THE LION OF THE DAY"

Though one other depository failed, the Fidelity's resistance had saved the city's banking structure.

The end of the actual panic by no means brought about a restoration of the status quo. The late prosperity had been sustained by borrowing. In five years national bank loans alone had increased $283,000,000 while deposits increased only $43,000,000. The liquidation of these debts was to prove a long and painful process. The most involved firms went down promptly. By the end of 1873 the number of failures for the year was 10,000. Business was slackening. Pessimism was in the air. Therefore the cheerful note with which the Insurance Company of North America began its annual report, dated January 1, 1874, must have been particularly enheartening:

"The year 1873 has been profitable, as will be shown by the exhibits herewith." The exhibits indicated a net gain of $420,057 for the fire business and a net gain of $368,811 for the marine business.

With many weak companies eliminated, with premiums increased and "the entire reorganization of the amounts at risk in the business centres of the large cities"—a lesson learned from Boston—the fire picture looked encouraging. Regarding the marine side the annual report explained: "The winter of 1872-3 was by far the most disastrous experienced for many years, and your Company suffered heavily in consequence. Many companies, both here and abroad, were obliged to close their doors, and competition was so materially lessened that no difficulty has been experienced in securing advanced rates during the last half of the year, thereby showing a reasonable profit. The Company is now so well known at home and abroad that its business is steadily on the increase, and gives promise of still further progress." Despite a declining American merchant marine, the North America had won its battle for survival in the teeth of foreign competition.

The directors expressed satisfaction over the new Pennsylvania law "for the proper regulation of Insurance Companies in this State." Dividends were resumed. During 1873 both the January and the July dividends had been passed owing to the Chicago and the Boston fires. With the resumption, in January 1874, no dividend has been omitted to the date of this writing. Moreover, the directors announced their determination to increase the capital stock of the company from $500,000 to $1,000,000, for which the stockholders had given their assent in 1872.[21]

The new shares were readily bought up, and the purchasers soon had reason to congratulate themselves. In 1874 business exceeded all expectations, returning the largest profit in the history of the company. To this the marine department contributed $525,242 and fire $356,854. The semiannual July dividend, the first paid on the increased capitalization, was $100,000, or 10 per cent.

The fire branch of the company's business attained a new dignity in 1874 when W. S. Davis of Worcester, Massachusetts, entered the company as second vice-president in charge of fire risks. Mr. Davis had been president of the Bay State Fire Insurance Company, destroyed by the Boston disaster. Vigorously he continued the policy of spreading risks to meet a possible occurrence of such a calamity. As a protest against "the very insatisfactory state of the Fire Department and water supply," the company closed its agency in Chicago. "On the other hand some new agencies have been made in Tennessee, North Carolina, Georgia and Texas."[22] The carpetbaggers' sun was setting and the South resuming the direction of its own affairs. In 1875 Mr. Davis organized the Southern Department, with an ex-Confederate soldier, Captain Edward S. Gay, of Atlanta, as manager. The same year the Pacific Coast Department was established under Jonathan Hunt of San Francisco. In 1876 the number of local agents "from Maine to California" was 1,300. In 1860 there had been about 40.

The advent of $500,000 of fresh capital was a tribute to the esteem in which investors held the North America. Times were growing harder and opportunities for safe investment yielding a fair return difficult to find. More remarkable still was the company's ability to double its capitalization in 1877, raising the total to $2,000,000 without decreasing the annual dividend rate of 20 per cent. At the close of that year the North America was able to report "the largest surplus over all liabilities [$2,426,626] of any American Insurance Company, and equal to that of any Foreign Company."[23]

This was despite the grimly deepening depression, pitiful suffering among unemployed and the bloodiest series of strikes the country has known. The labor trouble began on the Baltimore & Ohio railroad over a pay cut and quickly spread to other lines. Troops were called and pitched battles fought. For three days Pittsburgh was in the power of a mob. Frightened persons thought anarchy at hand. The loosening of the bonds of authority was felt by insurance. The National Board of Fire Underwriters lost its grip and, in the language of the North America's Annual Report, "practically dissolved." This precipitated a rate war in which "even large and strong Fire Companies" joined. But the North America held off, warning stockholders that the result would be a loss of revenue.[24]

In 1878 the depression reached its nadir, with more business failures than in the panic year of '73. This was the end. The last of the boom debts had been sponged out. In 1879 the skies began to clear, wheels to turn and the country to move into the green pastures of better times.

On the threshold of a new era, the North America's remark concerning the impotency of the National Board of Fire Underwriters represented a serious indictment. Unless insurance companies could keep their house in order public authorities would attempt to order it for them, for insurance was too closely knit to the public interest. The North America had hailed the law creating an insurance department as a part of the State Government of Pennsylvania. The object of this department was to insure the solvency of companies. Its requirements were not so strict as some that the North America voluntarily imposed upon itself. Yet neither this department nor any other public regulatory body in the country had touched the issue of rates, so vital to solvency. Insurance had attempted self-regulation in this respect without success. The lessons of Chicago and of Boston were ignored in a matter of months. Clearly, unless the insurance community proved capable of keeping premiums at a figure to insure solvency, state legislatures would step in. The result was not easily predictable. Insurance men shuddered at the thought of so technical a question in the hands of politicians.

7

In January 1878 Arthur G. Coffin refused re-election as president of the company which he had served for forty-six years, thirty-three as its head. Under his leadership assets had grown from $426,507 to $6,461,729. Mr. Coffin was induced to take a place on the Board of Directors, a post he held until he died in 1881, aged eighty-one.

Vice-President Charles Platt succeeded Mr. Coffin as president.

On the day that Mr. Coffin died the North America lost by death another of its veteran directors, William Welsh, a retired merchant, beloved, as was Mr. Coffin, for his philanthropies. He had been a

member of the Board for thirty-six years. Within recent years other
links with the past had been severed when death had taken Ambrose
White, a director for thirty-four years, Charles Taylor, who had
served thirty-six years, and John A. Brown, thirty-four. The Nestor
of them all, Samuel W. Jones, went to his reward in 1873 at the age
of ninety-two. Joining the board in 1807, Mr. Jones had begun a
service which lasted sixty-six years. What a panorama of insurance
history had passed before his eyes!

The company had long since outgrown the attractive building
erected in 1851, with a garden in the rear. In 1872 it had spread into
the building next door. Two years later the garden gave way to a
three-story addition. All this space was overcrowded in 1880 when
the property next door was purchased and plans drawn for a four-
story structure that should be the most imposing insurance edifice in
the United States. The new home—the company's eighth—was
occupied December 6, 1881. The cost, with furnishings, was about
$250,000.

President Platt's office, a stately chamber paneled in dark mahog-
any, contained the latest aids to executive convenience in the way of
electric push buttons and a speaking tube. Mr. Platt never mastered
the art of speaking through the tube. The only telephone in the
building was on a wall near the door of the president's sanctum.
This marvel of the modern world did not work very well. To make
themselves heard most users had to shout, or thought they did. Tir-
ing of the racket, Mr. Platt ordered "that contraption" removed to
the rear of the building. A little later typewriters were introduced.
Mr. Platt did not warm to the innovation and continued for several
years to have his correspondence prepared in longhand by a secretary.[25]

CHAPTER XI

The Marine Branch in Difficulty

I

On the fourth of May 1882, the schooner *George W. Lochner* arrived in Philadelphia from Caribbean ports. On board were the captain and the crew of the British bark *L. E. Cann* whom the *Lochner* had taken from an open boat fifty miles off Brunswick, Georgia, on April 27. Within sight at the time was the abandoned bark, half filled with water and nearly on beam ends. The rescued captain, whose name was Brooks, said that the *Cann* was from Tecoluta, Mexico, for New York. Knocked about by rough weather in the Gulf, the 601-ton vessel had begun to take water faster than the pumps could handle it. With seven and a half feet in the hold she was abandoned shortly before the fortuitous appearance of the *George W. Lochner*. Captain Brooks' story was such a common one—another old sailing vessel foundered—that the Philadelphia papers gave it only a squib.

The Insurance Company of North America displayed more interest. The cargo of the abandoned vessel had been underwritten for $120,000, of which the Philadelphia company held $60,000. Another feature of the case was the fact that the consignors of the *Cann's* cargo had within recent years collected insurance on goods shipped in four other vessels which had been abandoned at sea. A representative of the company interviewed Captain Brooks, whose manner did nothing to allay the suspicion that there was something peculiar about the loss of the *L. E. Cann*.

Fraudulent wrecks and fraudulent fires are a part of the normal histories of insurance companies. Of late, however, the number of queer wrecks had been running above average. The North America decided to look into the case of the *L. E. Cann*. Word was dispatched to a salvage firm at Norfolk to send a tug in search of the missing craft, on the chance that if Brooks had tried to scuttle his bark he might have done a poor job of it. There had been cases of honestly abandoned vessels staying afloat for weeks. The company also formally expressed its suspicions in a protest to the British consul in Philadelphia, alleging the vessel to have been unseaworthy at the start of the voyage and that the goods on the manifest were not aboard her.

On May 9 the salvage company's wrecking steamer *Resolute* returned to Norfolk to report no trace of the *L. E. Cann*. The North America asked that the search be continued. Meantime the British consul hailed Captain Brooks and the mate of the *Cann* who was the captain's brother before a navy court. The Brookses swore that their vessel was seaworthy when she left Mexico. They swore that the goods appearing on the manifest were in her hold. On May 15 the *Resolute* again returned to Norfolk empty-handed. The insurance company asked that the search be resumed and ordered its own seagoing tug *North America* southward to assist. On May 24 the navy court rendered its decision which, after a word of censure for not having tried to run into a port of refuge before the trouble became serious, held Captain Brooks blameless and returned his master's certificate. This seemed to leave the insurance companies holding the bag.

Two days before Captain Edward Gibbons of the *North America* received orders to take up the hunt for the *L. E. Cann* he had saved his employers a heavy loss by hauling off the sugar-laden bark *John Baisley,* which had grounded on the Delaware coast in a storm. Before he could get under way to the southward the Mallory Line steamer *Rio Grande,* Galveston to New York, turned into Delaware Bay with smoke pouring from her. The cargo of cotton was on fire. Having extinguished this, Gibbons proceeded south. A week later the company heard that the wreck of the *L. E. Cann* had been found aground on Cape Lookout, North Carolina. With two of her three masts and a portion of her decks gone, the derelict was towed to Norfolk and the hold pumped out so that the watersoaked but intact cargo could be examined.

The manifest which Captain Brooks had exhibited at the Philadelphia inquiry listed the principal items of cargo as rubber, vanilla beans, deerskins, coffee and tobacco. At Norfolk small quantities of some of these items were found, though in nothing like the amounts mentioned in the manifest. The bulk of the cargo consisted of items not mentioned on the manifest, as follows: 106 bales of broom grass, 151 bales of old rags, 210 bales of bones, 185 bales of sand and a heap of scrap metal. A little more sand or metal and the *Cann* would have gone to the bottom, rendering these disclosures impossible.

"The officers of the Insurance Company of North America," remarked the Baltimore *Underwriter,* "deserve great credit for the perseverance with which they pursued to the point of detection and exposure [the case of] . . . the bark L. E. Cann. . . . The incredible stories and the slippery conduct of the captain led to such well-grounded suspicion that the tug was sent in search of the vessel. An inspection of the hull showed that she had been scuttled by boring five 1¼ inch auger holes and five smaller ones in her hull, below the water line. There is evidence to show that the first mate of the Cann bored the holes, and the second mate held the light, and that in addition to the auger holes there had been a hole half a foot square cut in her port bow, near the keel. The captain of the Cann has disappeared."[1]

2

Other examples of the North America's war on insurance pirates could be cited. Salutary as this activity was, it did not reach the heart of the difficulties depriving marine underwriters of their share of the prosperity which had succeeded six years of depression in 1879.

"The Directors were confronted early in the year with the very grave question," recited the Annual Report dated January 1, 1881, "whether to allow the regular customers to leave for other companies, owing to reduced rates offered, or to retain the business at the best figures attainable, if not too low for safety, until such time as more remunerative premiums could be obtained. It was decided that the business of desirable character should be retained, and the result has been satisfactory. During the year several of the larger foreign companies have withdrawn from the country, and three American companies have retired from the business, so that there promises to be less trouble in the future in obtaining satisfactory rates.

"The results of Marine business can only be measured by a term of years, and almost every decade can be equally divided into good, fair, and unprofitable years. [In the decade just closed the North

Sea-Going Tug "North America"

One of instruments by which insurance company cut marine losses. *North America* aided vessels in distress, did salvage work, hunted insurance "pirates" who wrecked vessels to collect on policies. Photograph shows vessel run aground by master, Captain Edward Gibbons, to escape effects of Florida hurricane, about 1890.

Picture supplied by captain's son, Joseph E. Gibbons, Ridley Park, Pennsylvania.

America had shown only one losing year.] It should be remembered
that this Company has been actively identified with the commerce of
the country for eighty-eight years, during which period years of
disastrous losses did not deter the managements from a steady, on-
ward course; nor in like manner should we, their successors, be
alarmed by periods of diminished gains."[2]

The hope was short-lived. Instead of relief from foreign competition the report for the following year confessed:

"There has been an increase in the number of foreign corporations
which have established branches in this country, which adds materially to the difficulty in the way of advancing rates to a remunerative standard."

Something had to be done. "A meeting of Marine underwriters
was held in the city of New York to consider the demoralized condition of the business"—this was plain speaking—"and to devise
remedies for existing evils, which resulted in the formation of the
Association of Marine Underwriters."[3]

Forty years before, the fight for survival during the upheavals following the panic of 1837 had brought the marine companies together in a national organization which perished of neglect when
better times returned. Similar causes united them again in 1881.
Charles Platt bore an active part in this. He became chairman of
two important committees charged with recommendations concerning forms of policies, rates, loading of vessels, losses and averages.

Eighteen months later the North America still spoke of what the
National Association hoped to accomplish rather than what it had
accomplished. There was "promise" that "abuses which have crept
into the business" would be checked and "more remunerative rates"
established "at no distant date." Yet the existence of baffling impon-
derables which continued to siphon off profit was admitted. "It
seems impossible to give any correct theory of the cause of the numerous disasters which are of constant occurrence. . . . Collisions
and fires have greatly increased in consequence of a large number of
steamers which have taken the place of sailing vessels." The company
showed a preference for sail and assured its stockholders that, despite
the mounting tide of losses, every risk was "carefully scrutinized."[4]

A further effort to better the company's situation was made in 1882
by increasing the capital from $2,000,000 to $3,000,000.

"The insurance business of the future must be done to a great extent by companies possessing capital and reserve sufficient to enable them to ... compete successfully with the large foreign corporations. ... A few years ago coffee was imported from Brazil in vessels which carried from 3,000 to 5,000 bags. Steamers are now employed, the cargoes of which frequently reach 40,000 bags. Cargoes of 8,000 bales of cotton are now not infrequently found in place of 3,000 or 4,000, which was formerly the maximum. ... Your company receives a large share of this increased business and frequently is obliged ... to reinsure. ... The object of the increase of capital and surplus is to enable the company to retain a larger share of the business."[5]

The ensuing years of 1883 and 1884 were good ones, with profits for the marine account of $327,900 and $388,200, respectively. The company gave credit to the reforms worked by the National Association "not only in checking abuses in the business, but in maintaining rates of premium which prior to their efforts had fallen below the paying point."[6] Though continued improvement was anticipated the two good years were followed by two losing ones, the figures being (1885) $80,600 and (1886) $269,300. A tone of perplexity returned to the comment of the directors, troubled by "the frequency of fires on shipboard, mostly on cotton-laden vessels, for which it has been impossible to assign an adequate reason."[7]

3

The unsatisfactory state of the marine business sharpened interest in the eighty-odd-year-old French Spoliation Claims. In 1801 the United States had signed away the right of the claimants to undertake to recover from the French Government. As we have seen, the claimants at once turned to our Government for restitution. At one time or another numerous congressional committees recommended payment. Twice bills passed both Houses, to be vetoed by the presidents in office. The Insurance Company of North America played a leading part in keeping the subject alive. In 1885 its efforts were crowned with success. President Cleveland approved a bill recognizing the obligation of the United States to the claimants. This act, however, carried no appropriation, but referred the question of reimbursement to the Court of Claims.

This seemed fair enough. The North America overhauled its yellowing files reaching back into the administrations of George Washington. The result was a statement of claims for 181 separate losses at sea on which it had paid insurance aggregating $1,506,000. (In 1802 the North America had stated its claims to be approximately $2,000,000. For the most part the difference between that figure and $1,506,000 is accounted for by the recovery of $346,000 under the Florida Treaty of 1819 and certain smaller sums recovered otherwise.)[8]

The North America's 181 claims went before the court along with a host of others. In the fullness of time the court made ninety-eight awards in favor of the company, aggregating $747,047. Notwithstanding the difficulty after such a lapse of time in marshaling facts and evidence more than half of its claims had passed muster. This was noteworthy, considering that only 17 per cent of all claims presented resulted in awards.

The next step was to wait for a congressional appropriation. One came in 1891 for $1,304,000. In its disbursal $26,800 went to insurance companies and all the rest to claimants who were private underwriters or private individuals. The North America got nothing. Other appropriations, totaling $2,606,000, were made in 1899, 1902 and 1905. All this went to satisfy awards to private claimants; nothing to corporations. At the date of this writing, 1942, the North America's awards of $747,000 remain unpaid.[9]

In preferring the claims of individuals to those of insurance companies the Government followed the precedent of the so-called "Alabama Claims" against Great Britain for the damage done by Confederate raiders built in British yards. In 1872 a mixed international commission awarded the United States $15,500,000 which Britain paid in gold. Half of this amount was relayed to the owners of vessels and of cargo not protected by insurance. The balance remains in the Treasury. Nothing was paid to insurance companies. In the case of the North America, whose losses to English-built Confederate cruisers amounted only to $11,169, this was a trifling matter. For some companies which had paid out a million or more it was serious.

4

The Insurance Company of North America was a pleasant place to work. It had grown into an international institution without losing its character as a Philadelphia institution, faithful to the local traditions in which family dynasties play such a part. On the current Board of Directors was Francis R. Cope who rounded out thirty years' service in 1885 as successor to his father, the founder of the Pennsylvania Railroad, who had been twenty-five years a director; John Lowber Welsh, nephew of William Welsh who had served thirty-seven years; John A. Brown, whose grandfather of the same name had served forty-four. Director William H. Trotter had taken the place made vacant by the death of his brother. When W. H. Trotter died his son, Nathan, succeeded him. In 1880 Vice-President William S. Davis, in charge of the fire business, retired on account of ill health. His place was taken by T. Charlton Henry, a member of the Board since 1864 and a specialist in fire insurance. Mr. Henry was a great-grandson of Colonel Charles Pettit, the company's second president. In 1881 President Platt's son, William A., was promoted to second vice-president. His especial concern was marine risks.

Though Davis had been with the company only six years he had done a good job, and was rewarded with a half-pay pension for life. This was typical of the policy of the company which, in 1860, had established a fund "for the relief of decayed clerks." It was a policy Charles Platt was equipped by temperament to carry out and to extend. The magnetic young man who had come to the company before the Civil War had grown mellow and white-haired. "He was the milk of human kindness," one veteran employee has said. He declined to reduce the commissions to local agents below 15 per cent though three out of four other companies had done so. When a man did his best, though that best might fall short of perfection, Charles Platt would do his best to find a way to keep the man in employment. The president knew the personal histories, the private troubles of those who worked for him. The colored porter, William, was an institution at 232 Walnut Street. When he married, the company gave him a wedding present, and when a baby was born, William proudly wheeled the infant in to receive Charles Platt's blessing.

In this congenial atmosphere a weight of responsibility rested on T. Charlton Henry. With the marine business making money one year and losing it another—a heavy portion of these losses flowing from causes one could not put a finger on—the North America was sharing the lot of marine underwriters the world over during the decade of 1885-1895. More fortunate than some other marine firms, however, the North America had a profitable fire business to fall back on. It was Henry's lookout to keep it profitable.

The problems were numerous. Rate-cutting which was a part of the fight for survival during the depression of the seventies having broken down the authority of the National Board of Fire Underwriters, state legislatures began to take a hand. Up to this time insurance legislation, designed to protect the public from inadequately financed companies, had been beneficial. Now legislators ventured into other fields. Wisconsin enacted a "valued policy" law which other states began to copy. This provided that a policyholder suffering a total loss could collect the face value of his policy regardless of what might have been the actual value of the property destroyed. "The most adroit rogues could not devise a more efficient scheme to facilitate the burning of property," remarked the Insurance Commissioner of New Hampshire in 1881.[10]

In the large cities arson became a means of permanent employment for professional criminals. Insurance companies spent large sums in rewards and in the employment of attorneys and detectives to ferret out and punish firebugs. The situation also called for an increase in rates to meet the hazard. This was as necessary to protect the public as it was to protect the companies. National self-control of the rate problem having failed, regional control was substituted. New York City and the southeastern states organized tariff associations in 1882. Other sections followed and by 1884 the country was covered. The experienced and strong companies took the lead in this work. Opposition was from some, though by no means all, of the new companies. The inexperienced and poorly furnished insurance company was not the competitor it had been in times past, however. The public was learning, though slowly.

The formation of these sectional rating organizations necessitated conferences and compacts among the insurance companies; and these were things of which the public was suspicious. The word "trust" had lately taken on a new meaning. Great industrial combines were unpopular with the masses, and in many instances justly so. Already at work was the ferment destined to produce the Interstate Commerce Commission (1887) and the Sherman Anti-Trust Law (1890). Directed against insurance it took the form of the first "anti-compact" law, in Ohio, in 1885. The intent was to prevent understandings among agents and companies for the purpose of stabilizing rates. "Free competition" was the watchword. Such legislation over-looked the fact that no real monopoly did or was likely to exist in fire insurance. New companies could enter the business and were doing so. Long and costly experience had shown, for one thing, that unless they charged proper rates they could not remain there.

5

In the fall of 1884 a question was asked at a Board meeting about "the large proportion of the receipts of fire premiums which is ab-sorbed by expenses." At the following meeting President Platt undertook to give the answer.

Some seemed to think that the local agents should receive less than 15 per cent as their commissions. Though a majority of the companies paid less Mr. Platt did not think it good business. Among the North America's 2,200 agents the average annual earning was only $150. Small earnings were made by the men in small towns who often represented other companies as well. The general agent for New York City had a guarantee of $10,000 and actually made a great deal more. The business that agents controlled belonged to them, Mr. Platt said, and much of it would be diverted to other com-panies if commissions were cut.

The department offices at Hartford, Albany, Erie, Atlanta and San Francisco took an additional six cents from the premium dollar. Mr. Platt said the offices could not be run for less. "These [department] Managers have long been connected with the Company and in effect are its Executive Officers for their respective districts. Cheap labor cannot be utilized for these positions."

Three and a half cents went to support adjusters and field men whose travels carried them over the entire country, inspecting risks, checking on the activity and character of agents and adjusting losses. "The tendency of policyholders is to exaggerate their claims."

Advertising cost four and one-half cents. Taxes were placed at two and one-half. The early procedure, suggested by insurance companies themselves, of driving away competition by prohibitive taxation upon a company of another state had shown itself to be a pro-tector of weak companies. Taxation for revenue had been substituted. Pennsylvania taxed other-state companies 3 per cent on the business

CHARLES PLATT

Seventh president Insurance Company of North America, 1878-1909. Joining company in 1860 as secretary, his handling of marine accounts during Civil War gave him immediate prominence. Under his regime as president company's fire business passed marine in volume. Record for prompt and full payments at Chicago (1871) and Boston (1872) had much to do with this.

From a portrait, about 1880, artist unknown, owned by the Insurance Company of North America.

done in the state. Pennsylvania companies were charged 3 per cent on the business done in nearly all the other states.

These items totalled $31\frac{1}{2}$ per cent of receipts, and Mr. Platt did not see how the figure could be lowered without harm. Covering the same items the average for the fourteen largest American companies was 37 4/7 per cent.

Then Mr. Platt spoke of something he implied he would like to change but did not know how.

"In the large cities of New York, Philadelphia, Boston, New Orleans, Pittsburg and some others there is a class of men known as Brokers or middlemen, through whose hands a very large proportion of the business of Fire Insurance passes. These men by active personal solicitation secure the control of the business of most of the large Manufacturing Concerns and Mercantile businesses and it is now the exception to a rule when such risks are placed directly by the assured with the Companies. The reason is a plain one. When large amounts of insurance are required and any one Company will not assume more than a limited line it becomes a very troublesome business and requires constant attention. Brokers are now the recognized medium and must obtain licenses from the State Authorities."

In Philadelphia the brokerage rate was 15 per cent. In New York it ran as high as 25.

"Why not do away with this system? The reply is that no one Company can safely move in this direction for the result would be the alienation of the large portion of its business derived from Brokers."[11]

So much for the cost of writing fire insurance in 1884.

The following year Mr. Platt was able to announce that "a marked change for the better has taken place in the fire insurance business, due to enhanced rates and more rigid inspection of risks." In 1886 brokerage in New York was cut to 10 per cent. First Mr. Platt and then Mr. Henry made surveys of the European field with the result that agencies were opened in England, Belgium, Austria and Russia. The report for 1888 declared, "The Foreign Agencies have been quite successful, and show an excess of receipts over expenditures of $57,220.03."[12]

After the death of T. Charlton Henry in 1890, Eugene L. Ellison was made second vice-president in charge of fire. William A. Platt was raised to the vice-presidency. Mr. Ellison was forty-five years old. Beginning his business experience in a country bank in Delaware, where he was born, he later had joined the staff of the Enterprise Insurance Company of Philadelphia which was wrecked by the Chicago fire. After that he had entered the Harrisburg office of the North America, becoming assistant secretary of the company in 1884.

The Annual Report to the stockholders, dated January 1, 1892, made modest mention of an approaching anniversary rare in the annals of business corporations:

"The present year will complete the hundredth year of the Company's life. It was founded in 1792, and transacted a large and profitable Marine Insurance business; Fire Insurance being then but little practiced. Regular dividends were paid until the year 1800, when the heavy losses by French captures caused an intermission of seven years. In 1807 they were resumed, and continued until the English War of 1812-15, when again there were three years without dividend. In 1816 they were again resumed, and from that time until the present (76 years) there have been only four years in which no dividends have been paid. The average of the 99 complete years has been 12 40/100%, which is a remarkable result for so long a period. . . .

"The Fire Insurance Branch received but little attention in the early years of the Company's life, and even up to 1860 the annual premiums did not exceed $100,000. . . . At the present time they are over $3,000,000 per annum. In 1860 the total income from Fire and Marine premiums was $500,000 while it is now over $5,000,000; the entire properties of the Company were $1,100,000, while they are now nearly $9,300,000. . . ."

Possibly the authors hoped that this encouraging review of an institution which had withstood the vicissitudes of ninety-nine years might counterbalance less agreeable news which it was the duty of the Annual Report to convey. Despite the healthy volume of business fire losses for the twelve months just passed had been so tremendous as to reduce the net gain from that source to $44,413. To avoid depleting the surplus below $2,500,000, the annual dividend rate had been cut from 15 to 12 per cent. This was the second reduction in five years, the rate in 1886 having been 20 per cent.

6

Eighteen ninety-one was an off year for the fire branch, the profits of which had averaged $273,000 a year for the past decade. Without this and the earnings of the company's large and well-placed investments there would have been no dividends at all by 1892, for the marine branch had not found a way out of its difficulties. In the year 1889, $297,200 was lost on its operations. The three succeeding years returned profits, aggregating $445,100, but these were considerably depleted by the deficit in 1893, which was $301,000. The fact that 1893 witnessed another financial panic which reduced business in all lines did not explain the heavy loss. There had been too many such losses in years otherwise good for trade. Except for its marine business, the North America came through the panic handsomely. On January 1, 1894, the value of its investments had depreciated only $30,000.[13]

From these circumstances it was clear that the unprofitable nature of marine risks derived from something inherent in that business rather than from external factors, including one so profound as a panic and business depression. A search for causes began in earnest. Cotton had long since been singled out as a consistently poor risk. In its Annual Report for 1888 the North America noted that "a large and influential committee has been appointed from the London and Liverpool companies for the purpose of investigating the origin . . . [of cotton fires on shipboard] and is now acting in concert with a committee of American underwriters."[14]

No account of the committee's findings appears in the company's files. The cotton and other losses continued.

So did the search for underlying causes. A notation on the subject by Charles Platt, undated, but apparently written about 1890:

"In Philadelphia, New York, New Orleans, and Boston the Company employs competent Marine Surveyors, who report on the vessels proposed for insurance, but such survey cannot prevent loss. Vessels are reported under open policies, from China, Japan, Brazil, etc., and sometimes, the cable informs us of their loss by fire, or stranding, or some cause that has no connection with the character of the vessel.

"Great care is taken to reduce the Company's line by reinsurance.

At times, the amounts by any one vessel may, and do, aggregate, from different dealers, more than the Company will carry, but it will readily be seen how impolitic it would be to refuse to take a dealer's risk because the Company's line was full. . . .

"As to rates of premium, it must be borne in mind that one Company can no longer control them than can a grocer control the price of his wares, or an iron-merchant the price of iron. Demand and supply enter quite as much into the consideration of this business as in any other, and, just now, the supply of companies is in excess of the demand. Large and strong English companies are transacting business in this country. . . . As in any other trade, under similar circumstances, the prices are reduced—but, surely, no one would argue from this that a company such as the North America should allow itself to be driven from a business which it has successfully carried on for nearly one hundred years. . . .

"It must also be remembered that the sailing vessels of the olden time have passed away, and the commerce of the world is now carried on by steamers, of large capacity, and it is very possible that, as yet, underwriters have not been able to adjust their rates to the new conditions."[15]

Too obvious for a marine underwriter of the period to mention was the shrinkage of the American field due to the continuing reduction of our merchant marine, which in 1890 was 928,000 tons or smaller than it had been in 1810. The decline since 1880 had amounted to 386,000 tons.

Sugar as well as cotton was a notorious source of losses. How one importer of sugar, a well-known and highly reputable Philadelphia merchant, regarded insurance forms the basis of a story that has been told along Insurance Row for fifty years. This importer carried with the North America an open policy on sugar in transit from the West Indies. An officer of the company noted that the merchant was behind with his premiums. As the policyholder was prosperous it was assumed that the neglect had been due to inadvertence. A clerk was sent to ask for a remittance. The sugar dealer was indignant. "Certainly not!" he exclaimed. "I'll continue to do business with the North America as I've always done it: credit my premiums against my losses."[16]

Given enough customers like this the strongest company in the world would go broke in time.

CHAPTER XII

Enter Benjamin Rush

I

In March 1895 Vice-President William A. Platt died, leaving a
grieving parent to fill the position of nominal head of the marine
branch. One must say nominal head because President Charles Platt
carried on his own shoulders the real burden of that ailing department. While routine administration could be delegated, the gallant
old gentleman reserved for himself responsibilities dealing with constructive policy, the paramount object of which was to end the
marine deficits.

The quest for someone to keep the wheels turning while Mr. Platt
devoted his energies to larger things led to mention of Benjamin
Rush, manager of the average adjusting department of the old marine brokerage firm of Curtin & Brockie. The prospect was quite
young—twenty-five—but the position he held with Curtin & Brockie
was responsible. In all, Mr. Platt heard Rush so well spoken of that
he was asked to call at No. 232. The fatherly executive found himself
sizing up a sprucely turned out young chap whose manner could be
incisive and confident without bumptiousness. A few questions satisfied Platt of Rush's knowledge of marine law. This suggested an
ability to protect the interest of the company in the settlements of
losses. The young man was hired, and he began work on April 22,
1895. His title, assistant to the president, was new to the roster of the
old insurance company. It was the salary, rather than the title, that
attracted Benjamin Rush, however. Three thousand a year was more
than he had been getting at Curtin & Brockie's. Rush thought he
could marry on such pay, and six weeks after joining the North
America he did so. Looking back he thinks this gave him a deeper
interest in the welfare of the company than otherwise might have
been the case.

The assistant to the president learned his run-of-mill duties quickly.
The advantageous adjustment of a few minor claims attracted favor-

able notice. There was the case of a canned-goods shipment. The goods had been salvaged with the labels washed off. It seemed impossible to dispose of them except at a great sacrifice until Rush got an idea. The young assistant ate his lunches at a Horn & Hardart cafeteria. Why shouldn't this restaurant buy the labelless canned goods at a price that would be fair all around? Rush saw the manager and made the sale.

Little strokes of enterprise like this helped—but not enough. Rush's first year with the company proved the most disastrous for marine risks in the North America's one hundred and two years as a going concern. The deficit was $553,500.

"If this keeps up," thought Rush, "I'll be out of a job before long."[1]

The challenge was a personal one. Coming from a line of distinguished public figures, Benjamin Rush had committed the indiscretion of a departure from family precedent by entering business. His father, Colonel Richard Henry Rush, had raised and commanded the Sixth Pennsylvania Cavalry in the Civil War. His grandfather, Richard Rush, had served four presidents of the United States in various capacities including secretary of the treasury, attorney general, minister to Britain and to France. His great-grandfather, Doctor Benjamin Rush, had signed the Declaration of Independence, been surgeon general of Washington's army, and a member of the convention which framed the Constitution of the United States.

Preferring business, young Benjamin could not wait to go to college. Leaving the aristocratic Episcopal Academy at fifteen he entered the employ of an insurance brokerage house as an office boy. By the time he was old enough to vote he was an average adjuster, perhaps the youngest practitioner of that skilled calling in Philadelphia. He meant to continue to climb.

2

Losses being the business of an average adjuster, they formed a subject about which Rush knew a good deal and had a curiosity to learn more when he went to work for the North America. He did not suspect the abundant opportunity he would find to gratify that curiosity, however. But with losses breaking on every hand like bombshells his analytical mind went to work. Where did these appal-

THE COMPANY'S NEW HOME, 1880

This edifice at 232 Walnut Street in the heart of Insurance Row was the company's head office until 1925.

ling claims come from; and why? From what classes of ships? From what sea routes? From what categories of cargo? Rush's experience in brokerage houses had taught him to regard sailing vessels as hazardous risks for insurers; that West Indian routes, due to the prevalence of hurricanes and the preponderance of sail, rolled up high loss ratios; and that among the commodities cotton and sugar had a bad name. What were the actual figures as concerned the North America? Rush could find no figures, only general statements. Rush had long heard gossip on the Row that the North America was a good place to go for reinsurance—on a poor risk. Was this true? The books did not reveal: no figures. After he had been with the company about a year and a half and had begun to feel some concern for its future and his, Benjamin Rush inaugurated, on the quiet, a systematic investigation of the company's marine losses.

It was not long before the young man discovered that he had a bear by the tail. That the job should have turned out to be bigger than Rush bargained for is not surprising. The subordinate at 232 Walnut had laid himself out to solve a problem which was baffling some of the best minds in insurance on both sides of the water.

For bookkeeping purposes the North America divided its business into fourteen classifications, as they were called. Eight of these classifications were on the basis of routes: coastwise; transatlantic; West Indies; Far East; transpacific; west coast of South America; east coast of South America; Great Lakes. Five had to do with cargo: export cotton; petroleum; coffee; general cargo; miscellaneous. One related to reinsurance. Profit and loss figures were not kept on the separate classifications. About all the company knew was that premiums amounted to so much in a year, expenses so much, losses so much. The remainder was gain or loss. Which of the fourteen individual categories had made or lost money was not known, except in a general way as in the case of cotton. For instance it was thought in company councils that reinsurance tended to diminish losses. Rush had not gone very far until he began to suspect that it tended to increase them. The same way with petroleum. Another thing Rush learned from his inquiry was that fourteen classifications were not enough for his purpose. To get the real story he would have to subdivide the business into several times fourteen classes and set up books on each.

As a beginning he split carriers into sail and steam. Then he divided the steamers into three classes: those operating on first-class regular lines; on second-class lines; and as tramps. Covering the whole globe, this task in itself entailed a great amount of work. And it was only a start. Fortunately, however, by this time Rush was not working alone. Early in his researches he had met a young marine clerk named Henry W. Farnum who was also curious about the subject of losses. Rush and Farnum talked things over and presently began to work along together. They were joined by another clerk, a boy of nineteen named Thomas R. Young.

As time went on Harry Farnum, Tommy Young and Rush found they had more to do than they could take care of in office hours without neglecting the work they were paid for doing. They took to working evenings, after all but the janitors had left the big building. Rush was now sure that he was on the trail of something big. But before he could broach it to Mr. Platt he must be doubly sure, with everything checked and verified beyond power to upset. This entailed more work, and the harder the three young men worked the more remained to be done as the picture spread and ramified. Every day put them on the trace of something new. Weeks stretched into months, but they couldn't stop. Eventually they had broken down the company's marine business into 198 components. It was necessary to check the profit and loss performance of each of the 198 back through five years at least to obtain dependable data.

Before all this was completed Rush began his approach to Mr. Platt. Nothing was said about the 198 classifications into which the three young men had privately divided the business. To keep the discussion on familiar ground Rush mentioned only the original fourteen. He showed figures indicating that over a period of ten years eight of these classes had consistently made money and six had consistently lost. The losers were petroleum, general cargo, West Indies (largely sugar), cotton, miscellaneous and reinsurance.

This was the work of weeks, Mr. Platt not being the type of man one could sweep off his feet. Rush's figures indicated petroleum to be an even more flagrant loser than cotton. He would bring up the subject obliquely.

"What is our capital and surplus, Mr. Platt?"

"You know what it is."

"And what is the capital and surplus of the Oil Trust?"

Mr. Platt did did not know, precisely. Rush supplied the figure. It was many times the capital and surplus of the North America.

"Now if I were running the Oil Trust," the young man continued, "I would not, with those resources, spend money on insurance unless I knew I could profit by it. That is what the Trust is doing. It is deliberately making money off us, year in and year out. It carries insurance for no other reason."

"And what should we do?" asked Mr. Platt.

"Raise rates or drop the business," said Rush.

Mr. Platt did nothing so sensational as to drop the oil business. Nor did he raise rates. Yet the assistant was making an impression. In the spring of 1897 the boss sent him abroad to look over the marine end of the European agencies, which, in contrast to the foreign fire agencies, were not earning their salt. Rush returned to report that the home companies—English and Continental—were taking the cream and leaving the North America the skimmed milk. He recommended the virtual abandonment of the European field. The best opportunities for an American underwriter lay at home—provided unprofitable domestic business were spotted and weeded out and profitable given a place in the sun. By this time Rush was able to speak with some confidence and particularly on the subject of paying versus non-paying business, item for item, with figures running back far enough to clinch his arguments. The 198 classifications into which Rush had divided the company's marine operations enabled him to look into that opaque structure and to discern hitherto unsuspected facts concerning profit and loss, somewhat as the current marvel of the scientific world, Wilhelm Konrad Roentgen's x-ray, enabled one to look into the human body.

The eventual upshot was a request that Rush put in writing his ideas concerning the company's marine situation with suggestions for turning losses into profits. Mr. Platt promised to place the paper before the Board of Directors.[2]

3

There was the chance Rush had been working and waiting for. The result was one of the luminous documents in the modern history of marine underwriting:

"December 10, 1897.

"Charles Platt, Esq., Pres't.,
    "Philadelphia.
"Dear Sir:—

"In accordance with your request, I beg to submit my views upon the present state of marine insurance business, both generally and also as directly applicable to this Company—

"Also, upon the causes which have converted an exceptionally profitable business into one which has yielded no profit to underwriters generally for several years past—

"And, finally, upon the probability of the business again becoming profitable in the near future, and the steps, which, if taken, will bring about this result.

"GENERAL CONSIDERATIONS

"A review of the business of marine insurance generally, for say the past twenty years, will bring into prominent relief the following causes which have operated so disastrously to reduce the profits of marine underwriting.

"Although these causes could all be embodied under the head of 'Changed Business Conditions,' I nevertheless propose to so subdivide them as to make it possible to consider each one separately, as, by that means, we shall be better able to arrive at each one's individual effect upon the business, and, as the heading of this first sub-division indicates, I shall here deal only with 'General Conditions,' as it would be too great a tax upon your patience to follow into detail the results of all the causes which I propose to outline. With your permission, therefore, I propose to defer the consideration of details until we come to examine the condition of the business of our own Company.

"1st. It is an old insurance axiom that when any particular branch of trade fails to pay an adequate remuneration to its proprietors, then that particular trade will also be a losing one to underwriters.

"Let us see how this axiom applies to the present unprofitable condition of marine insurance.

"Twenty years ago the great majority of tonnage was in the shape of wooden sailing ships, of moderate size. These had been a very profitable investment for their owners, and had consequently been kept in good repair, and were well commanded and found, because their owners were making a large profit from their use. (It was no extraordinary thing for a vessel to pay for herself in two years.)

They were, therefore, profitable to underwriters both on hull and cargo, because their owners could make more money from employing them legitimately in trade than in any other way.

"But about twenty years ago this state of affairs began to alter rapidly under the operation of those changes of trade, the fruit of which we are reaping today; and the first noticeable alteration was the substitution of steamers constructed of iron. . . . The steamer could earn more money per ton per year than the sailing ship. Consequently each new steamer took just so much profit away from every sailing vessel . . . [until] very few of the old sailing ships were making any money.

"The result of this state of affairs was that . . . the sailing vessels, . . . although perfectly good as vessels, were perfectly bad as investments. . . . Many owners withdrew from business, others let their vessels run down until they were finally lost from neglect, and others knowingly destroyed them in order to collect the insurance money.

"Whenever a vessel was lost the cargo on board was usually more or less involved, consequently insurance on both cargo and hull became unprofitable.

"This state of affairs would have been offset by the profit to be made from insuring the steamers which had taken the place of the sailing vessels, had it not been for the fact that . . . transportation did not stand still with the advent of steam tonnage. . . . Engines were changed from single to compound, and then to triple expansion. Coal consumption was reduced . . . and the carrying capacity was enormously increased. . . . Many steamers built not ten years ago, and at that time embodying the highest art of the builder, are of no more value as investments than would be a stage-coach line between Philadelphia and Pittsburg. . . .

"The loss of invested capital by reason of these successive changes will probably never be accurately estimated. It must be measured in hundreds of millions of dollars, and marine underwriters were obliged to shoulder at least their share of this loss, to put it mildly.

"Another fruitful cause of increased loss to marine underwriters was the enormously increased hazard of collision, brought about by the vast expansion of commerce, which crowded the highways of the sea with vessels of great size, power and speed, many of them running on the schedule time of a railroad, through fair weather and foul. . . .

"I now come to the last and greatest cause of loss to marine underwriters. . . . I refer to

"COMPETITION

"It may seem a paradox to state that the unprofitable condition of marine insurance is due to the enormous profits which have been made in marine insurance; but it is none the less true. I will defer citing the profits made by this Company until I come to deal with its own particular affairs, but it will do no harm to glance at the profits of a few of the other large and ably managed marine insurance companies in past years.

"The Atlantic Mutual Ins. Co. of New York, a mutual organization, after paying dividends of 40% to its policy-holders annually, has accumulated a surplus estimated at about $2,000,000.

"The United States Lloyd's, after its reorganization . . . has paid liberal dividends. Today a share in its capital brings over four times its par value.

"The Boston Marine Ins. Co., organized in 1873, capital $1,000,000, after paying dividends of $1,830,000, has accumulated a surplus of over $1,100,000.

"Turning now to Great Britain:

"The British & Foreign Marine Ins. Co. organized in 1863, with a paid-up capital today, of £268,000, after paying liberal dividends (in 1896 25%), has accumulated a surplus of about £200,000.

"Similar results are shown by the statements of the Thames & Mersey Marine Ins. Co., organized in 1860; and the Sea Ins. Co., organized in 1875.

"These instances might be multiplied indefinitely, and although, per contra, during the last thirty years many marine companies have retired from business, it must be remembered that they lost money while others, under the same conditions, were able to make it; and that their want of success, therefore, should be charged to bad management and not to the business they were engaged in.

"It is also well to bear in mind that very few of the companies I have cited have made additions to their surplus in the last few years. Their profits have been largely made between the years of 1860 and 1890, and although they have continued to pay handsome dividends since that time, these latter dividends came out of the profits they had previously accumulated and interest on investments.

"These enormous profits bore their natural fruit in the fiercest competition . . . [which] manifested itself in the following ways:

"1st. Rates were enormously reduced in the efforts of each company to secure business. As an instance, on a certain class of business where ten years ago we used to secure a rate of

1%, we today secure 1/5 of 1%. Other rates have suffered corresponding reductions.

"2nd. Carriers were exonerated from the results of their own negligence.

"3rd. Claims were paid which should never have been admitted under the policy.

"4th. The policy itself was extended to cover losses which it was in the power of the assured himself and his agents to prevent—thus putting a premium on negligence and fraud.

"5th. The whole spirit which seemed to animate underwriters being: 'If I do not grant these admittedly vicious conditions, my neighbour will do so, and I will lose my business.'

"The result of this state of affairs you all know. The weaker companies were forced out of business, or absorbed by more powerful rivals. The stronger companies fought each other, until it has come to pass for the last few years that few of them have made any money on their underwriting account, and many iniquitous features have been introduced into marine insurance, which it will take some time to generally eradicate.

"So much for the past.

"Now as to the question: *Will marine insurance again become a profitable business in the near future?*'

"A legitimate business, for which there is a steady demand, will never be conducted on a losing basis as a permanent thing. Therefore, in the long run, the marine insurance business will pay a profit *to those who know how to secure it.* . . .

"[The way to secure it is to avoid] those classes of business which have been rendered unprofitable by reason of the causes I have cited, by retaining and extending those branches of the business which show a profit.

"It is not probable that any high percentage of profit will be made for several years, or until those companies which are transacting a reckless business are so filled with the fruit of their own devices as to be willing to inaugurate the necessary reforms. But, on a carefully selected business, I firmly believe a moderate, just profit can be made by those companies who have enough of the courage of their convictions to *avoid the bad business and to hold fast that which is good.*

"MARINE BUSINESS OF THE INSURANCE COMPANY
OF NORTH AMERICA

". . . During the decade beginning 1860 and ended 1869, this Company made in its marine business $764,500.

"Between 1870 and 1879 it made . . . . . . 2,075,400.
"Between 1880 and 1889 it made . . . . . . 604,800.

"Total . . . .$3,444,700.
"Between 1890 and 1897 it lost about . . . . . 450,000.

"Leaving an absolute net profit of . . . . .$2,994,700.
"Say $3,000,000 in the last thirty-seven years. . . .

"In the twenty years beginning 1860 and ending 1879, there were but two bad years, which together made a loss of $74,200.

"Since 1880, the years have given the following results:

	PROFIT	LOSS
1880	$ 51,700	
1881	253,200	
1882		$ 52,600
1883	327,900	
1884	388,200	
1885		80,600
1886		269,300
1887	81,600	
1888	201,900	
1889		297,200
	$1,304,500	$ 699,700
Profit		604,800
	$1,304,500	$1,304,500
1890	154,600	
1891	121,200	
1892	169,300	
1893		301,000
1894	63,500	
1895		553,500
1896		85,000
	$ 508,600	$ 939,500
Loss	427,900	
	$ 939,500	$ 939,500

"We thus see that the business began to change for the worse

about 1885, although the profit for the first five years of that decade
handsomely overcame the loss of the last five years, while the four
profitable years of the decade beginning 1890 were completely
swamped by the bad year of 1895—a year in marine insurance comparable only to the years of the Boston and Chicago fires in fire
insurance.

"NOW THE QUESTION IS: HOW AND WHERE HAS THIS FOUR OR FIVE
HUNDRED THOUSAND DOLLARS BEEN LOST, AND WHAT STEPS MUST BE
TAKEN TO REVERSE THIS RESULT?

"Every insurance company divides, or should divide, its business
into what are technically known as 'Classifications.'

"A classification is a sub-division made for the purpose of ascertaining which particular branches of your business are profitable and
which are the reverse. To illustrate, we will suppose that this Company did a business of $1,000,000 annually. Were no classification
made, it would be known at the end of the year whether the Company had made or lost money, but where and how this result had
been reached would be merely guess-work. . . .

"*The more complete and scientific is your classification, the better
will you be able to know the good business from the bad, and to act
on the knowledge so acquired.* . . .

"In past years the marine business of this Company has been
divided into thirteen sub-divisions or classifications, exclusive of the
Re-insurance Account. . . .

"The statistics of these classifications since 1885 show that EIGHT
OF THEM HAVE PAID US A STEADY PROFIT (certain ones not showing a
single loss IN THE PAST TEN YEARS), but that five of them, in connection with the Re-insurance Account, have made such a heavy loss as
not only to ENTIRELY OVERCOME the profit made by the other branches
of the business, but to account for the loss which the Company
has made in its marine business in the past ten years. The classifications showing a loss are the following:

Petroleum	Export Cotton
General Cargo	Miscellaneous Business
West Indies	Re-insurance Account

"The Re-insurance Account for the past ten
years shows that we have paid to the other companies for re-insuring us, the sum of $5,169,100
and have recovered from them 4,569,800
_____

Showing a profit to our Re-insurers of . . . . $ 599,300
or 11.59%

"It may be asked, Why is it that our Re-insurers have made so large a profit on the business we have given them, while the Company itself has lost money on the business it has retained?

"The answer is a twofold one.

"First. Because the Company has re-insured too large a proportion of its good business. . . .

"Second. Our Re-insurers received, in most cases, the exact rate of premium which we ourselves received from our Assured, free from the expense of conducting our business.

"As the expense of conducting our business is never less than 10% on the premiums received, this was of course a clear profit to them of that amount.

"I believe I have shown where the Company has lost money in marine business of the past ten years. I will . . . [now suggest]

"REMEDIES

in order to put the business on a steadily profitable basis. . . .

"FIRST—

"*Re-insurance Account*
"*The Company should be put in a position* to carry ALL ITS GOOD BUSINESS, no matter how great the risks on individual vessels. To this end a Re-insurance Fund should be created to equalize over a series of years any exceptionally heavy loss which would otherwise destroy the profit of any year in which it occurred.

"We would thus keep on our books not only the profit which we have lost in the past on our Re-insurance Account, but a much larger sum; for it is to be remembered that the Re-insurance Account in the past covered all the business, both good and bad, whereas we ourselves propose only to keep the good re-insurance.

"SECOND—

"*The business which our experience has proven to be hopelessly bad, must be gotten rid of.*

"I wish here to draw a distinction between two classes of bad business, as, in my judgment, they require different treatment.

"First. A business which has become unprofitable solely through a temporary reduction of rates below the paying point, but which otherwise is in a sound, healthy condition, I would by no means sacrifice. I would keep it on my books, and, as far as possible, I would re-insure it with those companies whose competition is responsible for the reduction in rates. This will afford them the necessary object lesson as to the unwisdom of their actions. And when the rates do go up to the paying point, we will be ready to secure the profit.

"But all branches of business which are, and must be unprofitable, by reason of vicious conditions which we by ourselves cannot reform, *must be cut off with a firm hand.* . . .

"If, at a later date, reforms are inaugurated, we can again secure our share of the business. . . .

"THIRD—

"*The classification system of the Company* should be extended and improved. A dozen or so of sub-divisions are entirely inadequate for a business of Two Million Dollars annually. The meshes of the net are so large that only the greatest sources of loss can be discovered. A good classification would disclose many sources of loss which we now do not suspect.

"FOURTH—

"A systematic effort should be made to extend and increase the paying business of the Company, especially in the direction of small policy business. The large accounts are, in my estimation, not apt to be so desirable, and the business of all well-organized trusts [monopolies] should be avoided. These latter expect to make a profit on their insurance. Their accounts are kept as carefully as those of any insurance company. Their resources are so great that they have no need of marine insurance, and in my experience they never engage in it except when they know that they can make a profit from their underwriters.

"FIFTH—

"All the recommendations which I have made should be undertaken in a careful and conservative spirit, without haste, and without delay, and when undertaken they should be pursued steadily and consistently until the end sought is attained.

"In these recommendations I have necessarily sketched a general outline only, as the discussion of all the details involved would consume many hours and would be out of place at the present time. But I feel confident that a steady pursuit of the policy of keeping and extending business which *we know to be good,* and getting rid of business which *we know to be bad,* cannot but result in the Marine Branch becoming profitable in the near future.

"BENJAMIN RUSH."[3]

4

Benjamin Rush's diplomat grandfather need not have been ashamed of that paper, which is the most original and searching analysis of the profit and loss feature of marine insurance of the period that has been brought to light. More than this, it is a masterpiece of tactful understatement, of persuasive advocacy. Take the remarks on the subject of classifications. From what is said the directors must have assumed this device for "ascertaining which particular branches of your business are profitable and which are the reverse" to be an established insurance fixture, Rush merely recommending that it "be extended and improved." Actually, the system described was Rush's invention. All through his letter the writer revealed less than he knew. He said as little as possible about the details of the reforms necessary to bring about what he had in mind. But he thought he said enough to get action; and in this he was right.

The letter went first to the Finance Committee and then to the Board of Directors. In a month plus two days—January 12, 1898—Benjamin Rush was elected second vice-president in charge of the marine branch, with a mandate to reorganize the business.

5

He made fur fly. "It seemed like a young revolution had hit the office," remarked Thomas R. Young in later years.[4] Twenty things were set in motion at once—each a job in itself. The petroleum business went out of the window, lock and stock—no new policies accepted on oil in transit. Other patently bad business was gutted to get rid of the more flagrant losers. This meant cotton and sugar for the most part. The complicated rate structure, a heritage of years, was torn down and rebuilt, premiums on losing lines being raised as much as 100 per cent. If assureds did not wish to pay them they could take their business elsewhere, as many did. These amputations diminished the company's marine volume 25 per cent in a year. Rush's 198-category classification system was officially substituted for the old fourteen-ply arrangement. Reinsurance was turned upside down. Business which Rush's classification x-ray indicated to be profitable was not offered for reinsurance when this could be avoided. Doubtful business was freely offered—in particular to rate-cutting companies, to give them a taste of their own medicine. Reinsurance was accepted on good business, rejected on bad. The reinsurance fund, advocated by Rush, was started at $75,000 to which $5,000 was added each month.

So much for a quick glance at only the principal courses of action which the new vice-president started. To get any one of them going involved many executive decisions and much administrative labor. Taken together they shook the old marine branch to its foundations, affecting the daily occupations of a personnel scattered over a good part of the world. To begin with Rush had beside him only two men—Farnum and Young—capable of sharing in the direction of administrative details. He got them raises in pay and they worked like Trojans. Veteran clerks with pens behind their ears peered dubiously from beneath green eye-shades, grumbling at the long hours but more especially at the new tasks Rush set for them. Sure no good could come from such radical changes, they took their criticisms to Mr. Platt whose door was open to high and low alike. Employees of the fire branch, who had come to look patronizingly on the unprofitable marine department, shook their heads and sighed that marine was going from bad to worse. Old clients of the company, one or two of them directors, demanded that Mr. Platt call a halt on the upstart innovator; their pocketbooks had been touched by Rush's rate-raising. With admirable tact the second vice-president managed to neutralize this pressure on the president, and to retain Mr. Platt's support at critical junctures. But for this the revolution would have been sabotaged in its early stages.

From the first Rush knew that he was in for a long pull. "It will take five years to show whether we're right or not," he told Young.[5]

Moreover, Rush knew that the results of his work would not show immediately on the profit side of the ledger. On the contrary deficits would increase for the time being. By cutting off petroleum business all oil revenue stopped while the company had to pay losses on oil policies which had two years to run. Similarly with sugar and cotton. During his first year Rush refused sugar and cotton business which would have brought premiums of $145,000—very needful for settling current sugar and cotton losses. Loud were the wails that poured into the ears of Mr. Platt. Rush stuck to his guns. "The way to retire from bad business is to retire from it." The aging president backed his spunky junior.

Another thing Rush saw at the outset was that the department managers would have to be taken care of to win their support of a program which at first would diminish the volume of business they handled for the North America. Managers were paid on a straight commission basis, some with a minimum guarantee. It made no difference to their pocketbooks whether the company made or lost money on what they wrote. When Rush cut off petroleum and refused $145,000 in sugar and cotton income, he deprived the department heads of a sizable amount of revenue. Unless Rush could remedy this condition he would lose some of his best representatives. Accordingly he devised what was called the "contingency commission" by which a manager should be paid a living salary but would make his real money from a cut in the profits on the business he brought in. If no profits, no cut. Thus it would be to a manager's advantage to write good business instead of merely any business.

Rush went to Boston to try his idea on Herbert Damon, the company's agent in that busy underwriting center. Damon also represented other leading companies.

"Herbert, how much do you make a year out of your North America account?" asked the vice-president.

Damon said he averaged about $5,500.

"Would you accept a salary of $5,500 plus expenses plus 10 per cent of what the company makes on your business?"

Damon said he would.

"Before you commit yourself definitely," cautioned Rush, "I must tell you that we will ask you to get rid of a lot of business you've been writing for us in the past; about a quarter of it in fact. But we will give you leads on new business to work up."

Rush mentioned several categories of business. "We've been losing on these risks," he said. "We want to drop them." He mentioned other lines which were profitable. "This business we want to hold and add to. You now limit your liability to $30,000 on a single line. We want you to double your line liability and cut out hedging on reinsurance. If the risk is good enough for us to insure, we want to keep the profits instead of handing them over to our rivals on a silver platter tagged reinsurance. In fact, on the accounts we tell you to hold, the North America will be glad to take everything over the old $30,000 limit."

Damon's enthusiasm subsided. He told Rush he couldn't go along with any such scheme. It looked too much like a paved road to bank-ruptcy. He was being asked to throw out accounts from which he derived some of his fattest fees and at the same time to increase his liabilities. Come a first-class marine disaster, he'd be wiped out, commissions and all, and saddled with a debt to the company he might be years working off.

"Why should I run any risk? I'm doing all right now, taking small lines and spreading the big ones around with reinsurance. That way one wreck can't put me out of business."

Rush countered with concrete proposals to protect Damon's agency and at length the Boston manager agreed to "take a chance."

"You won't be taking a chance," Rush reassured him.

Damon did not go the whole way. He agreed to raise his line lia-bility only $10,000. Rush tried to show him that he was putting a limit on his own income. And so it worked out. At the end of the first year Damon was making more money with his contingency fees than he had ever earned before. The second year he was eager to raise his line to $60,000. Of course in the background of this success was the North America's new classification system which had helped Damon to select the good risks.

As Damon's success was noted in the insurance world, other com-pany representatives became interested, enabling Rush to reorganize the departments on a contingency commission basis. Putting em-ployees in business with the company proved a great step toward promoting the success of the selective-risk program.[6] Everywhere agents went after new, profitable business. This led to the establish-ment of the New Business Department under Harry Farnum at the home office.

The idea was opposed at first. The solicitation of accounts was held to be undignified for an institution occupying the North Ameri-ca's commanding position. Yet Farnum obtained consent to make a trial. Tommy Young and Charles W. Churchman were called from their desks to conduct an old-fashioned door-to-door canvass of Chestnut Street. They brought back several acceptable accounts, largely at the expense of foreign companies. Young proved so good a solicitor that he was sent to Pittsburgh to try for a larger slice of the steel business, which was A No. 1 as a risk. He did so well that the trip was extended over the entire steel area. In Dayton he succeeded in getting the National Cash Register account from a worthy rival.

At the time this was one of the large insurance accounts of the country, and highly desirable because the Cash Register Company packed its goods carefully and paid bills punctually.

The following year, however, the rival got the account back. Young took a train to Dayton. One complaint was that the North America listed the Scandinavian-American Steamship Company as a second-class line, and accordingly charged a higher premium than on goods shipped via first-class lines. Young got the cash register people to say that the North America could have the business again providing the Scandinavian line were reclassified as first-class. Young called Rush on the telephone.

"Nothing doing," said the vice-president.

Young was sorely disappointed, though later he said: "That was characteristic of Rush. When he believed in a program he stuck to it through thick and thin, whatever the immediate disadvantage. It took nerve to turn down that account at that particular time."[7]

Benjamin Rush knew that unless he respected his own rulings others would be unlikely to do so.

6

Eighteen ninety-eight and 1899 were the years of transition. It may not be too much to say that they witnessed the birth of modern, scientific marine underwriting. They were anxious and critical years. There were times when the pressure from those wedded to the old methods was so strong that Rush thought he might have to throw in the sponge, quit the North America and make a fresh start elsewhere. The new business he brought in and the old business he gradually shifted from a losing to a paying plane in no way compensated for the loss of immediate revenue. Moreover, the new regime had been under way only three months when the Spanish-American War started. Fortunately that mercifully brief conflict was virtually uneventful from a marine underwriting standpoint.

The deficit for 1899 reached the staggering total of $764,412. This was in part because the company was still paying losses on a class of business it no longer accepted and in part because 1899 was a "disaster year" at sea. "No less than twenty-six Steamers," recounted the Annual Report, "have sailed out of various ports and never been heard from and seventy-nine Sailing Vessels have sailed away and

"NORTH AMERICA" TO THE RESCUE

This example of early spot-news photography shows the tug *North America* pulling free the ship *Comliebank* of Glasgow grounded on Cape Henlopen, Delaware, in a storm, about 1890.

From a photograph owned by and reproduced by permission of Joseph E. Gibbons, Ridley Park, Pennsylvanna, son of Captain Edward Gibbons, master of the North America.

never reached their destination, and there can be no doubt that the crews and passengers of these vessels are lost. It addition to this eighty-five Sailing Vessels and eleven Steamers were abandoned at sea. As a result of all the losses of the merchant marine of the World, during the past year, 1141 vessels, representing a tonnage of 820,000, were destroyed."

The report admitted that "in the face of the heavy disasters of the year ... it required some courage to persevere" in the course Rush had laid. The report closed with a note of optimism. All losses had been sustained in the first eight months of the year. Since September 1 the marine account had shown a profit which had increased month by month. "It is a reasonable supposition that the business is at last on a paying basis."[8]

Possibly some stockholders with good memories accepted this statement with an air of reserve. In years past similarly cheerful predictions had been unfulfilled. At the close of 1900, however, the company was able to report a marine profit of $241,513—the first in six years. In 1901 the profit was $360,447.

Rush had been in office four years. Believing the battle won, he submitted a concise account of his stewardship.

"During the years 1888/97 the Company lost as follows:

PETROLEUM:
Net premiums . . . . $ 286,859
Losses 479,713

Loss—10 years . . . . $ 192,854
A yearly average of . . . . . $ 19,285

GENERAL CARGO:
Net premiums 82,701
Losses 184,859

Loss—10 years . . . . $ 102,158
A yearly average of 10,215

COTTON:
Net premiums $3,711,510
Losses 4,511,458

Loss—10 years . . . . $ 799,948
A yearly average of 79,994

MISCELLANEOUS:
Premiums $1,300,242
Losses   1,568,645
                                   ——————————
Loss—10 years . . . . $ 268,403
    A yearly average of   26,840
SUGAR:
Premiums $1,315,600
Losses   1,598,900
                                   ——————————
Loss—10 years . . . . $ 283,300
    A yearly average of   28,330
                                                        ————————
                                                       $164,664
                                                        ————————
making a yearly total of say . . . $ 165,000
which, for 10 years, equals . . . $1,650,000
                                                    ——————————

"During the years 1900/1901, these classifications resulted approximately as follows:
Net premiums $1,030,000
Net losses   920,000
                                  ——————————
Gain . . . . $ 110,000

or, an average of $55,000 per year, so that we may say that our revision of our business has resulted in a saving of about $220,000 a year on these classifications alone, in addition to the saving in Reinsurance Account," which Rush put at $189,000 a year.

In two sentences Rush gave the credit for this transformation to the classification system. "It embodies over 200 subdivisions as against 13 [exclusive of reinsurance] previously in use, and it has therefore proved of great value in indicating what was good and what was bad business. Our underwriting course of action today is largely based on what it has taught us."

The New Business Department, which had had to fight its way against prejudice, was coming into its own. It, too, had set up a sort of classification system.

"We examine carefully the records of exports and imports of the country to see if we are getting our share. Then we secure lists of all persons or firms importing and exporting merchandise, and those engaged in a desirable business are communicated with, and their business secured, if possible. If not secured, a careful record is kept of the business of each merchant, for future reference, so that when opportunity comes he may be again approached on the subject. We have now on our files lists comprising about Four thousand names of merchants and others engaged in importing or exporting, many of whom we can hope to secure as policy holders of the Company."

The report closed with an allusion to that imponderable which the marine underwriter must ever take into account—luck:

"Finally we must not flatter ourselves that all the improvement is due to our own wisdom. Time and chance happen to all Companies, as well as all men, and it may be that good fortune has had much to do with the gratifying result."[9]

Luck may have been *a* factor in the pleasing results for 1900 and 1901 but it wasn't *the* factor. This is borne out by the circumstance that for nineteen consecutive years thereafter the North America made a profit on marine operations. This record of twenty-one years of uninterrupted marine operating profits has rarely been equalled by a single company in the long history of the industry. It was not made by luck. In 1897 Benjamin Rush had found the formula for success for which experts had been searching for fifteen years. It rescued the North America and changed the course of marine underwriting.

CHAPTER XIII

The Drama of San Francisco

I

WHILE the marine branch was weathering the vexed interval of 1885-1900, the fire branch lost money during only two of those sixteen years. Its profits for the period, aggregating $3,820,522, explain the ability of the company to continue a 12-per-cent annual dividend.

Fire was able to make money while marine sank deeper into the quicksands of deficit because fire kept abreast of the times. Electricity came in—for lighting, for power, for traction—creating a host of new problems. "There had begun to be a marked increase in losses in the better class of risks," writes one chronicler of the period. "The companies were suffering where they had felt most secure. Could the spirit of arson [much in the minds of insurance men at the time] be spreading among our best citizens? This was unthinkable. Then they suddenly awakened to a consciousness that the hidden enemy was *electricity*. The world had entered upon a new age."[1]

In August 1892 an emergency meeting of insurance electrical inspectors was called by the National Board of Fire Underwriters. The result was a code to govern installations. Fires from defective wiring fell off. So much for only one example of how fire insurance kept on top of its problems.

The rejuvenated National Board made fire prevention its particular work. Rate problems were left in the hands of the regional associations formed in the eighties. Companies contending for safe rates found themselves in conflict with the anti-monopoly zeal of state legislatures. Nor were legislatures the sole obstacles.

"The difficulty of reform is very great," noted the Annual Report of the Insurance Company of North America covering 1899, "owing to the large number of Companies which refuse to join any agreement, but remain outside with the hope of making a profit by shading premiums fixed by the old line Companies and also by the payment of larger brokerage and agency commissions. Adverse legislation in almost every state of the Union is also an important factor, and the conduct of the business is attended with more and more difficulty. The average legislator fails to recognize the difference between Trusts which are inimical to public welfare, and an agreement between Insurance Companies to charge certain fair rates for their policies."

Would another Chicago or another Boston be necessary to bring people to their senses? Perhaps not. The North America was able to conclude the report just quoted with the assurance that "a decided check in the downward tendency and demoralization of rates" had become apparent.

2

In 1895 the North America took an important step in the sharpening competition for good fire business by sponsoring the organization of a company known as the Philadelphia Underwriters. This corporation was a forerunner of the modern development through subsidiaries. The circumstances attending its creation were these.

In addition to his able representation of the North America as manager of the Western Department, in 1872 J. F. Downing had become general agent in the Middle West for the Pennsylvania Fire Insurance Company. For this company he built up an organization of local and state agents, field men and adjusters, which he ran from his headquarters in Erie, also the administrative seat of the Western Department of the North America. Earnings from the two companies made Downing a wealthy man. In 1894 the Pennsylvania decided to move its midwestern headquarters to Chicago with a new chief in charge.

Downing saw no reason why the organization he had created should go to this man as a gift. He suggested the formation of a new company, owned jointly by the North America and "one other Philadelphia fire insurance company," to take over the agency setup in question. His argument mentioned several advantages. Two agents in a community, working in the same interest, could obtain more business than one. The Phoenix of Hartford had recently placed a second agent in towns of importance. The Royal of London had established the Queen as its American subsidiary; and the Hartford of Hartford "has duplicated itself in the form of the New York Underwriters." Half interest in a second company would also give the North America advantageous reinsurance facilities. On top of this the new concern would start out with a midwestern field organization ready made. So argued Downing.[2]

The plan was adopted. The North America selected as its partner in the enterprise the Fire Association of Philadelphia, an insurance company formed in 1817 by volunteer firemen. Since 1871 when the volunteers had been superseded by professional firemen, the Fire Association had made great strides and in 1894 it was one of the large companies of the country. The offspring of this union began business on January 1, 1895, and was called the Philadelphia Underwriters. Immediately successful, it gradually extended operations to include other parts of the country.

In 1903 net fire premiums of the North America—the parent company—reached the new high figure of $4,994,000 of which $723,000 was profit—also a new high. It was, of course, a lucky year, with an abnormally low loss ratio. Insurance men know that two such years rarely come together. The instance in point was no exception. Nineteen hundred and four also proved a record year— but for losses. They totalled $3,284,900—$800,000 more than in 1903.

Four exceptional fires within a space of 115 days counted for the bulk of the excess: Yazoo, Mississippi, $32,744; Toronto, Canada, $126,107; Rochester, New York, $28,704; Baltimore, Maryland, $507,292.

The Baltimore conflagration was the country's most disastrous fire since Boston in 1872. At 10:48 on the morning of February 7 an automatic electrical fire alarm in a building at Liberty and German Streets gave the first notice. Firemen found a small blaze in the basement near an elevator shaft and were dealing with it, as they thought, successfully when a tremendous explosion wrecked the building and spread the flames. The cause of the blast was a mystery. Firemen called it a "smoke explosion." A stiff wind kept the flames beyond control until the following day. Seventy blocks, representing a loss of about $90,000,000, were burned.

Special Agent John O. Platt was summoned from an adjusting job in Roanoke, Virginia, to take care of the North America's losses at

Baltimore. A nephew of the president of the company, John Platt
had gone to work for it as an office boy in 1891 when he was seventeen years old. With two adjusters to help him, Platt cleaned up the
situation in six weeks and returned to Philadelphia with a mass of
interesting notes on building construction. Many of the buildings
burned were supposed to have been fireproof, a term then rather
freely used in insurance as well as in lay circles. Mr. Platt's observa-
tions and a great many others were incorporated in a 130-page study
issued by the National Fire Protection Association. The report began
with the assertion that "the old term 'fireproof,' so obviously a misnomer when applied to any sort of building, is herein discarded in
favor of 'fire-resistive.' "[3] The well-documented lessons of Baltimore
were helpful to underwriters, and had a good effect on future
building.

The North America took these big fires in its stride, paying losses
immediately and still returning a profit, on fire, of $157,000 for the
year.

At the suggestion of Benjamin Rush in December of the same year
(1904), the Alliance Insurance Company was organized to do a fire
and marine business. The capital of $500,000 was represented by
50,000 shares of $10 par. Though not strictly a subsidiary of the
North America, it was near akin. A majority of the Alliance stockholders were also stockholders in the North America. The management of the two companies was almost identical, Charles Platt being
president of the Alliance, Eugene L. Ellison and Benjamin Rush vice-
presidents, Greville E. Fryer (secretary of the North America)
treasurer, and Henry W. Farnum secretary. The new company used
the North America's corps of special agents. The reasons for setting
up the Alliance were the same as those mentioned by Downing
when the Philadelphia Underwriters was brought into being. The
main object on which Rush laid the most stress, however, was to
create a reinsurance facility for the North America which would
keep more good business in the family.

The new concern started off nicely. In 1905 it earned a fire profit
of $161,000, a marine profit of $36,000 and paid a modest dividend.
The North America, too, did well in 1905: fire profit $752,000—
another record-breaker—and marine profit $209,000.

Then came 1906—and the greatest "shock loss" in fire-insurance
history: San Francisco.

3

The earthquake struck on April 18 at 5:15 in the morning, Pacific time, or 8:15 Eastern time, knocking out all telegraph and telephone connections. Something over an hour later one Postal wire was opened to Chicago over which Philadelphia received the first jumbled details of the catastrophe. Succeeding bulletins mentioned the fires that were springing up among the shaken buildings. In an hour the Postal wire went dead—melted by flames as it later transpired. Not until afternoon was communication re-established from Oakland across the bay. By that time San Francisco was a furnace.

Newspapers banner-lined the word "Earthquake." The fire seemed definitely a secondary consideration—a mere burning of the debris of a city demolished by the convulsion. Thoughts running through the agitated minds along Insurance Row were reflected by this headline in the Philadelphia *Press:*

"NO FIRE INSURANCE FOR
BUILDINGS THROWN DOWN"

As most American companies were not permitted by their charters to write insurance against damage by earthquake, the burden of the article was that the companies would be liable for fire damage only. If a house were thrown down by the 'quake and then swept by fire, insurance could not be collected. But if that fire should spread to a house not damaged, or not badly damaged, by earthquake the owner could collect on his fire loss.

San Francisco burned for three days, leaving the richest parts of the city a ruin. Communication was still difficult, the North America not having heard a word from its San Francisco office. The East remained under the impression that the greater part of the destruction had been by earthquake. Insurance men in particular did not fail to take account of this. In any event their losses would be terrific—probably the greatest in our history. Towering, white-haired Charles Platt, seventy-seven years old, strode through the offices at 232 Walnut like a kindly grenadier, cheering up subordinates. He reminded them of Chicago, Boston and Baltimore. "And we don't intend to let San Francisco frighten us, either." To department managers he sent this telegram:

"IF THE ENTIRE CITY IS DESTROYED OUR SURPLUS AND CONTINGENT FUND WILL NOT BE EXHAUSTED. OUR LOSSES WILL BE AS PROMPTLY PAID AS THEY CAN BE ADJUSTED."[4]

On Sunday, April 22, Mr. Platt further clarified the position of the North America in one of his rare statements to the press:

"We have already wired our [San Francisco] representatives to draw at sight on us to pay every claim proved. This shows how we stand. But, of course, where buildings have been destroyed by the earthquake and not by fire no insurance will be paid. If the building was shaken down and the ruins then swept by fire a compromise will be reached and a just portion of the insurance will be paid. In the case of buildings blown up by dynamite by civil or military authorities we are exempted by a clause in our policy, but I think the companies will pay insurance as the buildings were destroyed in an effort to stop the fire."[5]

Exclusive of reinsurance, the North America's risks in San Francisco totaled $3,740,000; those of the Alliance $1,296,000; and of the Philadelphia Underwriters $712,000. Already machinery was in motion to meet the losses, whatever they might be. Cash was accumulated and Vice-President Ellison, in charge of the fire branch, was in conference with Special Agent Sheldon Catlin, of the Pittsburgh office, who had been chosen to superintend the adjustments and payments. Ellison and Catlin spent the greater part of Sunday, April 22, together. The special agent was a young man, newly married, who had been with the company only seven months. That he should have been selected to go to San Francisco is testimony of the excellent impression he had made in that short time. President Platt, in his statement to the newspapers, had laid down the company's general policy governing settlements. Ellison amplified this by telling Catlin to use his judgment, and to act in concert with "the leading and best companies." Ellison estimated the North America's maximum liability at $2,000,000, with those of the Alliance and the Underwriters in proportion. This was based on newspaper reports, which emphasized earthquake damage. There was still no word from the company's San Francisco office.

Catlin boarded an evening train for Pittsburgh. With his bride he continued toward the Coast to tackle the North America's end of what proved to be the biggest adjustment problem in fire-insurance history as expressed in dollars and cents; also the most complicated and controversial.

4

Shortly after Catlin's departure on Sunday, April 22, the North America received its first tidings from the San Francisco office. The telegram, dated Oakland, read:

"OFFICE AND RECORDS OF COUNTRY DEPARTMENT DESTROYED. NO MAIL OR WIRE CAN REACH CITY. ADDRESS 532 SAN PABLO AVENUE OAKLAND.
"JAMES D. BAILEY."[6]

James D. Bailey was the company's general agent in the San Francisco territory. A retired sea captain in his sixties, he was a jovial, expansive personality and a good business getter. But what his telegram neglected to say was more important than what it did say. Country records and office destroyed. Were the city records saved, then? And what about losses? Evidently the old captain's faculties were still pretty badly shaken.

On Monday, April 23, came a wire from J. K. Hamilton, a special agent attached to the San Francisco office:

"OUR LOSS ESTIMATED FROM CITY PREMIUMS ABOUT THREE MILLION. NO MESSAGE FROM YOU."[7]

Three million! Surely Hamilton was ignoring the distinction between earthquake and fire damage.

Further word from Hamilton placed the Alliance loss at probably $600,000. He omitted to say anything on the vital subject of relative earthquake and fire damage.

Mr. Platt's statement and the North America's general reputation for prompt and liberal settlements brought a reaction from other insurance companies. "We have reinsured your Company upon property in San Francisco," one wrote, "and we beg to advise you that this Company will pay only such losses as it may be legally liable for." These, the letter continued, would not include "any loss or damage by fire or otherwise, occasioned directly or indirectly by earthquake or other specially exempted perils." This seemed to mean that it intended to pay no losses at all in San Francisco. The company which sent this letter had been hard hit by the Baltimore fire. But other companies in better circumstances, also began to press the North America to be "reasonable."

The next word of importance from the Coast came on May 5 in a letter from Catlin written the day after his arrival. The company's safe had cooled off sufficiently to be opened and all but a few of the city records were found undamaged. Some of the other companies had been less fortunate—all their papers having burned to a crisp in the red-hot vaults. Continued Catlin:

"I find that the earthquake damage is comparatively slight in San Francisco, the great loss being occasioned by fire. We can count upon very little salvage."[8]

This was astonishing news. Wishful thinking doubtless having something to do with it, eastern underwriters were prepared to believe that not more than 50 per cent of the damage had been caused by fire, despite the protestations of the California newspapers.

The real blow came on May 6, in a telegram from Catlin which arrived nine minutes before midnight:

"ESTIMATE NORTH AMERICA [LOSS] FOUR MILLION FOUR HUNDRED THOUSAND GROSS, THREE MILLION TWO HUNDRED THOUSAND NET. ALLIANCE ONE MILLION TWO HUNDRED THOUSAND GROSS, ONE MILLION ONE HUNDRED THOUSAND NET. SALVAGE ESTIMATED TEN PER CENT INCLUDING EARTHQUAKE."

In a covering letter Catlin substituted exact figures for the round figures used in the wire and gave a modest account of the almost incredible amount of work he had done, under difficult circumstances, to obtain them. These figures, the adjuster pointed out, were not random guesses. They were scientific estimates which Catlin insisted further investigation would prove to be "very close." The adjuster reiterated his unpalatable assertion that earthquake damage was "small." "I understand there were no buildings of any particular value which collapsed before the fire. Those which did were those of greatest age, poorest construction and least value. There has been generally published a report that the companies might insist on deducting 40% from face of policies for earthquake damage through-out the city. My individual opinion is that any such average ratio would be absolutely unjust to assured."[9]

5

Catlin's dismaying figures brought a fuller realization of the situation. Should they stand up, North America had received its hardest single blow. Alliance was "burned up," in the language of one veteran employee: its net assets more than wiped out. Ample precedent existed for the relief of insurance companies in such desperate straits: bankruptcy. Already a few companies, less hard hit in San Francisco than Alliance, were taking steps toward that end. Charles Platt refused to consider the thought for an instant. Summoning the Alliance directors he laid the situation before them in its worst light. In addition to existing capital and surplus, $750,000 might be needed to keep the company going. This came to $15 for each share of stock outstanding. Without ado a $15 assessment was voted, $10—totaling $500,000—to be paid within thirty days and $5 to be paid when called for. Thus Alliance prepared to satisfy its San Francisco policyholders dollar for dollar if need be.[10]

The North America took steps toward the same end, though these were not of the heroic nature necessitated by the extreme plight of the Alliance. The sale of some securities and the pledging of others could care for the maximum losses of three million plus, if it should develop that policies were to be paid at face value.

It should be borne in mind that at the time they were taken these were merely precautionary measures. Until Catlin expressed the straightforward opinion that a deduction of 40 per cent from the face value of policies for earthquake damage would be unjust, there had been no serious thought of paying in full. Mr. Platt had made this clear in his statement to the press while the city was still in flames. The theory of part payment rested on high estimates of earthquake damage, which the eastern offices declined to relinquish. Ellison was in touch with the heads of several of the largest companies. Their view was that from 40 to 60 per cent should be deducted for earthquake damage. One large Philadelphia company put Ellison on notice that its attorney had given an opinion that the payment of earthquake losses would be illegal. Some of the North America's reinsurers continued to importune against full payment, and in one case to hint at recourse to law to avert participation in such a course.

Ellison refused to commit the North America. Sensing that the companies might have reason to revise their views on receipt of advices from their men on the spot in California, the vice-president wrote Catlin in considerable detail what was taking place on the eastern front. He asked Catlin to consult with the San Francisco representatives of "the best companies." "We fancy that any company that will refuse to pay for losses [fairly] adjusted . . . will soon be in bad odor." Ellison was writing in this vein when Catlin penned his protest against a 40-per-cent cut.[11]

The arrival of this protest in Philadelphia darkened the prospect still more. Ellison continued to report that other companies insisted that 40-per-cent cuts, at least, would represent fair adjustments.

At the other end of the line young Sheldon Catlin struggled amid difficulties which would have overwhelmed a more easily swayed or a less able man. Though many companies had set up temporary offices in Oakland, Catlin had established himself in Bailey's residence on the edge of the burned district so as to be more accessible to policyholders. They descended in droves. Within fifteen days a thousand claims were in his hands. The Bailey house was besieged by people wanting money and needing it. With the San Francisco office staff reorganized as an adjustment unit, Catlin took up the claims one by one. At times short of such simple necessaries as pens and writing paper, he worked from dawn to dusk, power having been shut off and lights forbidden by the army which had taken over the running of the ruined city. In such a situation no policy except firmness would have succeeded. Catlin was as firm and as straightforward with his home office as with the throngs clamoring for settlements. When Philadelphia questioned his figures on aggregate losses he defended them. He stuck to his estimate of 10 per cent for salvage. He reiterated the opinion that anything like an overall 40-per-cent cut would be unfair to policyholders and prejudicial to the reputation of the company. He asked for two expert adjusters from the East, specifying that they should be strong men physically.

"The damage by earthquake has, in my opinion, been greatly overestimated in Eastern reports," insisted Catlin. "From what I have seen as well as from careful investigation from the most reliable sources, I cannot see how there could have been over a 10% general damage at the outside. It is to be regretted that I cannot give you more encouraging figures but must of course tell you the truth as it appears to me. . . . It looks very much as if the weaker companies and even some of the larger companies which have been very hard hit are doing what they can to *maximize* the extent and amount of the earthquake damage.

"There is one particular section comprising two or three blocks where the buildings are untouched by fire but are in a very bad condition of collapse from earthquake alone. This section has been often photographed and the results are sent East as a fair illustration of the earthquake loss. These photographs are entirely misleading as that particular section comprised the limits of a former creek and pond which had been filled in and built upon and the buildings themselves are of cheap and poor construction."[12]

The home office had asked Catlin to report on what the other companies were doing. In almost daily letters he rounded out the picture as it unfolded before him.

"There are a number of independent adjusters here from the East and it looks as if they were acting under instructions to make as much as possible out of the earthquake damage. I am not trying to minimize the earthquake damage. I wish I could prove it to have been 50% but I can only report the situation as I believe it to be. Some of the representatives of companies very close to your office entirely disagree with me, whether from disinterested motives or not I cannot say."

Thus wrote Catlin on May 18, continuing: "Each company is acting on its own ideas and they differ very materially." Several companies had clauses in their policies specifically exempting them from damage by earthquake. One or two of these nevertheless were adjusting small losses on contents at undivulged and varying reductions. Another was denying all liability. A Brooklyn company with no earthquake clause was exaggerating earthquake damage. A Philadelphia company with which the North America had close relations had begun payments, "deducting a percentage (apparently whatever they can get) from the face of the policy, either as earthquake loss or for some other reason." Certain New York companies were named as doing the same. On the other hand the Hartford and the

London, Liverpool and Globe were paying small losses in full, taking 2-per-cent discounts for cash. The Aetna was paying without discount.

The plain-speaking adjuster gave his opinion of these proceedings.

"In my judgment the companies (even though they include some of the best) which are deducting a percentage from the face of their policies in settlement are not doing the right thing, although they maintain that it is perfectly justifiable and that their claimants make little complaint. It is comparatively easy, with those small policy holders who need the money badly, to obtain these reductions by paying immediately. But when it comes to the larger ones who can resist it they will demand full settlements and I think they will get them. There is simply no doubt that some of the oldest, fairest and most liberal companies are, in the face of such tremendous losses, adopting tactics which they never used before in order to save themselves."[13]

On the following day, May 19, Catlin added another installment. An adjuster from a Brooklyn company had brought in a claim in which the Brooklyn company, a second company and the North America all were interested. Catlin named the companies in his letter.

"This adjuster says the loss will be total without doubt and they have no evidences of earthquake damage, but we are asked to co-operate with the other two companies in a demand for a 30% deduction from face of policies for a settlement. He stated confidentially that his company is following that course in all cases and if the assured refuses to stand such a cut, he is told that he must wait indefinitely. He usually accepts the reduced amount rather than wait months for his money. This adjuster admitted that such action was really unjustifiable and unfair but, said he, 'we are going to shave them all down and get all that we possibly can out of this earthquake business; all of the big Companies are doing the same thing.'"

Catlin said that the North America was not doing it. He refused to co-operate with the Brooklyn adjuster.[14]

Three days later, on May 22, Catlin wrote with obvious satisfaction that he had something "pleasing to report."

"It appears that at least the following named companies are *not* taking advantage of the earthquake in order to 'shave' their losses, but are paying in full where legally liable: Aetna, Royal, Hartford, Continental and Liverpool, London & Globe. I have lately talked with the chief representatives of the Aetna, Hartford and Continental and they all say that the earthquake damage overall would be more than covered by 10% of values and declare it to be absolutely unjust to take a percentage off the face of their policies as so many companies are doing. . . .

"Many companies have not sufficient capital and surplus to pay their losses here and are mentally justifying themselves for their line of action. But for solvent companies there is in my judgment only one right course. We cannot afford, in my opinion, to act in accord with . . . [those who] are deliberately playing upon the earthquake feature in order to reduce their losses. . . . I recommend that you definitely instruct us to adopt the policy of the Aetna and other companies which are paying in full as liable."[15]

Without waiting for the instructions he solicited, Catlin took the bull by the horns. He began paying claims "where there are no earthquake or other complications." Under the head of "other complications" would have come the case involving the Brooklyn company which was insisting on a heavy deduction. And Catlin paid these claims in full, "just as the Aetna and L. L. & G. and others were doing."[16]

6

In Philadelphia Vice-President Ellison was having his troubles as well. Pressure against settlements in full increased rather than diminished, despite accumulating evidence that earthquake damage had not been nearly so high as first supposed. This pressure came from companies, some of which were linked to the North America as reinsurers. Several of these companies were in financial hot water, though this could have been relieved had they the courage to do as Alliance had done. The pressure came also from frightened North America stockholders. Many of these were also stockholders in Alliance who had already paid in $10 a share to save that company from the stigma of receivership and were liable for $5 more. They were moved by an understandable desire to avert an assessment on their North America stock. Had this happened some of the stockholders themselves might have been forced to the wall.

This was the state of affairs when Catlin's letters of May 18 and 19 arrived, containing sketchy details of the mixed character of the settlements being made by adjusters who were on the scene: some few settling in full; others clinging to the fiction (as Catlin put it) of high earthquake losses, and shaving accordingly. Catlin's spirited representations ran counter to what Ellison was hearing in certain home offices; and they would have been very bad reading for the scared and importuning stockholders. Moreover, Catlin was a new man; his judgment might be at fault. In response to Catlin's request, two other adjusters were on the way West. They were J. C. Johnston of Cincinnati and H. N. Friedley of Indianapolis, trusted men long in the company's service. Ellison desired to know whether they would support Catlin's ideas. In the meantime Ellison, himself, hesitated to accept them, and under date of May 25 forwarded the following instructions to San Francisco:

"We have given this subject much consideration and have consulted with many Companies, and have reached the conclusion, which agrees with their views, that it is our duty to our Companies to see that our policyholders bear some portion of the burden. We are called upon to make good losses for which we received no consideration from our policyholders, whether they suffered from the earthquake or not, and as in the case of the Alliance, we are calling upon our stockholders to contribute a large sum to help pay for losses, they in turn think it is only fair that policyholders should bear some portion of the burden and not expect us to bear it all. We therefore desire to avail ourselves of the privilege of settling our losses on the same terms as the Companies interested with us. . . .

"It is not necessary for us to proclaim what we are willing to do, or to say that we will pay any definite amount or percentage, but we can pay as others do, as the adjustments are made, under each policy as it comes before us. We are not at all fearful of any bad results that may come by reason of compromise settlements. You are therefore authorized to make such compromise settlements as may be made by such Companies as mentioned in your letter, and pay as they do."

Mr. Ellison said it was unnecessary for Catlin to proclaim what he was going to do because these were intended as tentative instructions merely.

"We are just in receipt of a request from a committee of the Strongest Companies to attend a meeting in New York to formulate a plan whereby an equitable and fair adjustment of the liabilities of the Company can be secured. This meeting is expected to include pretty much all of the Companies that can be reached. We suggest that this information be kept confidential for the present. We hope to write you definitely on Wednesday as to the course to be pursued. Meanwhile we can pay losses as other Companies are doing."[17]

Before Ellison got to the New York meeting, however, he read Catlin's letter of May 25, making a still stronger case for settlements in full and requesting definite instructions. After an exchange of telegrams Ellison consented to the payment in full of "uncomplicated" claims. Then the vice-president learned to his surprise that this was what the independent Mr. Catlin already was doing.[18]

7

On May 31 the meeting of underwriting executives, of which Ellison had spoken, was held in the offices of the Phenix Insurance Company of Brooklyn. As far as the North America was concerned the only result of that conclave was to expose the North America to some very undesirable publicity. It is necessary, however, to take up events in their order.

According to the list given to the New York newspapers and appended to the record of the meeting's deliberations, seventeen companies were represented—all by high officials. Though Mr. Ellison was present, the North America's name did not appear on the list of the seventeen subscribing companies. Nor did this list comprise, as Mr. Ellison had anticipated, the "strongest companies" in the East. Several of the stronger companies—then settling in full at San Francisco—were conspicuous by their absence. Of the seventeen concerns listed as present only five were ultimately to settle in full, taking at best a 2-per-cent discount for cash. Virtually all the other concerns were what Catlin would have called "shavers." So much for the company amid which Mr. Ellison found himself.

The meeting adopted a resolution on settlements, as follows:

1. Where a building had fallen before the fire reached it nothing should be paid.

2. Payment on buildings and on goods destroyed by the authorities subsequent to the conflagration should be held up pending investigation of each case.

3. To be settled by "reasonable compromise": buildings and goods destroyed by the authorities to check the spread of flames; buildings damaged but not destroyed by earthquake; cases covering property whose owners by reason of the destruction of their records were unable to supply proofs of value as required by the letter of their policies.

4. Other claims to be paid in full after proper deductions for salvage.[19]

Ellison forwarded the resolution to Catlin with the suggestion that it should "make the way easier to reach a satisfactory adjustment of our losses." He said it was the sense of the meeting that "reasonable compromise" cases be adjusted "on a basis of from 10% to 50%, depending upon the conditions of each loss." "We beg to assure you," Ellison added, "that we have no idea of dealing unfairly with our policyholders. At the same time it is only right that we see that the interests of the company are fairly guarded." Catlin was asked to say if there was anything in the resolution which he felt that he could not "honorably follow."[20]

Before anything could be settled between the home office and Catlin on that basis, however, the fat was in the fire. The New York resolution got a warm reception from the people and the newspapers of San Francisco. The newspapers were out to get all they could from the insurance companies—an attitude which would be more susceptible of criticism were it not for the fact that so many of the companies seemed out to pay as little as they could. On June 12 the representatives of 107 companies met in Oakland to take a definite stand on the resolution. Catlin and the other adjusters, Johnston and Friedley, represented the North America and the Alliance.

The session was not a tranquil one. A Brooklyn company led a fight to impose a straight 33⅓-per-cent cut on all cases in the "reasonable-compromise" category. After objections the figure was reduced to 25 per cent. During the debate the representatives of three of the seventeen companies officially represented at the New York meeting arose and said that their home offices were opposed to any horizontal cut. Each case should be settled on its merits. Thus far none of these three companies—Home, Hartford and Queen—had made any cuts at all. Every claim had been settled in full. Catlin would have liked to join in this repudiation of the horizontal-cut idea, for the North America and the crippled Alliance thus far had settled every claim in full. But just before going to the meeting Catlin had received a wire from Ellison that the North America was in favor of 33⅓-per-cent reductions in "reasonable-compromise" cases.

A vote was called on the 25-per-cent proposition. Representatives of fourteen companies whose policies contained earthquake exemption clauses were excused from voting. Of the others 32 voted against the cut and 61 in favor of it. Catlin cast the votes of the North America and the Alliance with the majority.[21]

As soon as the meeting was over Catlin, Johnston and Friedley jointly signed a telegram to the home office. They said they had voted for the cut "under instructions" though "our judgment [is] against it. North America apparently only solvent company supporting resolution. People here know company solvent and will not accept reduction as they will from others."[22]

The wire was followed by a letter in which the three adjusters urged a repudiation of the vote for the resolution. "It puts us in a position where we do not belong."[23]

This episode furnished the home office with the first clear statement of the position of Johnston and Friedley who had reached San Francisco only a few days before. Certainly the hope in the breasts of some of the stockholders had been that Johnston and Friedley could find grounds for dissenting from Catlin's insistence on settling in full.

The complete accord among the adjusters seems to have done much to convince Mr. Ellison that the New York meeting had made a mistake. The three adjusters were heartened by an immediate response from Ellison who acted on their telegram without waiting for the covering letter. "We leave this matter in your hands," wired Ellison, to settle losses as they should see fit. "We will be very glad to have you write us freely . . . [of] the policy being pursued by such companies as the Home, German-American, L. L. & G., Royal, Aetna, Hartford and others as our course will have to be largely in accord with those companies."[24]

It delighted Catlin to be able to report that the six companies named were honoring policies at face value, the German-American

GREATEST FIRE "SHOCK LOSS": SAN FRANCISCO, 1906

This disaster caused a heated controversy as to relative destruction by fire and by earthquake. For earthquake damage companies not liable. First reports greatly overestimated this damage. Twenty-seven of 105 companies paid in full; North America's share, $3,260,000. Forty-one companies paid over seventy-five cents on dollar, thirty-seven under.

Photograph by Underwood & Underwood.

refusing to take advantage of its earthquake exemption clause. Five of the companies had voted against the 25-per-cent cut. The German-American had been excused from voting.

Though Ellison's reversal of position came promptly, his telegram did not reach San Francisco in time to prevent the inclusion of the North America and the Alliance in the published list of companies declaring for cut-rate settlements. The San Francisco newspapers had some hard names for these underwriters. One headline:

71 COMPANIES
WILL BUNKO
THE POLICY
HOLDERS

THUS FAR ONLY THIRTY-TWO INSURANCE CONCERNS MAKE PRETENCE TO HONESTY.[25]

The figure 71 was a typographical slip for 61. There followed in blackface type a roster of the companies which had voted for the 25-per-cent cut. The list was republished throughout the country. Repercussions against the North America were immediate and unpleasant. J. F. Downing urged the company to publicize its disavowal of the 25-per-cent arrangement. This was done in a telegram to the New York *Journal of Commerce* and to the Chicago *Record-Herald* which was widely reprinted:

"Philadelphia, June 18, 1906.

"All reports from San Francisco, or elsewhere, representing that the Insurance Company of North America has proposed to settle its San Francisco losses on the basis of a flat reduction of 25%, or any other percent, are untrue. Not a cent less than strict honesty and square dealing demand will be offered the insured; anything different would be contrary to the uniform record of the Company for more than a hundred years. Every loss is being taken up, adjusted and paid on its merits, or as equal and exact justice may dictate. No more can be asked, and no less will be given. If, in any case, a deduction is called for on account of earthquake damage, which is not covered by a policy of fire insurance, no more than what is just and reasonable is asked or expected.

"Adjustments on the above basis are rapidly progressing.
"CHARLES PLATT"[26]

8

Adjustments and settlements so continued to the end. In all, the
North America paid $3,260,000 and the Alliance $1,032,000. These
figures reveal the almost uncanny accuracy of Sheldon Catlin's
estimates of May 7 which the home office had thought much too
high. At that time, after a week's survey of the situation, Catlin had
forecast losses of $3,195,000 for the North America and $1,111,000
for the Alliance.

During the first six weeks of his stay on the Coast there had
been times when Catlin feared that the penalty of his refusal to fall
in with the views of the majority on the ethics of shaving settlements would be dismissal. But he did not waver because he was
sure he was right, and sure that the home office was not getting the
true picture. Instead of firing his strong-minded adjuster, Vice-
President Ellison sent Catlin a $500 bonus and an offer of the joint
managership of the San Francisco office, with the idea of ultimately
succeeding Bailey. Catlin declined the post because he did not care
to make his home in the West. Advancement in the company came
steadily, however. In 1910 Catlin was elected assistant secretary, in
1916 vice-president. When he retired in 1941, Sheldon Catlin was
rated among the leading fire-insurance executives of the country.

San Francisco contributed a wealth of material to our growing
knowledge of the science of prevention. Of several studies of the
individual performances of the insurance companies involved, the
most complete and perhaps the most reliable is that of Professor
Whitney of the University of California. According to Whitney six
companies paid one hundred cents on the dollar. Twenty-one others
also paid in full, less 1- or 2-per-cent discounts for cash. The North
America and the Alliance are on this list. Nineteen paid ninety
cents and up. In that category Whitney places the Philadelphia
Underwriters, jointly owned by the North America and the Fire
Association of Philadelphia. Four companies settled for eighty cents
and up. One of these was the Fire Association of Philadelphia.
Twenty-eight paid seventy-five and up; eight below seventy-five and
up; eighteen less than seventy-five. Five companies went into re-

ceivership and eventually paid something. Four European companies denied liability because of the earthquake and paid nothing.

The record is better than those of Chicago and Boston, showing the increased strength of the companies. Nearly all concerns not settling in full excused themselves on ground of financial necessity. Had they been willing to make the sacrifices the Alliance demanded of its stockholders, it seems that most of them could have paid up. Because of a lack of public confidence some of the low-paying companies never fully recovered and all had hard sledding. Companies which settled in full, or close to it, were the recipients of a windfall of applications for insurance such as a disaster always puts in motion. After paying its regular dividend of 12 per cent, the North America closed the year with a working surplus of $1,042,000. Alliance was on its feet in three years' time when dividends were resumed on a 6-per-cent basis.

9

An interesting sidelight on the San Francisco conflagration was an exchange of letters between Charles Platt and Jacob B. Levison, then second vice-president of the Fireman's Fund Insurance Company of San Francisco. Relations between these companies were close. The North America had no marine department on the Pacific Coast, being content with a reinsurance agreement with the Fireman's Fund whose profitable marine branch was principally the inspiration of Mr. Levison. The San Francisco company was also heavily involved in local fire risks. When the blow fell it was clear that even the sternest measures of self-denial on the part of the company to keep afloat would fail without the co-operation of the policyholders.

A proposal was made to pay part of each valid claim in cash. For the balance policyholders were asked to accept stock in a reorganized Fireman's Fund Company. While policyholders considered the offer, the officers of the company passed anxious days and nights. Fearing a rejection Mr. Levison came to the conclusion that the company's marine branch should cut away from the fire branch and thus save something from the wreck. He believed that "no company would ever again be able to do both a fire and a marine business."[27] With the settlement controversy at its height, on June 16

Mr. Levison wrote Charles Platt a long letter outlining the reasons which had led to this conclusion:

"The majority of the companies interested in the San Francisco conflagration appear to be assuming the position, slowly but surely, that they are not liable to the full amount of their policies, and it looks very much as if ultimately, adjustment will have to be made along these lines. This is bound to result in a great deal of bitter feeling, newspaper criticism and hostile action, the effect of which cannot be otherwise than injurious to the large marine business of the old [Fireman's Fund] company here on the Pacific Coast. . . .

"I have seen unmistakable signs of dissatisfaction recently on the part of more than one of our large marine customers who also hold fire policies. . . .

"There is the important factor that this catastrophe and the heavy losses resulting therefrom will, in the future, place a marine underwriter operating for a company that does both a fire and marine business at a serious disadvantage as compared with one operating for an exclusive marine company. . . ."

To counteract the handicap Mr. Levison proposed to organize "a purely marine company with a limited number of shareholders and such of our office companies . . . as cared to come in." The North America was invited to subscribe. Additional stockholders would be the shipowning and mercantile community of the Pacific Coast generally, thereby securing their "active cooperation, interest and support."[28]

Mr. Platt replied:

"The plan you propose . . . does not appeal to me. . . .

"You will remember that I have been through a good many of these conflagrations, though, of course, none quite so bad as San Francisco. . . .

"I recall the condition of the marine insurance business after the Boston fire, where practically all the Boston companies doing fire and marine together were ruined and yet the North America, which suffered a loss of $1,000,000, stood, if anything, higher in the estimation of the public than ever before and our marine business increased largely. . . . I do not, therefore, agree with you that a fire and marine company will find its position weakened, as regards its marine business, by the fact that it also does a fire business. On the contrary,

I believe that its position will be largely strengthened. In other words, the transaction of a fire and marine business is, in my experience, a source of strength, rather than weakness.

"My own opinion would be that the Fireman's Fund Insurance Company should pay its San Francisco losses to the best of its ability and should continue both its fire and marine business under the old name. Five years from now, or even three years, the feeling of antagonism, or lack of confidence which you anticipate, will have disappeared. You must also bear in mind that companies doing an exclusive marine business have also their weak spots. A war, for instance, is liable to cripple them in a very short time. . . . Looking back over my experience, the number of marine companies which have failed has been quite as large, as to percentage, as the failure among fire companies. . . .

"I dislike extremely to write to you in this strain, in the midst of your many and great troubles . . . but I think it will do no harm to state my views plainly."[29]

By the time this letter was received the skies had begun to clear for the Fireman's Fund. In a stirring demonstration of confidence in the integrity of the home company and in the ability of its officers to outgeneral disaster, the suffering policyholders became shareholders in the reorganized company. Their faith was not misplaced. Jacob Levison took the presidency of the new organization and led it not only to solvency but to great success. On his retirement, after sixteen years at the head of the company, he wrote a book of memoirs for his family in which he called Mr. Platt's letter a "most remarkable" document, adding that his "prophecy has indeed come true."[30]

The system of underwriting outlined by the president of the North America is called "multiple-line coverage"—a new thing in 1906. It is the system upon which the Fireman's Fund built its recovery, and upon which the North America has erected its modern organization. By increasing the number of coverages a company broadens its service to the public and strengthens its structure so that a calamity in one particular field is less likely to embarrass the institution as a whole.

CHAPTER XIV

Improving the Other Fellow's Business

I

On January 25, 1909, the Board of Directors held a special meeting at which was adopted a resolution beginning:

"In the long and eventful history of the Insurance Company of North America nothing more momentous has occurred than the event we are met to record today, the lamented death of Mr. Charles Platt, who was for more than thirty-one years the President of the Company, and had ably, faithfully and zealously served it as Secretary, Vice-President and President since January 3, 1860. He passed away from us on Saturday morning, the 23rd inst., leaving our hearts full of sorrow."[1]

This last was no ceremonial phrase. One would search the archives of American industry for a long time to find a chief so dearly loved by all ranks as the grand old man who had laid down his burdens a few days short of eighty. Charles Platt would listen to the problems of an office boy as patiently as to those of a vice-president. The number of office boys who under his eye rose to responsible positions in the company seems to have justified the attention on practical grounds. Mr. Platt's nephew, John O. Platt, then assistant secretary and presently to be second vice-president in charge of fire, had begun as an office boy toeing the mark with the other apprentices.

The Board of Directors noted that Mr. Platt left his company in flourishing condition, representing a triumph over manifold calamities on sea and on land, the San Francisco conflagration being mentioned by name. All true. Two young subordinates, Benjamin Rush and Sheldon Catlin, had a good deal to do with incidents ministering to the company's prosperity and good name. The reputation for integrity which Charles Platt had preserved as a part of the North America's heritage made their tasks easier than otherwise they might have been. A body of legend associated with the old gentleman's name survives as an asset of the organization at this writing directed by men most of whom were schoolboys when Charles Platt breathed his last.

On November 3, 1909, Eugene L. Ellison was elected president of the Insurance Company of North America, and Benjamin Rush senior vice-president.

2

A continuation of reforms in the marine branch placed the prosperity of the company on the most solid basis in twenty-five years. The panic of 1907 caused scarcely a ripple. Between 1902 and 1909 marine premiums increased from $1,737,840 to $2,649,793. The 1909 marine profits were $497,748 against $696,473 for fire.[2] Although the downward trend of the American merchant marine had been arrested and our tonnage was slowly gaining, marine had a narrower field than fire in which to expand. Still, 40 per cent of the marine insurance placed in the United States went to foreign underwriters. Rush kept his eye fixed on that figure and continued to whittle it down.

The operation of the North America's constantly improved classification system by which good business was segregated from bad and rates maintained at a paying level had not gone unobserved. Other companies instituted systems directed toward the same end, though Rush's system, on testimony from impartial sources, had no equal for a number of years. This condition helped everyone. Less and less was the North America obliged to compete with ruinous rates.

With Rush and John O. Platt actively expanding their respective departments, it became the part of wisdom to provide them with additional capital. Consequently, in February 1910 the directors voted to increase the stock issue from $3,000,000 to $4,000,000 and at the same time to add $500,000 to surplus. In April this was ratified by the stockholders, 217,234 shares in favor to 39 shares opposed. The new issue was offered to stockholders at $15 a share and by July 1 all was taken and paid for. On that date the assets of the company stood at $15,446,877, including a net surplus of $3,341,-693.[3] The average price of North America shares in the open market during the month of July was about 20⅝.

An example of the perpetuation of the spirit in which Charles Platt had transacted business may be cited in the North America's connection with the greatest single peacetime marine loss in history, that of the *Titanic*. The White Star liner was the largest ship in the world and supposedly the safest. On her maiden voyage from Southampton to New York she struck an iceberg and sank on the night of April 14, 1912. Fifteen hundred and seventeen of the 2,223 persons aboard perished. There were lifeboats for a thousand persons only and these were unskillfully handled. Wireless telegraphy, then in its infancy, brought the *Carpathia* which picked up the survivors. Another ship equipped with wireless was nearer than the *Carpathia* but its operator had gone to bed.

The *Titanic* was insured for $5,566,820, of which $4,875,000 was regular coverage and $701,821 "disbursement insurance," payable only in event of a total loss. The English owners of the vessel had distributed the insurance among European companies, American underwriters getting only the leavings. These amounted to $140,000, regular coverage, of which $100,000 was held by the North America's old reinsurance associate, the Atlantic Mutual, and $40,000 by the United States Lloyd's. One hundred and twenty thousand of the disbursement coverage was held in America—$70,000 by the Aetna and $50,000 by the North America. The total loss of the *Titanic* seemed so improbable that the disbursement policies had been written at a rate of three-eights of 1 per cent, making the North America's premium for the $50,000 risk $187.50.

News of the disaster stunned the insurance community. Old-timers say there is no other word for it. The North America's participation had been handled by the New York brokerage firm of Johnson & Higgins. When a clerk got out the policy he noticed that it had not been signed by a representative of the insurance company. It was, therefore, invalid. Mr. Higgins got in touch with Henry W. Farnum, then manager of the New York office of the North America. Farnum called Mr. Rush by telephone.

"Sign that policy immediately and put it into effect," said Rush.[4]

Some of the lessons to be learned from the *Titanic* are obvious to a layman. Modern ship construction had been overrated. Thereafter ships were equipped with lifeboats and rafts for all aboard; abandon-ship drills were held; wireless underwent a boom; more rigid inspections were inaugurated.

The rigid inspections did not come in time to be of help to the *Montoswald*, a tramp steamer out of Newcastle-on-Tyne, however. The case is an example of the lax methods prevailing at the time. It illustrates the changed ways of doing business since the first years of the North America's history when the company employed a retired sea captain as "surveyor" to go over risks for seaworthiness. If the surveyor were otherwise engaged there were members of the Board of Directors competent to pass on the condition of a ship.

In January 1912 the *Montoswald* discharged at New York a cargo from Buenos Aires and dropped down to Baltimore for a cargo for Hamburg. The tramp was twelve years old and displaced 3,224 tons. Her hull had been in bad condition since stranding in Mobile Bay some months before. But the owners hoped to get her home where repairs could be made more cheaply. At Baltimore the *Montoswald* loaded grain below deck, lumber on deck and sailed on February 20. At Cape Henry the Chesapeake Bay pilot left her heading into a gale. The pilot carried back a letter which the captain had given him to mail.

That was the last seen of the *Montoswald*. In the fullness of time the North America paid a $20,000 claim on cargo. Later on the widow of the skipper of the lost ship showed this letter to the London Board of Trade:

> "S. S. 'Montoswald,'
> "22/2/12.
> "Chesapeake Bay.

"My dear Lizzie,
"By this time you will have heard that we are loaded for Hamburg, and no doubt we will come to the Tyne. I will be glad when we get home; coming to Baltimore I was three days in the ice, and we have had the same thing coming down. I want you to keep this letter as evidence, in case anything happens to the ship, as I wanted the ship dry-docked in New York and the owners would not allow it; as it is now we have 12 feet of water in the forepeak, and we are not out of harbour yet. Goodness knows whether we will reach home or not, but don't expect us any time, as I cannot give you any idea when we are due. We have the sailors at the hand-pumps now, so what it will be when we get out of the Bay I don't know. . . .
> "Your affectionate husband,
> "G. STANNARD."[5]

The inquiry which followed brought to light evidence to corroborate what the captain had written his wife of the condition of the vessel. Insurance was ordered refunded—and, one trusts, something done for Mrs. Lizzie Stannard.

3

The *Montoswald* case, and others similar, resulted in more rigid inspections from which the owners of hulls and of cargoes benefited as greatly as did the insurance companies. That is a distinguishing feature of an insurance company's business. When it helps itself it helps the assureds, and also the other way around. Benjamin Rush has set forth this philosophy very briefly.

"The mores of the insurance business," he said in a public address, "is that the first duty of our organization is to the policyholder rather than to the stockholder; to the body politic rather than to the body corporate; to those who are served rather than to those who do the serving. . . .

"Our three functions, therefore, may be briefly summed up as follows:

"First: Prompt payment of any insured loss which may occur.

"Second: Prevention of avoidable loss. And

"Third: Fitting of rate to risk. These are the three goal posts of the insurance business. . . .

"The method of attack on unnecessary losses by insurance companies is in brief to find out where a defect exists and then do away with it. As an illustration: A good many years ago the United States was shipping a large number of cattle to Europe. The rate of mortality loss reached as high as 7% on a voyage. After a study of the cause of these losses this Company was able to introduce an improved method of shipping and handling cattle whereby the rate in a very short space of time was reduced to ¼ of 1%, and thus seven pounds of beef out of every hundred (which had hitherto gone to feed the fishes) was preserved for the use of mankind."[6]

This was a simple case, though in his address Mr. Rush made it appear simpler than it really was. At the other end of the pole may be cited the vast and complicated case of cotton which the North America was years in working out.

4

When Benjamin Rush took charge of the marine branch in 1898 he characterized cotton as a "disastrous business." Our largest and most valuable export commodity, cotton was too big a thing, representing too much underwriting revenue, to abandon as petroleum had been abandoned. During the crop season of 1899-1900 world consumption was 13,500,000 bales of which the United States produced 9,142,000 bales and exported 6,090,000. The American crop was worth $335,000,000 and the portion exported $241,000,000. Cotton was probably the collateral behind more loans than any other produce of our soil. The planter borrowed to buy seed, fertilizer and labor; the storekeeper borrowed to pay for goods supplied the planter; the local banks borrowed from their city correspondents to lend to the planter and the storekeeper. When the crop was harvested the cotton buyers borrowed to finance their purchases, beginning another chain of borrowing which took the cotton through several hands to the manufacturer. For years Government economists had tried to rid the business of such heavy interest charges. They failed. Cotton ripened and was picked in the course of three or four months, but the world required at least a year to absorb it. In this situation the banker was as necessary as the cotton seed. After the harvest when most of the crop found its way into warehouses under pledge to him, he looked to insurance to protect his investment.

So on top of interest charges came insurance charges. At the beginning of the twentieth century cotton premiums ran close to $10,-000,000 a year. Yet this tremendous overhead, costing the owners of the cotton $27,000 a day, brought scant profit, or no profit, to the underwriters. In the five years ending in 1900 the North America's loss on export cotton alone had been $241,000, and on all cotton $201,000. The largest source of loss was "country damage"—waste in baling, storing and shipping to the seaports. In a nation proverbially prodigal with its bounteous resources the enormous waste of country damage to the cotton crop stood near the top of the list. For the 1904-1905 season the Government calculated the loss in this category at more than $5,000,000.

As the business represented potentialities too great to walk away from, Rush chose the alternative of trying to remold it. This was a large order. Dealing with tens of thousands of independent planters, ginners, warehousemen, transporters and buyers, most of them wedded to such time-honored fallacies as the belief that ignorant Negro labor was economical because it could be had for a dollar a day, was only one prong of the problem. The other pointed at the insurance community itself. Cotton underwriting was virtually controlled by a few powerful brokerage houses which had entered the picture in the eighties when the cotton crop passed the ten-million-bale mark and the cotton belt banks lacked the money to finance it. Eastern banks were appealed to. They introduced the New York insurance broker. The brokers parceled the risks among underwriters on a reciprocity-of-favors basis. Cotton had become big business and the reinsurance required considerable spread. It was common talk among the insurance people that most of the cotton underwriting was done over good food and wine at Delmonico's famous restaurant at 56 Beaver Street. Though a gamble with odds against the underwriter, cotton accounts nevertheless were sought, the underwriter hoping always he'd be lucky. If he weren't there was always the chance that the contact with the broker would lead to other accounts which would prove profitable. The situation resolved more or less into a dogfight of rate-cutting. Heavy losses made cotton rates always high, affording leeway for bargaining.

After vainly trying to get the brokers to take a long view of the situation and lend a hand toward modernizing the cotton business into a reasonably insurable risk at stabilized rates, Rush decided to go his own way and write his cotton insurance direct. This was easier said than done. No matter how successful the plan, Rush could hardly hope to get on his own the volume of reinsurance that came to him from the brokers. Although the North America was losing money on cotton, withdrawal meant the loss of a large immediate income, while payment of losses would continue for perhaps two more years.

"It was an unpleasant state of affairs to face," Rush later said, "but after due consideration, we came to the conclusion that the only sure way of quitting a losing field was to quit it."[7]

Policies were canceled wholesale. A number of the North America's directors were frankly critical, particularly as they contemplated the statements of cotton losses which had to be indemnified out of a dwindling income. At the same time Rush turned to the company's southern connections to make a start at redressing the balance. Captain Edward S. Gay, since 1875 manager of the Southern Department with headquarters at Atlanta, had been writing a fair amount of cotton business. On the whole the risks accepted by Captain Gay had turned out better than the business dumped on the company by the brokers. Studying the records of the southern office, Rush discovered that one of its most active agents was a Colonel Ed L. Wight, the fire representative at Albany, Georgia. After an interview with Wight in which he learned that the Colonel knew a great deal about cotton, Rush extended Wight's authority to include the writing of cotton accounts. Wight got the drift of what Rush was trying to do and entered upon his new assignment with zest because he thought it would be a great thing for his native Georgia. He preached this to local cotton growers and dealers. Working on a contingent fee, Wight soon gathered in the profitable business of the lately organized Georgia Cotton Company as well as a substantial number of other good accounts.

Wight's business grew so that he took in a partner, F. M. Butt of Augusta. Under home-office directions, Butt made a study of the unsatisfactory state of cotton insurance and began giving compressors, storers and haulers lessons in improved methods. This helped the cotton men; it helped the firm of Wight & Butt; it helped the Insurance Company of North America. After a tour of the cotton belt where he saw the slovenly manner in which the cotton was baled with inferior jute, Butt could believe the tales told of the small army of people on the docks at Liverpool, who supported themselves by gathering up loose cotton that fell from the faulty bales. The underwriters had to pay on the short-weight bales, and these losses were passed back down the line to warehouses and cotton growers in high insurance rates.

Butt traveled over a good part of the South spreading his gospel of more careful baling, storing and handling. He offered lower insurance rates to those who heeded his advice. Texas was coming into its own as a leading cotton-producing state. In time Wight & Butt established an office in Dallas, which, with branches in Houston and Memphis, became one of the noted cotton insurance agencies of the South.

In the early stages of the North America's contest further help was obtained from the New Orleans agent, an ex-Confederate colonel named Marshall J. Smith, seventy-four years old but full of fight.

Aside from the tremendous loss of loose cotton at this port, a great hazard was the open wooden docks which from the underwriters' point of view seemed to have been constructed to meet the requirements of perfect fire traps. Colonel Smith and his successor, W. J. Hardin, through many years worked with the New Orleans Dock Board to get rid of the old docks and to build modern wharves and warehouses equipped with sprinkler systems that have been models for cotton ports.[8]

5

Eastern brokers followed Mr. Rush's maneuvers with deepening interest. The North America found it necessary to cut rates in order to keep some of the new accounts out of the hands of the brokers from whom it had parted company. This rate-cutting was not very expensive to the North America because it was largely made on good risks which could stand it. The company also made a feint at cutting rates to get poor business, eventually letting this business go, however, to competitors. Thus in a few years the North America began to make money on cotton. Its five-year statement of 1904 showed a cotton profit of $292,000, of which $90,000 was on export, formerly the heaviest loser of all cotton categories.

The competitors' balance sheets did not present the same healthy aspect. One of them made a trip from New York to try to bring the North America back into the fold. A little more spread, such as the North America could offer, would bring down the average of losses and also get rid of the rate-cutting which reduced premium income. The visitor asked for the North America's peace terms.

"Five hundred thousand dollars cotton premiums annually on first-class risks, and my agents taken care of," Rush replied.

The New Yorker said the price was too stiff and the conflict went on.[9]

The North America's southern representatives continued their missionary work for more scientific handling of cotton at lowered insurance costs. Slowly this work bore fruit. A notable milestone was the construction in 1907 of the South Memphis Terminal, the most modern warehouse then in existence. Cotton stored in the South Memphis Terminal received an exceptionally low rate. The first year of operation its facilities were taxed to the utmost while near-by warehouses with inferior storage accommodations and higher insurance rates lost customers. Taking this lesson to heart, some warehouse owners began to invite underwriters to suggest improvements. Those who acted on the suggestions given were able to compete with the rates of the South Memphis Terminal.

About this time Galloway C. Morris, in charge of the Marine Loss Department at the home office, made an extensive tour of the cotton belt and brought back so dismal a picture of conditions that a more intensive program of improvement was inaugurated. Cotton fires are probably the most discouraging conflagrations firemen have to fight. Fires starting inside bales were attributed to spontaneous combustion. Penetrating a compressed bale with difficulty, water will seldom quench such a fire. An old insurance joke tells of the adjuster sent to a cotton fire. His home office received his expense account listing the usual charges, with this additional item: "3 gallons kerosene to put out fire, $.30." Startling but true: kerosene is about the only liquid light enough to penetrate a bale of cotton and smother a smoldering fire.

The rate fight was still going on. From Atlanta Morris telephoned that customers were being offered a reduction of 10 per cent on premiums. The home office said to meet the cuts—on good business. Poor business the competitors could have at their own unprofitable figures.[10] Meantime Rush made trips to New York, talking to underwriters and brokers as well, suggesting they get together on the cotton business and make it pay for all parties concerned. Underwriters whose cotton losses had been mounting were all for the idea. A few meetings were held with considerable talk but no action. As is often the way in insurance circles it remained for a disaster to bring matters to a head.

On December 22, 1908, the British steamer *Irada,* Galveston to Liverpool, carrying the most expensive cargo of cotton ever shipped to that time from the United States, foundered off the Irish coast. The cargo loss to British and American underwriters was $1,250,000. The premium had been pitifully low. Luckier than most of its competitors, the North America paid out only $17,267.20.

6

The sinking of the *Irada* resulted in the formation of the Cotton Reinsurance Exchange, on September 1, 1909. This was the first of the marine-insurance syndicates. Nine companies participated, six

English and three American—the Atlantic Mutual, United States Lloyd's and the North America. The syndicate was made up of a total of 104 shares. Of these two English companies owned twenty each or 19.23 per cent of the whole. The smallest participant owned three shares or 2.88 per cent. The North America owned fourteen shares or 13.46 per cent. The syndicate virtually took over the insurance of American cotton and continued the work of teaching cotton men how to reduce the hazards of their business, much as the National Board of Fire Underwriters had done in its field.[11]

"I consider the Cotton Reinsurance Exchange one of the most constructive jobs ever done in insurance," said Hendon Chubb of Chubb & Son, New York underwriters, in 1942.[12] Hendon Chubb is a brother of the late Percy Chubb who represented the Sea Insurance Company of Liverpool in the organization of the Exchange.

The first work of the Exchange was to survey all the cotton compresses and warehouses in the South. Rates were fixed accordingly. With most of the compresses and warehouses in a state that invited losses, the revision was upward on the whole. This put a premium on better methods. The Exchange followed up the rate revision by circulating plans for the improvement of presses and places of storage, for the better baling of cotton and for less wasteful handling in transit and on the docks. Where these plans were followed rates came down. Exchange experts demonstrated that spontaneous combustion in a cotton bale was impossible, though it was a long time before the myth died. Mysterious internal fires were usually from "fire-packed" bales—bales packed with sparks in them, which might smoulder for weeks before starting a conflagration in a ship at sea or in a warehouse. A spark, buried inside a bale, from a Negro's pipe or from a gin engine, was the cause of most "spontaneous combustion" fires.

The United States Department of Agriculture took cognizance of the work the Exchange was doing.

"Financing the cotton crop is one of the most difficult, and at the same time one of the most important problems confronting the southern farmer and the southern business man," read one of its *Bulletins*. "The banks are entirely willing to advance money on cotton on liberal terms when it is properly stored and insured."

The building and modernization of warehouses was urged, it being

EUGENE L. ELLISON

Eighth president Insurance Company of North America, 1909-1916. Joined North America in 1871 after company for which he was working became casualty of Chicago fire. He was essentially a fire underwriter.

From a portrait by Hugh Breckenridge, owned by the Insurance Company of North America.

pointed out that reduced insurance charges would defray a part of the cost. But this was only one advantage.

"It would be impossible to enumerate all of the benefits, direct and indirect, that might be derived from the inauguration of an ample and efficient system of storage houses. It would benefit not only the farmer but the merchant, the local banker, and other business men. A storage system properly operated and used would eventually free the cotton farmer from the present destructive credit system. It would improve conditions in the cotton market. Much 'country damage' and loss from unnecessary sampling would be prevented. Such a system would enable the farmer to distribute the sales of cotton throughout the year, and in this way avoid depressed prices. Under present conditions the farmer rushes his cotton to market as fast as it can be picked and ginned, and thus 'bears' his own market."[13]

This agitation was effective, and its results soon apparent. For the five years ending 1914 the North America's cotton profits were $572,-000. Other underwriters profited correspondingly as did the owners of the cotton. In 1916 the Exchange created the Cotton Engineering & Inspection Service to take over and continue the work of technical improvement. The achievements of this organization would comprise a story in themselves, affording further testimony in support of the fact that insurance seems to improve every business with which it has to do.

CHAPTER XV

THE FIRST WORLD WAR

I

ON JUNE 14, 1914, Mr. Rush and his daughter Charlotte reached home from a sojourn in Europe. Had someone mentioned the possibility of war they would have thought the speaker meant war between the United States and Mexico. In April our forces had occupied Vera Cruz. Nor was this situation altered when the newspapers of June 29 related that the heir to the Austro-Hungarian throne and his wife had been assassinated. The reigning house of Austria had a bloody history and within a few days this latest chapter was eclipsed in interest by such European goings on as the Caillaux trial in Paris and the violence of the English suffragettes.

On July 25 Austria came back in the news. An ultimatum had been delivered to Serbia, compliance with which would amount to a confession of complicity in the royal murder and a surrender of national independence. Austria-Hungary required an answer within forty-eight hours. Berlin backed Vienna. Serbia's answer was unsatisfactory and on July 28 Austria declared war on her small neighbor. Russian, German and French troops moved toward the frontiers. The British Home Fleet, which had been assembled for maneuvers, stood by. And yet the average European could not conceive of a general war.

Much less could Americans conceive of a general war—even the marine-insurance fraternity which would be affected the most vitally of all our business institutions. The Insurance Company of North America did not have in its files such a thing as a sample policy covering war risks. There was no precedent to guide the company's officers in preparing such policies. A war involving the great maritime powers of England, Germany, France and possibly Italy would be a phenomenon such as the world had not seen since the end of the career of Napoleon in 1815, just ninety-nine years before. Though the North America had spent its formative years amid that adventure, the fruits of the experience, could they have been revealed in a flash from archives which had not been glanced at for generations, would have been of slight service in 1914. Conditions had changed. War was not the same.

Yet the North America was not quite so ill-prepared as the majority of its contemporaries, because ten years before Benjamin Rush had had a hunch. He says it was just that—no prevision at all. These are the facts, however. In 1904 Japan attacked the Russian base of Port Arthur without a declaration of hostilities. Marine underwriters, surprised as badly as the Russians, took terrific losses in the early days of the war that followed. Though the North America lost little it occurred to Rush to insert a "war exclusion" clause in all his open policies. "Not that I thought a general war likely," he said later. "The truth is I could conceive of no such thing as a general war. Nevertheless, it occurred to me that *should* such a war break out suddenly it might cost us a million dollars. So I put the clause in."[1] He was one of the few American underwriters to do so.

Very rarely did the assureds object, they, too, thinking the possibility of war too remote to discuss. When one did object sometimes he had his way and the offending clause was omitted.

On July 25, the date of news of the Austrian ultimatum, Rush asked Galloway Morris, his second in command, to get out all the open marine policies then in force—some two thousand in number. A dozen clerks were pressed into service to examine each policy. With the exception of ten or twelve policies on wool, written in Boston, all these policies were found to contain the war exclusion clause. Rush ordered the wool policies canceled forthwith.[2]

These preliminaries attended to, the vice-president shut himself in his office to contemplate the possibility of war on a scale hitherto unknown—and to try to formulate a policy for the Insurance Company of North America. He had with him a book by Douglas Owen entitled *Declaration of War*. This thick volume, published in London in 1889, was considered the most complete underwriters' guide in existence on the subject of war.

For three or four days Rush was immured in his office. By the time he emerged the war seemed inevitable. Rush had his plan.

"How much of it did you get from Owen's book?" he was later asked.

"Very little," was the reply. "I had a feeling this war was going to be different from the others."[3]

Rush got his plan from his head—from his knowledge of the role insurance plays in the interchange of goods and services throughout the world, and from his speculation as to the part it would be possible for it to play in event war should engulf Europe. Some years later Mr. Rush briefly wrote down the considerations which influenced him in determining the North America's position:

"It was necessary for the Company to decide, and to decide quickly, as to the course they would pursue, and this decision involved the making of a prophecy as to which of the opposed belligerents would ultimately be successful [on the sea].

"Without hesitation they chose France, Great Britain, and their allies, as much on account of their belief in the righteousness of their cause as on account of their known maritime superiority.

"This was a momentous decision to make for had it turned out to be incorrect, the Insurance Company of North America would undoubtedly have sustained very serious losses, and might indeed have been seriously crippled, for a Maritime War is to a Marine Underwriter what a conflagration in a great city is to a Fire Underwriter—it presents an incalculable hazard.

"Having once come to this decision, the Company pursued with consistency the policy it had adopted. It placed its War policies, and certificates, in the hands of its agents with instructions to write both the hazards of Marine and War on merchandise carried by neutral and/or allied tonnage all over the world, with the exception of cargoes which were destined to the Germanic confederacy, which were contraband of war, or those cargoes consigned to neutrals which it was suspected were ultimately intended for enemy consumption."[4]

Thus with President Wilson ready to caution us to be "neutral in thought," the Insurance Company of North America prepared to take its positive stand on the side of the Allies. This was, of course, in harmony with the majority of American sentiment. It is one thing, however, to express sentimental interest in one side or another in a struggle, and quite another thing to prepare to back up that sentiment, as the North America was doing. Rush's decision called for participation in a war that might be fought on every ocean. The decision recalls the part of the North America in the struggles of

1793-1815 when the survival of the United States depended on our ability to keep our merchant flag afloat.

2

Now for an outline of the general situation during the crucial days of July and August 1914, after which the North America's specific part in it—already formulated in principle—will be considered.

As Europe rushed toward the precipice the intricate structure of international commerce, which a week before had seemed as firm as Gibraltar, began to fall apart. Austria's attack on Serbia (July 28) threw the European exchanges into panic. Repercussions in the United States were sharp, internationally held securities losing heavily. London and Paris bankers called on the United States for gold, and insurance rates on the yellow metal jumped from five cents on $100 to twelve and a half cents.

July 29 was a day of hope as English and French statesmen struggled to localize the conflict. Markets were quieter. But demands for American gold continued and the rate went to fifty cents a hundred.

On July 30 the belligerent attitudes of Germany and of Russia dimmed the peace hope. Foreign markets were demoralized and the New York Stock Exchange saw its worst day since the panic of 1907. "Insurance rates chaotic and quotations the highest ever known," remarked the conservative New York *Journal of Commerce*. There was a general refusal to cover German or Austrian ships. This sometimes took the form of quoting prohibitive war-risk rates—as high as 60 per cent of value. All war-risk rates were topsy-turvy. Placers from the New York brokerage offices stood in long lines before the marine desks of the various companies, shopping for rates or endeavoring to obtain coverage at any price possible for an assured to pay. Some of the companies refused all transatlantic risks. Overburdened cables brought word that in London the rate picture was as jumbled as it was here. Lights in insurance offices burned late that night. Weary men watched the situation grow more confused hour by hour.

The crash came next morning (July 31). The New York Stock Exchange suspended. Sailings of German and of Austrian ships were canceled. With some exceptions French and British passenger liners left on schedule, carrying many army reservists. Freighters of various nationalities were held up because of an inability to get insurance. Except to German and Austrian ports, war risks were quoted at 3 to 10 per cent, though few underwriters would accept business at any figure. Grain merchants notified European buyers that they would execute their contracts only on a free-of-all-risk basis. London came back with the statement that the shippers and sellers must undertake the insurance. The grain ships remained at the docks. The American liner *St. Louis* sailed with $11,025,000 worth of gold, the most valuable shipment on record up to that time. Most of it had been hastily transferred from German and British ships. Premiums were as high as $2 a hundred. Three days before they had been five cents a hundred. British underwriters took great losses when they reinsured at $2 risks they had taken at from five to fifty cents.

Then, in Europe, the dam burst. On August 1 Germany declared war on Russia. On August 2 Germany invaded Luxemburg. On August 3 Germany declared war on France. Italy, nominal ally of Germany and Austria, proclaimed neutrality. On August 4 Germany invaded Belgium and England went to war. The unthinkable was an accomplished fact.

It left shipping on our Atlantic seaboard in a situation that is impossible to convey in a word, though "embargo" comes fairly close. "Export blockade" was the expression used by the *Journal of Commerce* on August 8. Not since the days of Thomas Jefferson had our ports been so nearly sealed. A bank holiday having closed Lloyd's of London, that lodestar of marine rates was issuing no quotations. Independent American quotations ran as high as 25 and 30 per cent to cover war risks through the North Sea. Reports of German commerce raiders in the South Atlantic and the Indian Oceans sent South American rates to 20 per cent, rates to India and the Far East to 15 and 20. Quotations were by no means uniform for the same type of risk. One underwriter would ask 20 per cent for what another would take for 10. Moreover all quotations were largely academic. Few shippers could afford to pay them. Many underwriters refused coverage for large amounts at any premium, because of the temporary disappearance of the reinsurance markets in London. When Lloyd's reopened, its rates closely paralleled American quotations established during the holiday. On August 4 the rate from British ports to the United States was 10.5 per cent; on August

6, 21 per cent. North Sea rates were 25 and 30, South American 10 and Far Eastern 15 and 20.

Germany's plunge into war had sent German ships that were at sea scurrying for neutral ports. After a wild run dodging British men-of-war the outward bound *Kronprinzessin Cecilie* reached Bar Harbor, Maine, with a cargo of gold and a distinguished passenger list which incidentally included some prominent American marine-insurance men. The liner *Kronprinz Wilhelm,* ready to sail when the war came, behaved differently. Prospective passengers were got rid of and seamen set to painting her gray. Loaded with coal and ships' stores she cleared for Bremen. On deck appeared a large wooden box: an extra crank shaft, the officers said. Newspaper reporters thought it looked more like a gun. On the night of August 3 the *Wilhelm* slipped to sea with only legal lights showing. Two days later a newly arrived American freighter reported the *Wilhelm* far south of the route to Bremen. She had turned commerce raider. The incident gave point to rumors already filling the air with stories of captures by the British navy and sinkings by German raiders and German mines—stories impossible to confirm or deny because the cables were too busy to accommodate underwriters with reports on the movements of vessels at sea.

On August 14 the trade journal *Spectator* summed up the first fortnight of the war succinctly: "Practically no [marine] insurance is being written."

With hundreds of laden vessels tied up at docks or lying at anchor, wharves and waterside warehouses quickly filled to overflowing. Seaport railroad yards filled. Oncoming trains were headed off and the congestion extended to the freight yards of inland centers. Prices began to climb. A Norwegian steamer from Philadelphia, immured behind the Delaware breakwater, carried 6,000 tons of sugar which increased in value $50,000 in a day as sugar jumped ten points. Despite the small amount of shipping, ocean freight rates skyrocketed. A sugar refiner paid twenty cents a hundred pounds to bring his produce from the north coast of Cuba. Ten days before, the rate had been 8½. Fifteen dollars a ton was paid to carry coal from Norfolk to Buenos Aires, a rise of $11.25. At tidewater the coal cost $2.25. The mark-up of hull values had started. So much for a few subsidiary complications creeping into the insurance problem.

Nor was the paralysis of marine insurance by any means the sole

factor in the "blockade" of our coasts. The machinery of foreign
trade, of which insurance is only one wheel, had broken down. With
the international banking, credit and exchange systems frozen, American
exporters had difficulty disposing of their drafts.

As for insurance, the demand simply exceeded the supply. The
physical risks of a given voyage were incalculable. With hazards to
be met unknown, premiums were undeterminable. And what of
capital to protect such risks as an adventurous underwriter might
undertake? England, the leading insurance market, was a belligerent.
Germany, the next largest, was a belligerent and—for the
moment at least—a prisoner of the British navy. The Norwegian
market, while important, was too small to meet the needs of the
situation. That left the United States where marine insurance commanded
no such sums of capital as fire or life insurance. The financial
resources of American marine underwriters were unequal to the
sudden burdens placed upon them.

On August 10 an impressive committee of maritime and railroad
men and manufacturers appealed to the United States Government
to come to the relief of the insurance situation. Among the petitioners
were such personages as P. A. S. Franklin of the International
Mercantile Marine, Captain Robert Dollar, James J. Hill and James
A. Farrell, president of United States Steel. On the part of the Government,
Secretary of the Treasury McAdoo acted vigorously. On
August 14 a bill creating the Bureau of War Risk Insurance was before
Congress. On September 2 it became a law. Insurance was
offered on American vessels, their freight, passage moneys and their
cargoes, against loss or damage by war whenever it should appear
that coverage could not be obtained elsewhere at reasonable rates.
No fixed rates were established, the law providing that the bureau
should determine the rate for each voyage according to the character
of the vessel, the route taken and the nature of the cargo, in the
same way that private underwriters normally determine rates.

By the time the Bureau of War Risk Insurance began operation the
hysteria was over and the blockade was being broken. The fact that it
was known that the Government was going into the insurance business
as soon as it could get there had proved a factor helpful to this
end. Other help came from the British Government which offered insurance
protection to vessels and cargoes under the Union Jack. Another
circumstance, which seems to have been as important as either

of the two already mentioned, was the fact that underwriters were getting their bearings in a world turned upside down. They were beginning to be able to make calculations as to what their risks were. The main German battle fleet was bottled up at home. Eight or nine commerce raiders—cruisers and armed liners and merchant-men—were abroad, and reports thus far received of their depredations did not minimize the facts to say the least. The German Admiral von Spee was loose with a small naval squadron in the Pacific. Allied men-of-war were after von Spee and the raiders. The first raider caught up with, the former liner *Kaiser Wilhelm der Grosse,* was sunk off Africa on August 26.

By the middle of August rates had begun to drop. On August 27 the *Spectator* quoted war-risk premiums to the British Isles as low as 1 per cent on American ships, 2 per cent on others; to other European ports 3 to 10 per cent. The Bureau of War Risk Insurance, starting business a week later, accepted risks at about the market rates.[5]

3

When the declarations of war during the first days of August brought panic to the insurance market on both sides of the water, the North America issued a schedule of war-risk rates which for the North Atlantic approached the top quotations then prevailing—25 and 30 per cent. A limit of $75,000 on one bottom was established for North Atlantic risks, and $125,000 for other routes.

The steep North Atlantic rates were based on what turned out to be a faulty prediction as to German naval strategy. Mr. Rush thought the German fleet would steam out in force and fall upon commerce in the much-traveled waters about the British Isles. The Germans would have suffered losses, which must be counted on in any war, but they could have done tremendous damage. Rush knew the German shells to be a little lighter than those of the British. When the Germans did not appear at once he thought that possibly they were re-gunning their fleet. He asked our Navy Department how long it would take to complete such an operation. The reply was three months.

For fully two months Rush held to his belief in the imminence of a German raid in force—a view which incidentally had the support of several neutral naval experts. When the panic subsided the latter part of August and Atlantic rates dropped to 2 to 10 per cent, the North America kept its rates 3 to 5 per cent above the market. Elsewhere its rates followed the market. The Kaiser reasoned that with the French apparently beaten and the way to Paris open he could win the war without risking his fleet. But in September the French rallied on the Marne and sent the Germans rolling back from the gates of the capital. By this time British naval strength was preponderant in the North Sea. The Kaiser had lost his chance to deal British shipping a lightning blow. His fleet was bottled up. The North America reduced its rates to the level of the market.[6]

From the first the company gave effect to its policy of support to the Allies. When the stabilization of marine rates had broken the blockade of our coasts, a remarkably profitable trade with neutral countries surrounding Germany sprang up overnight. In the month of November our exports to little Denmark leaped to $7,101,000, which was more than the Danes ordinarily bought from us in a year. Shipments to Sweden jumped sevenfold to $2,558,000. Consignments to Norway were $2,318,000 against $477,000 for November 1913; to Italy $4,781,000, or nearly double those for the same month a year before. There was no serious pretense that the bulk of these shipments did not comprise war materials—copper, aluminum, oil—destined for Germany's war machine.

The North America did not touch this lucrative business. Consequently it was not involved in the diplomatic wrangles which followed when England began seizing vessels, some of them American, bound for neutral countries with contraband intended for German use. The Germans went to great lengths to keep this trade open, and they enjoyed considerable underwriting support. A brazen attempt to make trouble between the United States and Great Britain was the case of the *Dacia*. At the beginning of the war Congress had hastily passed a bill admitting foreign ships to United States registry. Americans of German antecedents bought the Hamburg-American merchantman *Dacia,* at Port Arthur, Texas. They loaded her with cotton and cleared for Bremen. A great hullabaloo was raised in certain circles about the rights of "peaceful commerce" under the American flag. But when the French, not the British as had been expected, stepped in and took charge of the *Dacia* as she neared the German coast, the cry fell rather flat. A few weeks later two other American cotton vessels, Bremen bound, were sunk by mines the Germans themselves had sown off their coasts.

This about ended attempts to ship to Germany direct. Shipments via Scandinavia declined, and our entry into the war in 1917 ended them as far as the United States was concerned.

In the early months of hostilities the surface raider rather than the submarine was the great menace to commerce. Germany began the conflict with raiders on every ocean and they gave good accounts of themselves. The activities of these vessels, as reported from various parts of the world, caused violent fluctuations in rates. In dealing with this situation the North America followed a policy which Charles Platt had used so successfully during the Civil War. It would accept business at moderate rates along routes where raiders were last reported, on the assumption that when the cargoes reached there the raiders would be elsewhere.

The strategy worked almost as well as it had fifty-five years before. By the spring of 1915 von Spee's squadron had been sunk off the Falkland Islands and all the original raiders disposed of. One of the last of them, the *Prinz Eitel Friedrich,* in China waters when war was declared, slipped into Norfolk, Virginia, on March 12 and accepted internment. On board was the crew of the American sailing ship *William P. Frye,* bound for England with grain, which the *Prinz Eitel* had sunk a few weeks previously. This was the first American ship to go to the bottom as a result of belligerent action. The North America paid a claim of $10,000.

For the period ending December 31, 1914, taking in the first five months of the war, the company's operations were remarkably successful. Owing to the war exclusion clause it had lost nothing on its common-risk open policies whereas certain contemporaries lost heavily. On war-risk business the company received $676,000 in premiums and paid $64,500 in claims. That is a loss ratio of 9.29. Anything under 50 would have been safe. Ordinary marine premiums were $2,947,000; losses $1,748,000.

4

New problems awaited the marine underwriter in 1915. With the fate of the surface raiders virtually sealed and the Allied blockade clamping down on her supply lines via neutral Europe, Germany announced the decision to use submarines against merchant shipping. This violation of international law was excused on the ground of Allied action against contraband destined for Germany via the neutral countries. The German announcement came on February 4. The United States immediately declared that the imperial government would be held to "strict accountability" for American "property endangered or lives lost."

Hitherto German submarines had been used only against British naval vessels. Mr. Rush made it his business to learn what he could of their tactics. The early submarines were of limited range. Their practice was to lie in wait for their prey on shelves under fairly shallow water. A study of the ocean floor showed that vessels bound for Liverpool or Bristol would be safer from such danger spots than ships traversing the Channel. The North America guided its under writing accordingly and maintained a low loss ratio until the Germans began producing larger U-boats which could operate anywhere in the waters about the British Isles.[7]

The first American victim of a German submarine was the tanker *Gulflight,* torpedoed on May 1, 1915. No lives were lost and the North America paid $9,260 as its share on the cargo. American indignation over the *Gulflight* was eclipsed on May 7 when the Cunarder *Lusitania* was sunk and more than a hundred Americans drowned. The North America paid a claim of $21,740. The sinking of the British steamers *Arabic* and *Ancona,* with further loss of American lives, heightened the clamor that we join the war. The North America paid claims on both of these ships.

By this time our material aid to the Allies was in full swing and the underwriting picture changing swiftly. During the first year of the war our exports to the Allied powers increased from $927,000,000 to $2,432,000,000. Our merchant marine engaged in foreign trade grew from 1,076,000 tons to 1,871,000. The value of vessels soared 50, 100 per cent and even more as coastwise steamers, lake steamers and hulks that had been long laid up were refitted and sent to sea. One exporter chartered for $90,000 a month an old steamer which he had had a chance to buy for that figure in August 1914. Freight rates advanced 500 per cent, and cargoes about 50 per cent in value. According to one observer of the scene:

"An underwriter instead of being called upon to cover the ordinary marine risk on a vessel valued at $400,000, on freights valued at $20,000, and cargo valued at $1,000,000, must furnish both marine insurance and war risk insurance on a $600,000 to $800,000 vessel,

$120,000 on freights, and $1,500,000 on cargo—two risks of $2,420,000 instead of one risk of $1,420,000 in pre-war days—an increase of $1,000,000 or about 70 percent."[8]

This 70-per-cent increase in the underwriting load was for one sailing only. Double and treble the number of sailings and one gets nearer the true dimensions of the problem in dollars. Nor does the mere matter of dollars tell the whole story. In addition to the extraordinary risks of war—submarines, mines and surface raiders—ordinary risks of the sea were greatly enhanced by the suppression of navigation lights, by hasty inspections, inadequately trained officers and crews, want of time for proper repair or overhaul, and other factors. Additional sources of cargo loss were thefts from warehouses and piers, damage due to speed or carelessness in handling and to insecure packing. In the emergency there was not time to see to those things.

Insurance had to take up the slack. In the beginning there was a woeful shortage of capital resources, plus a rate panic. As the panic subsided the British and United States Governments came in to supply additional capital facilities. Japan and Norway followed. In American insurance circles there was considerable shortsighted opposition to the American move, though most of the truly constructive marine leaders welcomed it.

"The Bureau of War Risk Insurance," said Benjamin Rush, "did a necessary job and did it well. Fortunately the Government benefited in this connection by the services of one of the ablest marine underwriters in the United States, Mr. Hendon Chubb."[9]

Hendon Chubb, whom Secretary McAdoo called to Washington to organize the Bureau, was the head of Chubb & Son, of New York, managing agents for insurance companies. Their largest representation was of English firms.

The government agencies actually wrote only a small fraction of the war-risk insurance necessary to keep the ships at sea, the North America alone writing more than half as much as the Federal Bureau. Great additions to private underwriting capital were necessary. Where such apparent opportunities for profit are present, capital is never lacking. The boom in shipping was followed by a boom in insurance, such as the country had not seen since the clipper-ship era. Old-line fire companies entered the marine field. New companies were formed. Scandinavian, Spanish and other neutral nationalities established themselves in the United States. The New York market, in which before the war not more than thirty companies were actively engaged, expanded to more than a hundred companies. A million dollars could be placed as easily as $200,000 a few years before.[10]

To a certain extent rates were influenced by the factor of sharpened competition, though the fortunes of war formed the main influence. By and large the situation shook down to following certain acknowledged leaders. As ever the London market, with its greater capital, prestige and experience remained the bellwether. Before the war the American leaders had been, by tacit agreement, Chubb & Son and the Insurance Company of North America. A part of the market now continued to follow Chubb and a part to follow Rush.

In the simplest terms the North America's rate policy was this. Rates were governed by the amount of liability the company had afloat on a given ocean route at any one time, as well as by the calculable chances of loss by hostile action. For example, the liability limit on the North Atlantic was from $3,000,000 to $4,000,000, according to circumstances. Records on accumulated liability throughout the world were constantly maintained. When the permissible limit anywhere was reached rates for that route would be shoved a notch above the current market. This had the effect of diverting business elsewhere and keeping the company's liability within prudent bounds.

The second feature in the maintenance of a rate schedule had to do with the calculable risks as a result of hostile action. In 1915 this meant principally submarines whose technique of destruction steadily improved, though actual sinkings came somewhat in waves. A period of heavy sinkings would be followed by a lull. The areas of severest destruction would shift from place to place. Rush studied this changing pattern as carefully as a naval strategist. As a result the North America maintained rates which were more uniform, less subject to abrupt fluctuations, than those of the market as a whole. When a lull came the North America's policy was not to follow the market down but to maintain existing rates in anticipation of a resumption of increased submarine activity. This would have the effect of reducing the company's liability. When the subs got busy again and rates rose, the company would be in a position to accept heavy lines and bring its liability up to the maximum with some assurance that when ships entered the danger zone the submarines would have returned to their bases to refuel or refit.[11]

The story is told on John Street in New York's insurance center of the shipper who divided his business almost equally between Chubb & Son and the North America. Often their rates varied considerably. At the end of the war the shipper figured up what he had paid each. The amounts were approximately the same. The North America's policy of comparatively stable rates in the long run just about balanced the schedules of competitors whose rates were usually in motion up or down.

Following a policy as old as the company itself, the North America tried to exercise diligence as to what it insured. This was not so simple as in normal times, and it insured some unseaworthy risks and took losses in consequence. But at the principal ports it maintained surveyors—the term had not changed since 1792—to inspect hulls wherever possible. At a time when nearly anything that could float was putting to sea this was a wise precaution. A lake steamer called the *Maryland* was in Cramp's shipyard in Philadelphia being made ready for a voyage across the Atlantic with scrap iron. Captain W. R. Jeffcott, a ship master with twenty-five years' sea experience behind him, had just joined the North America's staff. He reported the *Maryland* unfit for ocean travel.

"Can't you pass that ship, Captain?" someone in the home office asked. "We've been offered three times the regular premium."

The Captain said he could not, and wondered if it would cost him his job. The insurance went elsewhere. Two weeks after the vessel had sailed an SOS from mid-atlantic reported the ex-lake freighter breaking up in a storm. That was the last ever heard from the *Maryland*.[12]

In 1915 the company's war-risk premiums were $1,387,100 and claims paid $390,300, a loss ratio of 28.2. Ordinary premiums were $3,845,000; losses $2,189,900.

5

On February 8, 1916, Eugene L. Ellison, president of the Insurance Company of North America, died. He had joined the company the year of the Chicago fire, 1871, and had been its head since 1909. Benjamin Rush was elected to succeed Mr. Ellison. He was forty-six years old, the youngest but one of the nine men who had held that office since the founding of the company 123 years before.

At the same time John O. Platt, in charge of the fire branch, was raised to the senior vice-presidency, and Sheldon Catlin was made second vice-president.

At the next annual meeting, January 10, 1917, promotions were given to the men who, under Rush, bore the brunt of the burden of directing the home office and of the war effort. Galloway C. Morris was elected third vice-president in charge of marine, and T. Leaming Smith was appointed marine secretary. Morris, a native of near-by Chester County, Pennsylvania, born 1881, was educated at Haverford College. In 1909 Rush hired him away from Johnson & Higgins to head the North America's Marine Loss Department. Smith was born in New York City in 1886 and educated at Philadelphia's Episcopal Academy and at Princeton. He came with the North America in 1908 and at the start of the war was a clerk in the Automobile Department. Morris asked him to stay one night to help out the marine clerks in an emergency. He never got back to automobiles.

The other key men on the war staff were Henry W. Farnum, head of the company's New York office, and Herbert Damon, chief of the Boston office until ill-health obliged him to retire in favor of Thomas R. Young. It is noteworthy that in these critical years posts of responsibility were won by the two men associated with Rush in the revolutionary classification work of 1897—Farnum and Young.

The story of the year 1916 was one of increasing submarine effectiveness. Eighty-one thousand tons of shipping was sent to the bottom in January. In December the figure rose to 355,100 tons. The year's total was 2,328,000 against 1,438,000 in 1915. Not all these sinkings were by submarines, but most of them were. The chief other cause of destruction was mines, which German submarines began to lay late in 1915. This was a new technique. Surface ships sank a few vessels and one or two small ones were destroyed by bombs dropped from airplanes. Germany was building bigger and better submarines. She was handling them more skillfully and more ruthlessly. More often than not sinkings were without warning, leaving crews to their fates. Moreover, the U-boats invaded the Mediterranean where the placid and narrow sea lanes and the weakness of Allied countermeasures created a veritable paradise for the submersibles. True,

BENJAMIN RUSH

Ninth president Insurance Company of North America, 1916-1939. Chairman of the Board
since 1939. Architect of the modern company and one of great creative underwriters of his
time. Entered insurance business as an office boy at fifteen. At twenty-eight reorganized
North America's losing marine business. His method copied throughout world. In 1920 began
program of expansion and diversification which placed company in every branch of insurance
except life.

From a portrait by Vaughn Borie, owned by the Insurance Company of North America.

Italy was brought into the war on the Allied side but without much effect on the adverse situation.

Scant respect was paid to neutral flags, the Stars and Stripes excepted. Norway lost 192 vessels, or more than France. Sweden lost 52, Holland 26 and Denmark 52. Our losses were five, the same as in 1915. Germany's attention to the United States was largely confined to an extensive sabotage campaign in our munitions plants and to propaganda calculated to turn us from the Allies or to frighten us into shrinking from war in any event. Though propaganda was largely a failure, in the line of sabotage the Germans did fairly well.

This drain on shipping began to pinch, and the disheartening feature was that nothing the Allies could devise to stop the subs seemed to work. A boom was stretched across the English Channel from Folkestone to Cape Griz-Nez. At night the submarines went over it and in the daytime they went under it. Only twenty-two submarines were put out of business in the year, an increase of three over 1915. In the same time the damage done by submarines had doubled. In the face of this it seems unusual that war-risk insurance rates remained as low as they did. On December 1 they were 1½ per cent between the United States and Great Britain but shortly thereafter were raised to 2 and 3 per cent.

For the year the North America's marine premiums totaled $6,762,000, the highest in the company's history to that time. Of this amount $2,269,000 were for war-risk insurance. War-risk claims paid were $773,000, giving a loss ratio of 34.1. Common-risk losses were $2,605,000.

6

In the face of the depletion of world shipping in 1916 our own merchant marine grew to 2,191,000 tons, or double what it had been in July 1914. Our exports to the Allies amounted to $3,012,000,000 of which $1,290,000,000 were munitions. These statistics did not escape the German war lords, and early in 1917 the Kaiser was prevailed upon to stake everything on one cast of the dice and to declare unrestricted submarine warfare against anyone sending anything to the Allies.

This required months of persuasion, for the Emperor was afraid of stirring up a hornet's nest in the United States. The navy clique exhibited the impressive figures on sinkings for the last months of 1916. They exhibited data on dwindling British food stocks, rising prices, marine-insurance rates, ocean freight rates and so on. If this could be done by "restricted" submarine warfare, an unrestricted campaign would bring Britain to her knees in six months at latest Suppose the United States should declare war. What blows could she strike in six months? By these arguments the Kaiser was won over.[13]

On January 31, 1917, the German ambassador informed our State Department that unrestricted warfare would begin the next morning, thus leaving no time for debate. On February 3 the ambassador received his passport; diplomatic relations with Germany were at an end. On February 24 the country was inflamed by the publication of the Zimmermann Note, which had fallen into our hands. It was addressed by Herr Zimmermann, German foreign secretary, to the German minister to Mexico suggesting that Mexico and Japan be egged into attacking the United States. Annexation of Texas, New Mexico and Arizona was held out as bait to Mexico. Then came news of the sinking of the American vessels *City of Memphis, Illinois* and *Vigilancia.* (The North America lost $107,648 on the *Vigilancia.*) On April 6 we declared war.

Meantime German submarines seemed to be sweeping everything before them. Sinkings for January, the last month of the "restricted" phase, were 368,000 tons. February they leaped to 540,000, March to 593,000. Germany's answer to our war declaration was to sink 881,000 tons in April. Six more months of this and the prophecy of the German naval experts would be borne out: Britain starved into defeat before we could land a blow. Insurance rates to Britain and Mediterranean ports soared to 6, 8, 10 and even to 20 per cent. Panic threatened the market.

At a meeting of the Executive Committee of the Board of Directors, the suggestion was thrown out that the North America retire temporarily from the war-risk market. A few other American companies already were out. Precedent for the action existed in the North America's early history. It could be done again by the usual means of quoting no rates or rates that were prohibitive. Mr. Rush said such a course would be a blow to the North America's leadership from which it might take years to recover. More than that, the country was at war. Everyone must take chances and make sacrifices.

It was the company's duty to remain in the market. Nothing more was said on the subject.[14]

May brought a little better news. Sinkings dropped to 596,000 tons. Was this merely a periodical dip, or was the United States Navy making its weight felt? Anxiously underwriters scanned the cumulative June record from day to day. At the end of the month countenances were grave. Sinkings had risen to 687,000. July they went down again: 557,000. On August 1 the North America reduced rates on Allied vessels to the United Kingdom to 6 per cent; to Mediterranean ports, 8½, scaling down, in some instances, to 6½ per cent. Rates for neutrals were ½ to 1 per cent higher.

August sinkings dropped a little more—to 511,000—and in September there was cause for genuine optimism when sinkings fell to 351,000. November, with losses of 289,000, saw a desperate crisis passed. Not only were Britain and France being sustained. One hundred thousand American soldiers were in France and the greatest troop movement, in terms of numbers and distances, which the world had seen to that time, was under way.

This defeat, from which Germany was never to recover, was due to several factors. It was known that convoys afforded the best protection against underwater attack. The United States Navy gave Britain's battered and worn fleets the reinforcement which did most to turn the tide. Improvement of technique in the use of the depth charge, first used in 1916, and the introduction of the hydrophone for locating submerged U-boats by sound also had their place. For another thing the Germans simply could not keep up the pace they set in the spring of the year. Neither machines nor men could stand it. The Germans lost sixty-three submarines in 1917 as against twenty-two the year before. The losing nature of the fight was even more clearly shown by the fact that thirty-three of the sixty-three subs were bagged in the last four months of the year, when merchant sinkings were lowest.

The North America, and indeed insurance companies generally, felt the strain of that eventful year. North America's war-risk premiums were $5,185,600, and claims paid $2,750,100; a loss ratio of 53.4 as compared with 34.1 for 1916. Ordinary premiums were $6,226,000 and ordinary losses $2,635,000. Thus total marine premiums for the year were $11,411,049, exceeding the fire account for the first—and last—time since 1881.

7

On the seas the victory was won in 1917. The problem for 1918 was to hold what had been gained, to keep the U-boats in check while the land forces achieved the final triumph. This was done handsomely. January sinkings were 356,000 tons, a figure never attained again though the end of winter brought weather more favorable for submarine work. By April the total was down to 278,-000, by July to 260,000, September to 187,000. The "bridge of boats" across the Atlantic was maintained. The land forces went in and cleaned up. By midsummer the fabulous German military machine had cracked. In October it collapsed with a speed that amazed even the conquerors. On the eleventh of November all was over.

During the year marine underwriters were busier than ever though rates declined steadily. After the Armistice nominal war-risk premiums were maintained while the seas were swept free of floating mines. The job was done.

From 1914 to 1919, inclusive, the Insurance Company of North America had written war-risk policies with an aggregate net value (after cancellations) of $1,486,800,000. Gross premiums were $16,-858,000; net premiums, after commissions and expenses, $12,843,000; making an average rate of .86 per cent for the war. It was the low premium rate in effect after the Armistice that brought the company's average rate under 1 per cent. The average during the period of active hostilities was 1.15. Total net losses (after salvage) were $5,873,000, giving an all-over loss ratio of 45.8.

It is interesting to contrast these figures with corresponding statistical data on the Government's Bureau of War Risk Insurance. The Bureau wrote insurance totaling $2,067,308,000 against North America's $1,486,000,000. The Government collected $46,743,000 gross premiums and net premiums of $46,563,000 making the average rate 2.2 per cent. This high figure is misleading, however, inasmuch as there is only $180,000 difference between the Government's gross revenue and its net. Operating expenses were met by the taxpayers. They did not lose on the deal, however. When the Bureau wound up its marine insurance activities a profit of $16,600,000 was paid into the Treasury. Making a normal allowance for operating costs, it would still appear that the Government's average rate exceeded that of the North America. The explanation doubtless lies in the fact

that the Government accepted a greater volume of extremely hazardous and therefore high-rated business than did the company.

8

The fire branch of the North America also hung up a record during the war. Before going into that, however, it will be necessary
to catch up with the fire part of our story by reviewing a few matters
subsequent to the San Francisco calamity.

That disaster occasioned the largest fire deficit in the company's
history—$2,169,911. The following year of 1907 returned the largest
fire profit—$894,625. John O. Platt assumed full charge of the fire
branch in 1910, introducing a number of forward underwriting policies and administrative reforms. The closing of an epoch was
marked when J. F. Downing retired, in 1910, as manager of the
Western Department, a post he had held since the creation of that
department "a year before the peace at Appomattox," as the old
gentleman phrased it in a letter of farewell to his agents.[15] The
new manager was W. N. Johnson, fifteen years Downing's first
assistant. Under him the department headquarters were moved to
Chicago from Erie, Pennsylvania, where Downing had established
them in 1864.

The San Francisco fire, wherein a majority of the insurance com-
panied involved failed to redeem their pledges in full, was occasion
for a general boost in rates. Had this occurred before the fire it
doubtless would have been a signal for an uproar in a dozen state
legislatures which through their anti-compact and other laws were
taking an active interest in the conduct of insurance companies.
With the lesson of San Francisco before them there was scarcely a
murmur. This is not to say that official bodies had taken their eyes
off the fire companies. The New York Legislature's investigation of
life insurance in which Charles Evans Hughes distinguished himself
as the committee's counsel had made its searching report in 1906.
The result was a needed housecleaning of the life business, and a
centering of attention on *all* insurance companies. Within the next
ten years ten separate state investigations of fire companies were
made. The most important of the inquisitorial bodies, the Merritt
Committee of New York, published its report in 1911.

This document contained recommendations which Platt and other fire-insurance leaders had been advocating for many years. The committee went on record as opposed to the anti-compact laws and to arbitrary rate regulation by states. It urged that rating bureaus established by the companies be recognized by law and placed under state supervision.

The report was a salient factor in reversing a trend toward state interference which had begun about 1880. Designed to preserve free competition this activity actually had encouraged weakly financed companies. Kentucky was one state which without heeding the warnings of the Merritt report made its contribution toward progress indirectly.

A law passed in 1912 set up a board empowered to prepare rate schedules and made it unlawful for companies to use other rates. The State Insurance Board ordered a 20-per-cent reduction on dwellings to become effective on March 15, 1913. The leading companies threatened to withdraw from the State and while underwriters were conferring with the governor a $150,000 fire occurred in Hopkinsville, Kentucky. Twenty-three buildings were destroyed with only $50,000 insurance in force. Rebuilding could not be commenced unless loans were secured and loans in turn were not forthcoming without insurance. By March 10, 1914, forty-seven companies, including the North America, had withdrawn and industrial concerns were considering moving. Banks threatened to call $162,000,000 of liquor loans if insurance on warehouses were canceled. A compromise was reached under which the law was not enforced and the companies returned to the State. The act was later held unconstitutional.

In the year 1914 the fire branch lost money for the first time since the San Francisco year. There was no great conflagration. The largest single loss was $68,000 at Salem, Massachusetts. An abnormal accumulation of small losses, however, made up a total of $3,750,657 which was enough to put the fire branch $147,000 in the red. Such are the fortunes of the insurance business.

9

By the end of 1914 the war boom was on and Mr. Platt had a busy four years. The enormous industrial expansion and enhancement of all insurable property values was attended by a marked increase in the incidence of hazards. Plants were operated at a feverish rate. Machines were run almost continuously and repairs postponed beyond the period of safety. Buildings were hastily erected with small attention to fire prevention. Electric and heating installations were hastily done. Goods were stored and handled less carefully. Untrained men were put at work beyond their skills. Explosives, the greatest fire hazard on earth, were produced, stored and shipped in quantities hitherto unknown.

The fire branch came through it all with a truly remarkable record. Premiums rose from $6,074,000 in 1914 to $11,505,000 in 1918. The fire profit for 1918 was $2,359,000. In the biggest munitions disaster of the war, the work of German saboteurs at Black Tom, New Jersey, the explosion of 2,000,000 pounds of munitions was heard in Philadelphia ninety-three miles away. On this the North America sustained its heaviest strictly war loss—$132,000. In the Kingsland (New Jersey) munitions blast it lost $76,000. Its second largest single loss during the war period was $79,000 on a cotton fire in Paris, Texas. In the course of postwar settlements Germany eventually indemnified the company for the Black Tom and Kingsland losses to a substantial extent.

The satisfactory operation of the fire and marine branches enabled the directors to increase the dividend rate in 1916 from 12 to 15 per cent. This was the first rate increase since 1870 when the rate went from 12 to 20 per cent. In 1890 it was back to 12 where it remained until 1916. The amount of dividends had been increased in 1910, however, when the capital stock was raised from $3,000,000 to $4,000,000 without a change in the dividend rate. In 1917 the 15-per-cent rate was increased by an additional 1¼ per cent ($50,000), declared for the benefit of the American Red Cross. In 1918 the rate went to 16 per cent and in 1919 to 21½.

The fire branch held its wartime gains in business. In 1919 premiums went to $13,800,000 and during the gilded twenties to $26,-000,000 and more a year. Wartime gains were held because in the midst of that hurly-burly the fire branch was building for peace. One small but significant incident:

In 1916 Mr. Platt called in his adjusters and Mr. Rush, who had just become president, addressed them. He said he wanted them to make generous settlements; no hair-splitting; no technicalities; resolve doubts in favor of the assured. "Do the fair thing and not the technical thing."

There was printed on the backs of drafts sent in settlement of claims a short message over the signature of Benjamin Rush. It said that the loss had been settled to the best of the ability of the company, which meant to be fair. If the assured had any complaint he was asked to write.

For some time Mr. Rush received an average of a letter a month in response to this invitation. All involved small amounts. Few of the writers seemed to be chiselers.

The company believes that one of the results of this policy has been to reduce padded claims. Apparently the word has got around that it isn't necessary to pad a claim to get a fair shake from the North America.

CHAPTER XVI

NEW GROWTH

I

IN THE language of a contemporary with a flair for Shakespearean allusions, the victory of the Allies created a "brave new world" as a workshop wherein mankind could fashion a nobler destiny.

In the domain of statecraft there was the League of Nations to impart reality to Mr. Wilson's ideal of a world "safe for democracy." The arms limitation conference of 1921 and the Kellogg pact outlawing war seemed further steps in the right direction. Then, from causes unnecessary to try to indicate here, this elaborate machinery failed to do what was expected. The upshot was Hitler, his satellites and imitators; the humiliation of democracy at Munich; and, in 1939, an attack and unprepared democracy's decision to resist again rather than perish.

In the domain of business the brave new world of 1919 progressed sumptuously into the "prosperous twenties," one aspect of which was a fool's paradise of stock gambling which had its inevitable denouement in just ten years—1929.

But give business a few marks on the credit side. The twenties were not altogether a buying-on-margin saturnalia. There were examples of broad and solid expansion patterned in the light of extraordinary vision. Despite all that has happened they stand today as testimony that business *could* do its part to lend substance to the dream of a better world the statesmen of Versailles said was ours for the having. A case in point was the DuPont Company, which turned from the manufacture of explosives in which it had been engaged for more than a century to the little-explored empire of industrial chemistry and its adaptation to peacetime uses. Another illustration was General Motors. Another was the Insurance Company of North America.

2

It has been the endeavor of these pages to show something of how this company grew large from small beginnings. In 1792 there were only three kinds of insurance: marine, fire and life—and life was very new. Launching itself in marine, the aristocracy of insurance-dom, the North America took on fire as a sideline. As late as 1815 it was happy when the revenues from this branch paid the office expenses. The time came, though, when fire drew even with marine, then outstripped it, and in the troubled eighties and nineties preserved the dividends. Both marine and fire became enormously diversified, for the growth of insurance was the growth of America. A hundred new kinds of insurance, outside the confines of either marine or fire, came into existence. By 1919 instead of being able to count the available forms of insurance on the fingers of one hand, one could insure almost anything.

A man might wish to insure the bonds he had sent by registered mail; his payroll messenger against highway robbery; his country house against injury by a falling airplane or a flying meteor; the plate glass window in his store; his daughter's Cremona violin; his wife's furs and jewelry while traveling; himself against the defalcation of a cashier, the claims of an employee for compensation for injuries; or the possibility of a damage suit by a guest in his home who might slip on a cake of bathroom soap. Local agents of the North America were reporting that clients, and brokers acting for them, liked to do business where they could do it with the least trouble—which meant, other things being equal, placing all their insurance with one company.

English underwriters were the first to appreciate this. The new developments of insurance had been largely in fields known to the trade as "inland marine" (a misnomer as will presently be seen), and "casualty." The average marine charter permitted the writing of risks in the inland-marine category, though casualty risks required separate incorporations. By the end of the war several British companies had established casualty annexes in the United States. Our own Hartford set up the Hartford Accident and Indemnity. Benjamin Rush decided to meet this competition. He persuaded his Board that the North America should prepare to write virtually every known form of insurance except life.

The first step was to get in hand additional capital. The company being in tiptop condition this proved simple. On February 14, 1920, stockholders voted 301,813 shares to 0 to increase the capitalization from $4,000,000 to $5,000,000. One hundred thousand new shares were subscribed at $20 each, $1,000,000 of the proceeds being placed to capital stock and $1,000,000 to surplus. It is interesting to note that one of the three tellers who announced the result of the stockholders' referendum was Alexander J. Dallas Dixon, a grandson of Alexander James Dallas, an original North America stockholder whom the reader may recall.

This money was used to start on its career the Indemnity Insurance Company of North America, which began business in September 1920 with a capital of $1,000,000 and a surplus of the same amount. All the stock was owned by the Insurance Company of North America. Except in unusual cases fire agents for the North America acted also as agents for the Indemnity.

The field which the old company thus invaded was rapidly growing and about as varied as human experience. Individuals, partnerships and corporations were offered protection against hundreds of kinds of losses both direct (a cracksman enters your office and blows the safe) and indirect (a chauffeur in your employ driving your automobile hits a pedestrian who sues you). As in the case of the automobile accident much of the business is third-party liability, with all the complications that can entail: the insurance company (first party) protects the assured (second party) against damages to someone else (third party). An adjuster in the casualty field regards the work of a colleague in fire or marine as simplicity itself.

The principal items in the casualty field in 1920 included fidelity and surety bonds; public official bonds; contract and supply bonds; lost 'securities bonds; license and permit bonds; and various court and judicial bonds such as administrators' and executors'; guardians'; trustees' and referees'; appeal; attachment; replevin. Protection against theft, burglary or robbery in the home, office or plant comprised another category. Insurance could be taken against personal accident or disability; against public liability by automobile or elevator owners or by contractors or manufacturers. Automobile collision insurance was a very large item. Employers could find protection against workmen's compensation claims.

To the North America this was a new field. And the insurance fraternity as a whole lacked the backlog of casualty experience available to underwriters of marine and of fire risks. Most casualty lines were less than thirty years old, some less than ten. Men who had been in casualty all their lives, though possessing a decided advantage over newcomers, were still learning by trial and error. The business was where fire insurance was about 1850.

During its first full year of existence, 1921, Indemnity was active. It collected $3,335,000 in premiums but wound up with an underwriting loss of $608,000. In 1922 the parent company contributed another $1,000,000 to its subsidiary's surplus. That year Indemnity's premium income mounted to $5,578,000 and the underwriting loss moderated to $554,000. In 1923 prospects brightened. Premium income was $7,293,000, surpassing marine with $6,549,000. The underwriting loss fell almost to the vanishing point—$39,000. Moreover, Indemnity had brought an undetermined amount of business to the fire account simply because Indemnity agents and North America fire agencies were usually consolidated in the same individual. And Mr. Rush predicted even better things in the future.[1]

3

The expansion program did not end with embarking the company in the casualty business. It included the old standbys of fire and marine as well. To this end additional subsidiary companies were set up.

The first object was to get more business. When advocating the establishment of the Philadelphia Underwriters in 1894 that cagey old agency tactician, J. F. Downing, had pointed out that two representatives in a town could get more business than one. This still held true. Meantime, however, the number of agents which a company could maintain in one place had been limited—usually to two—by the regional associations or conferences.

These conferences were institutions in which a small company had the same say as a large one. This resulted in the limitation of agents. The only way the large companies could get around the regulation was to form affiliates or subsidiaries. With one affiliate the North America could place four agents where it had had two before; with two affiliates, six agents, and so on. The affiliates could operate with reduced overhead, having the benefit of the parent company's management, agency structure, inspection and loss-prevention services.

The second object of the subsidiary system was to enable the parent company to retain a greater proportion of its profitable business by reinsuring such business with subsidiaries.

The first step toward a subsidiary system had been taken in January 1895 when the Philadelphia Underwriters had entered the field under the joint proprietorship of the North America and the Fire Association. The second step was in 1904 when the Alliance, a subsidiary in fact if not by strict legal definition, was launched. These enterprises had been profitable, despite the staggering loss to Alliance in the San Francisco fire.

In December 1921 the North America acquired its second outright subsidiary—Indemnity having been the first—by the purchase of a majority of the stock of the National Security Fire Insurance Company of Omaha, Nebraska. This was a small institution of $250,000 capital, but with a valuable agency plant in its territory. Under the laws of Pennsylvania one fire-insurance company could not own another fire-insurance company, although it could own a casualty company. A fire company could, however, own a holding company which in turn could own another fire company. Therefore the Insurance Company of North America formed the Securities Company of North America which bought the National Security of Omaha. In 1923 the capital of the subsidiary was increased to $500,000.

For some years the North America had been chary of putting too much skill and energy into building up the Philadelphia Underwriters. Half of the profits went to a competing company. In 1923 a long series of negotiations was terminated whereby the North America purchased the Fire Association's interest in the Underwriters. Thereupon, through its holding company, the North America formed the Philadelphia Fire and Marine Insurance Company—capital $1,000,000, surplus $1,000,000—to take over the Underwriters' agency plant and business. In its first year the new company's operations showed a profit of $705,000.

During 1923 the Alliance, the National Security of Omaha and the Philadelphia Fire and Marine reinsured with the parent company risks representing a premium income of $6,238,817. The North America reinsured with the affiliates risks representing a premium income of $1,967,476, leaving a gain to the North America of $4,271,341.

Later we shall speak of the performances of the subsidiaries after 1923, where we now leave them. At this time, however, it may be helpful to note how the North America eventually rounded out its "fleet" of companies. In 1928 the Alliance Insurance Company was made a full-fledged subsidiary by the purchase of all Alliance stock excepting qualifying shares in the hands of directors. The same year the Alliance Casualty Company was formed with $1,000,000 capital and $1,000,000 surplus. In 1930 the North America purchased the sixty-five-year-old Central Fire Insurance Company of Baltimore with assets exceeding $4,500,000.

Thus the fleet consisted of: the parent company; four subsidiary fire and marine companies—the Alliance, the Philadelphia Fire and Marine, the National Security of Omaha and the Central of Baltimore; two casualty companies—the Indemnity of North America and the Alliance Casualty.

4

While getting its fleet under way the North America also played a leading role in the postwar development of its original line, ocean-marine insurance.

The war had the effect of re-establishing the American merchant marine, largely through Government construction. In 1919 our tonnage engaged in or available for foreign commerce was 10,300,000. In 1914 it had been just over a million tons. For the first time in half a century we were a real rival of Britain for the carrying trade of the world. It was the ambition of the Government, and the hope of most of our citizens, that the flag should stay on the seas, the United States Shipping Board transferring to private ownership the vessels to which it held title. The success of this project depended upon a number of things. For one, an adequate marine-insurance market, free of London domination, would have to be created. Part and parcel of any merchant marine is sufficient insurance capital, under the same flag, to protect it.

The Committee on Merchant Marine and Fisheries of the House of Representatives was wrestling with the problem. Its chairman, Congressman George Washington Edmonds, a Philadelphia businessman, got in touch with Benjamin Rush. Conferences between marine-insurance leaders and members of the committee followed. A program was devised for which Hendon Chubb, William R. Hedge, president of the Boston Insurance Company, and Mr. Rush were largely responsible.

The program had to do with hull insurance solely, the Government being interested only in the vessels and not their cargo. In 1920 three syndicates called A, B and C were organized.

Syndicate A consisted of forty-seven American insurance companies. The object was to inspect hulls for seaworthiness, to appraise damage after an accident and agree with the owners on a settlement. This organization filled a real need. It was shortly incorporated as a non-profit company under the title of United States Salvage Association. As such it exists today, performing a great service to American marine underwriters. Its surveyors are located throughout the world. They know what can and does happen to vessels at sea, how to repair them and what the cost of such repairs should be. They may be called upon for advice on damaged vessels or other information of use to underwriters in out-of-the-way foreign ports.

Syndicate B, comprising forty-seven American companies, was formed to insure the Government's mortgage interest in the vessels it sold. Premiums were fixed by a rating committee of the syndicate. After a year or two London began cutting its rates below those of the syndicate. The Shipping Board permitted ship purchasers to insure where the rates were lowest and permitted the syndicate to abolish its rate schedule, allowing constituent members to compete with London if they saw fit. This marked the end of Syndicate B's active operations.

Syndicate C had a different history. It is in existence today and, until after our entry into World War II, it handled virtually all the insurance written on American-owned or -operated ocean steamers of more than 500 tons. Rates are fixed by a committee. Forty-seven American and thirty-seven foreign companies, mostly English, participated in the syndicate at the outset. It was necessary to admit the foreign companies because American underwriting capital was insufficient to the task at hand. Originally the combined interest of the foreign companies was only 20 per cent of the whole, and the American interest 80 per cent. In the beginning the second largest single subscriber was the North America, with an interest of 7.2 per cent.

The Globe & Rutgers was first with 9.05 per cent. Eventually the North America became the largest participant, and so remains.

During the first three years of their existence Benjamin Rush served as chairman of the Board of Managers, or governing body, of the syndicates. His administration saw these organizations safely launched as an indispensable factor in the creation of our modern mercantile marine.

Building contracted for in wartime brought American tonnage to 15,900,000 in 1922, or 5,000,000 more than when the Armistice was signed. Upon American underwriters fell the bulk of the insurance burden of keeping as much as possible of that enormous fleet at sea—not alone for peacetime needs but also to provide military and naval auxiliaries in case of another emergency. The difficulties were enormous. American ships, paying the highest wages in the world to seamen, were thrown in competition with foreign vessels whose overhead was much less. Consequently our tonnage declined, but the remarkable fact is that it declined so little. In 1936 it aggregated 13,500,000 tons, though a large part of the ships were obsolescent. In that year President Roosevelt, with a weather eye on Hitler, launched a program of direct Government subsidies for new building and operation. In this farsighted move Syndicate C and the insurance community generally had their parts to play, as will be seen.[2]

5

The marine syndicates, which had the benefit of direction by the ablest minds in American underwriting, were concerned with hulls only. As to the cargoes carried in those American hulls, and others, insurance companies were left to act independently, each according to its own judgment. In 1919 there was business for everyone and premiums rolled in like a flood. The rehabilitation of a war-devastated and war-starved world had begun. European industry would be months, at least, in making the change-over from war to peacetime production. In the interim Europe itself would be a market for American products. The rest of the world would be a market. The demand was for foodstuffs, shoes, clothing, farm machinery, automobiles, household furnishings and about everything else required to put civilized society back on its own. In 1920 our exports were the highest in history—$8,228,000,000. In 1914 they had been $2,364,000,-

000. In 1921 this bubble burst. Europe was practically feeding itself again and making its own shoes. The collapse of foreign currencies made overseas trade a chancy business anyhow. In 1922 our exports were down to $3,831,000,000.

Before the deflation of 1921, however, insurance companies were headed for trouble. So great had been the rush to send stuff abroad that both forwarding and receiving ports were clogged. In South America docks became so congested that steamers could not unload for weeks. Before the war merchants and shippers had been content to insure against the ordinary perils of the sea, the incidence of which was predictable. Now they demanded protection against theft, pilferage, breakage, damage from salt water, ship's sweat, contact with other cargo and so on. In the lexicon of insurancedom the new factors were known as "extended conditions." It was not a term calculated to promote serenity of mind among the underwriting fraternity. Adequate experience on which to base rates for extended condition risks did not exist. Underwriters faced a situation as imponderable as insurance against the risks of wartime capture or destruction a few years before. Then the insurance market had been a seller's market; now it was a buyer's market. A war-expanded industry needed a large volume of business to keep going. In the scramble for it, rates were fixed by guesswork under bearish pressure to land business. The assurance of protection afforded an incentive to shippers to ship even more to already congested ports.

Inexperienced underwriters could not cope with such conditions. Nearly all the fire companies which had gone into marine insurance during the war boom closed their marine branches, wiser if not richer for their ventures. War-born marine companies folded, some unable to pay their losses in full. By 1924 the marine-insurance market was practically back to the old-established offices which had comprised it before the war. And only a few of these had much left of the undistributed surpluses of those fat years.

The North America was one of the few. Since 1920 it had been using a share of its surplus to promote the program of growth through subsidiaries. In addition to this it had come through the hectic postwar inflation and collapse, still making money from marine underwriting. True, there had been one bad year—1921—which was a bad year all around for American business. The North America's marine loss was $889,202, representing its first in-the-red year since

1899. This was more than made up in 1922 by a marine profit of $1,168,223. The marine profit in 1923 was $1,034,113 and in 1924 $475,113, despite the precarious nature of those years for the industry as a whole.

6

"An ounce of prevention is worth a pound of cure." Benjamin Franklin, insurance pioneer, loved to quote these words which express a fundamental law of underwriting. The archives of the North America reveal that as early as 1797 pilots and boatmen at home in those treacherous waters were retained under fee in Delaware Bay to reduce the likelihood of mishap to vessels. As time went on this service greatly improved, all the Philadelphia underwriters bearing a share of the expense. Nearly three generations later we encounter the sea-going tug *North America,* one or two of whose exploits have been mentioned in these pages, and which remained in service for twenty-five years. After the turn of the present century the marine underwriters' associations emulating the fire associations took up the work. The North America continued to do much on its own, as when it showed shipowners how to cut the mortality of cattle exported to the United Kingdom and the Continent of Europe from 7 to ¼ of 1 per cent.

Experience in the prevention of losses, as well as an uncanny knack for distinguishing good business from bad (thanks to unremitting attention to the classification system Rush introduced in 1898), were factors in the shrewd program which enabled the North America to do so well during the extended-condition and commodity-inflation crisis of 1919-1921. Extended conditions were here to stay. Analysis of a few years' losses convinced the North America that a high percentage of them were preventable. This the old company set out to accomplish by carrying the science of loss-prevention beyond anything then known. The result was the organization, in 1924, of the Marine Service Department under the supervision of Marine Secretary T. Leaming Smith.

Much preventable loss was found to be due to improper packing. With the advent of high postwar tariffs exporters and importers sought to save on this item. It was poor economy, for satisfactory delivery is a valuable asset to any business. From the assured's point of view prevention of a claim is better than the payment of one. That it is better from the insurer's point of view goes without saying—and so another link in the long chain of evidence that what is good for the underwriter is usually good for the purchaser of his wares.

The Service Department made a study of the packing and stowing of the following commodities: furs, automobiles, rugs, pianos, leather, hides, skins, cash registers and other business machines, plate glass, razor blades, cherries in brine, olives, vegetable oils, sausage casings, flour, cocoa, coffee, linseed, spices, tanning materials, linens, laces, embroideries, hats, gloves, silk, chemicals, toilet preparations, artificial flowers, veneer panels and doors, furniture, newsprint, tobacco, fresh fruit, canned goods, eggs, wines and liquors, cast iron pipe, tin plate, galvanized sheet, concrete reinforcing rods, horses, mules, rubber, heavy machinery and on-deck cargo generally.

North America's experts learned things about the shipment of some of these products which men who had been in the business a lifetime did not know. Firms whose names are known the world over were glad to adopt suggestions offered by the insurance company. Some interesting discoveries were made. To cite one at random: In the Argentine an importer of metal screws offered proof that the screws were arriving damaged by rust. It was salt-water damage. The North America paid for it and began an investigation. The screws were made by a well-known Connecticut manufacturer. They were shipped in watertight boxes of a type approved by the North America. Captain Jeffcott of the New York office of the Service Department watched the entire process of the manufacture and packing of a consignment of screws. He saw them on their way in airtight boxes. Opened in the Argentine they showed salt-water rust. Jeffcott went to Maine where the wood-pulp cartons, in which the screws were shipped, were made. There he found the solution to the riddle. The carton manufacturer was using salt water to wash his wood pulp. Enough moisture remained in the finished product to affect the screws.

The theft of valuable furs, particularly in connection with German shipments, was a source of heavy losses. The North America designed tamper-proof cases and saw the furs packed in them at Leipzig. At Bremen company representatives saw the cases on board ship and at New York other representatives saw them unloaded. Other North America men rode on the trucks which carried the cases from docks to the importer's warehouse where the cases were opened in the presence of a company agent. The thefts ceased.

Today an application for an open-policy account with the North America must be accompanied by a detailed report of the concern's packing methods made on a form supplied by the insurance company. An inspector from the Service Department then visits the applicant's packing and shipping department. If the work is up to North America standards the account is accepted. If not Service Department engineers submit recommendations which the applicant must follow or obtain his insurance elsewhere. The Department makes about a thousand such analyses a year.

Poor stowage and careless handling were other prolific causes of losses. The North America found that underwriters for years had been losing money on green hides from South America because they were not properly salted and brined during the long voyage. This attended to, the business became a paying one. In Pacific Coast ports valuable wood-veneer panels were stowed in holds with green lumber. The moisture from the lumber warped the panels. Careless winch work, unnecessary use of stevedores' hooks and use of the wrong type of loading slings were other damage causers. The North America has catalogued the various categories of cargo for each of the five principal types of slings. Steamship owners find it profitable to follow such directions. A British exporter of glass had consistently hard luck—until the North America suggested he change steamship lines.

When the North America was unable to work reforms in the intercoastal lumber and overseas flour trades, it dropped those lines until shippers perceived the advantage of instituting reforms. The German fur formula was tried without success on rugs from the Near East. A study of the situation, however, disclosed the extent of the risks involved and enabled the company to adjust its rate schedule accordingly.

The latter-day development of the Marine Service Department has been in the competent hands of R. Bruce Miller. The institution has earned its keep many times over, and has been of inestimable benefit to shippers. In 1928 preventable losses paid were $1,067,203 out of $2,796,548 received in premiums, making the loss ratio 38.2. Ten years later preventable losses paid were $496,341 out of $1,848,576 in premiums, making the loss ratio 26.08. As Mr. Miller points out this decline was achieved in the face of constantly diminishing rates over the period involved. If one were to compare the preventable losses with the value of goods insured, the decline in loss ratio would be considerably greater.[3]

7

After the war there was a remarkable growth of fire revenue. In 1919 net premiums were $13,826,000; in 1920, $19,613,000; in 1923, $22,789,000; in 1927, $26,382,000. Only one year in that eight-year span did the fire profits fall below a million dollars. In 1920 they were $4,465,000 and in 1927 $2,451,000.

Many factors contributed to this record. A weak link anywhere in the complex underwriting machine and it would have been impossible. Moreover, it would have been impossible had the policyholders who paid these premiums felt they were not getting their money's worth. Again, many factors contributed to that feeling of satisfaction on the part of the company's customers. It is our purpose here to consider only one of them, the Engineering Department of the fire branch, which roughly speaking is the opposite number of the Service Department of the marine branch though it covers more ground.

In 1916, in the middle of the war, expansion was largely in the field of industrial plants. The North America wanted this business, and also very naturally it wanted to know what the risks were. Accordingly John O. Platt, in charge of the fire branch, organized the Improved Risk Engineering Department. C. W. Johnson headed it. The object was to obtain technical underwriting information on manufacturing plants which would enable the company to increase its lines without increasing its loss ratio. Unusual features of construction, good or bad, were reported. Operational hazards were considered, and safeguards noted. This information was for company use only and it was in addition to the great volume of underwriting data on manufacturing plants which had been accumulating in the manuals for a hundred years, available to anyone.

This enterprise was profitable. It enabled the North America to expand in the right direction. Soon it became apparent that assureds welcomed information as to the weaknesses of their plants from an underwriting standpoint, and were willing to accept the North America's advice as to changes. Then it occurred to Mr. Platt to turn his inspectors loose on a few school buildings. To obtain other business the company had been obliged to carry a good many school buildings, though it was a losing proposition. The inspectors were able to make suggestions which diminished the loss ratio until schools entered the profitable class.

In 1922 the Improved Risk and Engineering Service was made over and the name changed to Engineering Department. A number of professional civil engineers with insurance experience were added to the staff. The operations of the department, extended to nearly all classes of risks, fell largely under three heads: (1) establishment of replacement valuation of insured property, (2) fire prevention and (3) rate analysis.

It was often found that an assured did not know the value of his plant or home. Consequently he did not know the proper amount of insurance to carry. If he wished to take the trouble to hire an appraiser he could find out what his holdings were worth but the North America offered this service free. This work brought the coinsurance clause into prominence. It was remarkable the number of laymen who did not (and perhaps do not today) understand what is meant by coinsurance.

To take a simple example. Suppose your house has a replacement value of $20,000. You insure it for $10,000. When you do this you become a coinsurer with the insurance company. You say, in effect, to the company: "You carry $10,000 on the place and I'll carry $10,000." To eliminate this coinsurance clause most companies require one to insure up to 80-per-cent of value. But in the present example you have insured only to 50 per cent of value, so coinsurance is operative. Suppose your $20,000 house burns down—total loss. The company pays in full, $10,000; and you pay in full, $10,000. But suppose you have a $5,000 fire. The company does not pay $5,000. It pays ten-sixteenths of $5,000 and you pay the balance. Had you insured for 80 per cent of value, that is for $16,000, the company would have paid in full the partial loss—sixteen-sixteenths.

Thus the wisdom of ascertaining the true value of the property insured and of carrying sufficient protection, based on that value. The rates on 80-per-cent coverage, eliminating coinsurance, are lower than those on a smaller coverage. The Engineering Department did a great deal toward bringing this home to the people who buy fire insurance.

Rates, as we know, are not fixed by the individual companies but by rating bureaus which they club together to maintain under official supervision. A company is powerless to grant an assured a lower rate unless he complies with certain fire-prevention requirements. The Engineering Department worked with assureds, showing them how they could make changes which would entitle them to lower rates in accord with the rating-bureau standards.

This brings us down to the engineering service as it exists today, under the direction of Warren J. Baker. Qualified engineers are stationed in or available to the company's twenty-eight service offices throughout the country. Frequently the services of these men are used also by the inland-marine division of the marine branch and the Automobile Department. The engineering service is definitely a part of the production force of the North America and its affiliates. The service works with agents in determining the insurance problems of a prospect: checking existing policies; inspecting the property; analyzing coverages, forms, rates, hazards and values. From the report forthcoming is shaped a program to meet the assured's needs, covering him for all hazards at the lowest practicable cost.[4]

8

On December 6, 1881, when Charles Platt, his four fellow officers and twenty employees moved into the new home of the Insurance Company of North America at 232 Walnut Street some of the stockholders shook their heads. They thought such roomy and expensive ($250,000) accommodations unnecessary for twenty-five persons. They were unnecessary: Charles Platt had built for the future.

In 1919 the home office of the company and its affiliate, Alliance, employed more than 300 persons. Old 232 was filled pack-jam: no room for another desk. Filled also was the building of the late Delaware Mutual next door, which the North America had purchased and renovated in 1915. The Board appointed a building committee to consider the question of new quarters and set aside $300,000 to start a fund to provide them.

In 1922 the need was more pressing. The Indemnity Insurance Company was in being and further expansion just ahead. Employees numbered nearly 500, the increase having been distributed among three additional leased buildings. The directors voted unanimously that proper housing for the company and affiliates should be provided; that future as well as present needs should be considered; and that the company should own the new building. These decisions were by unanimous vote. A site at Sixteenth and Arch Streets was chosen, though not by unanimous vote.[5] Two directors felt so strongly about this departure from tradition that they resigned. A stockholder stopped Mr. Rush on the street to say that he was on his way to his broker to sell all his shares. Some years later he stopped Mr. Rush again to say that he had bought them back at a higher price.

Courage to swim against the current of precedent and a vision of the geographical pattern of Philadelphia's future were necessary for a businessman to go west of Broad Street and north of the wall of the Pennsylvania Railroad tracks in 1922. For all its six changes of location in the course of 130 years, the North America's home office had never been farther than two and a half blocks from the two rooms at 119 South Front Street in which it began business.

In his argument for a new building Mr. Rush sketched the growth of the company since 1900; assets from $9,000,000 to $48,000,000; surplus from $1,600,000 to $13,000,000; annual premium income from $6,700,000 to $28,000,000. The premium increase had been 415 per cent. During the same period the six other leading fire insurance companies had shown an average premium increase of 136 per cent. The casualty business, predicted Rush, would grow enormously, yielding, "by modest estimate," $10,000,000 in premiums in 1931. (Casualty premiums in 1929 were $16,413,000.)

The building, added Rush, "should have value as an advertisement." This was a new thought, the company having begun its first national advertising campaign only a few months before—unless the series of newspaper notices by which the company announced the extension of its local agency system west of the Alleghenies in 1808 could be called such a campaign. "While the building should be thoroughly modern the architect should be advised to try and preserve a colonial atmosphere so as to take advantage of the past history of the Company which your officers have found to be of considerable value in securing business."[6]

Mr. Rush's suggestions to the architects, Stewardson & Page, of Philadelphia, included these words:

"We want offices in which George Washington would find himself at home."

THE COMPANY'S HOME, COMPLETED 1925

The new building was occupied on November 15, 1925. Its cost, including land, was $7,750,000.

If the Father of His Country could return, it is possible that he would find there as much that would be familiar to his eye as in any modern business building of comparable dimensions in the United States. The North America's eighth home fills most of the block bounded by Sixteenth, Arch and Cuthbert Streets and the Parkway. Sixteen stories high, the exterior is a modern adaptation of the Colonial Georgian school, executed in light granite, white limestone and red brick. The simple interiors of the executive offices on the twelfth floor are fitting successors of the chastely paneled room in Independence Hall in which the Insurance Company of North America was born. The directors' room contains the largest reproduction of a Duncan Phyfe table in the world—approximately twenty-one feet long and ten feet wide. In a frame on a wall of Benjamin Rush's office is the original policy insuring the brick barn at Mount Vernon against fire.

The approach to the Board room is through a museum of relics of the company's past. The creation of this interesting gallery was largely the work of John J. Connor, former secretary and treasurer, and of Clarence A. Palmer, advertising manager, both of whom were Charles Platt's office boys.

There are primitive hand-drawn, hand-pump fire engines which Washington himself may have seen clattering over the cobbles of Philadelphia's narrow thoroughfares; hose carriages; the earliest steam engines; firemen's uniforms; fire marks of the pioneer insurance companies. There are contemporary representations of early fires; prints and paintings of famous ships which have sailed under the protection of North America insurance. In glass cases are manuscripts from the pens of Ebenezer Hazard, John M. Nesbitt, Colonel Charles Pettit and other founders of the company; receipts and letters by the hands of such personages as George Washington, Benjamin Franklin, Doctor Benjamin Rush, Stephen Girard and John Fenno.

There is the finest collection ever assembled of specimens of a department of early American painting known to only a few assiduous connoisseurs. These are engine-sides, those decorative panels with which the pioneer firemen adorned their apparatus. The handiwork of the prolific Woodside, who painted street signs when no loftier employment for his brush offered, is present in abundance. Mr.

Palmer's rarest finds, however, are two panels by Thomas Sully, executed for fire companies in New York City. The unearthing of a new Sully is an item of importance in American art circles anywhere.

Larger than the North America's home office is the structure the company erected in New York City to house its metropolitan offices. Twenty-nine stories tall and costing nearly $5,500,000 this building was completed in 1933. It stands at 99 John Street in the heart of New York's insurance district. In 1941 half a million was spent on an addition. The San Francisco office at 222 Sansome Street was built by the company at a cost of $500,000 and opened early in 1938. The building at 232 Walnut Street, Philadelphia, was retained until the spring of 1942 as the local Philadelphia office.

CHAPTER XVII

Inland Marine

I

THE term "inland marine" originally meant what it said and was used to designate insurance against the ordinary risks attending transportation on rivers, lakes and canals as distinguished from blue-water risks. The introduction of steamboats boomed river business and was the greatest single transportation factor in the settlement of the Mississippi valley. The typical frontier recklessness with which those early river steamers were operated shocked the Insurance Company of North America which judged such matters by deep-sea standards. As related in an earlier chapter, the company was very conservative in the matter of accepting river risks. The wisdom of this procedure was borne out by the fact that the field does not appear to have been very profitable for underwriters before the Civil War.

After the war, boats were somewhat stauncher and more safely operated, but very soon the railroads became formidable competitors. In the eighties the river business had about played out. The North America and most of the other leading companies had ceased writing river risks. This was the state of affairs when Edwin C. Gibbs, of Cincinnati, called on Charles Platt in 1889. Gibbs was a son-in-law and partner of Captain George W. Neare, former steamboat master and owner, who had gone in the insurance business in 1865. Gibbs convinced Mr. Platt that his firm knew the river business; that there was still a place and always would be for river transportation; that proper insurance participation could restore the business to a paying basis. Platt named the firm of George W. Neare & Company, Cincinnati, the North America's river agents. The co-operation of other large insurance companies was obtained and the slow renaissance of river traffic began. Early efforts were discouraging. The morals of the trade were low. Insurance was an invitation to wreck a boat or jettison a cargo. Neare went after that sort of thing and weeded it out. Other enterprising insurance agents joined him. The trade revived.

The firm of Neare, Gibbs & Company, as it now is called, is in the third generation of the Neare family. It remains the principal river agent of the Insurance Company of North America and affiliates. The business written does not form an impressive part of the North America's annual total, but it is consistently profitable. Nor are underwriters the only gainers. A business that had gone to the dogs was restored for the benefit of the American economy as a whole— through the foresight of an insurance agent.[1]

The North America embarked in the Great Lakes business early, and apparently it has always been a fairly good line. A Lake Marine Department was established at Chicago in 1890. In 1922 the Western Marine Department was opened there to handle all marine business for the middle states. The Great Lakes Underwriting Syndicate, similar to Syndicate C of the ocean hull group, now handles all Great Lakes business on metal freighters. Were it not for the difference in management, operation, etc., all rates on the Lakes would be the same. These factors vary so, however, that some owners, on the strength of their records, obtain rates which are half of those charged others.

Harbor business on the eastern seaboard is largely handled by the Atlantic Inland Association. The North America is not a member because of a difference of opinion concerning underwriting principles.[2]

This situation was a contributing factor to the formation, in 1939, of the Coastwise, Great Lakes and Inland Hull Association, in which the North America took a leading part. Other prime initiators were Chubb & Son, the Atlantic Mutual and the Hartford Insurance Company. This is a rating organization, not a reinsurance exchange. About 80 per cent of the market writing the class of business involved belongs to it. Its field is roughly the Atlantic seaboard and the Lakes where it facilitates the insurance of American and Canadian hulls of values in excess of $50,000. Dry docks, marine railways and builders' risks are also under its jurisdiction. The Atlantic Inland Association relinquished to the new organization jurisdiction over vessels worth more than $50,000. On the Lakes the new organization covers passenger vessels, railroad-car ferries, dredges, barges and miscellaneous craft not handled by the Great Lakes Syndicate. The principal risks

Mississippi River Steamboat

River steamboats revolutionized the transportation of passengers and freight. Boats and cargoes proved poor insurance risks, however. The North America entered the field cautiously. Captain George W. Neare of Cincinnati, insurance agent and former steamboat master, with the cooperation of the North America and other companies, reorganized river traffic so underwriters could handle it. Model of packet named in his honor from the North America's collection.

involved in order of premium income are small tankers, oil barges, railroad floating equipment, ferry boats, dredges and coastwise cargo vessels under 500 tons.

Robert R. Dwelly represented the North America in the negotiations resulting in the formation of the Coastwise, Great Lakes and Inland Hull Association. In 1942 Mr. Dwelly, hull underwriter attached to the New York office, was elected chairman of the Association for the second time.

2

Not for a generation has the term "inland marine" been used in the natural meaning of the words. It is not applied to "lake risks" or to "river risks," now so designated to distinguish them from the types of underwriting which have pre-empted the old title. So varied and so extensive is this modern inland-marine business that at first glance it might appear to a layman as if the term has come to denote a catchall for about everything under the sun. Closer examination will shoot holes in this snap judgment. Numerous and disparate as are the items which comprise present-day inland marine, almost without exception they do not fall readily into the fields of ocean marine, fire or casualty underwriting. They form a distinct species of insurance.

In the later stages of the evolution of this species the Insurance Company of North America has played an important part. It remains far ahead of its contemporaries. The 1941 edition of the by-laws of the Inland Marine Underwriters Association lists by name twenty-four classes of insurable risks. In the files of the North America is one breakdown (according to cause of loss and size of risk) of its inland-marine accounts which divides the business into fifty-six major classes. Another analysis recognizes ninety-five types of risk. Skim the latter and one will note that, among other things, the North America insures:

Motion picture film; armored cars; bridges and tunnels; cattle; horses, racing and other; cameras; coin collections; fine arts; furs; gold- and silverware; golf clubs; undertakers' equipment; motor trucks and contents thereof; musical instruments; neon signs; outboard motors; jewelry; parcel post; baggage; salesmen's samples; radium; shotguns; theater tickets; almost anything in transit whether a trainload or the contents of a registered letter; vending machines; voting machines; wedding presents.

Net premiums from this business aggregated $4,639,000 in 1941. This was 12.5 per cent of the company's income, ocean marine supplying $7,712,000 or 20.2 per cent and fire $16,712,000 or 43.9 per cent. In 1941 ocean marine benefited by an increase in premium income owing to the war. Before Herr Hitler started out to subjugate the world, inland-marine revenue was ahead of that produced by its god-parent, ocean marine.

By rule-of-thumb definition inland-marine insurance primarily covers moving or movable property while fire insurance covers fixed property or property at fixed locations. The inland-marine business grew up under the aegis of marine rather than of fire or casualty because the marine underwriters were the only ones with experience in the risks of transportation. They are, and always have been, transportation insurers. In the early days virtually all transportation was by water, and so they became specialists in that. As land transportation developed, by pack train and wagon, by railroad, motor truck and airplane, it was natural that those wishing protection should turn to the marine underwriters. Overland risks were not identical with the perils of the sea but they were more similar to them than to the hazards with which the fire and, later, the casualty companies had to contend.

A secondary reason for the drift of land transportation business to the marine companies was that their charters permitted them to write it. Early fire and casualty charters—since broadened—restricted the companies to rather narrow fields.[3]

3

The cautious beginnings of the North America in the inland field did not apply alone to river steamboats. It will be remembered that in 1850 the company declined to insure pelts Chouteau & Company brought from the Rocky Mountains to St. Louis. Not until after Benjamin Rush had the marine branch under his wing did the company really go after the business which was to prove the forerunner of modern inland marine. The first policies were called salesmen's floaters, covering the samples of drummers; theatrical floaters, covering the scenery and costumes of traveling stage troupes; horse and wagon floaters, covering merchants' delivery wagons for the most part; and transportation policies, covering merchandise aboard common carriers within the limits of the United States. When San Francisco burned the company paid $2,000 on a theatrical floater to the Cherry Blossom Burlesque Company. The tourist floater policy, introduced in 1904, covered the baggage of nonprofessional travelers. In 1909 the company began insuring registered mail and parcels sent by fourth-class mail.

Revenue was small in the beginning. Registered mail premiums were $449.08 in the first year and fourth-class mail $13,280.32. The three forms of tourist policy brought in about $20,000 and horse and wagon about $15,000, making the total receipts for 1909 in the neighborhood of $50,000. In 1912 parcel post was introduced and Rush made a drive for that class of business. The result was successful and in 1914 the inland-marine account netted premiums of $250,000 with parcel post contributing half of the total.[4]

At that time the stray items comprising inland marine were in charge of a young clerk in the Marine Loss Department named Ludwig C. Lewis. A member of an old Philadelphia family, Lewis' grandfather had been a supercargo for the account of John F. Lewis & Company on the ship *Globe,* operated by Eyre & Massey in the China trade. The North America did Eyre & Massey's insuring. After finishing at the Episcopal Academy Ludwig started to work his way through the University of Pennsylvania. Work interested him more than study and in 1909 the boy left college and took a regular job with the North America. In Rush he found a boss who did not believe a college degree essential to success in business. An aggressive young fellow determined to get on, "Wig" Lewis built inland marine into an $877,000 account by 1918. In 1919 the company sent him to China on other affairs of the marine branch.

Back from the Orient in 1920 Lewis found inland marine an orphan—"everybody's business and nobody's business," as he said later. Ludwig C. Lewis made it *his* business and went to work like a man putting out a fire. Taking a bird's-eye view of the situation he saw the possibility of developing inland marine into virtually a new insurance field. As in any pioneering effort this would involve considerable risk until sufficient experience should make it possible to fix rates at adequate levels. Additional capital would be required to carry these risks. The safe way to get it was through new reinsurance contacts. This pointed the way to London, seat of the world's greatest accumulation of insurance capital, plus the greatest experience, plus the pioneering spirit. Lewis believed Lloyd's the place to go to solicit backing for his prospective venture in inland expansion. He went there and got the backing—in the form of reinsurance agreements.[5]

The major items in Lewis' program were transportation and motor-truck insurance. The first was an old underwriting problem, involving many headaches, the second a new problem.

In the early days the railroads and the express companies had a virtual monopoly of the insurance on the goods they transported. The regular underwriters did some business in this field, the North America being one of the first, but this did not amount to a great deal. The carriers' insurance rates were whatever they elected to charge. There was no uniformity and much discrimination. Railroad operators were not practical insurance men. In instances rates were reduced far below the safety point in bids for freight. Some of the roads went into bankruptcy and shippers' losses were not paid. The Government stepped in and through the Interstate Commerce Commission asserted authority over freight and insurance rates. This ameliorated the ills but did not cure them.

The time came, during the war period, when railroads as well as shippers were anxious for help with their insurance problem. The situation was made to order for progressive underwriters who could offer complete protection without complications at reasonable rates. The carriers insured only against losses due to their negligence. The underwriters must guarantee against losses from almost any cause. To meet this need the North America introduced a "comprehensive" transportation policy insuring goods in transit via Atlantic coastwise vessels, railroads, railway express or public truckmen. Three types of coverage were offered, varying in degree from limited protection against certain specified perils to "all risks" which covered loss from almost any "external" cause. "Internal" causes were excluded. One could not (and cannot now) insure milk against souring in transit or fruit against spoiling.

By the end of the war the motor truck had become a real factor in transportation, though its great development lay ahead. The North America was fortunate in anticipating this development. From the year in which they were introduced, 1920, motor-truck policies have represented a large premium volume in the inland field. Policies were devised covering every need. Motor-truck carriers' policies in-

Coming of the Railroad

The railroad, providing new means of transporting goods, expanded the field of investment. Most pioneer railroads disappointed their financial sponsors, the Pennsylvania Railroad, founded by a director of the North America, Thomas P. Cope, being an exception. Ever chary of early railroad investments, the North America's initial purchases of Pennsylvania stock were modest.

Illustration from a painting owned by William W. Matos, reproduced by permission from Robert S. Henry's Trains.

sure the carriers' liability for damage to cargo rather than the cargo
itself. Motor-truck owners' policies protect goods conveyed by trucks
under the same ownership.

4

In this way it was that the orphan of inland marine became a full-
fledged department of the marine branch. It grew lustily. Net
premiums (minus commissions and heavy reinsurance) were $1,743,-
000 in 1920; in 1926 $2,200,000; in 1928 $3,500,000. Despite losses
due to trail-blazing inexperience and on accommodation lines assumed to secure or to retain other business, profits were highly satisfactory. Transportation, motor truck, parcel post, horse and wagon
and other old classes were constantly improved. As delivery trucks
removed Dobbin from the streets and highways, about all that
remained of the horse-and-wagon business was the name. It became
the title under which race horses and other valuable stock were
insured against fire and the perils of transportation. One type of
policy issued by the company insures valuable stock against death
from sickness or accident. It includes provision for payment when
destruction of an animal becomes an act of humanity to end incurable
suffering.

Classes new in name as well as in fact were introduced: jewelry,
jewelry floaters, jewelers' block (jewelers' own jewels in his store);
furs, fur floaters; fine arts; musical instruments; property for exhibi-
tion purposes; film floaters; laundries and dry cleaners.

It was Lewis' ambition to have the North America known as "the
American Lloyd's," meaning that it would insure almost anything
against almost any peril. To this end odd and peculiar risks were
undertaken, for example:

Bridges—difficult as it may be to believe they fell in that category
when the North America began insuring them in 1925.

Trophies—a man has one leg on a golf cup and wants protection
while it is in his possession.

Wedding presents—a ninety-day coverage. By that time the young
people are expected to have a home to put the presents in. Then they
can get regular household-effects coverage.

Installment buying—policies offered protecting both seller and
purchaser. This classification proved a headache until ironed out.

Private railroad cars—proved the reverse. Underwriters were sorry to see the automobile push these magnificent equipages into the limbo. Most of them eventually went for a song to circuses or were broken up for scrap.

Imagination, initiative, astute underwriting judgment and fortunate timing combined to promote the inland business into quick prosperity. It came at a moment of swift new developments in transportation. By augmenting, and on short hauls almost superseding, the railroad, the motor truck gave new directions to the flow of commerce. The growth of the chain idea in retailing and in manufacturing provided incentive for further transportation expansion. The result was a self-perpetuating movement of goods. Quick and constant deliveries enabled retailers to buy hand-to-mouth. The days of full stockrooms were over. On top of this was the prosperity of the twenties and the enhanced wealth it brought to individuals. There was an increase of all kinds of personal property much of it small in bulk but high in value, which the owner occasionally carried on his travels. All this was grist for the mill of the inland underwriter.

Along in 1927 and 1928 it began to be apparent that the beanstalk of inland marine was growing too fast for its own good. It had encroached on the domains of fire and casualty. Fire and casualty companies began to protest, and protests being unavailing they began to fight back. Rates were driven down and acquisition costs increased. As an official of one company said, "My company writes $25,000,000 fire insurance and $1,000,000 [inland] marine. Our president does not propose to have our large fire business jeopardized by the marine. We are willing to pay practically any commission on marine in order to protect our fire business."[6] Another complication was the entry of new companies into the inland field. State insurance departments began to take heed of the protests from the fire and casualty offices. They feared that marine companies—not controlled by rating bureaus as were the fire organizations—would cut rates so low that the weaker of them would fail. The stock market crash of 1929 and ensuing depression, cutting fire premiums, made the situation increasingly acute.

With its own fire business and its own casualty affiliates, the North America was not vitally concerned over the basic issue, *per se,* of inland's trespassing on those preserves. But when repercussions of the squabble threatened to demoralize a prosperous business, the

North America took a hand in efforts to pour oil on the troubled waters. Attempts were made through the Interstate Underwriters Board, representing the fire companies, and the Casualty Committee, an organization of casualty underwriters, to define the jurisdictions of inland, fire and casualty. These efforts proving bootless, matters grew worse. The London reinsurance market, losing money because of the turn of events, began to exert a pressure for peace. Pressure from the state insurance commissioners continued. It became clear that unless inland cleaned its own house someone else would do it.

The fraternity chose reform from within. After more than a year spent in negotiation the principal companies engaged in inland business formed the Inland Marine Underwriters Association. This difficult achievement was largely the work of a few men: C. Curtis Macy of Appleton & Cox, managers for insurance companies; John C. Keegan, Providence Washington Insurance Company; Edwin J. Perrin, Automobile Insurance Company; Hawley T. Chester, Chubb & Son; and Mr. Lewis. The I. M. U. A. became a going concern in January 1931. It instituted reforms much needed in a business which had mushroomed so rapidly with a minimum of internal or external regulation. Rates and acquisition costs were stabilized, rebating and unfair discrimination done away with, and in general the business put on an even keel.

The way was paved to the settlement of the problem of jurisdiction. A Joint Committee on Interpretation and Complaint was formed representing fire, casualty and inland. This body promulgated a definition of marine insurance. The New York State Insurance Commissioner, who was about ready to swing the big stick, accepted the definition. Widespread adoption throughout the country followed. By this definition inland surrendered some rich accounts, particularly warehouse and storage-on-the-premises-of-assured risks which had been parts of the all-inclusive transportation coverage. The Inland Marine Department of the North America lost $1,000,000 worth of premiums—a mere bookkeeping transaction, however, for what inland lost the fire branch and the casualty affiliates gained.[7]

5

On April 3, 1925, John Kremer, secretary of the North America, opened a letter from R. Jones Rife, the company's agent at Duncannon, Pennsylvania, and read:

"Does the Insurance Company of North America write flood insurance? The Clarks Ferry Bridge Company will complete their new reinforced concrete bridge about June 1st and will be in the market for flood insurance. If the North America does not write it can you give me an idea where I can place a line on it?"[8]

John Kremer had come up through the fire branch, which did write flood insurance, though it had never taken a risk on a bridge that anyone could recall. The following reply was dispatched to Agent Rife:

"In general Flood insurance of this nature is rather hard to place but we shall be glad to give the proposition our attention but feel that we should have further information. We have already written to our special agent, Mr. Norman White, to make a complete inspection, and possibly you can furnish us with further particulars, such as the force of the current at various times of the year, together with full details of construction and if possible the contingencies which the engineer provided against in drawing the specifications for the structure."[9]

The result was a speedy accumulation of data, the work probably being hastened by the fact that an effort was being made to interest a rival fire insurance company, a strong and alert organization, in the risk.

The Clarks Ferry Bridge, spanning the Susquehanna at Duncannon, about fourteen miles above Harrisburg, would cost $600,000. Wholly of steel and concrete construction the fire risk was nil. In the opinion of bridge engineers, including the distinguished Ralph Modjeski, the flood hazard was slight. The new structure's immediate predecessor, a wooden bridge resting on stone piers, had burned in 1923 after standing seventy-five years. The bridge was an indispensable link in the main highway between Philadelphia and the West. In the last year of its existence a quarter of a million vehicles had passed over the old structure. Gross tolls for the new bridge were estimated at $100,000 a year. The owning company was amply financed and ably managed.

By the time this information was forthcoming Ludwig Lewis had taken the matter in charge. He foresaw bridge insurance as a possible string to the bow of inland marine. On May 27 the North America covered the Clarks Ferry Bridge for $500,000—$400,000 for fire, flood or ice damage; $100,000 for use and occupancy. Use and occupancy is an old fire term under which an assured is indemnified for loss of use of an insured object. The bridge company was covered in the amount of an estimated year's revenue. Following the cautious inland practice of the time, Lewis reinsured $340,000 of the $500,000 risk.

In November 1925 the North America insured its second bridge, a structure in Harrisburg. The coverage was broader than in the Clarks Ferry risk, insuring against damage by fire, lightning, flood, ice, strikes, "riots or civil commotion" and explosion. The total policy was for $915,000 of which the North America took $665,000, reinsuring $390,000 with outside companies and $125,000 within its own family—Alliance taking $50,000, Philadelphia Fire and Marine $50,000 and National Security $25,000. There being no form for bridge insurance a transportation form was altered to suit by means of scissors, paste and typewritten inserts. The result was used as a model for the first printed bridge forms.

The next large policy was written to cover the Bay of Biscayne Bridge at Miami, Florida, the North America's participation being $300,000. The insurance became effective June 13, 1926. Two months later a hurricane severely damaged the structure. The North America paid $114,000, the heaviest bridge loss it has sustained to date.

Bridge business grew rapidly. In the decade from 1931 to 1940, inclusive, the North America statistics indicate writings of $366,-000,000 of this class of insurance, although this amount includes numerous renewals and it is probable that not more than $100,000,000 was at risk at any one time. The company's interest in policies protecting the great bridges and vehicular tunnels in New York City have in some years exceeded a total commitment of $10,000,000.

The Biscayne Bay Bridge appears to have been the first to be covered against "all risks." After that loss this broadest coverage was abandoned for a time, conditions of insurance reverting to standard named perils, including in addition to those previously mentioned collision, rising waters, malicious damage, tornado, windstorm, earthquake and collapse. As time went on policies were extended in individual cases to include such remote hazards as stranding, sinking or settling of vessels or other objects, subterranean waters, water spout, tidal wave, cloudburst, sleet or ice storm, falling meteors, volcanic eruption, subsidence of earth or rock, piracy, banditry, vandalism, sabotage, anarchy and numerous variations of the foregoing. In this way "all risks" gradually came back.

Bridge rates are fixed by the Bridge Committee of the Inland Marine Underwriters Association. On November 7, 1940, this body met in New York. Before it appeared a number of underwriters fortified with arguments to support the contention that rates on risks about to be presented could be safely lowered in certain instances. Before the particular bridges could be considered, however, a flash from the Pacific Coast announced the collapse of the Tacoma Narrows Bridge in Washington. When the news of the disaster came over the wires the underwriters present forgot their interest in rate reduction for the moment and the committee quickly adjourned so that the members could devote their attention to the disaster. Tacoma Narrows was one of the most expensive "bridge failures" in history, to use the engineers' term for it. Insurance companies paid $4,000,000, of which the North America's net loss was less than $100,000.

It might be thought that a disaster such as the Tacoma Narrows would result in increased rates for other bridges. This has not been the case since bridges, unlike most other classes of property, are rated on their individual merits because of the wide variation in types of construction and the hazards to which they are subjected. Since 1940 standard bridge insurance has been an "all-risk" coverage subject to certain exclusions and warranties. While underwriters are no longer willing to insure against war perils under present (1942) conditions, they continue to cover the risk of sabotage, the charge for which has increased. The total cost of bridge insurance is therefore somewhat greater than prior to the Tacoma disaster though this flows from other causes.[10]

6

It is a far cry from bridge insurance to insurance on the motor trucks which rumble over them—representing another classification the company built from nothing to a net premium yield of more than $300,000 annually. This has been a difficult task—not to get the business, but to get the right kind of business. After twenty-two years' experience the greatest care in the selection of risks must be exercised. Though not what they once were, the hazards of the trucking business are still comparable to those existing in the early days of river steamboat traffic. In that instance the North America avoided losses by accepting few river risks. To have followed a similar course with regard to motor trucks would have been to neglect lines which Lewis believed, and correctly, would become heavy income producers. So the company went into motor trucks and learned by experience. Its confidential files embodying that experience are voluminous.

One of the great perils from which the motor-truck business safely emerged was a variety of organized crime which flourished during the prohibition era. Motor-truck robbery became a criminal specialty involving as distinct professional technique as the stagecoach and train holdups of other days. This technique originated in the "high-jacking" of trucks laden with liquor whereby one ring of bootleggers despoiled another. Insurance companies, of course, were not involved. Nor were the police greatly interested in a warfare among criminals usually without injury to law-abiding persons.

The time came, however, when these new highwaymen were not content to prey on liquor trucks which the bootleg barons had learned to protect with their own gunmen. Insurance records exist of truckloads of silk or furs worth in excess of $100,000. Loads worth a fraction of this sum were likely to be more valuable than liquor and almost as easily disposed of through underworld channels. Insurance companies have always been prepared to deal with a limited amount of crime and fraud. But here was a veritable crime wave directed at insured goods. The North America engaged detectives and investigators to work with the authorities. The following case illustrates their activities.

On the night of March 4, 1931, a truck containing raw silk insured for $10,000 was standing in a garage at Union City, New Jersey. The garage was in charge of a night attendant who was playing cards with two friends. Shortly after midnight a band of armed men interrupted the game. They gagged and trussed the card-players and locked them in an empty truck. The bandits took their time. They seemed in communication with confederates outside the building. Sometime before daybreak they drove away in the silk truck.

This was not all that happened in Union City that night. About

4 A.M. two policemen were making their rounds in a patrol car when the movements of a big dark sedan drew the suspicion of the officers. The patrol car halted and Sergeant Knight stepped out to question the occupants of the sedan. Three shots came from the sedan and Knight fell dead. The murderers stepped on the gas and escaped.

What was thought to have been the killers' car was later found abandoned. A part of the stolen silk was recovered from a sewer in Hoboken; evidently the stuff had become too hot to handle. This was all. The usual surveillance of silk centers, including suspected fences, yielded nothing. Stool pigeons' tips yielded nothing. This was the state of affairs when, eight months after the crime, an East Rutherford, New Jersey, policeman telephoned to William Verrinder, an investigator attached to the North America's New York office. As a former railroad detective and, later, an expert on truck robberies for a private detective agency, Verrinder had learned a great deal of the methods and the personnels of gangs which preyed on goods in transit. The East Rutherford policeman told his friend Verrinder they had a man who might interest him.

Verrinder went over. The prisoner was a pallid, fidgety little fellow who gave the name of Anthony Curto. The policeman had got him to talk, but lacking intimate knowledge of the facts had been unable to obtain a clear confession. Verrinder and his friend spent the night in Curto's cell. By morning the prisoner had admitted participation in the Union City silk job, and said he had driven the car from which Sergeant Knight had been shot. The bulk of the loot, he added, had been sold in New Haven, Connecticut. Curto named the other members of the gang and offered to give state's evidence in exchange for leniency.

This is a type of service insurance detectives constantly render the police. It is given confidentially. Insurance operatives' names rarely appear in the papers. A part of their usefulness lies in the fact that they are willing that the local police should have the credit.

Six men besides Curto went to prison. All were members in good standing of the prohibition-era criminal hierarchy. An effort was made to bag the higher-ups, the big-shot hoodlums who employed them, but this failed.[11] Nevertheless, one truck-robbing band had been removed from the scene. The end of prohibition in 1933 further diminished this type of lawlessness and the situation was gradually brought under control.

7

In February 1920 a brokerage firm in Baltimore wrote the Insurance Company of North America to inquire if it issued "those so
called 'All Risks' jewelry floater policies, such as are issued by London Lloyds. . . . They cover fire, theft, transportation and even carelessness in connection with jewelry, including the loss under entirely
unknown circumstances." The company replied it wrote no such
policy. "As a matter of fact we would not care to cover any such
risks as carelessness on jewelry."[12]

These communications were exchanged just before Ludwig C.
Lewis took charge of the newly created Inland Marine Department.
The company had been insuring jewelry in a limited way under its
old tourist floater. In 1926 Lewis extended the North America's line
to include practically unlimited protection for personal jewelry and
furs by means of a policy covering these valuables against almost any
risk, any time, any place. The first year's premiums were $109,000.
Before long they were $300,000 plus.

The company's jewelry business affords an interesting laboratory
for the study of human nature.

"And the upshot of it all," says Mr. Lewis, "is proof that the mass
of people are honest, though frequently careless. Mrs. A. reports the
loss of a diamond brooch. She has no idea what happened to it. We
pay the claim and begin a search for the brooch. Usually we find it.
What Mrs. A. really wants is her brooch, not our money. That goes
for assureds in all the various classes of inland-marine insurance.
The chiseler is the exception and we can take care of him."[13]

Arthur Adams, head of the inland loss department of the New
York office, directs the investigations which follow a reported loss.
In nearly 50 per cent of the cases the gems are recovered simply by
checking up on the assured's itinerary previous to the loss. The first
place an investigator will look is the wall safe. Most users of jewelry
are women. Panic frequently takes them when they cannot lay their
hands immediately on a ring or necklace. One will 'phone the
insurance company before looking carefully through her safe. After
the hurricane of 1938 had swept the North Atlantic coast a dozen
claims for missing jewelry were satisfied by searching the permanent
homes of the summer residents; they had not taken their valuables to

the seashore at all. Plumbing drains are other worth-while places to look for jewelry that has disappeared.[14]

Careful underwriting comes into play in the jewelry business. The character of the applicant is assiduously considered from a moral standpoint. Satisfied on that head the company goes into another matter professionally entitled "exposure." This means the extent to which the jewels are publicly known or displayed, making the owner a target for robbery, holdup or "unexplained disappearance." "Exposure must be considered above normal for actors and actresses," says R. Bruce Miller, second in charge of the Inland Marine Department. "Avoid the veteran divorcée, café society and glamour girls of all ages."

"Nature of schedule" is another factor. A desirable schedule affords balance and spread. A single diamond necklace valued at $100,000 is less attractive to underwriters than a schedule for the same amount containing thirty items valued from $500 to $10,000 each. Large stones worn by men are more conspicuous than similar stones worn by women. When offered separately they must be considered the greater robbery or holdup hazards. As indicated, however, carelessness and unexplained disappearance are the major perils. In 1940 they accounted for 72.8 per cent of all losses, thefts for 22.8 per cent, other causes 4.4 per cent.[15]

Cases illustrating two types of losses, and eventual recoveries, were those involving Mrs. Harry C. Glemby, whose tribulations received a great deal of newspaper notice at the time. Indeed, the publicity given the first loss led to the second one, a circumstance which underwriters list under the head of exposure.

Mrs. Glemby, the wife of a New York hair-net manufacturer, owned jewelry and furs insured for $329,600 by the North America's subsidiary, the Philadelphia Fire & Marine Insurance Company. On New Year's Eve, 1931, the Glembys, their four sons and ten guests occupied a table near the orchestra in the Empire Room of the Hotel Waldorf-Astoria. Among the jewels Mrs. Glemby wore were two emerald earrings, valued at $25,000 apiece. About three o'clock in the morning a member of the party noticed that one of the earrings was missing. A search about the table brought to light the small nut by which the earring had been screwed in place; but no earring was found.

The orchestra leader announced the loss. A spotlight was thrown on the remaining earring, to enable a finder to identify the one that was lost. No one came forward with the missing jewel. After all the merrymakers had gone home Pinkerton detectives went through the confetti and other debris on the Empire Room floor without avail.

Next day Mr. Glemby inserted advertisements in the newspapers offering a reward and notified the North America. A week later an attorney telephoned the New York office of the insurance company that he thought he had the earring. This assumption proved to be correct and a reward of $1,500 was paid by the company to the attorney who promised to pass the money on to the finder. The attorney's story was this. A woman friend of a client had found the earring at the Waldorf on New Year's Eve. She thought it a cheap imitation until she read the newspaper advertisement. Then she became alarmed and asked her friend to get in touch with a lawyer. The insurance company never learned the finder's name.

By these means the emerald earring was restored to the safe in the Glemby residence on January 11, 1932. This safe was in a closet in the third-floor hall between two doors. One of these doors opened into what was known as the front bedroom. The other opened into the rear bedroom, which Mr. and Mrs. Glemby used. One bathroom served the two bedrooms.

The earring remained in the safe for ten days, or until a few minutes after ten o'clock on the morning of January 21. At that time Glemby was shaving in the bathroom and Mrs. Glemby was in bed eating her breakfast from a tray. The door between the bath and the front bedroom was opened by Hameyer, the butler, beside whom stood a strange man. Before Hameyer could say anything the strange man drew a pistol. Hameyer made a grab for the gun and the strange man knocked him down with the butt of it. Then the armed man bound the hands of Glemby and Hameyer and marched them into Mrs. Glemby's bedroom. Mrs. Glemby was sitting up in bed with her hands tied behind her and another armed man standing guard.

"It's the jewelry we're after," one of the armed men said.

They were getting it. Mrs. Glemby's maid, Frieda Miller, knew the combination to the safe. She and a third robber were in the hall.

"Are the earrings there?" this robber asked Frieda.

The earrings were, of course—along with other jewels to the value of $298,575. A descriptive list of the lot fills three typewritten pages. The robbers took everything and, after binding Frieda, they departed.

The robbers were young, well dressed and well spoken. Communicating among themselves they spoke Italian. The leader had gained admission to the house by posing as Glemby's bootlegger.

The first break in the case came when they unearthed a woman stool pigeon, or informer, who offered to point out the robbers for a fee of $25,000. As the police had no such sum at their disposal, the insurance company offered to pay in case the woman's tip should prove good. This satisfied the female stool pigeon who indicated a band of men and women who frequented a popular first-class hotel in midtown.

The police planted several of their number in the hotel. One acted as a night clerk, others as elevator operators, bellboys and doormen. When they had obtained a pretty good line on the habits of the suspects Patrolman Abraham Gralla registered as Joseph Rothstein of Seattle and took a suite of rooms. Rothstein spent money freely and let it be known that he was a jeweler in New York to enjoy himself. He made a cocktail-room acquaintance of a personable young woman who called herself Helen Smith. Helen Smith was a member of the robber gang. She introduced Rothstein to her colleagues. Gradually it developed that although the Pacific Coast jeweler had come east for recreation, he would not avoid a business deal if the terms were right. Finally one of Helen Smith's male friends spread before Rothstein a veritable fortune in jewels. Rothstein recognized them as the Glemby loot, the items of which he had committed to memory.

After considerable dickering Rothstein's offer of $50,000 for the lot was accepted. The transfer was to be made in a taxicab at Broadway and Sixty-sixth Street at thirty minutes past noon on April 13. Rothstein was there on time. So were Helen Smith and another woman named Ruby Golet. Each woman carried a stout brown paper bag. The three stepped into a cab. Detectives surrounded the cab. The jig was up. Three men who had been shadowed for weeks were arrested elsewhere.

One woman's bag contained the Glemby jewels, the other's broken crockery of the same bulk and weight. The scheme had been to switch bags on Rothstein.

The company paid a reward of $10,000 to the New York policemen. It paid the informer her $25,000 fee. On April 16 William Verrinder and two other company detectives took the money to police headquarters. There it was re-counted in the presence of a police inspector. The company operatives and the police inspector drove in a police car to a well-known hotel, though not the hotel which Joseph Rothstein had frequented. There the party met a woman whom the police inspector identified. The money was handed over. The woman counted it—twenty-three one-thousand-dollar bills and four five-hundreds—and the Glemby case was closed, from an underwriting standpoint. Helen Smith and one of the men received prison sentences. Another prisoner committed suicide before trial. Ruby Golet and the third man were acquitted.[16]

8

The inland-marine account of the North America and affiliates remains in the hands of Ludwig Lewis who in 1924 was made assistant secretary, in 1929 marine secretary and in 1937 vice-president of the parent company. The next ranking officer of the department, R. Bruce Miller, was graduated from the United States Naval Academy in 1922. With the majority of his class he was permitted to resign his commission because of the reduction of naval personnel under the 1921 arms-limitation agreement. Miller joined the North America in 1925. Since 1940 he has been an assistant secretary of the company.

As related, the rapidly growing inland business was stabilized in 1931 by the creation of the Inland Marine Underwriters Association which the London market, as reinsurers, was definitely interested in bringing about. A few years later relations with London became strained again because of the British practice of issuing reinsurance contracts which favored non-members of the I.M.U.A. In 1938 a committee of influential American underwriters, of which Lewis was a member, journeyed to London. The Englishmen were reminded of the chaotic conditions obtaining before the organization of the I.M.U.A. The Americans declared that they would not continue to hold an umbrella over a business which London was tending to disrupt by favoring non-members of the I.M.U.A. American companies affiliated with the Association, which paid premiums for reinsurance at Lloyd's, expected nothing more than equal treatment. The Englishmen saw the point and put in their contracts a clause stipulating that rates, terms and conditions must agree with I.M.U.A. requirements. The possibility of another disagreeable situation was thus averted.

The threat of its recurrence has been rendered less likely by the healthy growth of the capacity of the American market. As late as 1937 the limit of this market on a single risk was about $6,000,000. The rest was reinsured. In 1942 it was possible for the American market to absorb $15,000,000 on a single risk, a circumstance enabling it to handle large and costly bridges and valuable art collections without the dependence on reinsurance that had formerly been the case. When the North America began to develop modern inland marine it was a heavy reinsurer, particularly in London. Such commitments were constantly reduced. In 1941 the North America and affiliates paid slightly more than $200,000 in inland reinsurance premiums. Total inland premium receipts for that year were nearly $5,000,000. Four classes—transportation, motor truck, jewelry and personal property—netted over $300,000 apiece. Ten other classes exceeded $100,000 each. No other group of American companies carried so large an inland-marine account, and none reinsured so little of it.

CHAPTER XVIII

THE RISE OF CASUALTY

I

In 1898 two hundred automobiles were manufactured in the United States and the new contraption, almost universally regarded as a passing and somewhat harebrained fad, entered the realm of underwriting. The first automobile insurance policy in this country was issued to Doctor Truman J. Martin of Buffalo, New York, protecting him against liability for damages to the persons or the property of others by reason of the operation of his motor car. The date was February 1, two weeks before the *Maine* was sunk. During the year several other owners of those snorting little vehicles fortified themselves with similar policies. They were made out on "team forms," designed for the protection of owners of horse-drawn conveyances from damages resulting from runaways, kicking or biting horses and so on. This type of insurance was then about ten years old in America.[1]

Doctor Martin's policy was written by the Travelers Insurance Company, the pioneer casualty company in the United States and in 1898 by all odds the richest and strongest institution writing casualty. The preponderance of Travelers' revenue came, however, from its life-insurance business. The companies depending on casualty solely comprised a hard-driven little band, fighting for toe holds in the insurance arena and frequently living from hand to mouth. The marine and fire offices did not touch casualty risks. From a lofty height they looked down on the struggles of their impecunious colleagues.

This patronizing attitude failed to retard the development of the automobile. More and more car owners were taking liability insurance. Next they began to seek coverage on the machines themselves, just as on any other property that might stand in their names. In 1902 a shipowner and customer of the Boston Insurance

Company, an old-line fire and marine organization, applied for insurance on an automobile while in transit from England where he had bought it. As a matter of accommodation the Boston filled out the policy on a "schooner form." This was the first automobile coverage, other than third-party liability, issued in the United States. United States Lloyd's followed with a policy protecting automobiles against fire or theft at all times and places. The Boston introduced a similar coverage and in 1904 paid its first large automobile loss—$9,500. The beneficiary was William Wallace, the company's vice-president. Mr. Wallace was driving to Worcester when the gasoline tank exploded.[2]

When the subject of automobile insurance was broached at 232 Walnut Street, President Charles Platt would have nothing to do with it. "I'll never insure a gasoline can on wheels, the noisy stinking things!"[3] Plenty of insurance men agreed with him. The trade journal *Spectator* came out for an insurance boycott of automobiles.

"The motormen—chauffeurs is the general term—driving automobiles are usually reckless, rushing madly past frightened teams without attempting to slow down, or frequently coming up from behind and passing without giving any warning whatever. Nervous horses are sure to be alarmed at such apparitions. . . . While they cannot prevent their policyholders from being run over by reckless chauffeurs . . . [underwriters] might serve the cause of public safety by refusing to insure anyone who has acquired the automobile habit."[4]

Benjamin Rush kept at his superior, however, coaching agents to request facilities for covering automobiles. In 1905 the old gentleman yielded and the North America became the third company to write non-casualty automobile insurance. That year 25,000 cars were made in the United States and 78,000 were in operation. The North America's policies covered fire and theft.

In 1907 collision insurance was added. The business grew and ramified. Theft rates were raised. In the days when an automobile was a rich man's plaything it was almost immune from theft because too conspicuous and too difficult to dispose of. By the end of the first World War this situation had changed altogether. Six million motor cars were on American roads. The North America proudly announced:

EARLY "ENGINE-SIDE"

Pioneer firemen spent money and pains to decorate their equipment. Good painters sometimes were employed to adorn "engine-sides." In the North America's gallery are two Sullys. This copy of Trumbull's painting of Washington at Trenton was rendered by John Woodside who also painted street signs in Philadelphia. Original in the North America's notable collection of this type of early American art.

"The North America automobile policy needs no introduction. . . . [It] offers broad protection to owners of both pleasure and commercial cars, also dealers and manufacturers . . . [covering] losses by fire, including self-ignition; transportation; theft of the car or equipment, including any damage while in the hands of thieves; damage sustained by collision with other cars, vehicles or objects; and property damage, being the legal liability of the owner for injuries done to the property of others (excluding all personal injuries)."[5]

2

From this it will be seen that in its zeal to satisfy the insurance needs of automobilists the North America at one point had crossed the line into casualty underwriting. Other marine and fire organizations were doing the same. Casualty insurance had come up in the world since the beginning of the century. In this metamorphosis the automobile, so largely a casualty item, had played a conspicuous part. The old companies faced the alternative of writing casualty or of seeing a fertile and expanding field pass wholly into the hands of competitors—the strictly casualty companies which no longer could be regarded as poor relations of the insurance family.

To meet this situation the North America took two steps.

First was to assume direct control of its automobile underwriting. In 1905 when Rush embarked the company in the automobile business he handed the account to the Philadelphia brokerage firm of Platt, Yungman & Company as managing agents. Platt, Yungman & Company did a good job. They kept the North America up with the procession, as nearly as that could be done without going all-out into the casualty field in which the company was restricted by charter limitations. During the regime of Platt, Yungman automobile was under the general supervision of the marine branch of the company. Its premium, profit and loss figures became a part of the totals submitted by the marine branch. On July 1, 1919, Platt, Yungman were relieved of their managerial responsibilities and the Automobile Department set up under the supervision of the fire branch.[6]

The second step was to form the North America's casualty runningmate, the Indemnity Insurance Company of North America, which began business September 15, 1920. Though from the outset Indemnity did a general casualty business, automobile was one of its heaviest lines. With the exception of personal accident, protecting the car owner against physical injuries to himself, and plate-glass insurance, all Indemnity's varied automobile policies were third-party liability. That is, they protected owners, garage keepers and dealers against liability for damages to the persons and to the property of others. The rest of the field was covered by the Automobile Department of the parent company. This embraced numerous coverages against property damage to the assured's car only, as well as damages caused by his car to the property of others.

John O. Platt placed the parent company's interest in the automobile business under the supervisory eyes of Sheldon Catlin who selected Chester M. Campbell to organize and run the new department. Campbell was one of the many who, down the generations, have made service to the North America a life work. He had gone to work for the company from a Philadelphia high school and had never had another employer.

In 1921 and 1922 Campbell ran into moral-risk problems growing out of the current hard times and the type of automobile policies then in use. These were "valued" policies, an outgrowth of marine practice, by which a car was insured for a stated amount. Owing to depreciation sometimes this amount was more than the machine was worth. Hard times brought the temptation of willful destruction or fraudulent disappearance. Losses were heavy. This policy was done away with in favor of the nonvalued form under which the company's liability was limited in event of total loss or of disappearance to the actual cash value at the time of loss, this to be ascertained by making proper deduction for depreciation. A stated-amount policy was retained whereby one could insure a machine for a stipulated sum provided that sum did not exceed the true cash value at time of loss. In practice the stated amount was often lower than the value.

By these means the Automobile Department became increasingly profitable. When the moral-hazard situation arose again during the depression years of 1930-1933, there was no repetition of suspicious claims on the scale of ten years earlier.[7]

In the meantime the North America's casualty affiliate, Indemnity, was having difficulty with its automobile lines, as with several other classes of business. Early-year losses were to be expected by a company starting from scratch on such an ambitious scale. As related in another chapter, during the first two and a quarter years of operation, ending December 31, 1922, these aggregated $1,388,000. In 1923 the deficit dropped to $39,000 and the turn was believed to be at hand. In 1924, however, Indemnity's loss mounted to $214,000. In 1925 the first profit—$59,000—was earned. This changed to a loss of $67,000 in 1926. In 1927 the profit was $60,000 and in 1928 it was $206,000, but this ended the good news. Losses ensued as follows:

1929	$ 146,000
1930	1,205,000
1931	1,084,000
1932	2,026,000

Nor did this represent the sum of the North America's casualty troubles. It will be recalled that in 1928, when it seemed as if Indemnity had rounded the corner, the North America expanded its casualty operations by creating a second casualty affiliate, the Alliance Casualty Company. Alliance Casualty dismayed its creators by losing money faster than Indemnity was losing it, the deficit being smaller only because Alliance Casualty's business was smaller. In 1929 the new affiliate dropped $436,645; in 1930, $695,542; in 1931, $590,961. Losses for the first five months in 1933 were $439,336, whereupon the parent company called a halt. Alliance Casualty was liquidated on May 31 that year. The net cost of the experiment was $2,311,-767.16.[8]

There was some sentiment in favor of calling it a day with Indemnity as well and getting out of casualty for good and all. One of the things that deterred Benjamin Rush, however, was the fact that the local Philadelphia office of Indemnity, in the able hands of Dodd Bryan, had consistently made money. Rush thought what Indemnity could do in Philadelphia it could do in the rest of the country provided the right man were at the helm. He delegated to Sheldon Catlin and Leaming Smith the task of finding that man. Catlin, a fire underwriter, and Smith, a marine expert, were somewhat taken aback by the assignment. Knowing little of the intricacies of casualty, they began combing the field for the casualty executive who seemed to stand at the top of his calling. Their choice fell upon John A. Diemand, who was building up the lately organized casualty affiliate of the Home Insurance Company.[9] Stocky, unhurried, easy to meet and easy to know, John Diemand had a small-town friendliness about him though he had never lived in a small town. Thirty of his forty-seven years had been spent in the casualty business. He assumed the office of executive vice-president of Indemnity in June 1933.

3

The history of John Anthony Diemand and the history of casualty insurance in the United States have much in common. From 1903 on the history of Diemand parallels the history of casualty. They grew up together, and consequently know each other well.

The men who launched casualty underwriting on these shores were mostly self-made—poor boys who fought their way against obstacles that would have discouraged the fainthearted. Samuel Appleton, son of a New England sea captain, was orphaned and left to shift for himself at fifteen. C. P. Ellerbe, a nineteen-year-old Confederate soldier whose father and two brothers had fallen in battle, trudged barefoot to his ruined plantation home after the surrender of Lee. Adversity could not down them, and to this quality they added imagination and daring.

The Columbus of casualty was James G. Batterson, one of the remarkable figures in our insurance annals. Born in Connecticut in 1823 he learned the stone-cutter's trade from his father and eventually laid up a comfortable fortune dealing in grave markers. Largely by self-education he became a Greek and Latin scholar. In the darkest days of the Civil War he was a personal friend of Abraham Lincoln. In 1864 he formed the Travelers Insurance Company to accept accident risks on wayfarers. Batterson was without practical insurance experience, and there was little available which would have done him much good. As the first accident underwriter in the United States, he picked his rates "out of the air," an expression old casualty men, including Diemand, still occasionally use. In 1866 Batterson added life insurance, concerning which dependable experience tables were accessible. This made it easier for him to pursue his casualty experiments which eventually included the automobile liability policy issued to Doctor Martin in 1898. When Mr. Batterson died in 1901 his company had assets of $33,813,000, most of which had come from life business, however.[10]

John A. Diemand was born in Philadelphia in 1886. His mother died when he was three and his father when the child was six. After two years in the home of a neighbor John entered Girard College, which Stephen Girard had devised to take care of indigent orphan boys. They were housed, fed and clothed the year round and given an education equivalent to that offered by a first-rate high school. This was young Diemand's home for nine years. The rigid discipline had no effect on the boy's sunny disposition. He played varsity baseball and soccer. Excelling in mathematics, manual training and mechanical drawing, he conceived an ambition to become a civil engineer.

Upon graduation in 1903 John applied for employment with the engineering corps of the Pennsylvania Railroad. While waiting for word he met a typewriter salesman he had known at Girard. The salesman asked the lad if he would demonstrate an Underwood to a prospective customer. Young Diemand, who had learned stenography at school, said he'd be glad to. The prospective customer was the Philadelphia Casualty Company. The head of the claims department dictated several letters which John recorded in shorthand and then rattled off on the Underwood. The subject-matter of the correspondence interested the youth. At the conclusion of the demonstration John asked for a job and got it. "Just keep on what you're doing," said the head of the claims department producing a fresh batch of dictation. The salary was $8 a week.

In 1903 the casualty business of the United States did not exceed $20,000,000 a year. The strongest company in the field, Travelers, derived most of its strength from life insurance. The strongest and most ably managed of the pure casualty organizations was the Fidelity and Casualty of New York, with assets of $5,700,000. Today it is the sole survivor of the early exclusively casualty companies. Though the Philadelphia Casualty had assets of $1,250,000, like most of its contemporaries it was little better than breaking even on underwriting operations. The Philadelphia wrote a fairly complete casualty line: accident and health; public liability, including team and automobile policies, contractors' and owners' liability; burglary; plate glass; credit insurance. The last-named was insurance against bad debts and a heavy loser. Incidentally it has never been profitable except on a very restricted basis. Most of the business was in cities. Small-town folk were not "claim conscious." It rarely occurred to one of them to ask damages for tripping over a loose board in a sidewalk.

In the claims department John Diemand was close to the vitals of the business. A good claims department cannot make a successful casualty company but no company can succeed without one. Diemand began to study the claims that passed through his typewriter and to observe the technique of adjusters. Employers' liability was a growing line, and a profitable one. The subject took the young stenographer to the law books for a course of reading on the legal relationship of master and servant.

For centuries the common law had regulated this association. When one person entered the employ of another he assumed all risks natural to that employment, including the danger of injury through the negligence of a fellow workman. With so much in the employer's favor there was no demand on his part for insurance. But this had begun to change. Various states were whittling down the protection afforded by the common law. An employer must surround dangerous machinery with reasonable safeguards. He must assume liability to one employee for the default of another. By 1903 the tide was running strongly for better protection for the workingman. Diemand's mastery of the legal background necessary to the settlement of employers' liability claims made him too valuable a man to keep at a keyboard. In 1907 he was promoted to examiner and in 1910 to the head of the claims department. Twenty-four years old, John Diemand was probably the most youthful casualty claims chief in the United States.

In the claims field young Diemand had a hand in the making of precedents and the building of experience data which are stones in the foundation of modern casualty underwriting. He saw rates develop and crystallize; saw them "picked out of the air" by those who had the proper talent. In 1907 the building of the Pennsylvania Station in New York offered a chance at an insurance plum—a contractors' and public liability account totaling as much as $15,000 in premiums. Diemand saw the Philadelphia Casualty's liability underwriter deep in blueprints which he did not understand. The liability man pushed them aside and let his instincts go to work. "I'll make it $3.50 per payroll hundred on employers' liability and $2.50 on public," he said. Those rates got the business. They turned out to be all right.

In 1910 the Fidelity and Deposit Company of Maryland absorbed the Philadelphia Casualty, retaining Diemand as head of claims. The merger was a landmark in the development of casualty insurance. The founder of F. & D., Edwin Warfield, subsequently governor of Maryland, was the father of corporate suretyship. Before his advent bonds required of persons holding public or private positions of trust—county treasurers, bank cashiers—were supplied by individuals, as were court and judicial bonds—bail, appeal, replevin, guardianship, administrators', etc. With this business just emerging from the log-cabin stage, Warfield saw the natural affinity between fidelity and casualty underwriting and took over the Philadelphia company.

Diemand remained in Baltimore three years during which he learned what surety and fidelity were about and saw casualty greatly expand. Insurable units were larger, thanks to the interest big business organizations had begun to take in accident prevention; automobile moved up, thanks to mass production introduced by Henry Ford. But the real boom flowed from the enactment of workmen's compensation laws giving the laborer still greater protection of life and limb. Casualty companies began reinsuring their larger risks and pooling experience. In this way the casualty community was drawn together. Lone-wolf, throat-cutting practices of an earlier day were superseded as casualty began to get solid ground under its feet.

In 1913 Diemand went to Chicago as claims chief of the Zurich General Accident and Liability Insurance Company, a large Swiss concern which had just entered the American field. The following year he added the superintendency of agents to his responsibilities. This was a new work for Diemand and an important one. The business was filtering into the small towns, mainly on the rubber tires of the motor car. In 1916 Diemand organized the eastern seaboard into a separate department for Zurich and became its head. In 1921 he became assistant manager for the United States.

Casualty was of age. Its volume had passed that of marine and was beginning to crowd fire. Gone was the superior air of the old marine and fire companies as one after another entered the casualty field, holding out attractive offers to old-school casualty men. The internal picture also was changing. Accident and health had been the big line in 1903 when Diemand started. Then came workmen's compensation. Now automobile took the lead. Many new coverages were introduced. In 1928 Diemand went with Southern Surety which was presently taken over by the Home. This was one way the old companies squeezed into the new pasture. Diemand was in charge of the Home's affiliate, Home Indemnity, when he joined the North America group.[11]

4

The years following the 1929 collapse were bad ones for the casualty and surety companies of the country. Some of the best-known organizations closed their doors entirely. Others weathered the storm through such expedients as borrowing from the Reconstruction Finance Corporation, utilizing convention values—that is, inflated values instead of market values of securities, as authorized by the National Convention of Insurance Commissioners—and adding to surplus by reducing capital.

The reason that these years were so disastrous for the nation's casualty and surety companies was by no means due solely to the contraction of the value of securities in their portfolios. That in itself would have been bad enough, but the added sources of loss that produced such devastating effects on the industry were depository bonds, under which public moneys on deposit in the banks were protected, and mortgage guaranty bonds, under which principal and interest of mortgages were guaranteed to the holders. Workmen's compensation presented a ruinous loss ratio, as did surety bonds, other than those above mentioned. The reduction in payrolls, due to irregularity of employment and reduced wage rates, resulted in a sharp shrinkage of workmen's compensation premium income, although loss payments amounted to as much as they did during the period prior to the contraction in premium income.

The year 1932 and the early weeks of 1933 witnessed the low point of the depression. Not since the 1870s had business been so nearly paralyzed, or the hearts of the people so stricken with despair. Of the sixty stock casualty companies licensed in New York forty-one lost money. Only eight, however, lost it at the rate attained by the Indemnity Insurance Company of North America. For every dollar received in premiums Indemnity paid out $1.16 in operating expenses and claims.

When Diemand took over as executive vice-president in June 1933, Mr. Roosevelt's New Deal was ninety days old and the morale

of the country immensely improved. Diemand knew the history of
Indemnity in much greater detail than it has been set forth in these
pages. The facts were available to anyone capable of reading such
annual handbooks of the profession as the *Casualty Experience Exhibit.* Wishing more precise and extensive data, however, Diemand
filled a box with Indemnity records and took it to the Maine woods.

Returning in September he sat down with Mr. Rush and unfolded a plan for reforming the company. The principle was the
same as in Rush's plan for saving marine in 1897: drop or reform
losing business; increase paying business; eliminate administrative
waste. It was a long-range plan, as Rush's had been. Rush had allowed himself five years but did it sooner; Diemand did not say
how long he would need. Rush told him to go ahead, with complete
authority. In this respect Diemand in 1933 had an edge on Rush in
1897. Rush spent much time in the exercise of diplomacy to gain
and to retain authority. Diemand got it on a platter.

"That is one of the great advantages of working for Mr. Rush," said
Diemand in a reminiscence of those days. "When he has confidence
in a man he lets him alone."

The remaining three months of the year Diemand spent watching
the machinery of the ailing company operate. One of the things
he wanted to know was how many of Indemnity's key people could,
with education and guidance, be made into successful casualty men.
Diemand was trying to reduce to a minimum the number of personnel changes of a sort that often slow a reorganization. The year
ended with a general improvement in the casualty situation throughout the country but no improvement at 1600 Arch Street. Indemnity
lost $2,037,000 or 18.1 cents on every dollar of premiums. This
brought the net deficit, since the inception of the company, to $7,-
882,080.

How were those $2,037,000 lost in 1933? All but about $18,000
were lost on four lines as follows:

	Earned premiums received	Paid overhead and claims	Percentage of loss per dollar rec'd
Automobile public liability .	$3,804,000	$4,716,000	24
Liability, not auto	1,190,000	1,680,000	41.9
Workmen's compensation .	1,145,000	1,699,000	48.4
Surety	654,000	1,232,000	88.4

In 1934 the new boss went to work on the underwriting situation, with the result that the company's net deficit was cut to $487,186. The percentage of loss per premium dollar on the four sick lines was reduced to:

Automobile public liability 10.6
Liability, not auto 27.5
Workmen's compensation 13.3
Surety 86.2

In 1935 Indemnity made a profit of $237,081, the first since 1928. In 1936 the company's net gain was $215,000, automobile public liability turning the corner with a profit of 3.5 per cent. Surety's loss was cut to 6.6 per cent. The company was still paying, however, for the shortcomings of its early years—meeting claims on poor risks accepted before Diemand took charge. By 1938 these were pretty well worked off. The profit of Indemnity went to $1,203,315, with three of the four erstwhile heavy losers over the top:

Automobile public liability . . . . + 9.6
Liability, not auto . . . . + 5.4
Workmen's compensation . . . . — 3.9
Surety . . . . +26.8

In 1940 they were all on the proper side of the ledger for the first time in the company's history. The hardest nut to crack, compensation, showed a profit of 1.5 per cent. In 1941 this went to 7.18. In the seven complete years of Diemand's stewardship Indemnity had earned $5,022,000.[12]

5

How did he do it?
These figures on workmen's compensation afford a starting clue:

Year	Earned premiums	Claims expense per premium dollar	Commissions and other production expense	General administrative expense	Inspection and bureau expense	Taxes, licenses, fees	Total expenses	Total losses—claims paid	Total outgo	Gain or loss
1933	$1,145,000	24.1	19.5	15.	3.5	1.9	64.	84.4	148.4	—48.4
1940	1,889,000	10.9	17.9	10.2	2.2	4.5	45.7	52.8	98.5	+ 1.5

It will be observed that the increase in premiums is not great, the changed times considered, and bears slight relation to the radical transformation of gain-or-loss figures. Diemand was not out for volume but for quality. Until 1936 he held the volume almost stationary, merely replacing bad business with good. At the same time he ran the business more economically, while improving administrative efficiency. All costs, saving taxes over which he had no control, were reduced. In claims expense the reduction was most marked. One reason for this was fewer claims. Good business does not produce so many claims. This is reflected most strikingly in the loss column where Diemand made the greatest saving.

The statistics on automobile public liability tell a slightly different story:

Year	Earned premiums	Claims expense per premium dollar	Commissions and other production expense	General administrative expense	Inspection and bureau expense	Taxes, licenses, fees	Total expenses	Total losses— claims paid	Total outgo	Gain or loss
1933	$3,804,000	14.3	24.6	8.3	1.2	2.	50.4	73.6	124.	—24.
1940	2,493,000	11.9	29.	8.8	1.1	4.1	54.9	42.9	97.8	+ 2.2

Here volume was reduced measurably as soon as Diemand assumed control, indicating that poor business was dispensed with faster than it could be replaced by paying business. Expenses rose on the whole, however, a deficit being changed into a profit by smartly reducing the loss total—a commentary on the class of new business brought in.

In the process of turning surety upside down—converting an 88-per-cent loss into a 33-per-cent profit—good business was acquired a little faster than poor business was thrown out. Some premium increase resulted. Expenses rose slightly during the operation, but losses were cut to the vanishing point.

In the case of liability other than automobile it was possible to double the volume of the business and house clean at the same time. Expenses were cut somewhat, but the real change was in losses which in 1933 took 71.3 cents of every premium dollar and in 1940 took 29.

Thus a little different medicine for each of the patients.

Aside from the four disastrous losers which were brought out of the woods were two minor losers, accident and health, both small lines. Health losses have been cut and the accident volume nearly doubled in an expectation of future profits. There were five paying lines in 1933: automobile property damage; automobile collision; property damage other than automobile; fidelity; burglary and theft. Here both profits and volume have been increased, the volume of property damage other than automobile more than 400 per cent. This required underwriting enterprise. Compensation and automobile insurance, where heavy losses were, is easy business to get. Perhaps this was one of the reasons Indemnity had so many bad accounts. Liability other than automobile, surety, fidelity and burglary is hard business to get. The customer has to be "sold." This gives new significance to the volume increases in those lines.[13]

6

In 1942 Indemnity classified its business under seventy-four heads, each representing a type of bond or policy. This represented an increase of thirteen since 1933. There were eighteen classes of fidelity and surety bonds; twenty-two burglary coverages; five plate-glass policies; six health and accident policies; fifteen policies covering public liability and property damage in connection therewith; two collision policies; three employers' liability policies and three combination policies issued jointly by Indemnity and the fire branch of the North America.

Indemnity's present underwriting policy is to meet all requirements of the insuring public, however unorthodox, so long as they seem reasonable. This has been accomplished by underwriting (1) new lines of insurance; (2) old lines of insurance on modern bases; (3) the unusual risk.

An example of (1) may be found in the action of the company's burglary department in originating all-risk coverage for money, securities and valuable papers. Because of exclusions in the standard-form fire-insurance policy, coverage was not available on accounts, bills, currency, deeds, evidences of debt, money, notes and securities. American policyholders were driven to seek this protection abroad. Taking advantage of an amendment to insurance law adopted some years before, the Indemnity Company's burglary department made available insurance on the items excluded from fire-insurance contracts. A money-and-securities-destruction policy was issued covering

destruction of valuable records, such as abstracts, deeds, blueprints
and other documents. An accounts-receivable policy was prepared
to cover loss due to the inability of a merchant to collect his bills because of the records thereof having been destroyed. Finally, a money-
and-securities policy was prepared to cover all loss of money and
securities.

In 1934 a new line of personal accident insurance was written
when the first policy was issued to the students of a private school
in Richmond, Virginia, undertaking to indemnify each of them up
to an amount of $500 for expenses arising out of an accident in which
they might be injured during the school year, whether in school or
at home. From this modest beginning the business expanded rapidly
until in 1942 the company was covering 30,000 students of private
schools located in nearly every state in the Union. In 1938 this plan
was extended to cover children attending summer camps. Here again
the business grew until nearly 9,000 children were covered during
the summer of 1941.

While hardly a new line, so-called excess insurance may be considered a new variation for most American direct-writing casualty
companies. An excess-liability policy is usually purchased by a large
public utility or other industrial enterprise which elects to carry for
its own account normal losses, say of not more than $25,000 each, and
insures its catastrophic losses with an insurance company. Although
a small amount of this business had been written in the United States
by so-called excess or reinsurance companies, practically none had
been written by direct-writing companies such as the Indemnity.
The company entered this field in 1936 and six years later was writing a sizable premium volume of such risks.

One of the ways of underwriting old lines of insurance in new
forms comprises the development of particular policies for particular
types of risk, that is, drafting a custom-built policy for a specific risk
rather than trying to force a general policy to meet a specific need.
An example is what the trade calls a C.O.L.T. policy—meaning
comprehensive owners, landlords and tenants—protecting the insured
against liability for injuries and damages sustained by others on premises owned, operated or controlled by the assured. This is a special
policy designed for corporate fiduciaries. It covers the fiduciary in any
capacity whether as owner, operator, trustee, receiver or otherwise.
Another example is the church burglary-robbery-and-theft policy

which was especially prepared to insure all kinds of church property against theft under practically all circumstances.

For many years automobile liability insurance had been written under policies which, as Diemand says, "followed the car rather than the individual." A particular car was covered whether driven by the owner or anyone else with his permission. This meant that insurance companies reflected in their rates the additional hazard of insuring people unknown to them and possibly not so desirable as the car owner for whom their policies were issued. At the request of one of its agents to develop an automobile liability policy to be written for a lower premium, the Indemnity Company brought out its selected-automobile-operators' policy which followed the individual rather than the car. It described no automobile but undertook to cover a named individual in any car that he might drive. Other individuals might be included in the policy at additional charges. This policy was put on the market at a rate from 20 to 25 per cent below the rate for standard policies. The company's experience with this class of business has been highly profitable. It should be added that in the course of time orthodox policies used by other casualty companies were broadened, so that today the coverage under such policies is closer to that given by the Indemnity Company's selected-automobile-operators' policy.

Indemnity's blanket liability policy for manufacturers was the first policy to be sold on a broad scale which undertook to insure against all aspects of legal liability. Prior to the announcement of this policy, a manufacturer was obliged to purchase at least a half-dozen independent, mutually exclusive liability policies in order to cover himself against the various phases of his legal liability. These forms were known as manufacturers' liability, elevator liability, contingent liability, products liability, contractual liability, etc. The Indemnity Company's blanket policy in a single insuring clause provided all the coverage which these six or more policies covered collectively and went beyond their scope by making sure that no phase of the policyholder's legal liability and no phase of his operations were left uncovered. The success of Indemnity with this form has had some influence upon its competitors who have brought out policies which approach the advantages of the blanket form.

Unusual risks may be defined as those which do not fit into any classification commonly observed and handled by underwriters. Being single risks with independent and individual characteristics, they do not lend themselves to the law of average in the formulation of rate or policy form. Thus they must be dealt with on their merits and frequently no precedent can be found for dealing with them. For these reasons they prove annoying to the orthodox underwriter and often prospective customers have been driven to the foreign markets to find what they need. The Indemnity Company undertook to attract these unusual risks and indicated its desire in advertisements in the trade press.

One example of an unusual risk is interesting not alone for its own sake but also as a reflection of isolationist sentiment in the United States during the years when Hitler and the Japanese were preparing to set the world on fire.

On December 21, 1935, a sales corporation entered into contracts with China to supply eighty airplanes for military purposes. Then the sales organization asked a firm of American aircraft manufacturers to make the planes. The manufacturing corporation hesitated to spend a large sum of money because it feared that the United States might place an embargo on the export of aircraft to belligerent nations. It felt that it could undertake this contract only if protected against loss in that event. In 1937 Japan attacked China and though the planes were desperately needed there was a great deal of agitation for an embargo on war equipment. After a careful study of all elements of the risk, however, the Indemnity Company wrote two bonds in combined penalty of $760,000, affording the manufacturer the guaranty he sought. The venture worked out satisfactorily to all concerned, the last of the eighty planes being shipped on August 21, 1941.

Another unusual risk rose out of the celebrated feud between the American Society of Composers, Authors and Publishers (A.S.C.A.P.) and Broadcast Music, Incorporated (B.M.I.), when B.M.I. music supplanted A.S.C.A.P. music in radio programs. The latter organization kept a sharp watch on B.M.I. to determine whether copyright laws had been infringed. For the protection of B.M.I. advertising agencies, performers, and others connected with radio stations over which B.M.I. music was broadcast, a policy in the amount of $500,000 was prepared undertaking to indemnify them for actions brought by A.S.C.A.P. on the ground of copyright infringement.[14]

7

When John A. Diemand took charge he found the business run more or less on fire principles, which do not work in casualty underwriting. This had its effect on the claims department as well as production and underwriting. In fire or marine insurance one nearly always knows the worst concerning a loss shortly after it happens. Casualty is different. Ultimate settlements may be drawn out over a matter of years. An infected eye which may seem of slight consequence when brought to the underwriter's attention can run into something serious—and expensive. Faulty estimates concerning claims were reflected in future underwriting. Suppose a man insured five trucks and in the course of the year had a number of accidents which the company estimated would cost $1,500. The policies expired and were renewed on a basis of a loss estimate of $1,500. But actually some of those cases went to court and by the time they were all settled the loss was $3,000, double the estimate. Thus the renewal rate had been too low, and the company was saddled with an account bound to prove unprofitable. This identical thing happened in hundreds of cases.

In 1924 Indemnity made reservations of $657,900 to meet losses in automobile public liability. Within three months actual losses paid and claims and suits outstanding aggregated $723,000 or 110 per cent of the sum set aside to satisfy them. In a year the total had risen to $796,000; in five years to $925,000. Still there were claims unsettled, and in 1931, at the end of seven years, losses paid and suits pending amounted to $930,000 or 141.4 per cent of the original provision.

Now glance at the automobile-liability business originating in 1933. It was larger than in 1924 and the sum set aside to satisfy claims was $2,541,000. In three months this had proved insufficient, losses, claims and suits totaling $2,630,000 or 103.5 per cent of the amount provided. At the end of a year, however, losses, claims and suits had shrunk to $2,295,000, or well within the amount provided. At the end of five years losses, etc., were down to $1,962,000 and at the end of seven years, 1940, to $1,949,000 or 76.7 per cent of the sum reserved.

Inasmuch as the 1933 business was put on the books before Diemand had made his weight felt, the subsequent developments bear testimony to his skill as a claims man. Insurance companies, like

SEAL OF THE COMPANY, ADOPTED 1794

The design was submitted, and probably executed, by Samuel Blodget, Jr., original promoter of the company and an amateur architect of more than local note.

individuals, can be habitual victims of nuisance suits and exorbitant demands, which they will compromise rather than fight. Diemand compromised nothing in this category. He took especial pains to determine whether, in his judgment, a claim was just. If he thought it was he paid on the spot. If not he fought it in the courts. The trend of decisions in the company's favor is indicated by the figures in the paragraph preceding. At first these tactics resulted in a sharp rise in the number of suits and much employment for lawyers. Then suits began to fall off. People learned that Indemnity seldom went into court without a good case. In 1941 the number of suits was smaller in proportion to the business done than in 1933.

In 1940 the casualty volume in the United States amounted to $1,103,000,000 in terms of premiums received. Of this $844,000,000 was written by the stock companies and $259,000,000 by the mutuals. Contrast these figures with the $20,000,000 total for 1903 and one gets an idea of the changes Diemand has witnessed in the casualty scene. Measured by assets in 1940 the Indemnity Insurance Company of North America ($35,279,089) ranked tenth among the stock companies in the United States. In premium income ($13,847,000) it ranked fifteenth and in ratio of earnings to premiums (6.8) thirty-first. So much for the rise from the lowly position it occupied in 1932.

For his part in the foregoing John A. Diemand likes to give credit to his grass-roots casualty past. The pioneering school of trial and error was a hard school but a good one for those who had the instinct to profit by its lessons. Almost literally, instinct seems (to a layman at least) to be the word for that peculiar gift Diemand still employs to get at the red and yellow and green lights concealed in the acres of statistics which comprise the experience record of present-day casualty. It is an inheritance from the time when a successful casualty man had to be able to smell a bad risk or to pick a rate out of the air.

Mr. Diemand also gives a great deal of credit to the pivot men in his organization. Herbert P. Stellwagen in 1941 succeeded Diemand as executive vice-president. A Brooklyn boy who worked his way through New York University and came out with a Phi Beta Kappa key, he was one of the pre-1933 employees whom Diemand retained. Vice-President Benjamin Rush, Jr., and Calvin Roberts, assistant vice-president, have revamped the agency system. Of the new men, Patrick F. Burke, now vice-president, made over the claims department.

Franklin Vanderbilt, manager of the New York office, a veteran of casualty's early days, is known wherever casualty men gather.[15]

8

While Indemnity was rendering automobile liability accounts profitable, the Automobile Department of the parent company was increasing its coverages to include protection against almost every conceivable form of property damage. Every now and then, however, a peril not specifically foreseen, but covered under the company's "comprehensive" policy, comes to light. In the spring of 1942 a man in Pennsylvania made a claim for the price of new upholstery after a skunk, pursued by a dog, had leaped into his car.

Since the adoption of the non-valued policy in the early twenties the operations of the Automobile Department have been uniformly profitable. Between 1936 and 1942 the amount of business more than doubled, raising the premium income from $1,397,000 to $2,937,000.

A factor in all this was the avoidance by the North America of the automobile finance business. Sixty-odd per cent of automobiles were bought on credit, the business being controlled by a number of so-called finance companies. These concerns insured in bulk, say 10,000 cars at a time. The underwriter had to take all or nothing. The result was that he accepted many bad risks. The business was so hazardous that the North America largely refused it. Two or three large insurance companies who pursued the opposite course sustained heavy losses.

Along in 1937 and 1938 the banks of the country, looking for outlets for their surpluses, began lending directly to the automobile purchasers in their communities as well as to finance companies. By making loans directly to purchasers the banks could get a better rate, while the borrower would pay no more—and he might pay less— for his money than if he got it via a finance company. Cars thus financed by local banks would be good insurance risks because the banks would know to whom to extend credit. The North America was alert to this underwriting factor.

In 1941 Chester M. Campbell, head of the Automobile Department since its creation in 1919, retired. His successor was Arthur V. Davenport, a North America career man whose only other employment was in 1917 and 1918 in the United States Army.[16]

CHAPTER XIX

DEPRESSION AND RECOVERY

I

DURING the heyday of "Coolidge Prosperity" Charles P. Butler, counsel for the Insurance Department of the State of New York, was lamenting to a fire-insurance executive the decline in careful underwriting.

The executive did not appear to be disturbed. "We don't have to figure as closely as we used to. There are days when I'd insure a burning building to get the premium to put in the stock market."[1]

The underwriter's jest contained all too much truth in essence. This was in keeping with the spirit of the times, of which insurance companies were by no means conspicuous exemplars.

The North America adhered to a policy conservative even according to insurance standards. In 1926 an Investment Department was created to work with the Executive Committee of the Board in keeping an eye on the security holdings of the company and its affiliates. In 1928 the question was, in the words of Mr. Rush, "*When* is it going to happen?" That the bottom would fall out of the inflated market was taken for granted. The North America continued its preparations. Cash balances were built up; speculative issues were combed out of the portfolio.

In 1928 the North America increased its capital stock from $7,500,000 to $10,000,000. The money was used to acquire actual stock ownership of the affiliated Alliance Insurance Company.

In the summer of 1929 Mr. Rush called on the president of a New York bank. The banker saw no cloud in the sky. The country, he said, was in for an era of great industrial expansion. Mr. Rush passed on into the office of the bank's elderly chairman of the board who had surrendered the reins of active management. "I have noticed," he told his visitor, "that when common stocks are sold on a 2-percent basis experienced gentlemen prefer bonds."[2]

Rush thought the same, and the holdings of the North America reflected that judgment. John W. Drayton had lately become head of the Investment Department. Drayton was thirty-five years old and a son-in-law of Mr. Rush. He had been with the company since 1927 and before that with the brokerage house of Graham, Parsons & Company. Drayton was only fairly established in his new post when, in October, the crash came.

"I don't mind admitting," he said later, "that it cost me a little sleep."[3]

Few persons having to do with securities got more sleep than they needed that winter, or, intermittently, for some years to come. And few institutions during that vexing period equaled the investment record of the Insurance Company of North America. In all the other major financial crises—1819, 1837, 1857, 1873, 1893, 1907—the North America had given good accounts of itself. Only twice—amid the dislocations following the maritime war with France, 1798-1800, and the panic of 1837—was it actually hard pressed in times when that was the common lot. The crash of 1929 and ensuing depression were as severe as any in our history, security declines as great and business failures as numerous. The North America came through it without a scratch because the Investment Department proved itself so capable a navigator of troubled financial waters.

2

Despite the market panic the company finished the year 1929 in better condition than it had begun it. As of December 31 the market value of securities owned was $77,780,000, an increase of $3,799,000; surplus over capital and all liabilities $40,337,000, an increase of $5,069,000; total assets $90,109,000, an increase of $4,834,000. In a letter to the stockholders directing notice to these figures President Rush wrote: "During the latter part of the past year extensive liquidations occurred in the stock market." After this choice piece of understatement Rush continued: "Owing to the fact that we had been expecting ... a reduction in security values ... we were well fortified by cash, government bonds and short term government notes so that when the break came we were able to avail ourselves of the low prices then prevailing."[4]

On a temporary rise in the market the following spring these securities were sold at a profit of $3,000,000.[5] At the same time the portfolio was gone over carefully and many changes made, common-stock holdings being reduced and those of preferred stocks and high-grade bonds increased. From these exchanges the company emerged with an over-all gain of $788,000.[6] To facilitate the purchase of the Central Fire Insurance Company of Baltimore the North America's capital was increased during the year from $10,000,000 to $12,000,-000. In the face of deepening depression, bringing down premium income from $33,793,000 to $29,884,000, the company once more improved its position during the year. Assets were $92,841,000, up $2,732,000; securities owned, $83,539,000, up $5,729,000; surplus, $44,-377,000, up $4,040,000.

Nineteen thirty-one was a dark year. Business continued to fall off, security prices to sink, unemployment to rise, breadlines to lengthen. Bank failures added to the distress. For the first time the North America's annual statements showed marked effects of these misfortunes. Assets shrank to $74,992,000, off $17,849,000; securities to $64,942,000, off $18,597,000; surplus to $28,044,000, off $16,-333,000.

Serious as those reductions were, the North America fared far better than American business in general and considerably better than most other insurance companies. The solvency of about sixty fire, marine and casualty concerns doing business in New York seemed in danger. To avert the possibility of failures the national convention of insurance commissioners authorized insurance com-panies to value securities above the market prices, according to a fixed schedule which became known as "convention values." New York and certain other states went further than mere authorization. Companies were required to use convention values in making up their official statements.

The North America, and a few other companies, adopted the practice of getting out two reports: one based on convention values, which was used where the officials would accept no other; another based on market values, which was offered elsewhere. Stockholders received the market-value report from which the figures in the paragraph foregoing are taken. The company's convention-value report for 1931 added $15,242,000 to the securities portfolio, making a total of $80,184,000. This brought the surplus to $43,287,000 and the total assets to $90,234,000.[7]

In 1932 economic conditions went from bad to worse. At midyear the Insurance Company of North America sent a statement to its stockholders, based on market values, which indicated further declines, as follows: assets $63,349,000; securities $52,573,000; surplus $18,054,000. By this time a number of companies were in such critical plight that only the use of convention values and loans from the Reconstruction Finance Corporation kept them afloat. Securities, however, had touched bottom. The last of the year brought recoveries sufficient to lift the North America's assets to $72,042,000, its portfolio of stocks and bonds to $58,798,000 and its surplus to $28,764,000. These were market values. The company's convention-values statement showed: assets $85,356,000; securities $72,111,000; surplus $41,988,000.[8]

The creeping improvement of security prices brought no general betterment of conditions. The wave of bank failures had been stemmed by R.F.C. loans only to be followed by a wave of hoarding and consequent weakening of the banking structure. Continued attempts of the R.F.C. to stave off disaster were largely nullified by publishing the names of borrowing banks, a procedure which further diminished the confidence of frightened depositors. Business activity ebbed to its lowest point. The North America's premium receipts for the year fell to $20,240,000, a decline of $14,761,000 or 40 per cent since 1928. Panic psychology was again taking hold of the people.

This touched off a renewal of bank failures in January 1933. In February the governor of Michigan declared a bank moratorium to save the situation in Detroit. Four other states proclaimed moratoria before the end of the month and seventeen additional states acted during the first three days in March. On Saturday, March 4, Franklin D. Roosevelt became President. On Monday he closed the remaining banks of the country. A week later the sound ones began to reopen under Government licenses. The last phase of the depression had passed its nadir.

At the end of 1933 the company showed assets of $75,165,000, an increase of $3,123,000; securities with a market value of $62,091,000, an increase of $3,293,000; surplus $33,202,000, an increase of $4,-528,000.

Two years later saw the high-water marks of 1930 left behind: assets $100,003,000; securities $85,870,000; surplus $57,567,000. In

1934 John Drayton was rewarded with a promotion to vice-president.

Changing conditions brought changes in the nature of the portfolio. Whereas in 1932, 39.8 per cent of the holdings were in cash and high-grade bonds and 13.4 in common stocks, in 1935 these proportions had altered to 24.6 and 20.8. This was the North America's investment reaction to the New Deal. As Mr. Rush later expressed it: "The New Deal was averse to evidences of debt. It wished to relieve the debtor. We thought it best to get more real ownership of real things: things in the ground, such as oil; things on the ground, such as manufacturing; large distributors of essential commodities, such as chain stores."[9]

During each year of the anxious period the company earned a profit:

1929	$7,759,000
1930	6,295,000
1931	5,625,000
1932	2,721,000
1933	2,292,000
1934	4,792,000
1935	5,699,000

Only one year—1933—did the company have to dip into its surplus to maintain the dividend level at $2,400,000. That year dividends exceeded actual earnings by only $108,000. In 1935 dividends were increased to $3,000,000 where they remained until 1941 when they were increased to $3,600,000.

So much for a record remarkable in the annals of corporate history for the period. The average person who nursed securities through those years may grasp something of the company's achievement by looking at it this way. At the close of 1929 the company's stocks and bonds had a market value of $77,780,000. At their lowest point, June 1932, those securities, or their successors in the portfolio, were worth $52,573,000. How many individuals or corporations carried their holdings through that period with proportionately so small a decline? Very, very few.

The behavior of the North America's own shares was interesting. Though not listed by the company, the stock was traded on the New York Curb Exchange. Never a speculative issue, North America shares nevertheless responded to the magnetic attraction of the boom and reached 87½, as of December 31, 1928. A year later, after the market crash, the shares sold for 72. In 1931 they closed at 32. December 31, 1935, they stood at 76½, a recovery record with few equals.

3

What the depression meant to the marine branch may be seen at a glance from the following figures, which are net:

	Premiums	Losses	Expenses	Gain
1929 . . .	$9,225,000	$4,168,000	$4,101,000	$956,000
1930 . . .	8,097,000	4,183,000	4,005,000	91,000*
1931 . . .	7,097,000	3,346,000	3,353,000	398,000
1932 . . .	4,664,000	2,467,000	2,789,000	592,000*
1933 . . .	4,846,000	2,083,000	2,555,000	208,000
1936 . . .	5,881,000	2,328,000	2,743,000	810,000

* Loss.

To say that marine followed the general business of the country on its downward slide tells only part of the story. True, exports and imports were off, providing less employment for the shipowners and the shippers who buy insurance. Though they dropped 50 per cent, premiums did not go down at the pace that the loss ratio went up; nor was it possible to reduce overhead expenses to the extent that premiums reduced themselves. Claims climbed because insurers put in for small amounts they would not have bothered about in days of prosperity. The sum of thousands of such claims mounted. Like everyone else steamship operators were cutting expenses. Vessels were not maintained as in easy times; less care was taken loading and unloading: these and many other factors built up the loss total. Fortunately for the company the Marine Service Department was coming into its own during this period, or losses would have been measurably greater. As they were they ran under the general average for marine insurers.

That many small claims rather than a few large ones were responsible for the depression losses seems clear from a look at the large individual claims during the years involved. In 1929 the profit was $956,000 despite the payment of five individual net losses exceeding $50,000 each and totaling $773,000. Two of these were the Great

Lakes' steamers *Briton* and *Kiowa* on which the North America paid $226,000 and $329,000 respectively. In 1930 losses of more than $50,000 each totaled only $530,800, yet marine operations as a whole showed a deficit of $91,000. In 1932 when the marine operations' deficit mounted to $592,000 only $101,200 was paid in losses exceeding $50,000 each.

During the depression and not taken account of in the receipts indicated above, the company was the beneficiary of awards arising from German depredations upon American commerce during the war. These were settled in Washington by a mixed commission composed of one German, one American and an umpire who also was an American. In 1927 the commission made awards to the North America totaling $7,569,000, which included principal and interest from the date of the Armistice in 1918. To 1932, $3,370,000 of this amount was paid. Since then payments were in smaller amounts, making a total of $5,603,000 to 1942. This is probably all the company will get.[10]

Claimants were treated liberally in these settlements. The theory was reparations for German-inflicted losses to neutral commerce; or after we were no longer neutral, to our non-contraband commerce. In practice this was stretched in at least one instance involving the North America to include a ship sunk in a collision with a French naval vessel which presumably would not have been where it was unless looking for a German submarine. The awards were satisfied from a fund created by the sale of German property in the United States seized by the Government during the war.

4

The effect of the depression on the fire branch may be summed up in the following statistics:

	Premiums	Losses	Expenses	Gain
1929	$24,559,000	$10,307,000	$12,158,000	$2,094,000
1930	21,747,000	11,264,000	11,598,000	1,115,000*
1931	20,659,000	9,612,000	11,090,000	43,000*
1932	16,220,000	8,432,000	9,142,000	1,354,000*
1933	15,393,000	6,864,000	8,528,000	1,000
1936	16,490,000	6,016,000	9,169,000	1,305,000

* Loss.

These figures tell a story similar to that of the marine data: premiums down, loss and expense ratios up. This came about without one large single loss during the depression period. In 1927 fire was hit by five sizable disasters: the Briggs Manufacturing Company fire at Detroit which cost the company $132,900; the Illinois windstorm, $238,400; the St. Louis tornado, $346,900; the Florida hurricane, $251,300; the Feather River Pine Mills fire at Oroville, California, $150,800. Yet the fire branch absorbed these losses and turned in a profit for the year of $2,457,000. In 1928 there was a $145,000 loss at Fall River, Massachusetts. After that no large single loss was met with until recovery was under way in 1934 when the Schenley Distillery fire at Louisville cost $267,400 and the Chicago Stock Yards conflagration $276,300.

As with marine an accumulation of small losses, then, was responsible for the ascending loss ratio. There is record of a claim for fifty cents to place a patch on the seat of a pair of overalls burned when a policyholder sat on a lighted cigarette. Numerous claims of from one to five cents were paid on public buildings. This is one of the banes of insuring public structures. For political reasons the insuring officials usually apportion the coverage among as many local agents as possible. In a western city insurance in the amount of $10,000,000 was divided among thirty-five agents who placed it with fifty companies. On a claim for $12 to repair wind damage to a schoolhouse roof the North America paid its proportionate share, which was two cents. It cost the company $7 in postage, stationery and labor. Settlement of a claim for $12,000 would have cost no more. Ridiculously small claims are a feature of public insuring at all times though the depression heightened this evil. Individual policyholders rarely submit trivial claims except in times when one has to watch every penny.

Premiums went off because of the reduction of insurable values due to depreciation, lower replacement costs and reduced inventories; and because of a continuation of the downward rate trend. The virtual stoppage of new construction also affected premium volume. The moral hazard increased though the North America did not think it suffered heavily from fishy claims. "Primarily we do not insure *things,* but the persons who own the things," was a maxim John O. Platt had drummed into his agents. This policy paid dividends during the bleak years of 1930-1933.[11]

5

The beginning of the year 1939 saw Indemnity out of the woods and in the front rank of casualty companies. Fire and marine were prospering, though confronted by problems of increasingly serious portent. Fire suffered from antiquated organization and practices touching the business as a whole; marine from the threat of war. Three months earlier Hitler had levied his tribute at Munich and sensible men knew that a blackmailer is never paid in full.

Concerning the problems of the fire business Mr. Rush made a remarkably frank statement on January 4, 1939. It was addressed to the North America's special agents assembled in Chicago.

The name of Benjamin Rush was as well known in the high places in London's underwriting circles as in New York or Philadelphia. No important insurance matter could be regarded as decided without ascertaining answers to the questions: "What is the North America's position?" or "What do you think Ben Rush will say?" Some who spoke thus familiarly of the president of the North America had never seen him. The world their field, insurance executives traveled a great deal in the pursuit of their calling, Rush being about the sole exception. Mr. Rush's travels were almost purely for recreation. Not since he was a young man had he made it a practice to appear at the annual gatherings of insurance men, big or little. He read his talk to the special agents in Chicago over a telephone.

"The whole insurance machine exists for the protection of and service to the policyholder. I am afraid there are still a good many men in the insurance business who allow their own personal and temporary interest to obscure this cardinal fact; and to the extent to which they do so they militate against their own success and instead of building up good will for the insurance business and for themselves personally they may build up hostility.

"When I first entered the service of this company as a company officer, I got the idea, from my environment, that the first thing we had to provide was earning the dividends for our stockholders, and it was only some years later when I realized that this belief was fallacious, and substituted for it the protection of and service to the policyholder, that the North America began to make progress. . . .

"Don't let old-fashioned prejudices make you close your eyes to possible opportunities.

"The fire-insurance companies as a whole missed a tremendous opportunity when casualty insurance was first being developed because the executive managers of many of those companies had only contempt for the casualty business, which I, myself, heard fire insurance men refer to as 'a low-down business of ambulance-chasing that no decent fire-insurance man could be expected to soil his fingers with.' Well, as a result of that state of mind we have a very large number of casualty companies in existence that would probably never have been started had the fire-insurance people been alive to their opportunities, and we see today fire-insurance companies (this one among them) operating casualty companies under separate charter, and we see the casualty premiums steadily climbing ahead of the fire-insurance premiums.

"It was one of the biggest missed opportunities that I know of in the insurance business, but there are others which insurance management is missing today, and that brings me to my second recommendation of considering the future needs of the insurance business as a whole—the indirect needs of the policyholder so to speak. This is really a head-office problem but I think you may be interested in our views on it.

"It would be greatly to the convenience of the policyholder, and in the long run would save him money in premiums, if the various states of the union were to permit multiple-line charters. At the present time a separate charter is required to do life-insurance business, another one to do fire and marine, another to do casualty business. In Great Britain all three are done under one charter. Leaving out of consideration for the moment the life-insurance business, if multiple-line charters were permitted in the United States for fire and marine and for casualty it would be greatly to the assured's convenience to have one policy covering all these hazards instead of possibly a dozen or more. He would not run the risk (as he now does) of falling between two stools, and failing to protect something on which he desired protection. It would, in the long run, cut down the cost of insurance for him in that it would only require the executive force of one company instead of two as is the case at present, and it would do away with the conflict which now exists between casualty companies and fire and marine companies as to which shall write what.

"I believe agents are already sold on this proposition or are at least neutral to it. I regret to state that most of the opposition comes from the fire-insurance companies and casualty-insurance companies themselves.

"They will tell you, if you talk to them, that it cannot be done in

AN EARLY FIREMAN AND FIRE-INSURANCE MAN

Benjamin Franklin founded the Union Fire Company in Philadelphia in 1736. Later he had a hand in forming Philadelphia Contributionship, a fire-insurance company which still prospers. After Franklin's death the Union decorated its hand pumper with the above likeness (about 1795) of the founder. The artist is unknown. Original in the North America's collection of early American art dealing with insurance.

America and this in the face of the fact which they know, that it has been done successfully in Great Britain for more than forty years; or, if they admit it would be a good thing, they want to postpone consideration of the whole matter to some future date—the real reason being that certain officers of the casualty companies and the fire companies feel that they might lose their jobs. As a matter of fact they won't lose their jobs. They would merely have to have a paymaster with a different name.

"In line with this, and as a preparation for it, comes the drawing up of broad coverages in one policy for the convenience of the assured. In Great Britain you can cover most of the hazards that are covered by fire insurance, inland-marine insurance and casualty insurance in one document. Think how convenient this is to the average policyholder, and how much expense it saves in policywriting and the mere mechanics of handling the business on the part of the company. So when you get a chance to talk this over with agents speak a good word for multiple coverage, and for broad coverage for the assured so that we can get a body of support back of us when we go to the legislatures for the necessary changes.

"I now want to call your attention to another weakness in the insurance business, which is solely the fault of insurance companies, and particularly the fire branches of the companies, and that is the obstinacy with which they stick to the full-coverage standard fire form.

"In marine insurance whatever degree of coverage you want, from absolute all-risk policies up to total loss only, you can get, paying the correct rate for each class of coverage. . . . In the fire-insurance business such a thing does not exist, and most of the fire companies are opposed to it because they feel they would get less premium, which might be true, although I do not believe it, because when the assured wants a special form he goes over to the London market and gets it. That premium would stay over here were it not for the obstinacy with which fire-insurance men stick to their present forms.

"How would you feel if you went into a tailor shop to order a golf suit and the tailor refused to make you any other kind except an old-fashioned frock coat with waistcoat and trousers to match. This is an equivalent case to that taken by the fire-insurance managements today. There is no reason in the world why if an assured wants to carry a certain percentage of risk himself he should not be permitted to do so irrespective of any co-insurance clause, and if he wants to cover the excess of $5,000 or $50,000 on his risk he should not be able to do it at an equivalent rate.

"I have had several large assureds in the United States come to me and ask for one policy covering all their liability wherever it might be in the world—certain parts in whole, certain parts on high excess—and I have been obliged to tell them it is impossible for us to give them such a policy although I thought they were entitled to it, and that they could get it if they applied to a good broker in touch with the London market. That is not a condition of things which I can look at with equanimity. We should be able to do for our assured here what has been done abroad successfully for many years."[12]

A little more than two months after the delivery of these remarks, that is, on March 16, 1939, the architect of the modern underwriting institution known as the North America group resigned the presidency of the parent company which he had served for forty-four years, twenty-three as its chief executive. That the active services of Benjamin Rush should not be lost, the office of chairman of the Board was created for him. John O. Platt succeeded to the presidency. At a testimonial dinner to the retiring chief Mr. Platt observed that during his predecessor's tenure as president annual premiums had risen from $11,000,000 to $44,000,000, investment income from $940,000 to $4,350,000.

"These material gains are outstanding," concluded Platt, "but the thing I like to realize with pride and gratitude is that no one has ever been asked to do anything that did not square with his instinctive feeling of fair dealing."[13]

When Mr. Platt was elevated to the presidency Sheldon Catlin became the ranking official of the fire branch. On his retirement in 1940 the post was assumed by Vice-President John Kremer. Mr. Kremer's great-great-grandfather, Simeon Toby, was president of the North America's first corporate rival, the Insurance Company of the State of Pennsylvania, and piloted that organization through the panic of 1837. Kremer served with various insurance companies before joining the North America as a special agent in 1910. Platt, Catlin and Kremer were the triumvirate which had brought the fire branch to the peak of its prosperity. Mr. Platt likes to stress the teamwork feature of this relationship. "It was simply a case of three men pulling together. In my young days I used to do a bit of boat racing. The *crew* did the job. It's no different with an insurance organization."[14]

6

John O. Platt cordially endorsed Mr. Rush's remarks to the special agents. For a full generation Platt had witnessed the gradual accumulation of conditions against which Rush inveighed. To earn a living a fire-insurance company was required to thread a maze of bureaucracy sufficiently complicated to bewilder a master of governmental red tape.

Part of it *was* governmental red tape. The forty-eight states had insurance laws, each differing from others, sometimes in important particulars. Insurance men themselves were in considerable part responsible for this condition. Many of the laws and the regulations of the state insurance commissions were on the books at the urgent behest of insurance men; and of recent years little or no legislation or regulation touching insurance had been enacted without some support from the insurance fraternity. The trouble was that the fraternity was often split as to what it wanted. On top of public laws, regulations and regulatory bodies, the insurance fraternity had piled some forty rate-making, regulatory and administrative bodies of its own creation. They ran all the way from national to regional and local organizations. This patchwork followed few rules of consistency.

The result was that what was required in one community might be optional in another and forbidden in a third. Thirty-two variations of five basic policy forms were used in forty-six states and territories. Forms might differ city by city, due to rules imposed by competing local brokers. In one state concrete blocks made a frame house, in another a brick house. Valued policies were prohibited in most states but mandatory in a few. A list of such disparities would fill a page of this book. The cumbersome overhead structure devised to administer the un-uniform rules governing fire underwriting was expensive to maintain. Yet it was maintained in the face of declining rates, brought about largely by what the fire organizations had taught their patrons in the way of fire prevention. The average rate for the United States was $1.07 per $100 of insurance in 1914. In 1920 it was $1.02; in 1930, 86 cents; in 1935, 71 cents; in 1940, 67 cents.

There was no thought in Mr. Platt's mind that rates could be the same in all sections of the country, even on the same type of risk. Hazards varied too greatly, as shown by experience. They varied in cities as close together as Minneapolis and St. Paul. Underwriters must take account of these differences, though the top-heavy bureaucracy they had built up to that end went further than the rule of common sense.

"The casualty business," remarked Mr. Platt, "with its simpler and more flexible setup was better adapted to changing conditions. Less hidebound by tradition, it met its problems better than fire."[15]

7

Agitation for streamlining the fire business brought about the "extended-cover endorsement" in 1936. Instead of issuing separate policies for windstorm, cyclone, tornado, hail, explosion, riot, civil commotion, aircraft, smoke or vehicle damage these perils were covered in a blanket endorsement attached to the fire contract. This was about the extent of the modernizing influence, however.

The goals Mr. Platt and his associates worked toward were administrative simplification and multiple-line writing: fire, marine and casualty all under the one tent. Having to act within the archaic framework of the business as a whole Mr. Platt found that there were limits to what he could accomplish.

This work had begun early. In 1926 the Eastern Department, established with headquarters at Hartford in 1868, was abolished and its functions drawn into the head office at Philadelphia. Swifter modes of communication made this possible. The result was the elimination of considerable duplication of labor. In 1932 the Southern Department at Atlanta, dating from 1875, was closed and its work taken to the head office. For some years the southern territory had been unprofitable for underwriters generally, including the North America. The North America instituted a thorough overhauling of its southern situation. The number of agencies was reduced. This reduced premium volume, but it also stopped the net loss in Dixie. At this stage expansion was resumed. In 1942 the South was profitable territory except for two states.[16]

The most significant change of the period, however, took place in New York City, for more than eighty years the most important single outpost of the company. Prior to 1932 the North America's organization in New York was a scattered affair. Marine held forth on Beaver Street in the Delmonico Building which the company had purchased after the famous restaurant of that name, a great gathering

John O. Platt

Tenth president Insurance Company of North America, 1939-1941. Vice-Chairman of the Board since 1941. Joined company as an office boy in 1891. Vice-president in charge of fire, 1910. As one of country's leading underwriters, quadrupled company's fire business and greatly increased its prestige in that field.

From a portrait by John C. Johansen, owned by the Insurance Company of North America.

place for maritime underwriters, had gone out of business. Fire was on William Street. The Indemnity Company was on John Street, which had become Manhattan's Insurance Row. Alliance Casualty was on Maiden Lane. Each office had its manager and staff, reporting directly to Philadelphia and enjoying the semi-autonomous preroga- tives which were traditional attributes of the metropolitan field.

January 1, 1932, marine and fire were consolidated under the gen- eral managership of Henry H. Reed, former New York marine manager. In June casualty came under Reed. The new organization was housed at 111 John Street awaiting the completion of the com- pany's skyscraper at 99 John.

Henry Reed joined the North America in 1907 as a lad out of St. Paul's School and has been with the company ever since, saving 1917 and 1918 when he commanded a battery of the 305th Field Artillery in France. He is a descendant of Andrew Reed of the firm of Reed & Pettit, merchants and underwriters, which was established in South Front Street, Philadelphia, thirty years before the founding of the Insurance Company of North America. John Pettit, the junior part- ner, was the father of Colonel Charles Pettit, second president of the North America. Colonel Pettit married Sarah Reed, a daughter of his father's business associate.

The New York arrangement proved a happy one. It went as far along the road toward Rush's and Platt's ideal of carrying all sorts of insurance to the customer in one parcel as the variegated and restrict- ive body of insurance law and regulation would allow. A broker would come in with a large and complicated risk. Reed would call to his desk Henry Thorn, marine manager, Charles P. Butler, fire, and Franklin Vanderbilt, casualty. Then and there the proper coverages were determined and distributed.

The consolidated office has made insurance history in other interesting particulars. In 1935 a broker came to Reed for all-risk coverage on the credit files of Dun & Bradstreet. Though the files were immensely valuable, Dun & Bradstreet had never been able to insure them adequately. Thorn could not handle it because marine companies are prohibited from issuing policies on property at a fixed location. Butler could not handle it because fire companies may not issue all-risk policies or, in New York, valued policies. They could insure the files only for the value of the paper and the cost of the clerical labor of transcribing the data thereon.

Reed vainly endeavored to interest fire executives in an effort to remove these disabilities. Turning then to the insurance laws he concluded that casualty companies were empowered to insure "valuable papers" on an all-risk valued basis. The law was intended to cover securities but it used the words "valuable papers." "Those files are valuable papers if I ever saw valuable papers," said Reed. A special form was worked out by Indemnity protecting Dun & Bradstreet in the amount of $2,000,000. It was the first such policy to be issued.[17]

8

Although New York was the scene of the first formal application of the nearest thing possible to multiple-line writing, the principle had been in practice informally for some years in the Pittsburgh office of the North America under instructions from Philadelphia.[18]

The drawing of the Eastern and the Southern Department functions into Philadelphia had worked so well that thought was being given to the Western Department at Chicago. Its territory covered eighteen states. Four hundred persons were employed at the Chicago headquarters which constituted, in fact, another head office. How to do away with the duplication of functions between Philadelphia and Chicago, and get better service to the company's patrons in the immense Chicago area? The Pittsburgh-New York formula seemed to be the answer. The job of bringing this about was turned over to Ludwig C. Lewis who tackled it with characteristic vim. "Service offices" were opened with limited powers in Omaha, St. Louis, Detroit, Minneapolis. Each had a manager who knew something of all kinds of business the North America transacted: fire, marine, inland marine, casualty, bonding. Under him were experts in those fields. Engineering remained at Chicago, but when an engineer was needed on a service-office problem he went out. The service offices were designed to solve the technical problems of the local agents within their several jurisdictions.

The scheme worked. More service offices were set up. In June 1940 the Western Department was abolished, the Chicago office being shrunk down to a service office with a personnel of 114. Engineering was split up and an engineer assigned to each of the various service offices in the Chicago area. Lewis went ahead and covered the country with service offices. Twenty-three were in operation in October 1940 when the North America made a formal announcement of the new arrangement which the *National Underwriter* called "one of the most aggressively up-to-date adaptations of procedure in the insurance world."[19]

In the meantime the company's agency system, which the service offices serve, had come in for attention. A part of Diemand's reorganization of the Indemnity Company was a combing-over of the agencies. A good share of this work fell to Benjamin Rush, Jr., whose jurisdiction was presently extended to include the agency setup of the parent company. Young Rush proceeded to knead the two systems into a cohesive whole. In 1939 Benjamin was transferred to the underwriting end of Indemnity. His brother Stockton took over the agencies. In 1940 Stockton became agency secretary of the North America with authority over the entire group. Stockton Rush's experience had been varied and general. In the marine branch he had served in Pittsburgh, a witness to the advantages of the consolidated-office idea. He was in Chicago with the fire branch during the metamorphosis of the unwieldly Western Department.

In June 1942 the number of agents serving the North America group in the United States was 15,187. Service offices numbered twenty-eight. The roster of the North America agencies which have been in the hands of the same family for more than fifty years is too long to reproduce in this place. A few examples must suffice. Josiah Maxcy of Gardiner, Maine, began writing insurance the year before the Civil War. The Josiah Maxcy & Sons Company is now administered by a son and a grandson of the original agent. C. A. Worthington heads the agency in Trenton, New Jersey, which his grandfather and a partner started in 1867. What seems to be the oldest agency continuously in one family is that of Miles N. Eckert & Sons, Allentown, Pennsylvania, established in 1844. Since 1884 the Eckerts have acted for the Insurance Company of North America. D. P. Miller started writing North America policies in Cumberland, Maryland, in 1875. His son, D. P. Miller, is writing them now. El Paso, Texas, came up to an Easterner's expectations of the wild and woolly West in 1887 when Philip C. Stevens entered upon his duties for the North America there. The agency has passed to the founder's son, Horace B. Stevens.

Despite its pride of lineage the North America is out after new blood. This is another of Stockton Rush's responsibilities. Competition for promising youngsters is so keen that casual and voluntary accretions to the force no longer suffice. Some years ago the company established a training school for beginners but it did not produce the results desired. Stockton Rush likes to get recruits directly from colleges, technical institutions preferred, or from the state fire bureaus. They learn by working. The usual routine is to bring them to Philadelphia for six months during which they are shifted from department to department. The unpromising ones drop out and the promising ones are sent into the field where they get to see a good part of this spacious country of ours. When a man is properly seasoned and has found his forte the company likes to send him back where he grew up. This is called "homesteading." It has been found that a returned native son usually has advantages over an outsider.[20]

Benjamin Rush, Sr., had long believed that the fire branch should be able to introduce something on the order of the "merit ratings" by which, at his direction, Indemnity had lowered the premiums of automobile drivers without accident records. Mutual fire-insurance companies were doing it and one or two small stock companies had taken up the practice with good results. In 1941 the North America obtained from the Pennsylvania Legislature an amendment to the company's charter permitting it to write "participating" fire policies. Under this the company can, in effect, declare dividends to policyholders. The action created quite a stir in insurance circles. To the date of this writing the company has made no use of the new power which was acquired merely as another forehanded preparation for changes in the fire business which the North America believes to be overdue.

CHAPTER XX

Hitler Fails to Surprise the Underwriters

I

Though the fighting part of World War I ended on the minute at 11 A.M., November 11, 1918, war perils to water-borne commerce did not terminate so abruptly. The waters about Europe and certain localities elsewhere were strewn with mines which during the four years past had sunk more ships than any other agency excepting submarines. Time was necessary to sweep them up. Consequently war-risk insurance continued, though at greatly diminished rates. While the bulk of the mines was cleared away in a matter of months, an occasional one, perhaps carried a thousand miles from where it had been sown, turned up as long as two years after the Armistice.

In the meantime war rates went either to literally nothing or to token quotations of one-fortieth to one-twentieth of 1 per cent, which underwriters express by the symbols "2½c%" or "5c%," meaning two and one-half or five cents per $100 valuation. The interesting point, however, is that war-risk insurance *was* continued in most marine contracts. Under the "extended conditions" lately introduced the war clause included coverage from warehouse to warehouse.[1]

In 1933 Adolf Hitler began to rearm Germany. In 1935 Italy attacked Ethiopia. England had only to close the Suez Canal and stand firm in the Mediterranean to save the kingdom of Haile Selassie. Mediterranean war-risk rates soared out of the token class, but subsided when Britain and France fobbed off on the League of Nations the job of stopping Mussolini. In 1936 Franco launched his conquest of republican Spain with the military backing of Hitler and Mussolini. The following year Japan fell upon China, expecting a victory as easy as that of Italy who in the course of her subjugation of Ethiopia had successfully defied British sea power.

The wars in Spain and in China proved the destructive power of the airplane and caused British and Continental underwriters considerable on-shore losses. What airplanes might do in event of the outbreak of a general war was brought home by the fact that goods valued at $500,000,000 on London's docks alone were protected by the warehouse-to-warehouse clause. In the fall of 1937 the International Union of Marine Insurance recommended the abandonment of this coverage. By February 1, 1938, it had generally been given up. In the light of hindsight it seems curious that the underwriters should have been so slow about it. The explanation lies in the psychology of the times. British and French statesmen hoped to preserve the peace by a policy of concessions to the aggressors. For his part Uncle Sam draped himself in the mantle of isolationism and passed the Neutrality Act.

The complacency of the British was not shared by a number of leaders of the American insurance market, who believed that the dropping of the warehouse-to-warehouse clause did not go far enough to meet the real dangers of the situation. Vice-President T. Leaming Smith, in charge of North America's marine branch, was in London in March 1938. He took the opportunity to discuss the situation with the leading English underwriters, pointing out as forcibly as he could the serious possibilities.

The transatlantic war-risk rate was one-twentieth of 1 per cent. The increasing of this and other token rates would tend to build a backlog against the "shock-loss" period in event of an outbreak of a general war. The shock-loss period covers the first month of hostilities when ships that have sailed under peacetime rates are exposed to wartime perils. In 1914 losses during this period had been heavy.

London underwriters, ordinarily the most astute in the world, remained under the spell of their government's policy of appeasement in 1938. "To give Hitler what he wants within reason is better than going to war." The Nazis took over Austria just before Smith reached London. The British Government construed it as an act "within reason." The British market insisted that the competitive situation would doom any attempt to create a backlog. If war-risk rates went up certain companies would merely reduce their ordinary rates in like amounts so that the over-all charges would remain the same. The English disinclination to take war rates out of the token brackets prevented a stiffening of rates on this side of the water.[2]

2

Likewise Mr. Roosevelt's attempts to prepare the country to meet the challenge of totalitarianism had tedious going. Nearly every request for Army or Navy appropriations was pared down. When the President resorted to indirection to attain his ends—military works for which appropriations had been refused undertaken as unemployment relief projects—he was accused of militarism and deception. Despite this, in 1936 the Maritime Commission was created to rehabilitate, through subsidies, our merchant marine as a potential military and naval auxiliary as well as a carrier of peacetime commerce.

This posed an underwriting problem which the Commission called Henry H. Reed, general manager of the North America's New York office, to Washington to help solve.

That an adequate insurance market under the same flag is essential to a successful merchant marine is a fact that hardly can be overstressed. With this in view the hull syndicates of 1920 had been created at the Government's request. In 1929, however, the Shipping Board, the Maritime Commission's predecessor, had entered into competition with the private market by insuring the Government's mortgage interest in vessels at losing rates which the market, naturally, could not meet. Though these rates had since been raised to market levels the Government was still in the insurance business. Reed asked that it return this coverage to the market, meaning Syndicate C of the 1920 group. The Government held out for a "watching interest" in mortgaged ships. It was agreed that this should be only 10 per cent of the insurance on such vessels, in no case exceeding $400,000, and that market rates should be charged. Reed accepted this as a fair compromise.

The capacity of Syndicate C was increased from $2,500,000 on single risks to $4,000,000. In the case of a few luxury liners this limit was exceeded, an example being the *Washington* which was covered for $6,050,000. In such cases the syndicate took its $4,000,000 maximum, the balance being placed mostly with member companies who assumed this extra risk in addition to their syndicate participations. The North America group's participation in the enlarged syndicate was 7.125 per cent, making a total liability of $285,000 on a $4,000,000 hull.[3]

By the summer of 1938 Hitler's guns-for-butter program had borne ominous fruit. The German nation again possessed the mightiest military machine in Europe, based on daringly new conceptions of the striking power of the airplane and the tank. These weapons had been tested in the fighting in Spain. Italy's armed forces possessed the advantage of battle practice in Ethiopia and in Spain plus the prestige of having bluffed down Great Britain. The only nation resisting with force the march of the aggressors was Russia who had sent planes to Spain and was doing much to keep China in the fight against Japan. True, Great Britain had started to rearm, but was miles behind Germany. Internally distracted France—where Pierre Laval had lately been foreign minister—sat down behind her monumental product of the military minds of 1917, the Maginot Line.

In this dispensation of affairs Herr Hitler moved toward his next objective, the dismemberment of Czechoslovakia whose frontier defenses had been outflanked by the occupation of Austria. In August the Fuehrer began to build up the crisis with screaming denunciations of fancied mistreatment of the German population of Czech Sudetenland. England urged "concessions"—by Czechoslovakia—in the interest of peace. Early in September German troops massed on the Czech frontier. German-inspired clashes broke out in the Sudeten territory. Hitler threatened to move in to "restore order," but to the surprise of almost everyone the Czech army moved in instead. The next day, September 14, Prime Minister Chamberlain of Great Britain flew to Berchtesgaden where he yielded to the Fuehrer's demand for a plebiscite on the Sudeten question. Europe already had seen something of Hitler's plebiscites. This, however, was to be an honest election to express the wishes of the Sudetens.

The only question was whether the Czechs would consent. On this seemed to hinge the possibility of war. It was sufficient to give marine rates a harder jolt than the Mediterranean crisis over Ethiopia.

American underwriters largely took the token rates previously referred to from "advisory" schedules issued from time to time by the American Institute of Marine Underwriters. On September 15 the rate committee of that body held its most serious session in years. In a confidential bulletin it acknowledged the disturbed condition of the market. Rates quoted by different companies showed so many disparities that a new advisory schedule was offered "merely as an indication of the rates various underwriters are willing to quote."

Full war-risk coverage on cargoes to or from German ports went to actual wartime levels for an endangered route: "Not less than 5%." Coverage excluding loss by British or French capture was quoted at 1 per cent. Full coverage to Italy was "not less than 2½%" and coverage free of British or French capture 1 per cent. No rate was quoted for German ships to or from United Kingdom or French ports; the Italian flag rate was 1½ per cent; British or French flag ½ per cent; other flags ⅜. Scandinavian rates went from the token class to ⅛ to ½ per cent, depending on the flag and the degree of coverage.[4]

All this was because the Czechs threatened to fight and there seemed a bare chance that Britain and France might help them after all. In any event next day, on September 16, the Institute committee advised the *doubling* of transatlantic *export* rates quoted in the previous day's schedule. Rates on imports were unchanged. Vessels coming toward our shores were going away from danger; those leaving our shores were approaching it.[5]

On September 22 Chamberlain, back in Germany to arrange the details of the Sudeten business as quietly as possible, received the shock of his life. Blandly the Fuehrer repudiated his promise of a week before. There could be no plebiscite; not even a make-believe election. Sudetenland must be forked over without formality by October 1 or Hitler would take it by force. So far as the record is available no foreigner in history has thus insulted to his face a British prime minister.

Followed days of feverish, fumbling "consultations" between Chamberlain and the French premier, Daladier; between British and French military men. Trenches were dug in Hyde Park, gas masks distributed in London. France called some army reserves.

The American insurance market prepared for immediate hostilities. The Institute recommended another doubling of all rates, Pacific as well as Atlantic, import as well as export; and that no rates be quoted for German or Italian vessels.[6]

On September 29 Hitler won his war of nerves. Chamberlain, Daladier and Mussolini met the Fuehrer in Munich, while Czech statesmen sat in an anteroom unspoken to. The Sudetenland was yielded. Affably Hitler soothed the sting of his affront of a week before. "This is my last territorial demand in Europe." On the balcony at 10 Downing Street Mr. Chamberlain declaimed: "It is peace in our time. Peace with honor!" To which Winston Churchill, scowling from an Opposition bench in Commons, observed: "We have sustained a total, unmitigated defeat."

War-risk rates collapsed like a punctured balloon: to and from the United Kingdom ⅛ per cent; the Continent ¼; Mediterranean ⅜, Axis steamers and Axis ports included.[7]

3

Six months after it was made Hitler tore up the Munich pact and erased Czechoslovakia from the roll of nations. Half of what had been left after Munich was annexed to the Reich, the remainder made a "protectorate" or given to Hungary.

This was in March 1939. The American insurance market began to prepare in earnest for the whirlwind. At the time of Munich underwriters depending on London for a part of their reinsurance had faced the possibility of cancellations. They determined to render themselves self-sustaining on war risks and to avert a repetition of the chaos of 1914. On March 27 the American Institute of Marine Underwriters handed this sizable job to a committee consisting of Percy Chubb II, of Chubb & Son, chairman; Henry C. Thorn, the North America; A. B. Grant, Thames & Mersey Marine Insurance Company; John W. Morrow, Home Insurance Company; and Fred Maccabe, Automobile Insurance Company.

The labors of these men brought forth the American Cargo War Risk Reinsurance Exchange consisting of 144 native and locally licensed foreign companies which comprised all but a small fraction of the American market. Foreign participation was approximately 30 per cent of the total. The Exchange was to work like any reinsurance syndicate. Rates binding on all subscribers were to be fixed by the Reinsurance Exchange. All companies were to cede to the Exchange their cargo war-risk commitments which would be distributed among the membership according to the amount of their participation. The North America's share of 10 per cent (7.6 for the parent company and the balance spread among affiliates) was the largest of any group of companies under common ownership. On May 1, 1942, with the war-risk picture looking anything but attractive, this participation was increased to 11 per cent.

So much for the preparations concerning cargo. War risks on hulls were undertaken by Syndicate C, representing practically the same companies, the capacity of which had been expanded in 1937 by the Reed agreement with the Maritime Commission.

This left only ordinary marine risks (as distinguished from war risks) for each company to handle independently. Ordinary marine rates are not subject to the fluctuations that characterize war-risk premiums.

After putting themselves in readiness to sustain the shock of war the underwriters tried to go further. The Chubb committee urged the Government to set up machinery for supplementing the private market as had been done by hasty improvisation after the storm had broken in 1914. Isolationist sentiment proved too strong in Congress, however, and this effort was bootless.

The Cargo War Risk Reinsurance Exchange began operation on June 10, 1939, with William D. Winter, president of the Atlantic Mutual, chairman, and Henry C. Thorn, New York marine manager of the North America, vice-chairman. Thorn was also chairman of the Rate and Underwriting Committee upon which the vital work of the Exchange devolved. He came to this task well seasoned by experience.

Born in Brooklyn, genial Harry Thorn began his insurance career as an office boy for Johnson & Higgins in 1903. As a placer he was in the thick of the underwriting panic during the opening weeks of the first World War, which he got another view of later on as an infantry lieutenant in France. In 1925 he joined the North America. An early and tireless advocate of proper preparation for an emergency, Thorn was chairman of the Institute committee which issued the advisory war-risk rates. Under the Exchange he prepared to carry on the same work, clothed with real authority over the market.

By this time British and Continental underwriters, too, had acted to stiffen rates. Moreover, the British and other European governments moved to support their private markets in event of war and keep afloat the commerce they should need so desperately.

These important steps were taken none too soon. Hitler's destruction of Czechoslovakia was followed by Italy's seizure of Albania. On the ruins of appeasement Chamberlain strove frantically to rebuild an eastern front against the Nazis who had marked Poland for their next victim. The integrity of Poland was guaranteed and an Anglo-French mission sent to Moscow in a tardy effort to cement an alliance with the Soviets. The mission declined to meet Stalin's price, which was the right to occupy the little border states of Estonia, Lithuania and Latvia. Adolf Hitler had no such compunctions and so struck a bargain with the man against whom the Fuehrer had breathed fire and brimstone for years. On August 23, 1939, the democracies were all but overwhelmed by announcement of a non-aggression pact between the Reich and Russia. On September 1 the German army set upon Poland with a fury that made the world gasp. A nation of 34,000,000 with an army of 1,500,000 was crushed in twenty days.

4

In the midst of these events the American Cargo War Risk Reinsurance Exchange did the work it had been created to do—did it well and effectively. Syndicate C handled the hull business in similar fashion. The "bedlam"—the word is W. D. Winter's[8]—of August 1914 was avoided.

In 1914 the insurance communities on both sides of the ocean had been taken wholly by surprise. Companies were not banded together in syndicates which fixed rates and general underwriting conditions. It was a case of every man for himself until, after the first few weeks, the American market settled down to taking its cues from the two leading underwriters of the day, Hendon Chubb and Benjamin Rush. On top of this the 1914 market was short of capacity to handle the enormous burden so suddenly and so unexpectedly thrown upon it. Until this capacity could be increased by the Government's War Risk Insurance Bureau and by the entry of other insurance companies into the marine field there was a tendency to base rates on scarcity rather than on risk.

None of these conditions obtained in September 1939. The marine underwriters were ready for Hitler; and they were about the only people who were ready. The market was not taken by surprise. For this salutary condition of affairs a considerable measure of thanks is due to the initiative of a few American leaders. Though less active than they had been twenty-four years before, the elder statesmen of the profession, Chubb and Rush, wielded much influence in the preparations to meet the crisis.

The American market possessed sufficient capacity due largely to the multiple-line idea in insurance development. Many marine companies were also in the fire and the casualty business. These activities provided additional assets. The two great syndicates, embracing 95 per cent of the marine-underwriting capital of the country, provided the organization.

Therefore the participation of the North America, or of any other marine-insurance company, in World War II becomes largely the history of the cargo and the hull syndicates in which the individual companies had submerged their identities. In earlier wars and crises each company was on its independent own, enabling the historian to trace individual performances. Success or want of it depended on the degree of competence of the respective guiding heads in the science of underwriting.

These pages have endeavored to show more than one example in which the underwriting judgment of responsible officers brought the North America through a time of stress with comparatively light losses whereas other companies sustained heavy losses; and occasionally it was the other way around. In the conflict which began on the first day of September 1939 the lot of one company was the lot of all, so far as war-risk insurance was concerned. The North America might confine its liability on a particular risk to $5,000 while other members of the Exchange accepted $1,000,000. In event of a total loss the North America's share would be $100,000—or 10 per cent, in keeping with its syndicate subscription. Conversely, the North America might take a $500,000 risk and in event of a total loss have to pay only $50,000.

During the fateful days of August and September the rate problem, so chaotic in 1914, was handled smoothly. Chairman Thorn and colleagues of the Underwriting and Rate Committee of the Exchange had their machinery ready. On July 20 a schedule had been issued fixing the premium to and from the United Kingdom and the Continent at ¼ of 1 per cent; Baltic ⅜; Mediterranean ⅜. These quotations, lower than those prevailing in April and May, reflected the expectation that Britain and France might be able to postpone or avert an outbreak by a display of shotgun diplomacy. Then came the bombshell of the Russo-German pact.

The news reached New York after the close of business on August 23. Next day the Thorn committee had its new rates ready. German and Italian steamers were treated drastically. No quotations for them were issued except in the case of voyages from or to their own ports. These were 2 per cent for imports to the United States and 5 per cent for exports. Rates for vessels of other registry from or to Axis ports were 1 and 4 per cent; from or to the Baltic ⅜ and ¾; from or to the Mediterranean, except Italy, 1 and 1¼. The United Kingdom rate in either direction remained at ¼.

Next day, August 25, rates for the German and Italian flags were lifted to 5 and 10 per cent, and on the twenty-eighth Axis ships were dropped entirely from the schedule of quotations. At the same time the United Kingdom rate went to 1 per cent; the Mediterranean rate to 2¾.

Hitler struck at Poland as day was breaking on September 1. The Rate Committee issued a five-line bulletin, effective at noon, *tripling* war-risk rates throughout the world, excepting only shipments confined to the Western Hemisphere or carried by American-flag vessels "not touching European ports or not via Mediterranean." These were unchanged. The prompt war declarations of Great Britain and France affected these rates little, those actions having been discounted by the September first bulletin. By September 15 United Kingdom rates had increased slightly: belligerent ships 7½; American ships 2½; other neutrals 3¾. By the end of the month, however, these quotations had eased to 5, 1½ and 3¾.[9]

By this time the shock-loss period was safely passed. It had been a much less painful experience than the underwriters had feared. Except in Poland heavy losses from surprise airplane raids on congested harbors did not occur. Sea losses were mostly on German ships. As in 1914 German vessels were instructed to dash for the nearest neutral harbor, United States ports excepted. Nazi vessels in our harbors had orders to get away if they could, and some of them managed it. In this way cargoes were diverted from their true destinations. Notwithstanding the considerable doubts expressed as to whether the underwriters were liable, the Exchange bore the cost of retrieving such goods and delivering them to the proper places. They acted under the quaintly phrased "restraint-of-princes" clause which had been in marine contracts since before the North America was born. It was assumed that the German captains were not free agents but were restrained by their "prince," i.e., Hitler, from finishing their voyages. This action by the Exchange was not followed by British underwriters who resisted such claims until overruled by the House of Lords.

The completion of delivery of such cargoes constituted the heavy item of the shock-loss period, which in all cost the Exchange about $1,300,000, the North America's share being $130,000.

The low rates quoted for American ships promised something in the way of a shipping boom, with attendant inflation of hull prices and freights and consequent complication of the underwriting problem as in the first World War. The promise was unrealized. The Neutrality Act placed an absolute embargo on munitions shipments to the belligerents. This tied up $80,000,000 worth of war materials ordered by the Allies before hostilities had begun. Some months previously Mr. Roosevelt had failed in an attempt to obtain the repeal of the Neutrality Act. As the next-best thing he proposed to amend it, so as to permit England and France to obtain war supplies here on a "cash-and-carry" basis. In this the President was successful though he paid a heavy price. By the amended Act, effective early in November, American ships were prohibited from entering the European war zone which was so defined as to exclude them from the ports of neutral Eire, Belgium, Holland, Denmark, Sweden and Norway south of Bergen. Though a few American vessels evaded this by changing to Panamanian registry and others found new routes open to them in the Pacific and elsewhere replacing British shipping diverted to cash-and-carry work, there was no demand for American bottoms as in 1914-1916.

When Hitler did not attack in the West after his lightning conquest of Poland the legend of the impregnability of the Maginot Line grew. The Allies did not attack and the conflict lapsed into a stalemate which the English called the "bore war." Sinkings of merchant vessels taking food and the sinews of war to the Allies were not impressive. To January 1, 1940, they averaged 195,000 tons a month. During 1939 the Insurance Company of North America received in war-risk premiums $1,557,000 and paid in losses $391,000, giving a very satisfactory loss ratio of 25.7. As the bulk of this represented the company's participation in the two syndicates it can be taken as the measure of American underwriting experience as a whole.

5

The warfare of inaction continued and on April 3, 1940, the Exchange quoted the lowest rates since the conflict had begun: 3½ per cent from and 4 per cent to the United Kingdom and the Continental coast from Brest to Holland; 2½ from and to France south of Brest; 3 per cent to and from Norway in belligerent vessels and 2 per cent in neutral; 2 per cent to and 1 per cent from the Mediterranean.

Six days later the bore war ended with Germany's meticulously planned and remarkably executed surprise invasion of Denmark and Norway.

On May 10 the full might of the German juggernaut struck in the West, beginning the battle which Adolf Hitler said would decide the fate of Europe for a thousand years.

Holland was overrun in five days, the Maginot Line breached at Sedan.

The Belgium Army surrendered on May 28, leaving the position of the British Expeditionary Force hopeless. With the French army demoralized and Paris in panic, the Germans swung toward the Channel to finish off the B.E.F. In delaying actions 10,000 Britons sold their lives so dearly that 380,000 of their comrades escaped by the miracle of Dunkirk. The infuriated Germans turned on the French who raised the white flag June 16.

Battered England faced the conquerors of the Continent alone. Would she prolong the struggle which the rest of the world deemed already lost? The Reichsfuehrer seems to have thought not. He rested his troops and angled for a surrender by negotiation. Winston Churchill, who had taken the helm from Chamberlain's futile hands, rallied his people. "Our policy? It is to wage war. Our aim? It is victory. . . . Hitler knows he will have to break us in this island or lose the war."

These tremendous events provided a sterner test of the insurance fraternity's organization for war than had the "shock" period of nine months before. Thorn's Rate Committee met almost daily, and a "watch" of two members, relieved every two hours, was maintained on duty throughout each business day to alter rates on certain voyages in keeping with the changing panorama of current history.

As Denmark, Norway, Holland, Belgium and France were overrun they were dropped from the rate schedules. Before Dunkirk premiums for the west coast of Britain went to 4 (import) and 6 per cent (export), with the rate for the more exposed east-coast and Channel ports marked "quoted on application." It was the task of the watch to entertain such applications. Actual rates quoted were as high as 12½ per cent. On June 10 Mussolini, in quest of cheap loot, declared war on prostrate France and desperate Britain. Mediterranean rates went on a quotations-on-applications basis, actually reaching on one day—August 19—the nigh prohibitive figure of 25 per cent.

In August Germany began the air assault calculated to soften England for invasion. During the hell that followed, the scheduled rate to the British west coast was 10 per cent. Elsewhere the quoted-on-application rate went as high as 15 per cent for London.[10]

Japan's established policy of opportunism was early taken into account by marine-insurance men. Before Germany went into action the rate to the Far East for neutral flags had been: via Panama Canal or transpacific ½ of 1 per cent; via Cape of Good Hope ¾. Belligerent ships were fractions higher. Hitler's first victories doubled these figures.

"Underwriters are taking an increasing interest in the risks to the Dutch East Indies and French Indo-China and the Far East generally," Fred Maccabe, of the Automobile Insurance Company and one of the founders of the War Risk Exchange, wrote in September. "To some it appears that Japan is preparing to move in, probably waiting for complete German success against England, but if that does not come pretty soon the Japanese may move anyhow."[11]

England held against the worst that Goering could send. By October the R.A.F. made the assault of the *Luftwaffe* too costly to maintain on a mass scale. Hitler's sixty-day delay in launching that assault was the Fuehrer's first tactical mistake of the war. Possibly because of it the first round in democracy's fight for survival was won in the skies over the British Isles. Nevertheless, Japan moved into Indo-China. Far Eastern rates advanced again, ranging from 1 per cent on United States vessels via Panama to 5 per cent on belligerents via the Cape.

So ended the year 1940. The North America's war-risk business for the twelve months stood as follows: hull premiums $202,600, losses $25,000; cargo premiums $3,273,000, losses $529,000; miscellaneous premiums $11,410, losses nothing. This made totals of $3,487,010 and $554,000, showing a loss ratio of 15.9.

CHAPTER XXI

Unfinished Business: Sequel to Pearl Harbor

I

On March 20, 1941, the directors of the Insurance Company of North America re-elected Benjamin Rush chairman of the Board and elected John O. Platt vice-chairman. John A. Diemand was elevated to the presidency of the company. The eleventh man to hold that office in a space of 148 years, Mr. Diemand had the distinction of being the first underwriter from the ranks of casualty to head one of the great insurance organizations of the world among whose activities casualty insurance was only an item.

At the time of his promotion Diemand was also president of the International Association of Casualty and Surety Underwriters, president of the Insurance Federation of Pennsylvania and a member of the executive committee of the Association of Casualty and Surety Executives. Most of his outside activities concerned education. A trustee of the Williamson Free School of the Mechanical Trades, in 1942 he accepted a similar position with Temple University. But the office affording the greatest satisfaction was that of a member of the Philadelphia Board of City Trusts which among other responsibilities handles the affairs of Diemand's alma mater, Girard College.

Mr. Diemand took charge of the North America at an interesting juncture—particularly for the marine branch. The low war-risk loss ratio of 1940 was already rising. German possession of the littoral from North Cape to the Pyrenees gave her submarines an enormous advantage not enjoyed in World War I. The airplane had proved almost as destructive to shipping as the U-boat. Another innovation was the magnetic mine which could be dropped from planes. Losses which had been kept within the safe bounds of 200,000 tons a month went to 400,000 tons after the blitzkreig of May 1940.

April 1941 witnessed the Nazi conquest of the Balkans. Sea losses climbed to 500,000. In May they were 600,000. In June the British

Government discontinued the publication of monthly totals. It was known, however, that three ships were going to the bottom for every one coming off the ways of British and American yards.

The United States was awakening to its peril. The fall of France brought the first compulsory military-training law in our peacetime history. A ban on war supplies to Japan virtually ended commercial intercourse with that nation. During England's darkest hour, in early September 1940, the President by a bold use of executive power exchanged fifty old destroyers for military bases on British soil from Newfoundland to Guiana. In March 1941 "lend and lease" of munitions was substituted for cash and carry. That German eyes had long been on Iceland was no secret. Within the year war-risk rates to that strategic island had more than doubled. On July 7 the President informed Congress of its occupation by United States troops.

In the meantime Hitler had once more made the world gasp by his daring, when on June 22, without warning and without a declaration of war, he attacked Russia. The Nazi grand strategy called for a quick knockout and then an irresistible smash at England.

Hitler did not wish to be too long about his Russian business because England waxed stronger daily. Goods flowed from America, "the arsenal of democracy," in an ever-growing stream. Sinkings were down as the United States Navy took charge of the waters between this coast and Iceland, freeing British fighting ships for other tasks. Rates eased and underwriting volume exceeded that of 1940.

Coming in the face of the stoppage of commerce with Japan and the loss of a heavy Mediterranean trade following the Balkan campaign, this increase was due to higher rates and to some extent to United States Government imports of war-essential commodities from which we might be cut off should the conflict spread to the Pacific. To facilitate the latter program American marine underwriters undertook storage risks on shore in conjunction with the ocean risks. The decision was a costly one, the largest single loss since the beginning of the war—$7,000,000—being sustained when a fire consumed an enormous stock of Government rubber at Fall River, Massachusetts.

It was a year of heavy single losses: $3,000,000 on the Greek steamer *Petalli,* laden with Turkish and Greek tobacco, sunk in a Nazi bombing raid on Piraeus; $1,500,000 on the Dutch freighter *Kota Nopan* destroyed near the Galapagos Islands; $750,000 on the captured British steamer *Speybank;* $500,000 on the United States freighter *Robin Moor* shelled and torpedoed in the South Atlantic. These were war-risk losses, met by the membership of the Cargo Exchange. The hull syndicate also experienced its heaviest loss since the beginning of the war when the grounding of the American liner *Manhattan* near Palm Beach, Florida, cost $3,000,000. But for fair weather and excellent salvage work it might have been twice that much.

The accident to the *Manhattan* and the Fall River fire represented ordinary-marine rather than war losses. The considerable increase in ordinary claims was due, in the main, to the usual wartime conditions: blackout of navigation lights; crowded ports; neglected repairs and overhaul; unseaworthy vessels pressed into service. Sorely short of tonnage the British were using everything they could lay hands on. The demand for American tonnage increased sharply. Though the Maritime Commission was doing an excellent job on new construction it was not enough and vessels long laid up were put to sea under our flag.

In the summer of 1941 the North America embarked into life insurance in a small way for the first time in 125 years when it was one of several companies to respond to the Maritime Commission's request to provide protection for merchant seamen whose services were as essential as those of the armed forces and frequently rendered at as great peril. The policies covered war hazards only. They paid $5,000 in event of death and in proportion for injuries. Steamship operators met the premiums.

When the approach of the early Russian winter found the Soviet armies badly used though intact and fighting, it began to dawn that Herr Hitler had made the second military miscalculation destined to influence the course of the war. But the die was cast and he must go through with the gamble. As the time drew near for Japan to play the part assigned to her, Hitler began stepping on the toes of the United States. Hitherto he had let us pretty well alone in the hope that native appeasers would do his preliminary work for him. In 1940 only four American-owned ships were sunk. Three were of Panamanian registry. The lone war casualty under our flag was a vessel destroyed in Australian waters by a mine. The *Robin Moor* incident (May 21, 1941) represented the first deliberate attack on the Stars and Stripes.

JOHN A. DIEMAND

Eleventh president Insurance Company of North America, elected 1941. First head of a great insurance organization writing diversified lines to rise from ranks of casualty underwriters. In point of volume casualty is greatest of modern insurance developments. Beginning as a stenographer at seventeen Diemand grew with it. Joined North America in 1933.

From a photograph by Henry G. Engels Studio, Montclair, New Jersey.

Between mid-August and mid-September three American-owned vessels under the flag of Panama were sunk on the supply route to Iceland. On September 3 the destroyer *Greer* had a brush with a submarine which revealed that the Navy had orders to shoot to keep this route open. On October 16 the destroyer *Kearney*, speeding to the aid of a freighter under attack in a convoy, received a disabling torpedo hit, killing eleven men—the first Americans to fall in combat under their own colors. October 31 the destroyer *Reuben James* went down with a loss of 98 lives.

Thirteen days later an aroused Congress scuttled the Neutrality Act. United States ships were permitted to arm and to enter the war zones. The demand for American bottoms caused craft forty years old to be made ready for the sea. Though rates for American-flag ships plying exposed routes advanced fractions to 1 per cent they remained below those for belligerents. On November 24 Henry Thorn wrote for the New York *Journal of Commerce* that "it may not be possible to maintain this differential much longer. . . . We are engaged in a shooting naval war with Germany right now . . . [and are] faced with more than the possibility of becoming an all-out belligerent in two more or less separate wars."[1]

So much for one underwriter's skepticism as to the outcome of the peace parley the Japanese had opened in Washington.

2

The institution which is the subject of this history regards November 19, 1792, as its birthday. That was the date of the meeting in Independence Hall at which the proposal to form "a Society called the Insurance Company of North America" was formally and finally ratified. November 19, 1941, therefore, witnessed the beginning of the company's one hundred and fiftieth year.

At that moment the eyes of the world were on Washington, D. C., which was something of a coincidence for so had been the eyes of Samuel Blodget, Jr., in 1792 when he was doing his part to get the Insurance Company of North America started on its way. We have observed how Blodget's dreams for the capital city were so far in advance of the times that he went to a debtors' prison for his pains. Could that early promoter and architect, who submitted the first design for the Capitol building, have enjoyed a view of the noble prospect of Pennsylvania Avenue in 1941 he might have thought the sacrifice worth while.

In November 1941, however, the world was not so concerned with the magnificence of Washington's public edifices as with what went on inside some of them. At one end of Pennsylvania Avenue our Secretary of State, Mr. Hull, was listening to a grinning little man named Saburo Kurusu who professed the amicable intentions of Japan—with a string tied to them: we must give Japan *carte blanche* in the Pacific. Naturally, Mr. Hull refused. At the other end of the Avenue Congress was grimly doing away with the Neutrality Act.

The next date memorable in the annals of the Insurance Company of North America is December 15. On that day, in 1792, the company's first office was opened and its first policies written.

Before this anniversary was reached in 1941 it turned out that Mr. Kurusu meant business. Our refusal to turn the Pacific over to Japan had brought the Sunday-morning assault on Pearl Harbor.

On December 8, the day after that attack, the United States declared war.

Plans which had been made to observe the company's sesquicentennial were scaled down or abandoned. Mr. Diemand announced that the first concern of the Insurance Company of North America was to help win the war. No small part of this effort, he continued, should be to increase the value of its service to the policyholders who in the days ahead would need all the protection they could get.

"In that spirit, then, let us examine the situation in the fire-insurance business." The president of the North America was addressing the insurance commissioners of the fifteen states which had constituted our Federal Union in 1792. They had been invited to Philadelphia as guests of the company. Mr. Diemand spoke with reference to the antiquated organizational structure of the fire business.

"In 1920 the total net premiums written by stock fire companies amounted to $890,000,000 as against a policyholders' surplus of $523,159,000, or $1.70 of premium for each dollar of policyholders' surplus," he told the fifteen commissioners.

"In 1930 the total net premiums written were $909,000,000 as against a policyholders' surplus of $1,384,000,000, or 66 cents of premium for each dollar of policyholders' surplus.

"In 1940 the total net premiums written were $917,000,000 as against a policyholders' surplus of $1,488,000,000, or 62 cents in premiums for each dollar of policyholders' surplus.

"In other words, in twenty years we have seen the ratio of premiums written to policyholders' surplus decline from $1.70 to 62 cents."

The term "policyholders' surplus" embraces both capital and surplus. Diemand's figures were for American stock companies as a whole. Corresponding data for the North America group showed a ratio decline from $1.76 to 37 cents. The virtual standstill in premiums over twenty years did not mean that no more fire insurance was being written in 1940 than in 1920. Much more was being written but at lower rates due to fire prevention measures largely fostered by the companies themselves. With no more business (in terms of premium income) to get but more money (in terms of policyholders' surplus) to spend getting it, acquisition costs were rising to a point where the rates prevailing shortly would be unable to support them. Diemand called for a wholesale simplification of the fire setup, with its maze of boards, bureaus, laws and regulations, in part the creations of the insurance companies and in part the creations of state legislatures.

In reply to those who argued that the situation would correct itself eventually Diemand contended that "in wartime the ordinary processes of evolution are not sufficient." He urged action "now."[2]

3

Notwithstanding defects inherent in the way the business was conducted, the fire branch of the North America made a good showing in 1941. Net premiums were $16,712,000, an increase of $1,471,000 or 9.6 per cent over 1940. With private building greatly restricted by priorities on materials, the increase was due for the most part to expansion of the defense effort. This brought a general increase of losses both in frequency and severity, due to the abnormal rate of production, the introduction of new manufacturing hazards and the employment of less skilled workmen. Despite these conditions, and a series of severe wind and hail storms in the Middle West, the company's losses for the year rose only 5.9 per cent. This indicated an excellent individual performance on the part of the North America, for the war had not made fire underwriting the syndicate proposition that marine insurance was.

The progressive increase in the value of plants given over to war work was greatly augmenting the burdens of the fire insurance business when the thunderclap of Pearl Harbor redoubled them. The inevitable rise in the cost of materials and of wages was another factor. At the outset of this war the money tied up in the facilities turning out explosives, tanks, planes, guns, machine tools, foodstuffs and the like exceeded that at the end of World War I. By the nature of things there were heavy concentrations in certain areas. In more than one such area the insurable values exceeded $100,000,000. Never before has such a burden been placed on the fire-insurance business. Dealing with these large lines became the responsibility of Ludwig C. Lewis and his associate Bradford Smith, fire secretary of the company.

War damage is excluded from basic fire contracts. The events in England, nevertheless, brought the question of war damage to private property before us. The Federal Government took up the matter and as a result, beginning in the fall of 1941, the situation was canvassed at a series of conferences between Government officials and representatives of the insurance industry. The insurance men felt, representatives of the North America concurring, that indemnification for war damage was a public function which could best be handled by the Government. This had been the experience of England.

Accordingly after Pearl Harbor the War Damage Corporation was created to function as a joint venture of the Government and of private enterprise. The Government—that is all the people—accept the lion's share of the liability of this form of war-risk insurance. Certain liability is assumed by the private companies. The administration of the business, issuance of policies, collecting of premiums, settling of claims, etc., is to be handled by the machinery of the private companies. Any other course would be a wasteful duplication of functions.

In the setting up of this organization signal recognition was given the service offices of the Insurance Company of North America. The system these offices embody, begun during Mr. Rush's tenure as president, developed during Mr. Platt's and finished during Mr. Diemand's, represented something unique in insurance administration. North America was quite proud of it and one could hear at 1600 Arch Street the prediction that here was something other companies would have to come to or slip behind the procession. It became evident that the service offices could perform an important function for the War Damage Corporation. The result was that the Corporation appointed as its fiduciary agents the North America's twenty-eight service offices, strategically situated throughout the country. James E. Hitchcock, assistant secretary, set up the organization to take care of the business the service offices assumed for the War Damage Corporation. The premiums written by these offices for the Corporation exceeded $6,000,000 during the first five weeks of operation.

The necessary suppression of one of America's greatest industries—the manufacture of motor vehicles for private use—had extensive repercussions on the insurance fraternity. The North America's part of this problem fell to Arthur V. Davenport, guiding hand of the Automobile Department.

Most motor cars were sold on credit, the finance companies controlling the placing of the fire, theft and collision insurance on each car. When the automobile plants were turned over to full-time war work on January 1 and the stocks of finished cars on hand placed under a Government rationing order, premium income from this source of insurance was practically eliminated. Insurance companies carrying the accounts of the national finance companies were faced with the necessity of running off existing liability with very little new income from that source. As has been related the North America never attempted to write the business controlled by the national finance companies, preferring to develop its business through local agencies. Thus the North America largely escaped the situation with which companies carrying the accounts of national finance companies were faced.

Gasoline and rubber shortages are restricting the use of automobiles, particularly in the East where gasoline rationing became effective at the beginning of the summer of 1942. This will grow as the war goes on. It is already affecting collision, fire and theft premium volume as cars wear out and cannot be replaced. Some owners may exhibit a tendency to drop their automobile insurance before they have to lay up their cars.

Preparation for war compelled Herbert P. Stellwagen, executive vice-president, and Benjamin Rush, Jr., vice-president, to undertake obligations for the Indemnity Company more extensive than were deemed posible in times of peace. In the realm of corporate surety-ship, the company initiated or participated in contract bonds of huge amount covering the construction of planes, tanks, ships, and other war essentials. The company kept for its own account liabilities to the full amount of its statutory limitation to make it possible for manufacturers and contractors to meet the credit requirements of the Government in connection with the handling of contracts running to millions of dollars. In the performance of this considerable task the directing heads of Indemnity felt themselves fortunate in being able to call on the knowledge of Carroll W. Laird, assistant secretary of the company in charge of the Surety Bond Department.

In the casualty field, workmen's compensation and liability policies were written on projects which dwarfed anything in the peacetime experience of the company. Huge chemical plants were created, cantonments were built, and industries grew up, some of them employing as many as 20,000 or 30,000 men. Facilities had to be created to handle claims arising from these operations and, more important, to provide the necessary accident-prevention work which would facilitate and expedite production. The company's engineer, Assistant Secretary A. W. Meinke, has estimated that on one job Indemnity's safety experts were able to keep at work an average of sixty-nine workers a day who would otherwise have been laid up by injuries. That is quite a saving of man power.

An interesting development in connection with workmen's compensation and liability insurance on projects administered by Government departments and agencies involved an arrangement whereby premiums were computed on a cost-plus basis without consideration for the agent's or broker's commission. The policyholder himself made a service contract with a broker or agent and paid him his commission direct. This meant that the companies' premium contained allowances for losses, loss expense, taxes and general overhead but excluded an allowance for commission. This philosophy of premium construction was originated by the War Department and was soon adopted by the Navy Department, Maritime Commission and other Government agencies and bureaus. The plan was utilized by all casualty companies in the United States in connection with Government work. In insurance circles it gives rise to the speculation as to whether the idea may later be applied to normal peacetime operations.

The Indemnity Company, like many other casualty companies, construed its liability contracts so as to cover the various activities of civilian-defense organizations. By a narrow construction of the policy contract those might have been excluded from coverage. In a new personal-liability policy published in the summer of 1942 the insuring clauses specifically include without additional premium any liability arising from the policyholder's participating in civilian defense activities.

The war obliged the company's casualty underwriter, Assistant Vice-President James M. Crawford, to change his attitude toward certain types of risks which in normal times had been considered too hazardous. Accordingly, casualty policies were issued covering the operations of loading shells, the manufacture of fuses, flares and other explosives. Further, the company undertook to provide liability insurance against new types of obligations imposed on private manufacturers and operators by their contracts with the Government. In general, the company's underwriting procedure moved at a faster and more venturesome tempo.

One problem which beset the Indemnity Company, and for that matter all casualty companies, was the question of the hazard of war risk under various types of policy. Some years ago most casualty policies had lost their war-risk exclusions so that the declaration of war found the companies obliged to respond for war damages under plate glass, burglary, workmen's compensation, and probably other forms of policy contract. Nevertheless, the premiums collected did not anticipate war losses. Plans were initiated to overcome the shock of such losses through co-operative effort on the part of all companies engaged in the business. At the present writing, such plans have not matured. As a further safeguard against the possibility of such losses occurring in advance of common action to absorb them, the Indemnity Company in its semiannual statement of June 30, 1942, set up a special war reserve of $500,000, this being in addition to its general voluntary reserve of $1,000,000 over its capital and surplus.[3]

Though Pearl Harbor changed the complexion of marine-insurance affairs overnight that change came too late in the year to have much influence on the 1941 figures. The North America's net marine premiums were $12,462,000, an increase of 25 per cent over 1940. Of these $4,639,000 were inland-marine premiums, having little to do with water-borne risks. The balance was from ocean marine. Of this,

$5,013,000 were war-risk—$4,046,000 cargo, $905,000 hull and $61,000 miscellaneous. War-risk losses were $1,825,000 cargo, $339,000 hull and $3,400 miscellaneous, giving an over-all war-risk loss ratio of 43.2 against 15.9 for 1940.[4]

In keeping with the North America's traditional policy of concentrating ultimate responsibility, a small home-office staff takes care of the executive direction of the war effort of the marine branch. Its chief is Leaming Smith who advanced from clerk to company officer during World War I and who did a good deal of spade-work toward the preparation for the current conflict. The second in command is Marine Secretary G. Brinton Lucas. A native Philadelphian and a graduate of the Episcopal Academy, Lucas joined the North America in 1909 when he was twenty years old. He won his spurs with F. M. Butt & Company, of Dallas, Texas, successor to Wight & Butt, and general agents for the company's cotton business. Recalled to Philadelphia in 1915, Lucas handled the home-office end of the cotton account during the first World War. Under Mr. Lucas is Assistant Secretary Henry W. Farnum, a son of the Henry W. Farnum associated with Benjamin Rush in the classification revolution of 1898 and in the war work of twenty-five years ago.

Sixty per cent of the company's marine war business goes through the New York office. The office next in importance is at Boston, where Australian and South American wool imports are the big items. The Boston office is in charge of the veteran Thomas R. Young and his associate Donald Warren.

4

The one hundred and fiftieth Annual Statement of the Insurance Company of North America, dated March 18, 1942, showed net assets of $116,796,307.20. Securities consisting "largely [of] listed stocks and bonds which are readily saleable . . . comprise some 83% of the Company's assets," observes the Statement. According to market prices of December 31, 1941, the value of these holdings was $96,928,-451.52 which, despite recent declines due to the war news, was $12,220,629.35 above book value. Add to the securities cash in banks plus premium balances payable within ninety days and 94 per cent of the company's assets are accounted for. Investment profit for the year was $3,745,529.

This showing was a result of the usual ceaseless activity on the part of the Investment Department. The Executive Committee of the Board held fifty-two formal meetings with John Drayton[4a] and many informal discussions. As a result the following portfolio changes were made, as summarized in the Annual Statement:

"The number of issues eliminated was 30, of which 13 were sold and 17 matured, were redeemed or exchanged. Also holdings of 17 separate issues were reduced in amount. In the same period there were additions to 31 issues already held, and purchases of 49 issues not held at the beginning of the year, so that at the close of 1941, holdings in the portfolios stood at 356 separate issues of 228 issuers. These changes resulted in the elimination of investments in 12 companies and the addition of investments in 25 companies. In addition to the reviews of securities held in the various portfolios reports on 47 companies or issues were prepared for the Committee, and 50 reports were made on general economic subjects."

The personnel of the Executive Committee for 1941 was indicative of the caliber of the Board of Directors. It consisted of: Samuel D. Warriner, chairman of the board, Lehigh Coal & Navigation Company; Clarence M. Brown, chairman of the board, Pittsburgh Plate Glass Company; Joseph Wayne, Jr., chairman of the board, Philadelphia National Bank; James D. Winsor, Jr., partner, Biddle, Whelen & Company, brokers; George S. Munson, attorney; Edward Hopkinson, Jr., partner, Drexel & Company; Philip C. Staples, president, Bell Telephone Company of Pennsylvania.

The year's net operating profit of the company was $5,768,976 before taxes and after taxes $4,721,577. Dividends were $3,600,000—$3 a share or 30 per cent of par which remains $10. This was a dividend increase of 50 cents over the 1940 disbursement. On December 31 the closing quotation for North America shares was 77.

In their statements for 1941 the North America's subsidiaries reported assets as follows:

Indemnity Insurance Company of North America .	$37,135,559.17
Alliance Insurance Company of Philadelphia . . .	10,775,735.84
Philadelphia Fire and Marine Insurance Company .	6,200,201.90
National Security Insurance Company (Omaha, Nebraska)	3,066,940.09
Central Insurance Company of Baltimore	4,211,856.17

Add these sums to the $116,796,307.20 that represents the parent company's assets and one gets $178,186,600.37. Deduct $27,452,666.28 for inter-company obligations and one has $150,733,934.09, the total assets of the North America group on December 31, 1941.[5]

This gives it second place among the insurance groups (those writing life excepted) of common ownership in the United States. The largest group is that of the Hartford Insurance Company, with assets of $202,372,271. Third is the Aetna group, with assets of $82,752,816.

These are the top three so-called ownership groups in which the parent company owns all the stock of its subsidiaries. Another type of insurance combination is the ownership-and-management group, in which the dominant company manages the affairs of certain other companies without owning a majority of their capital stock. Among such groups the Home and the America Fore manage assets in excess of those of the North America group though they do not own all those assets.

The 1942 edition of *Best's Insurance Reports,* a severely factual volume the reverse of extravagant with its encomiums, has this to say of the North America:

"The Company is the oldest capital stock fire and marine insurance carrier in the United States. It enjoys an enviable reputation and the distinction of being the first ranking fire insurance company of the country from the standpoint of policyholders' surplus."[6]

5

To attempt to predict the ultimate effect of Pearl Harbor on the marine business of the North America would be as risky as a forecast of the outcome of John A. Diemand's pointed warning to the fire-insurance business to clean house as a wartime service to the country. Those are chapters for a later chronicler.

Perspective is necessary to the writing of history. This is a thing that cannot be improvised. It comes only in due course from the womb of time. Time is also charged with the function of bringing forth, piecemeal and from a hundred quarters, facts which historical judgment, tempered by perspective, must assemble into a pattern.

These lines are written seven months after Pearl Harbor. There is no perspective. Each day's newspapers pour facts into our laps, and every now and then one of them is of genuine importance. It influences the contour of the pattern. But to know which of these facts are important is usually beyond the capacity of contemporary discernment. Did the Coral Sea battle, in which the striking power of both sides was provided by carrier-based aircraft, mark a turning point in the Pacific struggle—or, indeed, in naval warfare, like the engagement of the *Monitor* and the *Merrimac?* One day we shall know. Is the United States Government's handling of the marine war-risk insurance problem an example of unwise usurpation of the prerogatives of private business as is sometimes said? Or is it the only thing possible in the emergency?

On June 30 the Insurance Company of North America was assessed $154 for its share of a total loss of $1,400 on the cargo of an airplane en route to an overseas destination. No other particulars can be disclosed. But since the claim was for war-risk insurance the loss could have been due only to enemy action. So far as John Street can remember this is the first air-borne cargo war-risk loss sustained by the American market. What will it mean in the sum total of war experience? Freak loss or forerunner of something more serious?

Pearl Harbor brought the greatest upheaval in war-risk rates since the panic of August 1914. It was attended by no semblance of panic, however. The well-tested machinery of the Reinsurance Exchange did the job almost as a matter of routine. Henry Thorn was spending the Sunday afternoon at his home in suburban Bronxville. He began telephoning members of the Underwriting and Rate Committee of the Exchange. Hardly a war-risk rate from the United States to any point on the globe remained unaffected. The great changes applied to United States ships, which passed into the belligerent class. The premium for the route to neutral Portugal went from $1\frac{1}{2}$ per cent to 5; to Egypt via the Cape from $2\frac{1}{2}$ to 9; to Calcutta via Panama or transpacific $1\frac{3}{4}$ to 10; Australasia $1\frac{1}{4}$ to $7\frac{1}{2}$. In this hemisphere rates on voyages connecting North, South and Central America and the West Indies went to 1 to 3 per cent. The previous spread had been $\frac{1}{8}$ to 1. The Atlantic and Gulf coasts of the United States were deemed virtually secure, however. The coastwise rate of one-twentieth of 1 per cent was raised only to $\frac{1}{4}$.[7]

The shock loss, nearly all in the Pacific, was much greater than that of September 1939. As yet not fully determined, it may run as high as $10,000,000 on cargo. The largest claim paid was $1,785,000 on the Norwegian steamer, *Ravnaas,* India for the United States, bombed in Philippine waters. Cargo on board the Philippine-flag *Sagoland* which suffered a similar fate cost the companies who comprise the Exchange $1,632,000. The United States liner *President Harrison* seized at Shanghai carried cargo covered for $378,000.

Ships all the way from a few hours to a few days out of port were ordered to harbors of refuge along the American Pacific coast, in Hawaii, Australia, India and Java. As in the cases of the German ships in 1939, the underwriters took care of the unloading and, where possible, the forwarding of cargoes to the proper destinations. The Australian Government is relieving the insurance companies by purchasing about $2,500,000 worth of cargo diverted to Australian ports. About $3,000,000 worth of cargo in Japan and $2,000,000 in Manila, awaiting trans-shipment, form a complicated claims question and a potential liability.[8]

By the end of the shock period rates had undergone several readjustments in the light of the changing war picture. A few quotations were down (examples: the Caribbean area; Pacific coast to Hawaii); but more were up. The Atlantic coastwise rate was $\frac{1}{2}$, up $\frac{1}{4}$, on the strength of a few scattered sinkings. This represented a serious underestimate of the submarine menace along our eastern seaboard. By the end of February the coastal rate was $2\frac{1}{2}$ per cent for tankers and 2 for other vessels; the middle of March 4 and $3\frac{1}{2}$; the middle of May 6 per cent for cargo vessels.

Early in May tankers were dropped from the rate schedule because most of the business had gone to the Government's insurance agency. The actual Exchange rate on tankers was 50 per cent above the regular scale which, on June 25, showed a maximum rate of $12\frac{1}{2}$ per cent. This maximum applied to voyages between the Atlantic seaboard and the Gulf, involving the perilous trip around the tip of Florida. The rate on vessels taking the "outside" course in the range between Norfolk, Virginia, and Eastport, Maine, was 10 per cent; those using the sheltered waters of Chesapeake Bay, Delaware Bay, Long Island Sound and Cape Cod Bay, 5 per cent. Short voyages in protected waters were rated as low as $\frac{1}{4}$ per cent.

Meantime rates elsewhere had advanced: Caribbean area to 10 per cent; Portugal $7\frac{1}{2}$; Egypt via the Cape 15; Calcutta 25; Australia via Panama 15; via transpacific $7\frac{1}{2}$.[9]

THE COMPANY'S NEW YORK PROPERTY
Erected, 1933, at 99 John Street in the heart of the Metropolitan insurance district.

On May 1 the North America increased its Exchange subscription to from 10 to 11 per cent. Coming at so critical a juncture in the history of marine insurance as well as of our country this increase amounted to a striking vote of confidence in the future.

In the spring of 1942 the Government entered the marine war-risk business. Though by no means nominal, its rates were sufficiently below the market to attract virtually all the business on hulls and some of it on cargo.

In 1939 when the private market was putting its affairs in order to meet the impact of war, underwriters advised that in their judgment it would be prudent for Congress to authorize the setting up of insurance machinery. In the summer of 1940 a start toward this end was made. But as the law enacted forbade the taking of risks on contraband, virtually no insurance was written under it. The pinch was not felt until the fall of 1941 when the necessities of the situation obliged the private market to make larger commitments than cautious underwriters cared to make. Pearl Harbor supplied the needed incentive to congressional action and, effective April 1, 1942, a Government insurance agency with extraordinary powers was authorized.

It was called the Division of Wartime Insurance of the War Shipping Administration, a subsidiary of the Maritime Commission. Percy Chubb II became the director, thus assuming a position similar to that his father held in 1914 as head of the War Risk Insurance Bureau. This similarity did not go too far, though. The Government insurance agency which Hendon Chubb directed during World War I operated on a commercial basis. Its function was to add needed capacity to the market and to help stabilize rates. The stabilizing process did not take the form of crowding rates down to figures the private companies could not meet. As we have noted the Government's rates on the whole were higher than those charged by the North America.

The law creating the 1942 agency breathed a different philosophy. "Nominal" rates could be charged whenever in the judgment of the Maritime Commission this course "would be of material benefit to the war effort" or (and this is important) "to the domestic economy of the United States."[10]

The result was the immediate quotation of rates about 50 per cent below the market. As the submarine campaign off our Atlantic coast and in the Caribbean increased in intensity the market rate went up in an attempt to avoid ruinous losses until, in some cases, it was three times the Government rate.[11]

As a consequence the Government got a large part of the business. Its losses for the first three months were more than the richest private insurance company on earth could stand as a regular thing. Forty million dollars were given the Division of Wartime Insurance on its organization. Five weeks later the House of Representatives approved of additional appropriation of $210,000,000 from the public funds.

During World War I naval protection to shipping was such as to keep rates at levels which could be passed to consumers without disastrous inflation of prices. This is not the case now. Authority to fix rates with reference to the needs of "the domestic economy" was designed as a measure to keep living costs down. It is helping to do it. The load falls on all of us. That is where it belongs, considering the fact that all but a fraction of the merchant tonnage of the world is in war service. So goes the argument of those who approve of the Government's way of handling the war-risk insurance question.

It should be borne in mind that the Government handles war risks only. Ordinary marine risks remain wholly in the hands of the private companies, operating individually rather than as members of syndicates. Nevertheless, rates are more or less uniform. They have risen only about 50 per cent since 1939. This takes care of the increased dangers to ordinary navigation: blacked-out coasts, deferred repairs, and so on.

6

This account of the Insurance Company of North America ends almost as it began: at a time of national peril. It is the lot of underwriters, however, to deal with perils as an everyday thing, whereas the rest of us experience them only once in a while. Virtually the first twenty-two years of the North America's life were spent amid conflict on the seas. Its part in keeping the American flag afloat during that troubled era was noteworthy; and if the flag hadn't been kept on the seas between 1793 and 1815 it would fly nowhere now.

A company thus living by dint of surviving hazards learns the arts of self-protection. In this way it is able to protect others. Charles Platt's reminder to the colleague who after the San Francisco fire wished to divorce his prosperous marine business from his hard-hit fire business is worth recalling. Mr. Platt said a war could be very hard on a marine company, and that at such a time fire income would be desirable. Building on that idea Benjamin Rush put the North America into every branch of insurance except life. He spread his risks. As a result, on the eve of its one-hundred-and-fiftieth anniversary the Insurance Company of North America is able once more to assume a place in the struggle of our country at war and to take in its stride its portion of the losses that flow therefrom.

THE END

OFFICERS AND DIRECTORS

OFFICERS AND DIRECTORS

OFFICERS OF
THE INSURANCE COMPANY OF NORTH AMERICA
1792 TO 1942

CHAIRMAN OF THE BOARD:

Benjamin Rush . . . . . Mar. 16, 1939

VICE-CHAIRMAN OF THE BOARD:

John O. Platt . . . . . . Mar. 20, 1941

PRESIDENTS:

John M. Nesbitt . . . . . Dec. 11, 1792 — Jan. 13, 1796
Charles Pettit . . . . . Jan. 13, 1796 — Jan. 9, 1798
Joseph Ball . . . . . . Jan. 9, 1798 — July 8, 1799
Charles Pettit . . . . . July 8, 1799 — Sept. 3, 1806
John Inskeep . . . . . Oct. 1, 1806 — April 5, 1831
John C. Smith . . . . . April 5, 1831 — June 22, 1845
Arthur G. Coffin . . . . July 1, 1845 — Jan. 14, 1878
Charles Platt . . . . . Jan. 14, 1878 — Jan. 23, 1909
Eugene L. Ellison . . . . Nov. 3, 1909 — Feb. 8, 1916
Benjamin Rush . . . . . Mar. 7, 1916 — Mar. 16, 1939
John O. Platt . . . . . Mar. 16, 1939 — Mar. 20, 1941
John A. Diemand . . . . Mar. 20, 1941

ASSISTANTS TO THE PRESIDENT:

John J. Connor . . . . . Mar. 19, 1936 — Dec. 31, 1940
Sheldon Catlin . . . . . Dec. 31, 1940

VICE-PRESIDENTS:

Charles Platt	Jan. 13, 1869 — Jan. 14, 1878
T. Charlton Henry	Nov. 2, 1880 — Aug. 31, 1890
William A. Platt	Nov. 4, 1890 — April 1, 1895
Eugene L. Ellison	Jan. 13, 1897 — Nov. 3, 1909
Benjamin Rush	Nov. 3, 1909 — Mar. 7, 1916
John O. Platt	Mar. 7, 1916 — Mar. 16, 1939
Sheldon Catlin	Jan. 9, 1929 — Dec. 31, 1940
Galloway C. Morris	Jan. 9, 1929 — Feb. 14, 1939
John Kremer	Jan. 9, 1929
T. Leaming Smith	Jan. 9, 1929
John W. Drayton	Mar. 22, 1934 — Sept. 23, 1942
Ludwig C. Lewis	Mar. 18, 1937
John A. Diemand	Mar. 17, 1938 — Mar. 20, 1941

RESIDENT VICE-PRESIDENT AT CHICAGO:

W. P. Robertson	May 14, 1940

ASSISTANT TO THE VICE-PRESIDENT:

Galloway C. Morris	Feb. 14, 1939

ACTING VICE-PRESIDENTS:

William S. Davis	June 4, 1878 — Oct. 5, 1880
George H. McFadden	April 17, 1895 — April 7, 1896
Robert M. Lewis	May 6, 1890 — Nov. 4, 1890

SECOND VICE-PRESIDENTS:

William S. Davis	Mar. 3, 1874 — June 4, 1878
William A. Platt	Jan. 12, 1881 — Nov. 4, 1890
Eugene L. Ellison	Nov. 4, 1890 — Jan. 13, 1897
Benjamin Rush	Jan. 12, 1898 — Nov. 3, 1909
John O. Platt	June 7, 1910 — Mar. 7, 1916
Sheldon Catlin	Mar. 7, 1916 — Jan. 9, 1929

THIRD VICE-PRESIDENTS:

Sheldon Catlin	Jan. 12, 1916 — Mar. 7, 1916
Galloway C. Morris . . .	Jan. 10, 1917 — Jan. 9, 1929

ASSISTANT VICE-PRESIDENT:

Charles F. Rupprecht . . . Nov. 14, 1939 — June 30, 1940

ASSISTANT FINANCIAL VICE-PRESIDENT:

Robert E. Jefferys . . . . . Mar. 18, 1937

SECRETARIES:

Ebenezer Hazard	Dec. 11 1792 — Jan. 13, 1800
Robert S. Stephens	Feb. 28, 1806 — June 12, 1832
Arthur G. Coffin	June 19, 1832 — July 1, 1845
Henry D. Sherrerd	July 1, 1845 — June 1, 1858
Matthias Maris	Nov. 2, 1858 — April 3, 1860
Charles Platt	April 3, 1860 — Jan. 26, 1869
Matthias Maris	Jan. 26, 1869 — Jan. 12, 1881
Greville E. Fryer	Jan. 12, 1881 — Nov. 4, 1890
T. Houard Wright	Oct. 6, 1908 — Jan. 10, 1912
John Kremer	Aug. 6, 1918 — Jan. 9, 1929

SECRETARY & TREASURER:

Greville E. Fryer	Nov. 4, 1890 — July 27, 1908
T. Houard Wright	Jan. 10, 1912 — July 15, 1918
John J. Connor	Jan. 9, 1929 — Mar. 19, 1936
Edmund H. Porter	Mar. 19, 1936 — Mar. 11, 1940
J. Kenton Eisenbrey	Mar. 21, 1940

ASSISTANT TO THE SECRETARY & TREASURER:

John J. Connor . . . . . Dec. 31, 1940

MARINE SECRETARIES:

T. Houard Wright	July 5, 1893 — May 7, 1901
Henry W. Farnum	May 7, 1901 — Oct. 6, 1908
T. Leaming Smith	Jan. 10, 1917 — Jan. 9, 1929
Ludwig C. Lewis	Jan. 9, 1929 — Mar. 18, 1937
G. Brinton Lucas	Mar. 18, 1937

AGENCY SECRETARY:

R. Stockton Rush	Sept. 10, 1940

FIRE SECRETARIES:

Silas H. Schoch	Mar. 19, 1936 — Mar. 16, 1939
R. Stockton Rush	Mar. 16, 1939 — Sept. 10, 1940
Bradford Smith, Jr.	Sept. 10, 1940

TREASURER & ASSISTANT SECRETARY:

John J. Connor	Aug. 6, 1918 — Jan. 9, 1929

ASSISTANT SECRETARIES & ASSISTANT TREASURERS:

Edmund H. Porter	Dec. 13, 1927 — Mar. 19, 1936
J. Kenton Eisenbrey	Mar. 19, 1936 — Mar. 21, 1940
Curtis L. Clay	Mar. 20, 1941
Algernon Roberts	Mar. 20, 1941

ASSISTANT SECRETARIES:

Alexander M. Walker	July 1, 1845 — Feb. 20, 1847
Matthias Maris	Feb. 23, 1847 — Nov. 2, 1858
E. P. Hollingshead	Nov. 29, 1859 — Feb. 9, 1864
Charles H. Reeves	Aug. 10, 1869 — Jan. 14, 1874
Greville E. Fryer	Jan. 14, 1874 — Jan. 12, 1881
Eugene L. Ellison	Jan. 16, 1884 — Nov. 4, 1890
John H. Atwood	Nov. 4, 1890 — April 2, 1901
T. Houard Wright	May 7, 1901 — Oct. 6, 1908
John O. Platt	Jan. 16, 1907 — June 7, 1910

Henry W. Farnum	Oct.	6, 1908 — April 4, 1911
Sheldon Catlin	June	7, 1910 — Jan. 12, 1916
John Kremer	Jan.	12, 1916 — Aug. 6, 1918
Galloway C. Morris	Jan.	12, 1916 — Jan. 10, 1917
Edmund H. Porter	Oct.	7, 1919 — Dec. 13, 1927
G. Brinton Lucas	Jan.	9, 1924 — Mar. 18, 1937
Ludwig C. Lewis	Jan.	9, 1924 — Jan. 9, 1929
C. William Johnson	Jan.	9, 1924
Albert C. Shaffer	Jan.	13, 1926 — July 1, 1933
Percy W. Clark	Jan.	12, 1927 — Dec. 13, 1931
Henry C. Thorn	Jan.	11, 1928 — Mar. 19, 1936
Silas H. Schoch	Jan.	15, 1930 — Mar. 19, 1936
Drury P. Malone	Jan.	15, 1930 — Nov. 14, 1939
David G. Cameron	Jan.	15, 1930 — Jan. 12, 1932
Chester M. Campbell . . .	Jan.	15, 1930 — Aug. 1, 1941
Robert P. Hare, Jr.	Mar.	21, 1935
Stewart T. Dunlap	Jan.	12, 1937 — Aug. 1, 1941
R. Stockton Rush	Mar.	19, 1936 — Mar. 16, 1939
J. Kenton Eisenbrey	Mar.	19, 1936 — Mar. 21, 1940
James E. Hitchcock	Dec.	8, 1936
Bradford Smith, Jr.	Dec.	8, 1936 — Sept. 10, 1940
Arthur V. Davenport . . .	Mar.	16, 1939
William P. Woodroffe . . .	Mar.	16, 1939
Henry W. Farnum	Mar.	21, 1940
R. Bruce Miller	Mar.	21, 1940 — Aug. 22, 1942

ASSISTANT TREASURER:

Curtis L. Clay	Jan.	6, 1920 — Mar. 20, 1941

DIRECTORS OF
THE INSURANCE COMPANY OF NORTH AMERICA
1792 TO 1942

Adams, Robert	1807-1808	Archer, Samuel	1816-1828
Allibone, S. Austin . . .	1847-1857	Ash, James	1800-1804

Ashley, John 1803-1803
Aspinwall, George W. . 1851-1853
Astley, Thomas . . . 1809-1839

Baker, John H. 1801-1801
Ball, Joseph 1792-1803
Barclay, John 1792-1793
Bayard, Andrew . . . 1798-1805
Bell, Thomas 1797-1800
Bevan, Matthew L. . . . 1822-1841
Biddle, Henry W. . . . 1891-1923
Blight, Peter 1794-1800
Blodget, Samuel, Jr. . . 1792-1799
Breck, Samuel . . . 1795-1797
Boggs, James 1805-1808
Bowen, William E. . . 1848-1866
Brengle, Henry G. . . 1923-
Brockie, William . . 1870-1890
Brooks, Samuel . . . 1835-1853
Brown, Clarence M. . 1922-
Brown, Israel 1803-1803
Brown, John A. . . . 1828-1872
Brown, John A. . . . 1881-1901
Brown, John H. . . . 1807-1816
Buckley, Edward S. . 1882-1910
Buckley, Edward S., Jr. . 1910-

Carrow, John G. . . . 1811-1813
Carson, G. Assheton . 1893-1913
Catlin, Sheldon . . . 1933-
Chaloner, William . . 1838-1838
Cheston, J. Hamilton . 1939-
Clapier, Lewis . . . 1802-1803
Clarke, Edward S. . . 1862-1898
Clement, M. W. . . . 1933-
Coates, Edward H. . . 1885-1921
Coffin, Arthur G. . . 1846-1881
Comegys, Cornelius . 1804-1804
Conyngham, David H. . 1796-1800
Cooke, Jay 1928-1932
Cope, Francis R. . . . 1855-1904
Cope, Thomas P. . . . 1829-1854

Cottineau, Dennis . . . 1801-1801
Cox, Paul 1799-1799
Coxe, Daniel William . . 1800-1805
Craig, John 1793-1799
Cramond, William . . . 1792-1800
Crawford, James . . . 1797-1800
Cummings, William . 1863-1867
Cunningham, Graham P. 1881-1881
Curwen, Samuel M. . . 1921-1932
Cushman, Charles W. . 1869-1880

Dale, Richard 1803-1803
Damon, Albert F. . . . 1874-1887
Dickson, James N. . . . 1851-1866
Diemand, John A. . . . 1940-
Donath, Joseph . . . 1803-1819
Donnaldson, John . . 1798-1799
Downing, Jacob . . . 1804-1804
Duane, James M. . . . 1890-1903
Dunn, Thomas . . . 1810-1813

Elliott, William T. . . . 1913-1917
Ellis, Rudulph 1911-1915
Ellison, Eugene L. . . 1909-1916
Emery, Samuel 1795-1797
Elmslie, Alexander . . 1801-1801
English, Thomas . . . 1803-1808
Evans, Cadwalader . 1801-1801

Field, Samuel 1874-1890
Fisher, James C. . . . 1798-1800
Fitzsimons, Thomas . 1794-1794
Forde, Standish . . . 1794-1797
Foster, William . . . 1829-1840
Francis, Thomas W. . . 1796-1807
Frizzell, Charles F. . . 1922-1933
Fry, John, Jr. 1794-1796

Gardiner, John, Jr. . . 1801-1803
Gates, Thomas S. . . 1915-1921
Gest, William P. . . . 1915-1933
Godfrey, Lincoln . . 1903-1916
Godfrey, William S. . . 1916-

Gourdon, Ferdinand . . 1797-1797	Kuhn, C. Hartman . . 1895-1940
Gowen, James E. . . . 1936-	
Gribbel, John . . . 1929-1936	Large, Ebenezer . . . 1800-1804
Griscom, Clement A. . 1870-1901	Large, John 1806-1815
	Latimer, Thomas . . . 1808-1824
Haga, Godfrey 1800-1825	Leamy, John 1792-1806
Harper, Charles A. . . 1826-1835	Lee, Elisha 1932-1933
Harris, Joseph S. . . . 1886-1893	Leedom, Richard . . . 1809-1813
Harrison, Charles C. . . 1885-1895	Leibert, John 1809-1813
Harrison, George . . . 1803-1803	Leisenring, Edward B. . 1933-
Harrison, George L. . . 1854-1885	Lewis, Robert M. . . . 1882-1899
Harvey, Isaac, Jr. . . . 1808-1810	Liversidge, Horace P. . 1938-
Harwood, Robert . . . 1803-1811	
Hawkins, Henry . . . 1800-1803	McCall, Archibald . . . 1794-1807
Henry, Alexander . . . 1799-1847	McConnell, Matthew . . 1792-1792
Henry, Bayard 1904-1926	McCrea, James 1801-1801
Henry, Charles W. . . 1890-1903	McFadden, George H. . 1887-1922
Henry, T. Charlton . . 1864-1890	McKean, Thomas . . . 1877-1898
Hodgdon, Samuel . . . 1802-1813	McKean, Thomas, Jr. . 1898-1906
Hollingsworth, Jehu . . 1794-1794	McKissick, John . . . 1810-1813
Hopkinson, Edward . . 1887-1935	McMurtrie, William . . 1794-1795
Hopkinson, Edward, Jr. . 1936-	Madeira, Louis C. . . . 1867-1880
Hoskins, Francis . . . 1846-1857	Markoe, Francis . . . 1812-1813
Houston, Henry H. . . 1884-1887	Mason, John 1854-1874
Humphreys, Abel . . . 1802-1802	Meeker, Samuel . . . 1802-1803
Hutchinson, S. Pemberton 1921-1929	Mifflin, Samuel 1804-1809
	Mifflin, Thomas . . . 1801-1802
	Miller, John, Jr. . . . 1803-1803
Imbert, Felix 1801-1801	Miller, Magnus 1792-1799
Ingraham, Francis . . 1799-1800	Milligan, James 1801-1801
Inskeep, John 1802-1834	Moore, Thomas L. . . . 1792-1799
	Morris, Effingham B. . . 1918-1933
Jenks, John Story . . . 1885-1923	Moylan, Jasper 1792-1792
Jenks, John Story, Jr. . . 1923-	Munson, George A. . . 1934-
Jessup, Alfred D. . . . 1866-1873	
Johnson, Lawrence . 1897-1905	Nairac, Peter 1801-1801
Johnson, R. Winder . 1905-1910	Neff, John R. 1841-1863
Jones, Samuel W. . . . 1807-1873	Nesbitt, John M. . . . 1792-1795
	Newbold, Arthur E. . . 1899-1920
Keating, J. Percy . . . 1901-1920	Newbold, John S. . . . 1881-1887
Keith, Samuel 1805-1806	Nicklin, Philip 1794-1800
Krumbhaar, Lewis . . 1812-1813	North, Joseph 1801-1802

Oldden, James 1798-1800

Packard, Charles S. W. . 1901-1937
Palmer, John 1808-1819
Parker, Jeremiah . . . 1803-1803
Pearce, Mathew 1802-1803
Pepper, John W. . . . 1906-1918
Perry, Charles 1817-1822
Pettit, Andrew 1806-1837
Pettit, Charles 1792-1806
Platt, Charles 1872-1909
Platt, Charles, Jr. . . . 1900-1916
Platt, Charles, 3rd . . . 1916-1918
Platt, John O. 1919-
Poyntell, William . . . 1801-1811
Prager, Michael 1792-1793
Pratt, Henry 1795-1795
Price, Thomas C. . . . 1847-1881
Purves, G. Colesberry . . 1903-1923

Ralston, Robert 1793-1799
Ramsay, William . . . 1809-1813
Read, James 1800-1822
Read, William 1797-1800
Rhoads, Samuel . . . 1803-1807
Rogers, Charles H. . . . 1877-1884
Ross, John 1792-1796
Rundle, Richard 1796-1796
Rush, Benjamin . . . 1916-

Sansom, William . . . 1795-1797
Sewall, Arthur W. . . . 1920-1939
Simpson, John 1800-1800
Smith, Edward 1807-1857
Smith, John C. 1831-1845
Smith, Robert 1794-1800
Smith, Samuel F. . . . 1830-1862
Sperry, Jacob 1802-1803
Staples, Philip C. . . . 1937-
Sterett, Samuel 1795-1798
Stewart, Walter 1792-1796

Stille, John 1800-1840
Stokes, William 1802-1802
Straus, Emanuel 1887-1897
Swanwick, John 1792-1794

Tagert, Joseph 1802-1813
Taylor, Charles 1836-1873
Taylor, James 1803-1808
Taylor, William H. . . . 1932-1938
Thomas, Jacob M. . . . 1840-1853
Tingey, Thomas . . . 1794-1794
Townsend, J. Barton . . 1918-1928
Trotter, Edward H. . . 1858-1872
Trotter, Nathan 1898-1915
Trotter, William H. . . 1873-1898

Vaughan, John 1794-1798

Waln, Jacob S. 1805-1824
Waln, S. Morris 1852-1870
Waln, William 1802-1802
Warder, John 1801-1801
Warriner, Samuel D. . . 1922-1942
Wayne, Joseph, Jr. . . . 1924-1942
Weir, Silas E. 1823-1828
Welsh, John Lowber . . 1879-1886
Welsh, William 1842-1878
West, Francis 1793-1799
Wharton, Robert . . . 1804-1805
Wheeler, Charles . . . 1874-1883
White, Ambrose . . . 1839-1873
White, John 1825-1848
White, John P. 1867-1868
Whitney, George . . . 1882-1885
Wikoff, Jacob C. . . . 1801-1831
Wilcocks, John 1794-1794
Williams, David E. . . . 1942-
Willing, Richard . . . 1805-1806
Winsor, Henry 1873-1889
Winsor, James D. Jr. . . 1917-
Winsor, William D. . . 1889-1917
Wood, Richard D. . . . 1841-1869

INDEMNITY INSURANCE COMPANY
OF NORTH AMERICA

OFFICERS IN 1942

PRESIDENT: John A. Diemand

EXECUTIVE VICE-PRESIDENT: H. P. Stellwagen

VICE-PRESIDENTS:

T. Leaming Smith
Benjamin Rush, Jr.

John W. Drayton
Patrick F. Burke

ASSISTANT VICE-PRESIDENTS:

Calvin S. Roberts

James M. Crawford

ASSISTANT FINANCIAL VICE-PRESIDENT: Robert F. Jefferys

SECRETARY: Frank A. Eger

TREASURER & ASSISTANT SECRETARY: J. Kenton Eisenbrey

ASSISTANT SECRETARY & ASSISTANT TREASURER: Algernon Roberts

ASSISTANT TREASURER: Edward S. Buckley, III

ASSISTANT SECRETARIES:

Horace B. Montgomery
Edgar W. Miller
W. Edgar Kipp
Carroll W. Laird

Arnold F. Bliss
William J. Schiff
Thomas F. Cass
H. Woodward Childs

DIRECTORS

CHAIRMAN OF THE BOARD: Benjamin Rush

VICE-CHAIRMAN OF THE BOARD: John O. Platt

Edward S. Buckley, Jr.
William S. Godfrey
Clarence M. Brown
Henry G. Brengle
John Story Jenks
James D. Winsor, Jr.
Edward B. Leisenring
M. W. Clement

Sheldon Catlin
George S. Munson
Edward Hopkinson, Jr.
James E. Gowen
Philip C. Staples
Horace P. Liversidge
J. Hamilton Cheston
John A. Diemand

THE ALLIANCE INSURANCE COMPANY
OF PHILADELPHIA

OFFICERS IN 1942

PRESIDENT: John A. Diemand

VICE-PRESIDENTS:

John Kremer
T. Leaming Smith

John W. Drayton
Ludwig C. Lewis

ASSISTANT FINANCIAL VICE-PRESIDENT: Robert F. Jefferys

SECRETARY & TREASURER: J. Kenton Eisenbrey

MARINE SECRETARY: G. Brinton Lucas

AGENCY SECRETARY: R. Stockton Rush

FIRE SECRETARY: Bradford Smith, Jr.

ASSISTANT SECRETARIES & ASSISTANT TREASURERS:

Curtis L. Clay

Algernon Roberts

ASSISTANT SECRETARIES:

C. William Johnson
William P. Woodroffe
James E. Hitchcock
Henry W. Farnum

Robert P. Hare, Jr.
Arthur V. Davenport
R. Bruce Miller

DIRECTORS

CHAIRMAN OF THE BOARD: Benjamin Rush

VICE-CHAIRMAN OF THE BOARD: John O. Platt

Clarence M. Brown
James D. Winsor, Jr.
Edward S. Buckley, Jr.
William S. Godfrey
Henry G. Brengle
John Story Jenks
Edward B. Leisenring
M. W. Clement

Sheldon Catlin
George S. Munson
Edward Hopkinson, Jr.
James E. Gowen
Philip C. Staples
Horace P. Liversidge
J. Hamilton Cheston
John A. Diemand

PHILADELPHIA FIRE AND MARINE
INSURANCE COMPANY

OFFICERS IN 1942

PRESIDENT: John A. Diemand

VICE-PRESIDENTS:

John Kremer

T. Leaming Smith

John W. Drayton

Ludwig C. Lewis

ASSISTANT FINANCIAL VICE-PRESIDENT: Robert F. Jefferys

SECRETARY & TREASURER: J. Kenton Eisenbrey

MARINE SECRETARY: G. Brinton Lucas

AGENCY SECRETARY: R. Stockton Rush

FIRE SECRETARY: Bradford Smith, Jr.

ASSISTANT SECRETARIES & ASSISTANT TREASURERS:

Curtis L. Clay

Algernon Roberts

ASSISTANT SECRETARIES:

C. William Johnson

William P. Woodroffe

James E. Hitchcock

Henry W. Farnum

Robert P. Hare, Jr.

Arthur V. Davenport

R. Bruce Miller

DIRECTORS

CHAIRMAN OF THE BOARD: Benjamin Rush

VICE-CHAIRMAN OF THE BOARD: John O. Platt

Clarence M. Brown

James D. Winsor, Jr.

Edward S. Buckley, Jr.

William S. Godfrey

Henry G. Brengle

John Story Jenks

Edward B. Leisenring

M. W. Clement

Sheldon Catlin

George S. Munson

Edward Hopkinson, Jr.

James E. Gowen

Philip C. Staples

Horace P. Liversidge

J. Hamilton Cheston

John A. Diemand

NATIONAL SECURITY INSURANCE COMPANY

OMAHA, NEBRASKA

OFFICERS IN 1942

PRESIDENT: Edgar M. Morsman, III

VICE-PRESIDENTS:

John A. Diemand
John Kremer

John W. Drayton
T. Leaming Smith

SECRETARY & TREASURER: J. Kenton Eisenbrey

ASSISTANT SECRETARIES:

Russell H. Petefish
Curtis L. Clay

Algernon Roberts

DIRECTORS

CHAIRMAN OF THE BOARD: Edgar M. Morsman, III

Benjamin Rush
A. L. Reed
Ford E. Hovey
A. A. Lowman
Willard D. Hosford
Clarence M. Brown
James D. Winsor, Jr.

I. W. Carpenter, Jr.
H. M. Bushnell
Russell H. Petefish
Gilbert C. Swanson
James L. Paxton, Jr.
Carl H. Brinkmann

CENTRAL INSURANCE COMPANY OF BALTIMORE

BALTIMORE, MARYLAND

OFFICERS IN 1942

PRESIDENT: Charles H. Roloson, Jr.

VICE-PRESIDENTS:

Bernard A. Grob
John Kremer
T. Leaming Smith

James H. Cupit
John W. Drayton

SECRETARY: Thomas Hughes

AGENCY SECRETARY: Richard Teano

ASSISTANT SECRETARIES:

J. Kenton Eisenbrey
F. Addison Fowler

Curtis L. Clay
Algernon Roberts

DIRECTORS

Frank J. Roll
Frank Novak
Charles H. Roloson, Jr.
Charles H. Baetjer
George W. Schoenhals
John A. Gebelein
Sheldon Catlin
John Kremer

T. Leaming Smith
John W. Drayton
Robert G. Merrick
John McC. Mowbray
John J. Ghingher
Robert O. Bonnell
Edwin A. Spilman
James H. Cupit

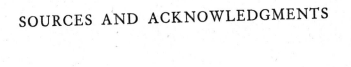

SOURCES AND ACKNOWLEDGMENTS

SOURCES AND ACKNOWLEDGMENTS

IT IS hoped that the documentary Notes in this volume have afforded some clue to the course and the nature of the research which underlies it.

The book is derived almost entirely from contemporary sources. In the main these consist of the records of the company; of newspapers and insurance trade journals; of the personal recollections of officers and employees of the company. The company's records were used from 1792 to the present time; newspapers over much of the same period; trade journals on and off from the time of the founding of that branch of journalism by *Tuckett's Monthly Insurance Journal* in 1852. The help that persons now living could give bore on a later period, naturally. John J. Connor went to work for the Insurance Company of North America in 1876; John O. Platt in 1891; Benjamin Rush in 1895. Their appearance on the scene marks about the beginning of the gradual introduction of oral testimony to supplement, explain, interpret and generally enrich from a narrative point of view the written records.

Other sources, though secondary, were very helpful throughout the work. J. A. Fowler's *History of Insurance in Philadelphia for Two Centuries* comprises a painstaking record of insurance in Philadelphia from the colonial times to 1882. The book is hard to read but worth the patience required. Another early compilation, dealing more particularly with the subject immediately under review, is Thomas H. Montgomery's *History of the Insurance Company of North America,* published in 1885. Mr. Montgomery was a former employee with a fondness for the company's eighteenth-century archives. His account of the steps that led to the organization of the North America, and of the first decade of its existence, is useful. The rest is rather sketchy. The published histories of other fire and marine insurance companies have been read. To clarify a point or two William D. Winter, president of the Atlantic Mutual Insurance Company, permitted an inspection of some of that company's files for the Civil War period. Insurance men connected with other companies, and brokers and agents, some with and some without North America connections, were consulted on occasions. Of help was the extensive monograph collection in the Library of the Insurance Society of New York.

The research necessary to the development of the narrative from its beginning to roughly 1920 was conducted almost wholly by my wife, Bessie Rowland James. Over a period of nearly two years she spent an aggregate of several months in Philadelphia. Most of this time was devoted to an exploration of the company's records. For the first fifty years of the North America's history these are so full as to present an embarrassment of riches. It is possible that they comprise the most nearly complete and intimate picture extant of how American business was conducted during the initial half-century of the life of the republic. My wife and I feel that this account does these archives less than justice. We hope that other students will be able to make use of them in the development of phases of our early business and economic history for which we could find no room or too little room in this book.

The officers of the Insurance Company of North America gave us access to its records without restriction as to their use.

I have tried to write this story as my wife and I have seen it shape up from the evidence. As our eyes are not those of insurance professionals it follows that this is a lay chronicle. The officers of the North America, uniformly so cordial and helpful to us, should not be taxed for its shortcomings. In rendering the account there has been no soft-pedaling of what appeared to constitute errors of judgment on the parts of company officers or directors during the course of a crowded century and a half. Never, in our many and extended conversations with present-day officers, has my wife or have I received a suggestion that this be done. One present officer expressed regret that something I proposed to write should show certain rival insurance companies in a comparatively unfavorable light. This is mentioned to absolve everyone except myself from responsibility for any such utterances.

The last chapter, and to a certain extent the next to last chapter, of the book represents an attempt to make history of a Niagara of current events. Tries like this never come off successfully. In this case it was impossible to give some facts because they are military secrets. Others are simply unavailable. And all the remainder is very difficult to evaluate at such close range. Nevertheless I took a stab at setting down a few things which may possibly be of some little assistance later on to someone undertaking a history of marine, fire or casualty insurance during World War II.

To mention all the officers and employees of the company who have helped us would be to repeat a long list of names which will be found in the Notes. We cannot forbear, however, a specific acknowledgment of the services of John J. Connor, one of Charles Platt's office boys who became secretary and treasurer of the company. Many years ago Mr. Connor began to take an interest in the historically valuable manuscripts concerning the North America's early years and to see to their preservation. Another acknowledgment in the same tenor is due to Algernon Roberts, currently assistant secretary and assistant treasurer of the company. Incidentally, Mr. Roberts is a direct descendant of Colonel Charles Pettit, the company's second president, a fact which he prevailed on me to exclude from the text of the history. Henry C. Thorn, marine manager of the New York office, lent a helpfully annotated collection of material from newspapers, magazines and other sources bearing on marine-insurance preparations for the present war. Thanks are also due to Miss Clare M. Doris of Philadelphia who acted as my wife's and my secretary during this work.

We wish to express our sense of obligation to the Philadelphia Free Library, to its librarian, Franklin H. Price, and his staff; to the Library Company of Philadelphia, its librarian, Austin J. Gray, and his assistant, Barney Chesnick; to the Historical Society of Pennsylvania, and its secretary, William Reitzel; to the Library of the Insurance Society of New York and its librarian, Miss Mabel Swerig; the Library of Congress; the New York Public Library; the Library of the State of New York, Albany; and the Public Library of Pleasantville, New York. We are grateful to A. E. Snyder of Philadelphia for the loan of his scrapbook and collection of histories of early Philadelphia.

For editorial suggestions (a phrase some of us writers use when we mean tips on how to straighten out awkward sentences) I am indebted to D. Laurance Chambers, president of the publishing house which is getting out this book, and to Elizabeth Frink, Patricia Jones and Elisabeth Yager of its staff in Indianapolis.

M. J.

Pleasantville, New York
September 4, 1942.

NOTES

CHAPTER I

[1]George Rothwell Brown, *Washington, a Not Too Serious History* (1930), 22; *Dictionary of American Biography*, II, 380-381.

[2]George Washington to Daniel Stuart, April 8, 1792, "The Writings of George Washington Relating to the National Capital," *Records of the Columbia Historical Society*, XVII, 55.

[3]Thomas H. Montgomery, *A History of the Insurance Company of North America* (1885), 96 *et seq.*

[4]Minute Book, I, I-II, Universal Tontine Association, Archives of the Insurance Company of North America, Philadelphia; *American Daily Advertiser* (Philadelphia), March 22, 1792; J. A. Fowler, *History of Insurance in Philadelphia for Two Centuries, 1683-1882* (1888), 43.

[5]*Dictionary of American Biography*, II, 380.

[6]Various letters, June and July 1792, between Samuel Blodget, Jr., and Ebenezer Hazard, Universal Tontine records, Archives of Insurance Company of North America. For brevity the source will henceforth be designated as Company Archives.

[7]Montgomery, 14-27; Fowler, 23-24.

[8]Montgomery, 11-13; Directors' Minutes, I, December 1792, Company Archives.

[9]Charles Pettit to J. M. Nesbitt, December 15, 1792, Museum of the Insurance Company of North America, Philadelphia.

[10]First Marine Blotter Book, Company Archives.

[11]Directors' Minutes, December 1792-January 1793, *ibid.*; Cash Book, December 1792, *ibid.*

CHAPTER II

[1]First Marine Blotter Book, Company Archives.

[2]Directors' Minutes, March 25 and 27, 1793, *ibid.*

[3]*American Daily Advertiser* (Philadelphia), May 3, 1793.

[4]Directors' Minutes, May-July 1793, Company Archives; *American Daily Advertiser*, May 3, 1793.

[5]Ebenezer Hazard to Thomas Patten & Company, July 24, 1793, Letter Book A, Company Archives.

[6]Ebenezer Hazard to Jedediah Morse, September 20, 1793, Cramond, Phillips and Croydan correspondence, 1789-1801, Gratz Collection, Historical Society of Pennsylvania (Philadelphia).

[7]Nathan Hazard to Ebenezer Hazard, September 30, 1793, Insurance Company of North America Museum, Philadelphia.

[8]Ebenezer Hazard to John M. Nesbitt, September 23, 1793, Miscellaneous Papers, Company Archives.

[9]John M. Nesbitt to Ebenezer Hazard, September 24, 1793, Company Museum; same to same, September 26, 1793, Folder 53, Company Archives; Ebenezer Hazard to John M. Nesbitt, September 27, 1793, Company Museum.

[10]Ebenezer Hazard to John M. Nesbitt, October 12, 1793, *ibid.*

[11]Various letters between Ebenezer Hazard and John M. Nesbitt, October and November 1793, Folder 53, Company Archives.

[12]J. Thomas Scharf and Thompson Westcott, *History of Philadelphia* (1884), I, 470.

[13]Ebenezer Hazard to John M. Nesbitt, November 9, 1793, Folder 53, Company Archives.

[14]*American Daily Advertiser* (Philadelphia), March 20, 1794.

[15]Directors' Minutes, December 1793 to March 1794, Company Archives.

[16]Directors' Minutes, December 1792 and January 1793, *ibid.*; *American Daily Advertiser* (Philadelphia), December 31, 1792, January 1, 3, 4, 5 and 7, 1793; Montgomery, 36-38.

[17]Directors' Minutes, December 1793, January-March 1794, Company Archives; Montgomery, 38-44; Fowler, 48-50.

CHAPTER III

[1]Montgomery, 28-34, 61; Scharf & Westcott, III, 2115.

[2]Receipt Book, 1793-1798, 122, Company Archives.

[3]First Fire Blotter Book, *ibid.*; Montgomery, 61-64.

[4]*Ibid.*, 72-74; Fowler, 623-25; Charles K. Knight, *History of Life Insurance in the United States* to 1870 (1920), 52; John Inskeep to Elias Boudinot, December 3, 1816, Letter Book 1815-46, 28, Company Archives; same to same, February 13, 1817, 30, *ibid.*

[5]Directors' Minutes, October 12, 1795, *ibid.*

[6]*American Daily Advertiser* (Philadelphia), April 18, 1796.

[7]Ebenezer Hazard to Jedediah Morse, May 13, 1796, Historical Society of Pennsylvania (Philadelphia).

[8]Five years later, on May 26, 1801, the Board of Directors computed the company's losses to the British at $1,060,155. See Directors' Minutes of that date, Company Archives.

[9]Insurance Company of North America to John Fry, Jr., March 3, 1800, Letter Book A, 101, Company Archives; Robert S. Stephens to James MacKenzie and A. Glennie, June 4, 1800, Letter Book II, 28, *ibid.*

[10]Index of Spoliation Claims, Folio III, 38, Company Archives; Charles Pettit to Jared Ingersoll, June 9, 1797, same to Thomas Murgatroyd, June 12, 1797, Letter Book A, 33-34, *ibid.*; Fowler, 56; Scharf and Westcott, I, 484.

[11]Directors' Minutes, October 8, 1796, Company Archives.

[12]Directors' Minutes, January 9, 1795, *ibid.*

[13]Directors' Minutes, August 10, 1795, *ibid.*

[14]Index to Spoliation Claims, Folio III, 38, *ibid.*

[15]Directors' Minutes, June 23 and September 1, 1794, *ibid.*

[16]Directors' Minutes, November 17, 1794 and March 16, 1795, *ibid.*

[17]Directors' Minutes, July 29, 1794; Ebenezer Hazard to Robert Morris, November 13, 1794, Folder 43, Company Archives; Directors' Minutes, December 15 and 22, 1794, January 15 and September 15, 1795, January 9, 1797, *ibid.*

[18]Directors' Minutes, January 15, 1795, *ibid.*; Montgomery, 103.

[19]William Eldredge to Insurance Company of North America, Folder 46, papers dated 1797, Company Archives.

CHAPTER IV

[1]Blotter Book H, Company Archives.

[2]Charles Pettit to John Hollins, July 29, 1801, Letter Book A, Company Archives; *United States Gazette* (Philadelphia), January 5, 1802; Scharf and Westcott, I, 512.

[3]Joseph Ball to Joseph Larcom, February 16, 1799, *Columbian Centinel* (Boston), April 3, 1799. As will presently be set forth in the text Mr. Ball had temporarily succeeded Colonel Pettit as president of the Insurance Company of North America.

[4]Robert S. Stephens to James and William Perot, November 10, 1801, Letter Book A, 226, Company Archives.

[5]Insurance Company of North America to John Fry, Jr., March 3, 1800, Letter Book A, 101-102, *ibid.*

[6]Ebenezer Hazard to John Fry, Jr., April 28, 1798, Letter Book A, 62, *ibid.*

[7]Charles Pettit to John Fry, Jr., March 3, 1800, Letter Book A, 100, *ibid.*

[8]Charles Pettit to John Fry, Jr., August 9 and October 6, 1801, Letter Book A, 204 and 215, *ibid.*

[9]Charles Pettit to Forsythe, Smith & Co., agents for the North America in Halifax, August 20, 1800, Letter Book A, 123, *ibid.*

[10]Charles Pettit to John Fry., Jr., August 9, 1801, Letter Book A, 204, *ibid.*

[11]Directors' Minutes, March 29, 1803, *ibid.*

[12]Stockholders' Minutes, January 4, 1804, *ibid.*; see also Charles Pettit to William Savage, April 29, 1804, Letter Book A, *ibid.*

[13]Stockholders' Minutes, January 4, 1804, *ibid.*

[14]David & Philip Grim to Messrs. Watson & Paul, February 4, 1799, Manuscript Letter at the Philadelphia Library Association.

[15]Fowler, 69.

[16]Directors' Minutes, March 11, 1806, Company Archives. The amount of the Phoenix Company's holding of North America stock seems unascertainable because the North America's stock book for 1799-1806 is missing.

[17]Charles Pettit to William Savage, April 29, 1804, Letter Book A, *ibid.*

[18]Directors' Minutes, December 1805 and January 1806, *ibid.*

[19]Dated April 10, 1804, Miscellaneous Papers, *ibid.*; Receipt Book, 1793-1798, 322, *ibid.*

[20]Charles Pettit to David H. Conyngham, June 16, 1803 and January 24, 1805, Letter Book 1802-1806, 117 and 265, *ibid.*

[21]Directors' Minutes, June 21, 1803, *ibid.*

[22]Directors' Minutes, February 25 and March 11, 1806, *ibid.*

[23]Directors' Minutes, September 1, 1806, *ibid.*

CHAPTER V

[1]*Pennsylvania Magazine of History and Biography*, XXVIII, No. 2, 131-33.

[2]Stockholders' Minute Book, 1803-1857, 17, Company Archives.

[3]Fowler, 72.

[4]John Inskeep to James Mackenzie & A. Glennie, February 11, 1808, Letter Book 1806-15, Company Archives.

[5]John Inskeep to a correspondent whose name is not given but who seems to

have been William Savage, the North America's agent in Jamaica, September
11, 1807, *ibid.*

[6]John Inskeep to William Savage, November 19, 1808, *ibid.*

[7]John Inskeep to James Mackenzie and A. Glennie, February 9, 1809, *ibid.*

[8]*Ibid.*, May 9, 1809; Directors' Minutes, March 20, 1809, Company Archives.

[9]John Inskeep to James Mackenzie and A. Glennie, May 9, 1809, Letter
Book 1806-1815, *ibid.*

[10]*Ibid.*, July 29, 1809.

[11]Financial statements contained in Directors' Minutes for December 29,
1807; July 11, 1808; July 10, 1809; July 9, 1811, Company Archives.

[12]Scharf and Westcott, III, 2128; *The Delaware*, Harry Emerson Wildes
(1940), 256; Directors' Minutes, August 10, 1810, Company Archives.

[13]*Ibid.*, July 11, 1808.

[14]*Ibid.*, January 9, 1809.

[15]Old Memorandum Book, Company Archives.

[16]Stockholders' Minutes, January 13, 1812, *ibid.*

[17]Fowler, 100.

[18]Stockholders' Minutes, July 13, 1812, Company Archives.

[19]John Inskeep to James Mackenzie and A. Glennie, August 15, 1812, Letter Book 1806-15, *ibid.*

[20]Directors' Minutes, January 11 and 25, 1813, *ibid.*; Stockholders' Minutes, January 11, 1813, *ibid.*; Directors' Minutes, July 12, 1813, January 10
and July 11, 1814, *ibid.*; John Inskeep to G. W. Campbell, Secretary of the
Treasury, April 30, 1814, *ibid.*

[21]John Inskeep to Alexander Glennie Sons & Company, August 19, 1814,
Letter Book 1806-15, *ibid.*

[22]Directors' Minutes, September 14, 1814, *ibid.*

[23]Stockholders' Minutes, January 9, 1815, *ibid.*

[24]Directors' Minutes, July 10, 1815, *ibid.*

[25]Directors' Minutes, September 27, 1815, *ibid.*

[26]Directors' Minutes, February 22, 1815, *ibid.*

[27]An unpublished genealogy of the Stotesbury family courteously lent the
writer by Mrs. Frances Butcher Mitchell, a daughter of E. T. Stotesbury and
a great-granddaughter of Captain Arthur Stotesbury.

CHAPTER VI

[1]Stockholders' Minutes, July 10, 1815, Company Archives.

[2]Charles Pettit to John Hollins, January 28, 1797, Letter Book A, *ibid.*

[3]Directors' Minutes, January 30 and August 8, 1797, *ibid.*

[4]Directors' Minutes, March 31, 1797, *ibid.* For material on the origin of the
Philadelphia Hose Company the writer is indebted to the researches of Clarence
A. Palmer, advertising manager of the Insurance Company of North America.

[5]Davis & Reid to Insurance Company of North America, January 18 and
24, 1798, Folder 54, Company Archives; Montgomery, 64.

[6]Directors' Minutes, April 19, 1798, Company Archives.

[7]Andrew Ross to Charles Pettit, March 1804, Folder 56, *ibid.*

[8]Policy dated August 18, 1804, *ibid.*

[9]Directors' Minutes, October 7 and 22, November 3 and December 1, 1807, *ibid.; The Insurance Field,* October, 1917, 6; Montgomery, 66.

[10]John Inskeep to Thomas Wallace, May 20, 1808, Letter Book 1806-1815, Company Archives.

[11]John Inskeep to Thomas Wilson, whose address is not given but who seems to have represented the company in a Pennsylvania town, June 16, 1808, Letter Book 1806-15, *ibid.*

[12]John Inskeep to James Ewing, June 3, 1808, *ibid.*

[13]John Inskeep to James Ewing, November 3, 1809, *ibid.*

[14]John Inskeep to Andrew Ross, February 16, 1818, Letter Book 1816-46, *ibid.*

[15]John Inskeep to Andrew Ross, May 29, 1818, *ibid.*

[16]John Inskeep to Andrew Ross, January 4, 1819, *ibid.*

[17]John Inskeep to Frederick Fritz, May 8, 1820, *ibid.*

CHAPTER VII

[1]Andrew Jackson to John Hutchings, April 25, 1816, John Spencer Bassett (editor), *Correspondence of Andrew Jackson* (1927-33), II, 241.

[2]Directors' Minutes, January 16, 1816, Company Archives.

[3]*Ibid.,* January 8, 1816; Stockholders' Minutes, same date; Directors' Minutes, July 8, 1816; Stockholders' Minutes, same date, *ibid.*

[4]Semiannual statements, January and July 1819 to 1823, Directors' Minutes, *ibid.*

[5]John Inskeep to James Giles, February 2, 1820, and to Henry Pratt, same date, Letter Book 1815-46, *ibid.*

[6]Correspondence concerning the Widow Roberts and with Stephen Kingston is fairly voluminous. These letters are representative: Charles Pettit to Mrs. Roberts, June 12, 1806; John Inskeep to same, November 15, 1810, Letter Book, 1806-15, *ibid.;* Inskeep to Kingston, September 4 and 24, 1816, Letter Book 1815-46, *ibid.*

[7]Stockholders' Minutes, July 9, 1821; Directors' Minutes, January 7, 1822, *ibid.*

[8]Directors' Minutes, June 15, 1824; Stockholders' Minutes, July 12, 1824, *ibid.* The sum paid Daniel Webster, the sources and amounts of whose corporation fees have become of interest to historians, has not been found by the present researchers, but it seems possible to reckon fairly closely from the following data appearing in the citations just mentioned: the directors reported the net recoveries, after deducting expenses, to be $303,190. The rewards to Jaudon, Stephens and Valentine total $8,810, leaving $20,933 spent elsewhere. Generously estimating incidentals at $933, it seems likely that the balance went to Webster.

[9]Directors' Minutes, July 12, 1824, Company Archives.

[10]Directors' Minutes, December 16, 1831; *ibid.,* April 12, 1825; *United States Gazette,* December 29, 1825.

[11]Scharf & Westcott, I, 432.

[12]John Inskeep to Board of Directors, May 21, 1831; Directors' Minutes, same date, Company Archives.

[13]*Insurance Monitor,* September 1879.

[14]Stockholders' Minutes, January 9, 1832, Company Archives.

[15]Directors' Minutes, July 9, 1832, *ibid.*

[16]Nicholas Biddle's correspondence, preserved in the Library of Congress, is evidence that the banker consciously brought on the panic of 1834 in an effort to destroy Jackson and to save the Bank of the United States. The story is told in detail, with citations, in Marquis James, *Life of Andrew Jackson.* See II, 350-388, in the two-volume edition or pp. 645-680 in the one-volume edition.

CHAPTER VIII

[1]Fowler, 135; Directors' Minutes, January 14, 1839; July 8, 1839; January 10, 1842; July 11, 1842; Stockholders' Minutes, January 10, 1842, Company Archives. It is possible to give only an approximation of the deficit in January 1842, as the company's securities portfolio had not been devalued at that time. Holdings carried at cost or at par aggregated $616,772. The July 1842 statement marks these down to current values, which totaled $326,088. The condition of Mr. Biddle's bank is admitted by Scharf and Westcott, I, 658, local historians who were partial to Mr. Biddle, ordinarily.

[2]Fowler, 144.

[3]F. C. Oviatt, "The Historical Study of Fire Insurance in the United States," *Annals of the American Academy of Political and Social Science* XXVI, No. 2, 164; Oscar S. Nelson, *Fire Insurance Adjustment Problems in the United States* (1930), 20.

[4]Fowler, 152-156.

[5]John C. Smith to Walter R. Jones, April 8, 1844, Letter Book 1815-1846, Company Archives.

[6]An indenture of settlement, dated August 10, 1807, *ibid.*

[7]Arthur G. Coffin to Edward Brooks, October 3, 1839; Directors' Minutes, October 3, 1849, *ibid.*

[8]Directors' Minutes, February 26, 1850, *ibid.*

[9]*Biographies of Successful Philadelphia Merchants,* published by James K. Simon (1864), 182-185. The assertion in this account that Mr. Cope never insured any of his ships is in error.

[10]Directors' Minutes, September 23, September 26, 1845; October 6, 1846; May 4, May 18 and October 19, 1847, Company Archives.

[11]Disaster Book, 1849-1851, 41, 45, *ibid.*; Henry R. Gall and William George Jordan, *One Hundred Years of Fire Insurance, Being a History of the Aetna Insurance Company* (1919), 91.

[12]Stockholders' Minutes, January 12, 1846, Company Archives.

[13]Charles Platt to W. West Lewis, April 3, 1849. From the Platt Family Papers by courtesy of John O. Platt, Philadelphia.

[14]A book of marine mishaps bearing no title and beginning with an entry dated February 19, 1849, Company Archives.

[15]Frank Morton Todd, *A Romance of Insurance, Being a History of the Firemen's Fund Insurance Company of San Francisco* (1929), 18.

[16]Disaster Book, 1849-1851, 147, Company Archives; Fowler, 381.

[17]Directors' Minutes, April 6, 1852, Company Archives.

[18]Fowler, 174.

[19]*Ibid.,* 200.

[20]Stockholders' Minutes, January 14, 1856; January 11, 1858; January 10, 1859; January 9, 1860, Company Archives.

[21]Directors' Minutes, May 1, 1855, *ibid.*
[22]Directors' Minutes, November 13, 1860, *ibid.*

CHAPTER IX

[1]Board of Philadelphia Marine Underwriters Minute Book 1861-1871, January 12, 1861, Company Archives.
[2]Directors' Minutes, January 14, 1861, *ibid.*
[3]Board of Philadelphia Marine Underwriters Minute Book, 1861-1871, January 18, 1861, *ibid.*
[4]Directors' Minutes, April 19, 1861, *ibid.*
[5]The date or circumstances of the capture or the amount of the company's loss does not appear. Directors' Minutes, February 11, 1862, makes allusion to the *Rowena* as having been taken "last summer."
[6]A. G. Coffin and five others to Gideon Welles, August 7, 1861, Board of Philadelphia Marine Underwriters Minutes, Company Archives; Fowler, 224-225.
[7]Directors' Minutes, May 7, May 21, October 29, November 26, December 24, 1861, Company Archives.
[8]J. R. Wucherer to Gideon Welles, October 10 and 11, 1862, Board of Philadelphia Marine Underwriters Minute Book, *ibid.*
[9]Charles Platt, presumably to W. W. Lewis, November 25, 1849, Platt Family Papers, Philadelphia, by courtesy of John O. Platt.
[10]Charles Platt's system for circumventing Confederate raiders has been mentioned to the writer by several veterans of the North America who knew him, notably his nephew John O. Platt and Benjamin Rush.
[11]W. S. Foster, Oak Park, Illinois, to B. R. James. Mr. Foster started to work as an office boy in the Erie office of the North America in 1885. When the Western Department was moved to Chicago in 1910, he went along. He retired with the title of associate manager in July, 1935. He has since written two technical works on insurance which have become salesmen's handbooks.
[12]In the *Journal of Commerce* (New York) of September 13, 1916, was published a speech by A. W. Damon, president of the Springfield Fire and Marine Insurance Company, in which he credited Alexander Stoddart of the New York Underwriters Agency for the invention of the daily report system in 1866. The claim was immediately disputed by W. S. Foster, at that time assistant general agent of the North America at Erie, Pennsylvania. Mr. Foster wrote Mr. Damon about a meeting between Mr. Downing and Mr. Stoddart in New York, probably around the turn of the century. "Downing, who invented the daily report?" Mr. Stoddart asked. "I don't know, who did?" Mr. Downing said. Mr. Foster claimed for Mr. Downing that he had begun using the daily report in 1864. At any rate, to Mr. Stoddart belongs credit for pushing the universal adoption of the daily report by insurance companies when they looked upon it as an "impracticable scheme."
[13]Fowler, 233, computes the total damage from Confederate naval action to January 30, 1864, at $13,300,000. This includes the losses to the British-built raiders.
[14]Figures on Philadelphia companies from Board of Philadelphia Underwriters Minutes, February 4, 1876, during the "Alabama Claims" settlement, Company Archives; those of Atlantic Mutual from Report of Trustees of that

company dated October 3, 1877, Atlantic Mutual Insurance Company records, New York City.

[15]Stockholders' Minutes, January 8, 1866, Company Archives.

CHAPTER X

[1]Quoted from Allan Nevins, *The Emergence of Modern America* (1928), 32.

[2]Stockholders' Minutes, January 14, 1867, and January 13, 1868, Company Archives.

[3]Solomon Huebner, *Development and Present Status of Marine Insurance in the United States*, Annals of the American Academy of Political and Social Science (Philadelphia), XXVI, 261-262; William D. Winter, *A Short Sketch of the History and the Principles of Marine Insurance*, published by The Insurance Society of New York (1935), 16.

[4]Stockholders' Minutes, January 14, 1867, Company Archives.

[5]*North America Almanac* (1869), 13, 23.

[6]Directors' Minutes, February 25, 1868, Company Archives.

[7]Lloyd Lewis and Henry Justin Smith, *Chicago, the History of Its Reputation* (1929), 119; *The Chronicle* (an insurance trade journal), November 30, 1871; New York *Tribune*, October 23, 1871.

[8]Directors' Minutes, March 10 and May 19, 1868, Company Archives.

[9]The figure $650,056.33 for losses in the Chicago fire is the total of 180 claims paid according to the label on a box containing the original documents in the Insurance Company of North America Archives. The January 1872 report of the directors gives the amount of losses as $623,769, which is the figure often subsequently used. It seems to indicate merely the losses adjusted to the date of that report.

[10]Gall and Jordan, 114-116.

[11]Company Archives.

[12]New York *Tribune*, October 23, 1871.

[13]Stockholders' Minutes, January 1872, Company Archives.

[14]A memorandum, dated May 26, 1925, Western Department files, *ibid.*

[15]*Report of the Commissioners . . .* [on] *the Great Fire in Boston* (1873), 571-572.

[16]Philadelphia *North American*, November 11, 1872.

[17]Philadelphia *Press*, November 11, 1872.

[18]Philadelphia *Inquirer*, November 12, 1872.

[19]*The Chronicle* (insurance trade journal), November 14, 1872.

[20]Directors' Minutes, September 20, 1873, Company Archives.

[21]Annual Report, January 1, 1874, *ibid.*

[22]Annual Report, January 1, 1875, *ibid.*

[23]Annual Report, January 1878, *ibid.*

[24]*Ibid.*

[25]John J. Connor to Bessie Rowland James, the wife of the writer, who conducted most of the research for this volume. See "Sources and Acknowledgments," *ante.*

CHAPTER XI

[1]Baltimore *Underwriter*, July 20, 1882; Baltimore *Sun*, May 6, 9, 11, 13, 16 and 19, 1882; Philadelphia *Ledger*, May 5, 12, 13, 15, 25, 30, 1882; New York *Herald*, January 11, 1886; a scrapbook of unidentified contemporary

newspaper clippings in the records of the Atlantic Mutual Insurance Company, New York; Stockholders' Minutes, January 1, 1883, Archives of the Insurance Company of North America. This story had a curious sequel. A part owner of the cargo brought suit for the amount of his insurance, $71,000. He claimed that he had purchased and insured in good faith rubber and other items to that value. The sellers were merchants of Vera Cruz, Mexico. As proof of his belief in the value of the cargo he showed that after the bark was loaded he had advanced the merchants $24,000. A court awarded the owner $5,000 which was the value of all the rubber, etc., consigned to the assured that was found on board.

[2]Annual Report, January 1, 1881, Company Archives.

[3]Annual Report, January 1, 1882, *ibid.*

[4]Annual Report, January 1, 1883, *ibid.*

[5]Fowler, 276.

[6]Annual Report, January 1, 1884, Company Archives.

[7]Annual Report, January 1, 1887, *ibid.*

[8]Directors' Minutes, February 3, 1885, and October 5, 1886, *ibid.*

[9]Edward M. Biddle, general counsel of the Insurance Company of North America, to B. R. James.

[10]Harry Chase Brearley, *Fifty Years of a Civilizing Force*, 74.

[11]Directors' Minutes, November 4, 1884, Company Archives.

[12]Stockholders' Minutes, January 1, 1886, January 1, 1887, January 1, 1889, *ibid.*

[13]Annual Report, January 1, 1894, *ibid.*

[14]Annual Report, January 1, 1888, *ibid.*

[15]A copy of Charles Platt's memorandum on the effort to discover the causes of marine losses was found among the early papers of Benjamin Rush. Apparently it was a part of the data collected by Mr. Rush when he took up the quest in 1895.

[16]Galloway C. Morris to B. R. James.

CHAPTER XII

[1]Benjamin Rush to B. R. James.

[2]Thomas R. Young, Allen Knight, John J. Connor and Benjamin Rush to B. R. James.

[3]Benjamin Rush to Charles Platt, December 10, 1897, Papers of Benjamin Rush. This letter has been printed as a pamphlet, though as far as the author has been able to discover no previous use of it has been made by a writer of insurance history.

[4]Thomas R. Young to B. R. James.

[5]*Ibid.*

[6]Benjamin Rush to B. R. James and to the writer.

[7]Thomas R. Young to B. R. James.

[8]Annual Report, January 1, 1900, Company Archives.

[9]Benjamin Rush to Charles Platt, January 7, 1902, Papers of Benjamin Rush.

CHAPTER XIII

[1]Brearley, *Fifty Years of a Civilizing Force*, 80.

[2]J. F. Downing to Charles Platt, November 13, 1894, Directors' Minutes November 14, 1894, Company Archives.

[3]*The Baltimore Conflagration, Report of the National Fire Protection Association* (1904).

[4]J. F. Downing, circular letter to agents of the Western Department, dated April 21, 1906, Papers of Sheldon Catlin, Philadelphia. When the North America moved into its new building in 1925 certain old and historically valuable files were destroyed. Mr. Catlin happened to see a box containing the San Francisco fire papers marked for destruction. Because of his association with that episode he had the box sent to his home. He kindly turned it over to my wife in the course of her research for this volume.

[5]Philadelphia *North American*, April 23, 1906.

[6]James D. Bailey to Insurance Company of North America, April 22, 1906, Papers of Sheldon Catlin.

[7]J. K. Hamilton to Insurance Company of North America, April 23, 1906, *ibid.*

[8]Sheldon Catlin to Eugene L. Ellison, May 1, 1906, *ibid.*

[9]Sheldon Catlin to Eugene L. Ellison, May 7, 1906, *ibid.*

[10]Directors' Minutes, May 14 and 17, 1906, Alliance Insurance Company Archives.

[11]Eugene L. Ellison to Sheldon Catlin, May 7, 8 and 12, 1906, Papers of Sheldon Catlin.

[12]Sheldon Catlin to Eugene L. Ellison, May 18, 1906, *ibid.*

[13]*Ibid.*

[14]Sheldon Catlin to Eugene L. Ellison, May 19, 1906, *ibid.*

[15]Sheldon Catlin to Eugene L. Ellison, May 22, 1906, *ibid.*

[16]Sheldon Catlin to Eugene L. Ellison, May 26, 1906, *ibid.*

[17]Eugene L. Ellison to Sheldon Catlin, May 25, 1906, *ibid.*

[18]Sheldon Catlin to Eugene L. Ellison, May 26, 1906; Eugene L. Ellison to Sheldon Catlin, May 28, 1906, *ibid.*

[19]New York *Journal of Commerce*, June 1, 1906.

[20]Eugene L. Ellison to Sheldon Catlin, June 1, 1906, Papers of Sheldon Catlin.

[21]Johnston, Friedley and Catlin to Eugene L. Ellison, June 15, 1906, *ibid.*

[22]Johnston, Friedley and Catlin to Insurance Company of North America, June 12, 1906, *ibid.*

[23]Johnston, Friedley and Catlin to Eugene L. Ellison, June 15, 1906, *ibid.*

[24]Eugene L. Ellison to Johnston, Friedley and Catlin, June 13, 1906, *ibid.*

[25]San Francisco *Examiner*, June 13, 1906.

[26]Papers of Sheldon Catlin.

[27]Jacob B. Levison, *Memories for My Family* (Privately printed, 1933), 137.

[28]Jacob B. Levison to Charles Platt, June 16, 1906. Copies of the Levison-Platt letters were supplied by Mr. Levison, this correspondence not having been preserved in the files of the Insurance Company of North America.

[29]Charles Platt to Jacob B. Levison, June 25, 1906, *ibid.*

[30]Levison, 137.

CHAPTER XIV

[1]Directors' Minutes, January 25, 1909, Company Archives.

[2]Annual Reports, 1902 and 1909, *ibid.*

[3]Directors' Minutes, February 1 and April 8, 1910; Report to Stockholders, September 6, 1910, *ibid.*

[4]Henry C. Thorn to B. R. James. Mr. Thorn was then connected with Johnson & Higgins.

[5]Board of Trade Inquiry into loss of S. S. *Montoswald*, London, August 22, 1913.

[6]An address delivered by Benjamin Rush before the American branch of the Newcomen Society of England, October 27, 1938, and printed in pamphlet form by the Princeton University Press under the title of *Romance of Insurance*. The Newcomen Society is a scientific body which takes its name from Thomas Newcomen from whom James Watt got the idea for his steam engine.

[7]Benjamin Rush to B. R. James.

[8]Records of Southern Department, Company Archives.

[9]Benjamin Rush to B. R. James.

[10]Galloway C. Morris to B. R. James.

[11]While the Cotton Reinsurance Exchange was the first workable reinsurance syndicate, it should be recorded that apparently an effort was made in the late eighties by underwriters to get together and settle on rates for export cotton. In the files of the North America is a copy of a "Cotton Tariff and Agreement signed May 17, 1888." No one interviewed could throw any light either on the origin or the fate of the "agreement." The several pages referring to rates and classes of ships are preceded by a brief outline of the purposes of the agreement which, in part, reads:

"We, the undersigned, on behalf of our respective organizations hereby agree . . . that we will not accept any direct insurance or re-insurance on cotton risks . . . for the season 1888-9, at less than the rates of premium named in the tariff hereto attached. . . .

"We also agree not to withdraw from this understanding unless by mutual consent. . . .

"And we further agree that we will loyally uphold the spirit, as well as the letter, of this undertaking."

The names of the signer organizations do not appear.

[12]Hendon Chubb to B. R. James.

[13]Bulletin No. 216, United States Department of Agriculture (1915).

CHAPTER XV

[1]Benjamin Rush to the writer.

[2]Galloway C. Morris, T. Leaming Smith and Thomas R. Young to B. R. James.

[3]Benjamin Rush to B. R. James.

[4]*Marine History*, a paper written and published privately by Benjamin Rush.

[5]Principal sources used for marine-insurance situation from July 28 to September 15, 1914: New York *Journal of Commerce;* New York *Times;* various trade journals, notably the *Spectator* and *Weekly Underwriter;* William F. Gephart, "Effects of the War Upon Insurance," Volume VI in *Preliminary Economic Studies of the War* issued by Carnegie Endowment for International Peace (1918), 176-180, 197-200; J. Russell Smith, "Influence of the Great War on Shipping," Volume IX in *Preliminary Economic Studies of the War* issued by Carnegie Endowment for International Peace (1919),

49 et seq.; Benjamin Rush, *Marine History;* conversations with various insurance men including Mr. Rush, Galloway C. Morris, T. Leaming Smith and Henry C. Thorn.

[6]Benjamin Rush to the writer.
[7]*Ibid.*
[8]J. Russell Smith, *Influence of the Great War on Shipping.*
[9]Benjamin Rush to the writer.
[10]Winter, 26.
[11]T. Leaming Smith to the writer.
[12]W. F. Jeffcott to B. R. James.
[13]R. H. Gibson and Maurice Prendergast, *The German Submarine War,* 1914-1918 (1931), 120-121.
[14]Benjamin Rush to the writer.
[15]J. F. Downing to Agents in the Western Department, February 21, 1910, Western Department correspondence, Company Archives.

CHAPTER XVI

[1]Statement of Benjamin Rush to Directors, January 1924, Papers of Benjamin Rush.

[2]Material on the hull syndicates of 1920 derived from the records of the syndicates at their headquarters, 99 John Street, New York, and from conversations with Henry H. Reed, general manager in New York of the Insurance Company of North America and affiliates.

[3]Principal sources for material on Marine Service Department: "Progress Report," dated April 29, 1938, by R. Bruce Miller; "Loss Prevention in the Field of Marine Insurance," a historical survey of the Department, dated May 8, 1939, by Mr. Miller; Lecture No. 13, Marine Course, Insurance Company of North America Student Classes.

[4]Section on Engineering Department of the fire branch compiled from various items of company literature on the subject including a memorandum by W. J. Baker, present chief of the department. The writer is also indebted to Morrison Harris, one of Mr. Baker's engineers.

[5]Directors' Minutes, February 9, 1922, Company Archives.
[6]*Ibid.,* August 8, 1922.

CHAPTER XVII

[1]*Three Score Years and Ten* (1935), a pamphlet history of Neare, Gibbs & Company; W. J. Gildsdorf to B. R. James.

[2]Lecture No. 6, Marine Course, Insurance Company of North America Student Classes.

[3]Earl Appleman, *Inland Marine Insurance* (1934), 7.
[4]Benjamin Rush to B. R. James; Ludwig C. Lewis to the writer.
[5]Ludwig C. Lewis to the writer.
[6]Lecture No. 21, Marine Course, Insurance Company of North America Student Classes.

[7]Ludwig C. Lewis and R. Bruce Miller to the writer. See also papers entitled "Forces that Lead to Tariff Rates and to Organization in the Inland Marine Field" written by Ellis T. Williams and by F. C. Lawton in competition for

the Waldemar J. Nichols Award, 1937. Copies are on file in the library of the Insurance Society of New York. The paper of Mr. Williams, an employee of the Insurance Company of North America, won the award. I am also indebted to Mr. Williams personally for many helpful services in connection with this volume.

[8]R. Jones Rife to John Kremer, April 2, 1925, Company Archives, Inland Marine Department, Philadelphia.

[9]F. A. Keller to R. J. Rife, April 9, 1925, *ibid*.

[10]The writer is indebted to Assistant Secretary R. Bruce Miller of the North America for patient and valuable assistance in combing and interpreting the company's files on bridge insurance from which the material on that topic appearing in the text was taken.

[11]William Verrinder to B. R. James; R. Bruce Miller to the writer; New York *Daily News*, April 9, 1933; New York *Daily Mirror*, August 12, 1934.

[12]Baldwin & Frick to Insurance Company of North America, February 18, 1920; the company's reply dated February 19, Company Archives, Inland Marine Department, Philadelphia.

[13]Ludwig C. Lewis to the writer.

[14]Arthur Adams to B. R. James.

[15]R. Bruce Miller to B. R. James.

[16]The narrative of the Glemby jewel robbery was compiled from the North America's extensive files on the case.

CHAPTER XVIII

[1]Edson S. Lott, *Pioneers of American Liability Insurance* (1938), 35; Eugene F. Hord, *History and Organization of Automobile Insurance* (1920), 17-19.

[2]*The Spectator*, June 25, 1925, and June 11, 1904.

[3]Henry H. Reed to B. R. James.

[4]*The Spectator*, May 14, 1903.

[5]*What the Insurance Company of North America Writes*, 40, an advertising pamphlet published by the company in 1919.

[6]John Kremer and Arthur V. Davenport to the writer.

[7]Arthur V. Davenport to the writer.

[8]Figures on the Alliance Casualty Company's operations are taken from that company's annual reports to the Insurance Commissioner of Pennsylvania, 1928 to 1933, inclusive.

[9]T. Leaming Smith to B. R. James.

[10]Lott, *passim*.

[11]John A. Diemand to the writer.

[12]See Note 15, below.

[13]See Note 15, below.

[14]John A. Diemand to the writer.

[15]The account of John A. Diemand's reformation of the Indemnity Company comprising sub-chapters 4 and 5 and a considerable part of the sub-chapter 7 of the text has largely been worked out by the writer from the statistics appearing in *Casualty Experience Exhibit*, 1932 to 1940, inclusive, and *Best's Fire & Casualty Aggregates & Averages*, 1941. For other data supplied from the company's files on request and for numerous statistical services

in connection with this volume I am indebted to Frank A. Eger, secretary of the company, and to Assistant Secretary H. Woodward Childs, who was Mr. Diemand's office boy at the Fidelity and Deposit of Maryland. Although Mr. Diemand personally was consulted and answered many questions he seemed anxious that I get the story from other sources.

[16]Arthur V. Davenport to the writer.

CHAPTER XIX

[1]Charles P. Butler to the writer. In 1932 Mr. Butler joined the North America as New York manager of the fire branch.

[2]Benjamin Rush to the writer.

[3]John W. Drayton to the writer.

[4]Benjamin Rush to the stockholders, January 27, 1930, Company Archives.

[5]Benjamin Rush to the writer.

[6]Benjamin Rush to the stockholders, January 26, 1931, Company Archives.

[7]Annual Statement, 1931, *ibid.*

[8]Annual Statement, 1932, *ibid.*

[9]Benjamin Rush to the writer.

[10]T. Leaming Smith, G. Brinton Lucas and Curtis L. Clay to the writer. Mr. Lucas is marine secretary and Mr. Clay assistant secretary and assistant treasurer of the company in charge of marine losses.

[11]John O. Platt and John Kremer to the writer.

[12]Remarks of Benjamin Rush to special agents of the North America at Chicago, January 4, 1939, Papers of Mr. Rush

[13]Remarks of John O. Platt at a dinner to Benjamin Rush, March 16, 1939, Papers of Mr. Platt.

[14]John O. Platt to the writer.

[15]John O. Platt, John Kremer and Charles P. Butler to the writer.

[16]Stockton Rush to the writer. Mr. Rush is agency secretary of the company.

[17]Henry H. Reed to the writer.

[18]John O. Platt to the writer.

[19]*National Underwriter*, October 3, 1940.

[20]Stockton Rush and E. W. Miller to the writer.

CHAPTER XX

[1]S. D. McComb, "Marine War Risks," *Best's Fire and Casualty News*, October, 1940; T. Leaming Smith and Henry C. Thorn to the writer.

[2]T. Leaming Smith to the writer.

[3]Henry H. Reed to the writer.

[4]Bulletin No. 147, War Risks, American Institute of Marine Underwriters, September 15, 1938.

[5]Bulletin No. 148, *ibid.*, September 16, 1938.

[6]Bulletin No. 153, *ibid.*, September 26, 1938.

[7]Bulletin No. 157, *ibid.*, September 30, 1938.

[8]"War Insurance Problems," an address by William D. Winter before the Export Managers' Club, New York City, February 20, 1940, Library of the Insurance Society of New York.

[9]American Cargo War Risk Reinsurance Exchange, Schedule 12, July 20, 1939; Schedule 14a, August 24; Schedule 14c, August 25; Schedule 16, August 28; Bulletin, September 1; Schedule 19, September 15; Schedule 21, September 30.

[10]Examples of quoted-on-application rates furnished by Henry C. Thorn.

[11]*Best's Fire and Casualty News*, October, 1940.

CHAPTER XXI

[1]Henry C. Thorn, "War Risks Again Dominate the Marine Insurance Field," New York *Journal of Commerce*, December 29, 1941. This article was written on November 24, more than a month before its publication. It comprises a review of the year to that date in the marine-insurance field. The writer is indebted to it for considerable material appearing in sub-chapter 1 of the text.

[2]John A. Diemand, an address to the insurance commissioners of the fifteen states which comprised the Union in 1792, Philadelphia, January 27, 1942.

[3]The writer is especially indebted to Ludwig C. Lewis for rounding up the greater part of the material from which an endeavor has been made to summarize in the text the war's effect to date on the fire, automobile and casualty business and to sketch the formation of the War Damage Corporation.

[4]Annual Statement for 1941, Company Archives, plus certain supplementary data from the files of the marine branch of the company.

[4a]Vice-President John W. Drayton died suddenly of a heart attack on September 23, 1942. He was forty-eight years old and had served as a corporal in the first World War. Mr. Drayton's management carried the North America through the depression of 1929-1933 with a remarkable investment record. He was engaged in wartime problems of a similar nature when death intervened.

[5]Annual Statement for 1941, Company Archives.

[6]*Best's Insurance Reports, Fire and Marine*, 1942, 333.

[7]American Cargo War Risk Reinsurance Exchange, Schedule 58, December 10, 1941.

[8]*Ibid.*, Loss Records.

[9]*Ibid.*, Schedule 61, January 26, 1942; Schedule 65, Amendment 4, March 14; Schedule 71, May 14; Schedule 77, June 25.

[10]Public Law 523, Seventy-seventh Congress, Second Session, H. R. 6554.

[11]War Shipping Administration, Division Wartime Insurance, Bulletin No. C-1, April 13, 1942; Bulletin No. C-5, June 17.

INDEX

INDEX

Adams, Arthur, head of New York Inland Loss Department, 297
Adams, John, 25, 51, 59, 60, 61
Adams, John Quincy, 91, 117
Aetna Engine Company, 98
Aetna Insurance Company, 122, 136, 137, 138, 164, 219, 220, 224, 232, 366
Alabama, 151, 152, 153, 156
Alabama Claims, 179
Alliance Casualty Company, capitalization, 270; losses and liquidation, 307, 337
Alliance Insurance Company, organization, capitalization and officers, 211; early profits, 211; risks in San Francisco, 213; losses in San Francisco, 214, 215, 226; stockholders' assessment, 216; payment of claims, 226; recovery, 227; reinsurance agent, 269, 293; company purchases stock, 270, 323; assets in 1941, 365
Alwine, L., cabinetmaker, 22
America, subject of first policy, 22
American Cargo War Risk Reinsurance Exchange, 346, 347, 348, 350-351, 367
American Daily Advertiser, 89
American Fire Insurance Company, 143
America Fore Insurance Company, 366
American Institute of Marine Underwriters, 344, 345, 346
American Insurance Company, 129
Ancona, 252
Anglo-French mission to Russia, 347-348
Ann McKim, 125
Antwerp Claims, 89, 90

Appleton, Samuel, casualty underwriter, 308
Appleton & Cox, managers for insurance companies, 291
Arabic, 252
Arms Limitation Conference, 265, 301
Association of Casualty and Surety Executives, 354
Atlantic Inland Association, 284
Atlantic Insurance Company of New York, 129
Atlantic Insurance Company of Philadelphia, 129, 132
Atlantic Mutual Insurance Company of New York, 131, 141, 154, 156, 194, 232, 240, 284, 347
Australia, 368
Austria, in World War I, 242, 245; in World War II, 342
Automobile Insurance Company, 291, 346

Bailey, James D., San Francisco agent, 214
Baker, Warren J., heads Engineering Department, 279
Ball, Joseph, elected director, 17; on committee of reparations memorial, 61; president of Union, 69, 70; president of company, 73
Baltimore & Ohio Railroad, 135, 159, 171
Baltimore fire, 210
Baltimore *Underwriter*, 176
Bank of North America, 16, 20, 23
Bank of Pennsylvania, 29, 85, 127, 128
Bank of the United States, 17, 38, 114-115, 118, 124

413

Barbon, Nicholas, London dentist, first fire insurer, 40

Barclay, John, director, 77

Barton, William, stockholder, 28

Bassett, E. J., Aetna agent, 164

Batterson, James G., casualty underwriter, 308

Battle of Gettysburg, 154

Battle of New Orleans, 93

Battle of Vicksburg, 154

Bayard, Andrew, director, 69

Bay of Biscayne Bridge, 293

Bay State Fire Insurance Company, 171

Belgium, 246, 352

Best's Insurance Reports, 366

Beynroth, William, holder of first fire policy, 42

Biddle, Clement, scrivener, 56

Biddle, Nicholas, attorney, 87; president of Bank of the United States, 115; backs Henry Clay, 124; creates artificial depression, 124; president of insolvent bank, 127-128

Binney, Horace, company attorney, 120

Black Tom munitions disaster, 263

Blodget, Samuel, Jr., career and interests, 11-12, 30; manages Boston Tontine, 12; stock salesman for company and first director, 17; private underwriting, 29-30; recommends fire business, 40; promotes life business, 44; designs company seal, 56; resignation, 71; in debtors' prison, 71

Board of Philadelphia Marine Underwriters, functions, 131-132, 148, 149, 150, 151

Boggs, James, director, 85

Bonaparte, Napoleon, 58, 80, 91

Bonar, L. J., Mansfield agent, 166

Bonhomme Richard-Serapis engagement, 94

Boston fire, 167-169

Boston Insurance Company, 271, 304

Boston Marine Insurance Company, 194

Boston Tontine, 11, 12, 15, 16

Boudinot, Elias, policyholder, 45

British & Foreign Marine Insurance Company, 194

Brooks, Captain, 174-176

Brooks, Edward, St. Louis agent, 133, 134, 137

Brown, Clarence M., director, 365

Brown, John A., director, 173

Brown, John A., (II), director, 180

Bryan, Dodd, Philadelphia agent, 307

Buchanan, James, 148

Buehler, William, Harrisburg agent, 151, 155

Bureau of War Risk Insurance, functions, 248; first rates, 249; government supplies capital facilities, 253; amount of writing, 253; statistics of underwriting, 260

Burke, Patrick F., vice-president of Indemnity, 321

Bustard, John, Louisville agent, 104

Butler, Charles P., counsel for New York State Insurance Department, 323; New York fire manager, 337

Butler, Pierce, Senator from South Carolina, 78

Butt, F. M., Georgia agent, improves methods of handling cotton, 237

Butt, F. M., & Company, 364

Caillaux Trial, 242

Caldwell, James M., Wheeling agent, 104

California, relinquished by Mexico, 139; during the Gold Rush, 140-142

Campbell, Chester M., head of Automobile Department, 306, 322

Carpathia, 232

Case, C. H., Chicago agent, 164

Casualty Committee, 291

Casualty Experience Exhibit, 313

Catlin, Sheldon, sent to San Francisco, 213; estimates losses, 215; fights reduction of payments, 215-216, 218; settles claims, 217, 220; refuses San Francisco position, 226; elected assistant secretary, 226; vice-president, 226, 256, 334; supervises au-

Catlin, Sheldon—*cont.*
tomobile department, 306; selects casualty executive, 307; retires, 226
Central Fire Insurance Company of Baltimore, 270, 325, 365
Central Pacific Railroad, 159
Chamberlain, Neville, 344, 345, 347, 352
Chesapeake-Leopard engagement, 80, 81
Chester, Hawley T., 291
Chicago fire, 163-165
Chicago *Record-Herald*, 225
Choate, Rufus, 143
Chouteau, Pierre, & Company, fur traders, 134, 286
Chronicle, The, 168, 169
Chubb, Hendon, underwriter, 240; organizes Bureau of War Risk Insurance, 253; organizes government syndicates, 271; influences preparations for 1939 crisis, 348
Chubb, Percy, 240
Chubb, Percy, II, 346, 369
Chubb & Son, underwriters, 240, 254, 284, 291, 346
Chubb Committee, 346, 347
Churchill, Winston, 346, 352
Churchman, Charles W., solicitor, 203
Cincinnati, first professional fire department, 162
City of Memphis, 258
City Tavern, 18, 20, 21, 60, 61, 73, 74, 112
Civil War, preparations, 148-149; blockade, 149; Confederate privateers, 150, 151, 152, 153-154; the Confederates in Pennsylvania, 154; losses inflicted by Confederate cruisers, 156
Clapier, Lewis, director, 69
Clarke, Julius L., Massachusetts Insurance Commissioner, 167
Clarks Ferry Bridge, 292, 293
Clay, Henry, 91, 124
Clayton, John M., 143
Cleveland, Grover, 178
Cline, John Valentine. *See* Valentine

Clinton, George, 25
Coastwise, Great Lakes and Inland Hull Association, 284
Cochrane, British admiral, 91
Coffin, Arthur Gilman, early career, 132; presidency, 132; encourages writing of fire risks, 136-137; urges extension of local agencies, 144, 147; discourages Chicago fire risks, 162, 163; resignation and death, 172
Collett, Captain John, first life-insurance policyholder, 44
Columbia Fire Company, 98
Columbian Insurance Company, 157
Congressional Committee on Merchant Marine and Fisheries, recommends postwar program of hull insurance, 270
Connor, John J., secretary and treasurer, 281
Constellation, 59
Constitution, 59
Continental Congress, 16
Continental Insurance Company, 220
Conyngham, David, 21, 30, 33, 74
Conyngham, Nesbitt & Company, first policyholder, 22, 74
Cooke, Jay, financier, 169
Cooke, Jay & Company, 159, 169
Cope, Francis R., director, 180
Cope, Thomas P., career, 22, 135; director, 125, 135, 136; death, 144
Copson, John, underwriter, 19-20
Cotton Engineering & Inspection Service, 241
Cotton Reinsurance Exchange, 239-241
Coulthard, William, clerk, 22, 31, 32, 33
Crawford, James M., assistant vice-president of Indemnity, 363
Crittenden, John J., 143
Curtin & Brockie, marine brokers, 187
Cushing, Caleb, 143
Custis, George Washington Parke, 122

Dacia, 250

Daladier, 345

Dale, Richard, director, 69

Dallas, Alexander James, stockholder, political career, 14, 28, 34, 92; promotes tontine, 14; writes petition for incorporation, 36

Dallas, Alexander James, Jr., 87

Damon, Herbert, Boston agent, 202-203, 256

Dancing Assembly, 14, 24, 35

Davenport, Arthur V., head of Automobile Department, 322, 361

Davis, William S., second vice-president, 171, 180

Davis & Reid, insurance agents, 100

Decatur, Captain Stephen, the elder, 60, 109

Declaration of Independence, 15, 16, 17

Declaration of War, Douglas Owen, 243

Deflation of 1921, 272-273

Delaware Breakwater, 120

Delaware Insurance Company, 69, 73, 85, 87, 129

Delaware-Le Croyable engagement, 60

Delaware Mutual Insurance Company, 156, 279

Delmonico Building, 236, 336

Depression of 1929, 289

Diemand, John Anthony, early career, 309-312, 354; vice-president of Indemnity, 307-308; adapts Rush's reform plan to casualty, 312-315; introduces casualty principles, 319-320; assigns credit for success, 321; elected president, 354; sesquicentennial address, 358-359; urges simplification of fire setup, 359

Division of Wartime Insurance of the Shipping Administration, organization, philosophy and practice, 369-370; appropriations, 370; as anti-inflation measure, 370

Dixon, Alexander J. Dallas, 267

Dollar, Captain Robert, 248

Dominick, Captain George, 50

Downing, Jerome F., early career, 155; manages Western department, 155; inaugurates daily reports, 155-

Downing, Jerome F.—*cont.*
156; favors Chicago risks, 163; advocates subsidiaries, 209, 268; urges public disavowal of San Francisco reductions, 225; retirement, 261

Drayton, John, head of Investment Department, 324, 365; vice-president, 327

Drew, Daniel, broker, 169

Dudley, Jephthah, Frankfort agent, 104

Dun & Bradstreet, 337, 338

DuPont Company, 265

Dwelly, Robert R., New York hull underwriter, 285

Eckert, Miles N., & Sons, Allentown agents, 339

Edmonds, George Washington, Congressman, 270

Eldredge, William, pilot, 56-57

Ellerbe, C. P., casualty underwriter, 308

Ellison, Eugene L., early career, 184; second vice-president in charge of fire, 183; vice-president of Alliance, 211; problems of San Francisco fire, 213, 216, 217, 220, 224; instructions to Catlin, 221-223; president, 231; death, 255

Elmslie, Alexander, director, 72

Enterprise Insurance Company, 165, 184

Episcopal Corporation, 44

Equitable Society of London, 44

Erie Canal, 135

Erie Railroad, 159

Erskine, Baron David Montague, British envoy to U. S., 84

Everett, Edward, 143

Ewing, James, Trenton agent, 106

Eyre & Massey, shipping firm, 287

Fall River fires, 330, 355

Farnum, Henry W., works with Rush on marine-loss investigation, 190, 201; heads New Business Department, 203; secretary of Alliance, 211; manager of New York office, 232, 256

Farnum, Henry W., (II), assistant secretary of marine, 364

Farrell, James A., 248

Fellowship Company, 41

Fidelity and Casualty Insurance Company, 309

Fidelity and Deposit Company of Maryland, 311

Fidelity Insurance Trust and Safe Deposit Company, 169, 170

Fire Association of Philadelphia, 143, 210, 226, 269

Fireman's Fund Insurance Company, 227-229

Fire Office of London, 40

Fisher, Samuel W., first secretary of Insurance Company of the State of Pennsylvania, 39

Fitch, John, mechanic, 133

Fitzsimons, Thomas, director, first president of Delaware Insurance. Company, 69

Florida, 153, 154, 156

Florida Treaty of 1819, *179*

Flying Cloud, 138

Ford, Henry, 311

Foster & Cole, Boston agents, 168

Fowler, John A., insurance historian, 145

France, Republic guillotines rulers and declares war, 27; offers safe-conduct to neutral ships, 28; friendship to U. S., 34, 46; seizes ships, 47, 48; break with U. S., 50-51; restrictions on commerce, 58; X Y Z papers, 59-60; war with U. S., 60; peace treaty, 61; conflict with England, 80; in World War I, 246, 250, 259; policy of concessions, 341, 342, 344; in World War II, 351, 352

Franco, General, 341

Franklin, Benjamin, 20; organizes fire companies and mutual company, 41, 85, 88, 99, 274

Franklin, P. A. S., 248

Franklin Insurance Company, 143

French Spoliation Claims, 68, 178, 179

Friedley, H. N., adjuster, 221, 223, 224

Friendship Company, 41

Fritz, Frederick, Reading agent, 109

Fry, John, Jr., director and London agent, 62, 65

Fryer, Greville E., secretary-treasurer, 211

Fulton, Robert, inventor of steamboat, 133

Gallatin, Albert, financier, 37, 91

Garrigues, William, fire surveyor, 42, 43

Gay, Captain Edward S., Southern Department manager, 171, 237

General Motors Corporation, 265

Gênet, Edmond, minister from France, 28, 34

George Tavern, 77

George W. Lochner, 174

Georgia Cotton Company, 237

German-American Insurance Company, 224-225

Germany, in World War I, 242, 245, 246, 248, 249, 250, 251, 252, 257, 258, 260; rearmament, 341; in World War II, 342, 344-346, 348, 350, 353, 354, 355, 356

Gibbons, Captain Edward, 175

Gibbs, Edwin C., Cincinnati agent, 283

Girard, Stephen, financier, French sympathizer, 34; opposes action on Jay Treaty, 49; on committee submitting memorial for reparations, 61; director of Union, 69; ransoms packet, 88; death, 128; founds Girard College, 132

Girard Bank, 128

Girard College, 132, 309, 354

Glemby case, 298-301

Glennie, A., London agent, 83, 84, 89-90

Glennie, Alexander, Son & Company, London agents, 115

Globe & Rutgers Insurance Company, 272

Gold Rush, 140-142

Good Intent Hose Company, 99

Grant, A. B., 346

Grant, Ulysses S., 169

Great Britain, government insurance business, 12, 248; seizes French vessels in Napoleonic Wars, 25; answers French safe-conduct offer, 29; seizes American shipping, 30-34; eases restrictions, 46; advantages of Jay Treaty, 47-48; Continental blockade, 58; adheres to Jay Treaty, 58; reparations, 58, 65, 67, 86; increasing friendship with U. S., 61-62; break with U. S., 66; supreme sea power, 68; conflict with France, 80; Orders in Council, 81, 84; refuses to ratify Erskine's pact, 84; increasing tension with U. S., 87; war declared, 87; land action in America, 91-92; treaty, 93; in World War I, 246, 248, 250, 259; policy of concessions, 341-342; in World War II, 342, 344-346, 351, 352, 353

Great Lakes Underwriting Syndicate, 284

Greene, General Nathanael, 57

Green Tree Company. *See* Mutual Assurance Company

Greer, 357

Grout, Jonathan, inventor, 85

Gulflight, 252

Haile Selassie, 341

Hamilton, Alexander, 17, 18, 27, 28, 47, 54

Hamilton, J. K., San Francisco special agent, 214

Hand-in-Hand Fire Company, 41

Hand-in-Hand Insurance Company. *See* Philadelphia Contributionship

Hardin, W. J., New Orleans agent, 238

Hartford Accident and Indemnity Company, 266

Hartford Convention, 93

Hartford Insurance Company, 210, 219, 220, 223, 224, 266, 284, 366

Haven, Joshua P., California agent, 142

Havens & Smith, shipping firm, 132

Haydock, Robert, plumber, casts fire marks, 42

Hazard, Ebenezer, early career, 12-14, 138; invites Blodget to extend tontine to Philadelphia, 12; personal appearance and tastes, 13; secretary of Tontine Association, 14; holds subscription book for stock, 17; secretary of the company, 18; manages office during epidemic, 31; correspondence, 31-34, 49, 64; dealings with Morris, 54-55, 72; office hours, 55-56; salary raise, 56; resignation, 71

Hazard, Nathan, 32

Hedge, William R., 271

Henry, Alexander T., career, 103; advocates expansion of western agencies, 103-104, 107; dies, 137

Henry, T. Charlton, vice-president in charge of fire, 180, 181, 183

Hibernia Fire Company, 41

High Court of Admiralty, 62, 66

Hill, James J., 248

Historical Collections, 13

Hitchcock, James E., assistant secretary, 361

Hitler, Adolf, 265, 331, 341, 345, 346, 348, 350, 351, 352, 353, 355, 356

Holland, 257, 352

Hollins, John, merchant, 97, 98

Home Indemnity Insurance Company, 312

Home Insurance Company, 223, 224, 307, 312, 346, 366

Hopkinson, Edward, Jr., director, 365

Hopkinson, Francis, 72

Hopkinson, Joseph, attorney, 72, 80, 120

Hopkinsville fire, 262

Hoxie, Joseph, 136

Hughes, Charles Evans, 261

Hull, Cordell, 358

Hunt, Jesse, Cincinnati agent, 104

Hunt, Jonathan, Pacific Coast Department Manager, 171

Illinois, 258

Indemnity Insurance Company of North America, organization and capitalization, 267; early premiums

Indemnity Insurance Co.—*cont.*

and losses, 268, 306-308, 312-316; heavy automobile line, 305, 306; problem of exceptional losses, 307, 312; policy, 316-317; unusual risks and new forms, 316-319, 338; no claims compromised, 320; ranking, 321, 331; encourages accident-prevention work, 362; wartime obligations, 362-363; war reserve, 363; civilian-defense policy, 363; assets in 1941, 365

Independence Hall, 15, 16, 17, 281

Industrial inventions and innovations, 158-159

Ingersoll, Jared, attorney, 26, 71, 72

Inland Marine Underwriters Association, 285, 291, 294, 301-302

Inskeep, John, career, 72, 77-78; president, 77; hopes to avoid war, 80-81; opinion of embargo, 82-83; correspondence with British agents, 83, 84, 89-90, 92; fortifies company finances, 85; appoints western agents, 104; personal responsibility, 104-105; correspondence with agents, 105-109; insists on fire-preventive measures, 108; prepares for peacetime marine problems, 110-113; salary increase, 114; works for payment of foreign claims, 116; recognition of services in French indemnity, 119; resignation and retirement, 120-121

Insurance

Development of:

lotteries, 13; private "underwriting," 19; consideration of moral hazard, 107; reinsurance policy, 129-130; unearned premium reserve introduced, 130; valued policies, 181; regional rate control, 181; anti-compact law, 181-182; syndicates, 239, 271-272, 349; subsidiary system, 268-270; multiple-line coverage, 332, 333, 334, 336, 348-349

Automobile:

development of underwriting,

Insurance, Automobile—*cont.*

303, 304; moral risk problem, 306; automobile finance business problems, 361

Casualty:

development, 267-268, 303, 305; growth of incorporated casualty annexes, 266; items of field, 267; fights inland marine, 290-291; employer's liability, 310; volume of underwriting, 311, 312, 320-321; difference of claims from fire and marine, 319-320; flexibility, 336

Fire:

history of insurance and prevention, 40-41; headquarters in Philadelphia, 13-14; early competitors, 18; relationship to fire companies, 41; and hose companies, 98-99, 100; fire prevention, 98, 108-109; new factors in risk, 121; state supervision, 130; state investigations, 261; rates raised after San Francisco, 261

Inland Marine:

development, 266; risks, 283; modern meaning of, 285, 286; relation to marine, 286; problems of transportation risks, 288; factors promoting underwriting, 290; opposed by fire and casualty, 290-291; motor-truck business menaced, 295; hazards of jewelry coverage, 298

Life:

tontines, 11-12; history, 44; pioneer projects in Boston and Philadelphia, 11, 14; New York legislature investigation, 261

Marine:

early headquarters in Philadelphia, 13-14; history, 19; private underwriting in America, 20-21; boom, 68; center of marine underwriting shifts, 112; strength of Philadelphia underwriters, 119; as aristocracy of underwriting, 138; after the

Insurance, Marine—*cont.*
    Civil War, 157; marine com-
    panies decrease after war, 273;
    fluctuation of rates during World
    War II, 345, 346, 349, 351-352,
    353, 355, 367, 368, 370
American companies:
    "Insurance Row," 73; expect
    spoliation claims, 113; in panic
    of 1837, 127-129; mutualiza-
    tion, 129; comparative assets,
    130; after St. Louis fire, 137-
    138; westward expansion, 144;
    war rates raised, 150; postwar
    marine slump, 157, 161; in Chi-
    cago, 163; losses in Chicago fire,
    164-165; affected by Boston fire,
    168; rate war during 1873 panic,
    172; competition curbed, 182;
    problem of brokerage rates, 183;
    regional associations, 208; expect
    little fire damage in San Francis-
    co, 212; reaction to San Fran-
    cisco fire, 214-220; New York
    meeting, 222-223; publicity,
    223; Oakland meeting, 223-224;
    relative settlements, 226-227;
    effect of *Titanic* disaster, 232;
    fight North America's cotton re-
    forms, 238; agents limited by re-
    gional conferences, 268; compe-
    tition on cargo rates, 272; in-
    crease in premiums from 1900,
    280; resume river risks, 283; de-
    velop casualty writing, 303; dur-
    ing the depression, 325; prepare
    for cancellation of British rein-
    surance, 346; in World War II,
    349; undertake storage risks,
    355; ownership and ownership-
    and-management groups, 366
English companies:
    early underwriters, 19; competi-
    tion with Americans, 20; nature
    of risks, 21; send agents here in
    peacetime, 112; reason for pros-
    perous marine underwriting,
    160; weed out American fire
    risks, 166-167; at beginning of
    World War I, 245; lead postwar

Insurance, English companies—*cont.*
    boom, 254; establish casualty an-
    nexes, 266; cut rates below syn-
    dicates, 271; press for settlement
    of inland-marine problem, 291;
    forced to agreement by I. M. U.
    A., 301-302; multiple-line char-
    ters, 332, 333, 334; argue against
    shock-loss backlog, 342; stiffen
    rates, 347
Insurance Company of North Amer-
    ica
Reflection of National Events:
    company organized in early years
    of Republic, 15; stand in Napo-
    leonic wars, 28-29; supports
    Washington on Jay Treaty, 48;
    in campaign to secure British
    reparations, 48-49; writes war-
    risk insurance, 49-50; interest
    in *Mount Vernon* case, 51; ac-
    tion against Robert Morris, 55,
    67, 71-72; "settling agents" ap-
    pointed, 58, 62, 63; suspends war
    risks on French vessels, 60;
    French Spoliation Claims assumed
    by government, 61; memorial to
    Congress, 61; contribution to
    embargo victims, 82; suspends
    writing marine risks, 84; during
    the embargo, 84-87; studies proj-
    ects for decreasing navigation
    hazards, 85; claims against U. S.
    and other nations, 86; during the
    War of 1812, 89-91; postwar ex-
    pansion, 93-94; westward exten-
    sion, 96, 103-104; first national
    advertising, 104; normal activi-
    ties resumed, 113; problems of
    peace, 111-113; in the 1819 de-
    pression, 115; expects French
    Spoliation Claims, 115, 116, 143;
    claims against Spain, 116-117;
    claims assumed by U. S., 117;
    meets monopolistic legislation,
    121-122; during panic of 1833,
    124; part of French claims paid,
    125; during panic of 1837, 127-
    129; policy of reinsurance, 130-
    131; conservative transportation

Insurance Company of North America—*cont.*

Reflection of National Events—*cont.*

risks, 133-134; during Mexican War, 139; during the Gold Rush, 141-142; faces difficulties of general expansion, 144; in panic of 1857, 146; preparations for war, 147; during the Civil War, 149-156; offers financial assistance to bank, 169; war on insurance pirates, 174, 176; foreign competition, 176-177; settlement of French claims, 178-179; during panic of 1893, 185; sponsors organization of corporation, 209-210; during the San Francisco disaster, 212-227; reforms cotton insurance, 235-239; supports Allies, 244; operations in first months of war, 251; wartime rate policy, 254-255; refuses to retire from war-risk market, 258; business during war, 260; postwar expansion, 265-270; in the deflation of 1921, 273; studies science of loss-prevention, 274-277; first advertising campaign, 280; aids formation of rating organization, 284-285; during the depression of 1929, 324-328; receives German reparations, 329; goal of multiple-line writing, 336-338; nature of war participation, 349; sesquicentennial, 357-358; first air-borne cargo war-risk loss, 367

Corporate Structure:
Resolution of organization, 16; "Plan" of capitalization submitted and adopted, 16-17, 18; fight for charter of incorporation, 36-39; charter granted, 39; encroachments on capital, 69; capital restored, 76; reputation of stock, 79; postwar surplus, 113; surplus policy, 118; capital tapped and restored, 119; guards capital account, 125; shrinking

Insurance Company of North America—*cont.*

Corporate Structure—*cont.*
surplus, 127-128; reduction of shares to par, 128-129; retains joint-stock form, 130; surplus increase, 130; mutualization suggested, 139, 142; shares restored to former par, 143; capital increased, 143, 170, 171, 177, 231, 263, 267, 323, 325; first subsidiary organized, 209; more subsidiaries organized, 268-270; holding company formed, 269; assets in 1941, 364; assets of subsidiaries in 1941, 364; assets of North America group, 366

Administration:
election of officers and directors, 17-18; bookkeeping, 23; board meetings suspended during epidemic, 30-31; office routine, 35; office hours, 55; adopts seal, 56; changes in personnel, 71-72; administrative improvements, 85; contributions for volunteer and relief work, 150; hundredth-year review, 184; bookkeeping classifications, 189; stockholders fear San Francisco assessment, 220; promotions during war, 256; Engineering Department established, 278-279; issues two reports, 325; training school and "homesteading," 340; 150th Annual Statement, 364-366; Executive Committee for 1941, 365

Offices:
at 119 South Front Street, 18, 21-22; project for building, 24, 35; at 107 South Front Street, 35, 73; at 98 South Second Street, 73; 40 Walnut Street, 86; sixth home, at Walnut and Dock Streets, 125; at 60 Walnut Street, 143; eighth home, 173; at Sixteenth and Arch Streets, 279-280; new building, 280-

Insurance Company of North America—*cont.*

Offices—*cont.*
281; company museum, 281-282; office buildings in New York and San Francisco, 282

Local agencies:
beginning, 96-98; Charleston experiment, 100; argument against, 101, 103; functions, 104; western agents appointed, 104; instructions issued, 105-107; prove worth, 107; threatened by legislation, 121; mode of payment, 122; agencies spread risks, 144; loss of Southern agencies expected, 147; Southern business cancelled, 150-151; Civil War expansion, 151; administrative decentralization, 155; Pennsylvania State Central Agency and Western Department organized, 155; Eastern and New York State Departments organized, 161; agents' commissions raised, 161; Southern and Pacific Coast Departments organized, 171; growth of local agency system, 171; expenses of local agents, 182; expense percentage of premiums, 182-183; Western Marine Department established, 284; abolishes Eastern Department and reorganizes Southern Department, 336; New York organization consolidated, 336-337; Western Department abolished, 338; service offices established, 338; family agencies, 339; service offices as fiduciary agents of War Damage Corporation, 360-361

Automobile Insurance:
early underwriting, 304-305; Automobile Department established, 305, 306; valued policies dropped, 306; growing profits, 306; increased coverage, 322-323

Insurance Company of North America—*cont.*

Fire:
investigation of fire insurance, 40; fire underwriting voted, 42; first policies, 42-43; first month's premiums, 43; first fire advertising, 43; rising premiums on fire, 43; expanding business, 67; fire branch encouraged, 85; growing profits, 95; fire prevention, 98, 162; profits, 107; kind of risks written, 107; prestige items, 109; larger source of income, 114; line of New York risks rejected, 136; business grows, 136; loss in New York fire, 136; losses in St. Louis fire, 137; losses in Philadelphia fire, 143; largest single loss up to 1852, 144; reconsiders concentration aspect of fire risks, 144; expansion of fire business, 151; early effect of war on fire business, 151; expansion, 155; during postwar boom, 161; increasing disasters, 161-162; supports cause of professional fire departments, 162; losses in Chicago fire, 163; settlements, 164, 165; effects of Chicago fire, 165-167; publicity about Boston fire losses, 168; effect of Boston fire, 168; during 1873 panic, 170; keeps abreast of times, 208; problem of rate-cutting, 209; shock losses in 1904, 210; effect of Baltimore fire, 211; during San Francisco fire crisis, 212-227; San Francisco losses, 226; during World War I, 262-264; business increased by casualty business, 268; Fire Engineering Department established, 277; increase in fire revenue, 277; work toward elimination of coinsurance, 278; improvement of school risks, 278; during the depression, 329-330; shock losses in 1927 and 1934, 330; agitation for streamlining, 331-334, 335-

Insurance Company of North Amer-
     ica—*cont.*

  Fire—*cont.*
     336,358-359;extended-cover en-
     dorsement, 336; charter amend-
     ment for writing participating
     fire policies, 340; business during
     1941, 359-360
  Inland Marine:
     attitude toward river transporta-
     tion risks, 132-133; river-risks
     agency, 133; instructions on riv-
     er risks, 134; classification of in-
     land marine risks, 285-286; rev-
     enue, 286; early floaters and poli-
     cies, 286-287; growing premi-
     ums, 287-289; comprehensive
     transportation policy, 288-289;
     motor-truck policies, 288-289;
     classes of risks, 289-290; defini-
     tion, 291; first bridge risks, 293;
     Tacoma Narrows shock loss,
     294; motor-truck business, 294-
     296; fight against highjackers,
     295; jewelry business, 297-298;
     reduction of reinsurance, 302
  Life:
     included in "Plan," 18; branch
     ignored, 18; experiments with
     policies, 44-45; promotion ig-
     nored, 45; life insurance re-
     sumed, 356
  Marine:
     concentration on marine risks,
     18; first policies, 22-23; early
     rates, 35-36; policy of dividing
     risks, 51; projects to reduce local
     marine hazards, 56-57, 119-120;
     business develops with merchant
     marine, 138-139; war clause add-
     ed to marine policies, 149; Platt's
     policy of avoiding raiders, 153;
     losses to Confederate raiders,
     153-154; after the Civil War,
     157, 160; marine business during
     panic of 1873, 170; the *L. E.
     Cann* case, 174-176; unprofita-
     ble business, 176-178, 185-186;
     attempt to find causes, 185;
     Rush's analysis of marine losses,

Insurance Company of North Amer-
     ica—*cont.*

  Marine—*cont.*
     194-199; formula proves suc-
     cessful, 207; reinsurance agree-
     ment with San Francisco, 227;
     during panic of 1907, 231; loss
     on *Titanic*, 232; adopts more
     rigid inspection of marine risks,
     232, 234; first marine-insurance
     syndicate, 239-240; no prece-
     dent for war-risk policies, 242;
     schedule of war-risk rates, 249;
     no risks on German-bound ship-
     ping, 250; avoidance of raiders,
     251; Marine Loss Department,
     256; postwar marine business,
     273-274; Marine Service Depart-
     ment, 274, 328; inspection of
     packing and shipping methods,
     276; Great Lakes business, 284;
     during the depression, 328-329;
     rates reflect European events,
     341, 344, 345; staff directing
     war-loss, 364; Pacific shock loss,
     367-368; exchange subscription
     increased, 369

  Investments:
     Turnpike Company stock, 53;
     own shares, 53; lottery subscrip-
     tions, 53; bottomry and respon-
     dentia loans, 53-54, 114; Bank
     of Pennsylvania shares, 54;
     United States bonds, 65, 85, 91;
     stock of other companies, 85;
     standing Committee on Finance
     appointed, 85; western securities,
     96; investment income after War
     of 1812, 112-113; change in in-
     vestments, 123-124; invest-
     ments in early steam projects,
     135; motives for investments,
     135; first railroad shares, 135-
     136; Investment Department
     created, 323; conservative poli-
     cy, 323; security values during
     1929 depression, 324-327; port-
     folio changes during depression,
     325; investment reaction to New

Insurance Company of North America—*cont.*
Investments—*cont.*
Deal, 327; security values in 1941, 364; portfolio changes in 1941, 365
Receipts and Losses:
first month's premiums, 26; in 1793, 29, 35; in 1794, 52; in 1795, 52; in 1796, 53; in 1797, 59, 101; in 1798, 60; 1799, 60, 65; 1800, 60, 65; in 1801, 60, 65; in 1802, 66, 103; in 1803, 66; in 1804, 66; in 1805, 75; in 1806, 79; in 1807, 84; in 1808-11, 87; in 1812, 107; in 1813, 91; in 1814, 91; in 1815, 93; in 1816, 114; in 1817, 114; in 1818, 114; in 1822, 109; during Gold Rush, 141; in 1863, 154; in 1864, 155; in 1873, 170; during World War I, 255, 257, 259; during World War II, 351, 353; of fire branch, 123, 139, 161, 185, 210, 262; of marine branch, 139, 195-197, 205-206, 251, 363-364
Dividends:
in 1793, 29, 35; in 1794 and 1795, 52; in 1796 and 1797, 53; in 1798, 1799, 1800, 1801 and 1802, 65; in 1805, 75; in 1806, 76, 79; in 1808, 86; in 1809, 1810 and 1811, 87; in 1812, 87, 89; in 1816, 113; in 1817, 113-114; in 1818, 114; in 1819, 1820, 1821 and 1822, 115; in 1824, 118-119; in 1825, 119; in 1829, 1830 and 1831, 120, 123; in 1832, 123, 125; in 1833, 1834, 1835, 1836 and 1837, 125; in 1839, 128; in 1842, 129; in 1844, 1845 and 1846, 139; in 1847 and 1848, 142; in 1856, 1857, 1858 and 1859, 146; in 1861, 149; in 1862, 151; in 1863, 154; in 1872, 165; in 1873, 168; in 1874, 170, 171; in 1892, 184; in 1906, 227; in 1916, 1917, 1918 and 1919, 263;

Insurance Company of North America—*cont.*
Dividends—*cont.*
in 1933 and 1935, 327; in 1941, 365
Insurance Company of the State of Pennsylvania, organization and incorporation, 38-39; officers and directors, 39; in *Mount Vernon* case, 51; joint memorial for reparations, 61; retains joint-stock form, 130, 156, 334
International Mercantile Marine, 248
Interstate Underwriters Board, 291
International Union of Marine Insurance, 342
Interstate Commerce Commission, 181, 288
Irada, 239
Italy, in World War I, 246, 250; in World War II, 341, 347

Jackson, General Andrew, 92, 93, 111, 117, 124, 125, 127
Jackson, Francis James, British envoy to U. S., 84
James-Manchester Company, Cleveland agency, 155
Japan, in World War I, 243, 253; in World War II, 341, 344, 353, 356, 357, 358
Jaudon, Samuel, merchant, 117
Jay, John, 46, 47
Jay's Treaty, 47, 48, 49
Jeffcott, Captain W. R., marine surveyor, 255, 275
Jefferson, Thomas, 16, 18, 27, 30, 48, 79, 80, 81, 82, 83
Jewell, Marshall, 164
Johnson, C. W., 277
Johnson, W. N., second Western Department manager, 261
Johnson & Higgins, New York brokers, 232, 256, 347
Johnston, J. C., adjuster, 221, 223, 224
Jones, John Paul, 69, 94
Jones, Samuel W., director, 173
Jones, Walter R., 131

Kaiser Wilhelm der Grosse, 249
Kansas-Nebraska Bill, 146
Kearney, 357
Kearsarge, the U. S. S., 156
Keegan, John C., 291
Keith, Samuel, director, 69
Kellogg Pact, 265
Kenney, 56
Kentucky, demonstrates danger of state interference with insurance rates, 262
Kimball, C. C., Eastern Department manager, 161
Kingsland munitions disaster, 263
Kingston, Stephen, Spanish agent, 116, 117
Knowles, Charles R., New York State Department manager, 161
Kremer, John, vice-president, secretary, 291; experience in fire branch, 292; succeeds Catlin, 334
Kronprincessin Cecilie, 247
Kronprinz Wilhelm, 247
Kurusu, Saburo, 358

Laird, Carroll W., assistant secretary, 362
L'Ambuscade, 28
Lancaster, 135
Lassley, John, merchant, 133
Latimer, George, 38
Laval, Pierre, 344
League of Nations, 265, 341
Leamy, John, director, 21, 23, 36, 116
L. E. Cann, 174-176
Lee, Peter, Pennsylvania agent, 104
Lee, General Robert E., 154, 156
Legrand, Claudius F., 43
L'Enfant, Major, 11, 101
Levison, Jacob B., 227-229
Lewis, John F., & Company, 287
Lewis, Ludwig, C., vice-president, early career, 287; builds up inland-marine account, 287-289; secures British reinsurance agreements, 288, 301; ambition for company, 289; helps form I. M. U. A., 291; encourages bridge and motor-truck business, 292-295; extends protection on valuables, 297; promotions,

Lewis, Ludwig C.—*cont.*
301; reorganizes Western Department, 338; opens service offices, 338; handles heavy factory fire accounts, 360
Lewis, Mordecai, first president of Insurance Company of the State of Pennsylvania, 39
Lightning, 138
Lincoln, Abraham, 146, 148, 149, 150
Little Belt-President incident, 87
Livingston, Edward, 143
Lloyd, Edward, 19
Lloyd's of London, 19, 160, 246, 288, 297
London Coffee House, 20
London, Liverpool and Globe Insurance Company, 219, 220, 224
Louisiana Purchase, 79, 81, 96
Lucas, G. Brinton, marine secretary, 364
Lusitania, 252

McAdoo, William Gibbs, 248, 253
Maccabe, Fred, 346, 353
McCall, Archibald, director, 21, 39
McConnell, Matthew, director, 14, 18
McCoy, John, Chillicothe agent, 104
McDowell, Dr. John, Ohio agent, 104
MacKenzie, James, London agent, 83, 84
Macy, C. Curtis, 291
Madison, James, 83, 90
Maginot Line, 344, 351, 352
Maine, 303
Manhattan, 356
Marine and Fire Insurance Company of Philadelphia, 71, 73, 129
Maris, Mathias, secretary, 168
Maritime Commission, 343, 356, 369
Marshall, John, 102
Martin, Dr. Truman J., first automobile-policyholder, 303, 308
Mason, Senator from Virginia, 47
Maxcy, Josiah, Maine agent, 339
Maxcy, Josiah, & Sons Company, 339
Meade, General George G., 154
Meinke, A. W., assistant secretary of Indemnity, 362

Mercantile Mutual Insurance Company, 136
Merchants' Coffee House, 112
Merritt Committee of New York, recommendations, 261-262
Mifflin, Samuel, 109, 115, 133
Mifflin, Thomas, 39, 72
Miller, D. P., Cumberland agent, 339
Miller, D. P., (II), 339
Miller, R. Bruce, heads Marine Service Department, 276; second in charge of Inland Marine Department, 298, 301; assistant secretary, 301
Modjeski, Ralph, bridge engineer, 292
Monroe, James, 46, 47, 48, 51
Montoswald, 233-234
Moore, Thomas L., director, 18
Morris, Galloway C., career, 256; heads Marine Loss Department, 239, 243; third vice-president in charge of marine, 256
Morris, Robert, organizes Bank of North America, 20; career and speculations, 54, 71; financial difficulties, 54-55, 74; in debtor's prison, 67, 101; company takes action against, 67; payment of company debt, 72; honored by hose company, 99
Morrow, John W., 346
Morse, Jedediah, geographer, 31
Mount Vernon-Flying Fish case, 50-51, 53
Mount Vernon policy, 102, 281
Moylan, Jasper, director, 14, 18, 24
Munson, George S., director, 365
Mussolini, 341, 345, 353
Mutual Assurance Society, 41, 78, 143

National Association of Marine Underwriters, 177, 178
National Board of Fire Underwriters, 166, 171, 172, 181, 208
National Cash Register Company, 203-204
National Convention of Insurance Commissioners, 312
National Fire Protection Association, 211

National Security Fire Insurance Company of Omaha, 269, 270, 293, 365
Neare, Captain George W., insurance agent, 283
Neare, Gibbs & Company, river agents, 283
Neptune Hose Company, 99
Nesbitt, John Maxwell, early career, 16-17; promotes tontine, 14; heads committee investigating project of insurance company, 16; organizer of Bank of North America, 16; elected director and president, 18; on committee to plan new building, 24; leaves Philadelphia during epidemic, 30; visits Philadelphia, 33; voted salary, 35; salary increase, 56; resignation, 57; death, 74
Neutrality Act, 342, 351, 357, 358
Neuville, Baron de, minister from France, 109
New Deal, 312, 327
New Orleans Dock Board, 238
New York Board of Marine Underwriters, 149
New York Central Railroad, 159
New York Curb Exchange, 327
New York fires, 122, 136
New York Insurance Office, 20
New York Journal of Commerce, 225, 245, 246, 357
New York Stock Exchange, 169, 245
New York Underwriters, 210
Nixon, Henry, stockholder, 133
North America, 175, 274
North America Almanac, 162, 163
Northern Pacific Railroad, 159, 169

Ohio Life Insurance Company, 145
Oldden, James, director, 72
Old Insurance Office, 20
O'Leary, Jeremiah, 163
Owen, Douglas, 243

Palmer, Clarence A., advertising manager, 281-282
Panic of 1819, 114-115
Panic of 1837, 126, 127, 130, 136
Panic of 1857, 145, 146
Panic of 1873, 169-170, 171

Pass & Stow, metal-working firm,
42
Peale, Charles Willson, 57
Pearl Harbor attack, 358
Penn, William, 19
Pennsylvania, credit, 127; insolvency,
128-129; regulates insurance, 170;
creates state department of insur-
ance, 172
Pennsylvania Fire Insurance Company, 209
Pennsylvania Railroad, 135-136, 144,
154, 158, 159
Perot, Elliston, merchant, 62
Perot, James, Bermuda agent, 62
Perot, John, merchant, 62
Perot, William, Bermuda agent, 62
Perrin, Edwin J., 291
Pettit, Andrew, director, acting president, 76
Pettit, Colonel Charles, early career,
57; director, 18; gives porter, 22;
on committee to plan new building,
24; president, 57; urges insurance
companies to request reparations,
61; correspondence with Fry, 65-
66; financial report to Savage, 69-
70; fights to keep company intact,
70-71; leave of absence, 73; works
off losses, 74; plans Baltimore fire
agency, 97-98; extends fire insurance to Washington, 101-102;
death, 76
Phenix Insurance Company of Brooklyn, 222
Philadelphia, first seat of government,
14; yellow fever epidemic, 30-34;
commercial supremacy threatened,
79; fortifies against British, 92; decline as port, 111, 112; artificial
harbor, 120; financial capital, 127;
bank difficulties, 127; bank run of
1838, 127-129; fire, 142; fortifies
against Confederates, 154
Philadelphia & Lancaster Turnpike
Company, 53
Philadelphia Board of Trade, warns
against weak companies, 145
Philadelphia Casualty Company, 309,
310, 311

Philadelphia Contributionship, 41,
143
Philadelphia Fire and Marine Insurance Company, 269, 270, 293, 298,
365
Philadelphia Fire Association, 99
Philadelphia Hose Company, 99
Philadelphia Insurance Company, 69,
73, 129
Philadelphia Underwriters, 209, 210,
213, 226, 269
Phoenix Insurance Company, capitalization and charter, 69; offices, 73;
as a company stockholder, 75-76;
sells own stock, 85; mutualization,
129; first news of Alabama, 151;
at the Chicago fire, 164; increases
agencies, 209-210
Phoenix of London, 100
Pierce, Franklin, 143
Pinckney, C. C., 51
Platt, Charles, early career, 140, 152-
153; characteristics, 173, 180; secretary, 153; stratagem to avoid
Semmes, 153; salary increase, 156;
vice-president, 160; acting president, 160; correspondence with
Chicago agents, 164-165; president, 172; in Association of Marine
Underwriters, 177; notation on
marine losses, 185-186; undertakes
constructive policy for marine
branch, 187; persuaded to support
Rush's reforms, 190, 191, 201;
president of Alliance, 211; during
San Francisco fire, 212; statement
of company's policy, 213, 214, 216;
disavowal of partial settlements,
225-226; correspondence with Levison, 227-229; advocates multiple-
line coverage, 229; resumes river
risks, 283; disapproves of automobile insurance, 304; death, 230-231
Platt, John O., special agent at Baltimore fire, 210-211; promotions,
230; senior vice-president, 256; in
charge of fire branch, 261; organizes engineering department, 277;
policy, 330; president, 334; sim-
plifies administration of fire busi-

Platt, John O.—*cont.*
    ness, 335-337; vice-chairman of the Board, 354
Platt, William A., second vice-president in marine branch, 180; vice-president, 183-184; death, 187
Platt, Yungman & Company, brokers, 305
Polk, James K., 143
Port Arthur attack, 243
Potts, Samuel I., Washington agent, 109
Poyntell, William, director, 85
Presbyterian Ministers' Fund, 44
Prinz Eitel Friedrich, 251
Proclamation of Neutrality, 27, 28, 46
Providence Washington Insurance Company, 291

Queen Insurance Company, 210, 223

Randolph, Edmund, 48, 51
Ratshillar, Antoine, blacksmith, 73
Rawle, Francis, 20
Reconstruction Finance Corporation, 312, 326
Reed, Andrew, 337
Reed, Henry H., New York general manager, 337; works toward multiple-line coverage, 337-338; advisor to Maritime Commission, 343
Reed & Pettit, merchant-underwriters, 337
Reeves, Charles H., special agent, 164, 165
Reuben James, 357
Rife, R. Jones, Duncannon agent, 291, 292
Robert Morris Hose Company, 99
Roberts, Calvin, assistant vice-president of Indemnity, 321
Roberts, Mrs. Maurice, 116
Robin Moore, 356
Rockefeller, John D., 158
Roosevelt, Franklin D., 272, 312, 326, 343, 351, 355
Ross, Andrew, Washington agent, 101, 102, 107, 108, 109
Ross, John, director, 18

Ross' Wharf, 22, 28
Royal Insurance Company, 210, 220, 224
Runnells & Manchester, Cleveland agency, 155
Rush, Dr. Benjamin, 31, 32, 188
Rush, Benjamin, early career and characteristics, 187-188, 204; assistant to the president, 187; begins investigation of marine losses, 189-191; discovers poor risks and increases classifications, 190; recommends abandonment of foreign marine agencies, 191; reports analysis of marine profits and losses, 192-199; second vice-president in charge of marine, 200; reorganizes marine branch, 200-201; originates contingency commission, 202-203; establishes New Business Department, 203; organizes Alliance and acts as vice-president, 211; senior vice-president, 231; reforms cotton underwriting and handling, 235-239; inserts war exclusion clause in marine policies, 243; formulates company's war policy, 243-244; expects German commerce raiding, 249; studies submarine tactics, 252; opinion of Government Bureau, 253; president, 255; refuses to retire from war-risk market, 258; policy of fire settlements, 263-264; advocates multiple-line underwriting, 266, 371; helps form Syndicates, 271; chairman of Board of Managers, 272; plans for new building, 280; encourages inland-marine business, 286-287; persuades Platt to write automobile insurance, 304; gives account to brokers, 305; appoints casualty executive, 307, 312; anticipates stock-market crash, 323-324; statement of fire problems, 331-334; resigns presidency, 334; chairman of the Board, 334; introduces Indemnity merit ratings, 340; influences preparations for 1939 crisis, 348; re-elected chairman of the Board, 354

Rush, Benjamin, Jr., vice-president of Indemnity, 321; reorganizes agency system, 339; transferred to Indemnity underwriting, 339
Rush, Charlotte, 242
Rush, Richard, 188
Rush, Colonel Richard Henry, 188
Rush, Stockton, agency secretary, 339; in charge of apprentices, 339-340
Russell, Jonathan, 91
Russia, in Russo-Japanese war, 243; in World War I, 242, 245; in World War II, 344, 348, 349, 355, 356

St. Louis, 246
St. Louis fire, 137
St. Louis tornado, 330
San Francisco fire, 211-212
Sansom, William, director, 53
Savage, William, Jamaica agent, 69, 70, 82
Savannah, 133
Scandinavia, in World War I, 248, 250, 251, 253, 257; in World War II, 352
Sea Insurance Company, 194, 240
Securities Company of North America, 269
Semmes, Raphael, 152, 153
Serbia, in World War I, 242, 245
Shenandoah, 156
Sherman, John, Senator from Ohio, 158
Sherman Anti-Trust Law, 181
Sherrerd, Henry D., secretary, 132, 142; suggests war exclusion clause, 148; president of Insurance Company of State of Pennsylvania, 148
Shipping, in the Napoleonic wars, 49, 60, 63-64, 80; boom, 68, 78; during the War of 1812, 88-89; postwar trade, 110-111; increase of merchant marine, 125; river traffic, 133; steam transportation, 133; clipper ships, 138; during the gold rush, 140-142; after the Civil War, 157-160; of cotton, 235, 238; during World War I, 245-251, 252,

Shipping—*cont.*
256-259; in the postwar period, 270-274; steamboat boom, 283; no boom during early World War II, 351
Shipping Board, 271, 343
Smith, Bradford, fire secretary, 360
Smith, Captain, marine surveyor, 35
Smith, John Correy, early career, 121; director, 120; president, 121; liberalizes fire policy, 122; introduces increasing excess in hand, 123; reduces salary, 128; sponsors reinsurance, 131; death, 132
Smith, Marshall J., New Orleans agent, 237, 238
Smith, T. Leaming, Automobile clerk, 256; marine secretary, 256; supervises Marine Service Department, 274; recommends Diemand, 307; advises increase of war-risk rates, 342; in charge of marine war risks, 364
Smith, William, apothecary, 121
Smith, the Reverend William, 44
Southern Surety Company, 312
South Memphis Terminal, 238
Spain, Government of, 58, 63, 341
Spanish-American War, 204
Spectator, 168, 247, 249, 304
Spee, Admiral von, 249, 251
Stalin, Josef, 348
Stannard, Captain G., 233-234
Stannard, Mrs. Lizzie, 233-234
Staples, Philip C., director, 365
Stellwagen, Herbert P., executive vice-president of Indemnity, 321
Stephens, Robert S., secretary, 72, 117, 121
Stevens, Horace B., El Paso agent, 339
Stevens, Philip C., El Paso agent, 339
Stewardson & Page, architects, 280
Stewart, General Walter, director, 14, 18, 52
Stotesbury, Captain Arthur, surveyor of vessels, 94
Stow, John, metal-worker, 42
Stuart, Gilbert, 57
Stuyvesant, Pieter, 41

Sully, Thomas, 98, 282
Swanwick, John, director, 34, 37, 39
Syndicate A, 271
Syndicate B, 271
Syndicate C, 271-272, 343, 347, 348

Tacoma Narrows Bridge, 294
Tate, William, Nashville agent, 104
Taylor, Charles, director, 173
Thames & Mersey Marine Insurance
  Company, 194, 346
Thorn, Henry, early career, 347; New
  York marine manager, 337; on A. I.
  M. U. committee, 346; vice-chair-
  man of Reinsurance Exchange,
  347-348, 367; expects America's
  entry into war, 357
Thorn Committee, 347, 349-350, 352,
  367
Tilghman, Edward, attorney, 26, 27
Titanic, 232
Toby, Simeon, 334
Tonti, Lorenzo, 12
Travelers Insurance Company, 303,
  308, 309
Treaty of Alliance, 27, 28
Treaty of Ghent, 93
Trotter, Nathan, director, 180
Trotter, William H., director, 180
Tuckett, Captain Harvey G. P., actu-
  ary and publisher, 145
Tuckett's Monthly Insurance Journal,
  144; campaign against irresponsible
  companies, 145

Union City holdup, 295-296
Union Fire Company, 41, 99
Union Insurance Company, 69, 70,
  73, 129, 156
Union Pacific Railroad, 159
United States, 59
United States, effect of Napoleonic
  wars on, 45-48; treaty with France,
  61; assumes French Spoliation
  Claims, 61; debt to the company,
  68; embargo and effects, 81-83;
  non-intercourse act, 83; Madison's
  proclamation, 83-84; settlement of
  the west, 95-96; Civil War inflation, 159; at war with Germany,

United States—*cont.*
  258; organizes insurance syndicates,
  271-272; in the insurance business,
  343; defense preparations, 355; declares war, 358; introduces new
  philosophy of premium construction, 362; marine war-risk business,
  369; differences between 1914 and
  1942 government insurance agencies, 369-370
United States Insurance Company, 73,
  129
United States Lloyd's, 194, 232, 240,
  304
United States Salvage Association, 271
Universal Tontine Association, prospects and promotion, 14; meetings
  of subscribers, 15, 16

Van Dam, Anthony, clerk of New
  York Insurance Office, 20
Vanderbilt, Cornelius, 158, 159
Vanderbilt, Franklin, casualty man-
  ager, 322, 337
Valentine, porter, 22, 31, 33, 56, 73,
  117
Verrinder, William, investigator, 296,
  300
Vigilancia, 258

Wallace, Thomas, Lexington agent,
  104, 105
Wallace, William, vice-president of
  Boston Insurance Company, 304
Waln, William, director, 72
War against Mexico, 139
War Damage Corporation, 360, 361
Warfield, Edwin, governor of Mary-
  land, 311
War of 1812, early effect on marine
  insurance, 66; wartime stimulation
  of trade, 78; tension between Eng-
  land and U. S. increases, 87; dec-
  laration of war, 87; American ac-
  tion on sea and land, 88; British ac-
  tion, 91-92; peace, 93
Warren, Donald, Boston associate
  manager, 364
Warriner, Samuel D., director, 365
Washington, Bushrod, 102, 103

Washington, George, 12, 13, 25, 27, 28, 30, 46, 47-48, 51-52, 72, 103
Washington Insurance Company, 129
Washington *National Intelligencer*, 108
Wayne, Joseph, Jr., director, 365
Webster, Daniel, 117, 143
Welles, Gideon, 151, 152
Welsh, John Lowber, director, 180
Welsh, William, director, 172
Wharton, John, director, 77
White, Ambrose, director, 173
White, J. Chester, company's first Civil War soldier, 150
White, Norman, special agent, 292
Wight, Colonel Ed L., Southern Department manager, 237
Wight & Butt, 237, 364
Willing, Thomas, financier, 38
Willing & Francis, mercantile firm, 51
Wilson, Woodrow, 244, 265
Winsor, James D., Jr., director, 365
Winter, William D., 347, 348
Winthrop, Governor of Massachusetts, 41

Woodside, John A., artist, 99, 281
World War I, Sarajevo, 242; Austrian ultimatum, 242-243; declarations of war, 246; events at beginning of war, 245-251; first submarine warfare, 256-257; unrestricted submarine warfare, 257-259; peace, 265
World War II, precipitating events, 341, 342; Czechoslovakia crisis, 344, 345-346; European action, 350-357; Pacific action, 367, 368
Worthington, C. A., Trenton agent, 339
Wright, James, New York agent, 137
Wucherer, J. R., letters to Welles, 151-152

X Y Z Papers, 59, 60

Young, Thomas R., works on Rush's investigation, 190, 201; solicitor, 203; head of Boston office, 256, 364

Zimmermann Note, 258
Zurich General Accident and Liability Insurance Company, 311